Lecture Notes in Computer Science 14690

Founding Editors

Gerhard Goos
Juris Hartmanis

Editorial Board Members

Elisa Bertino, *Purdue University, West Lafayette, IN, USA*
Wen Gao, *Peking University, Beijing, China*
Bernhard Steffen ⓘ, *TU Dortmund University, Dortmund, Germany*
Moti Yung ⓘ, *Columbia University, New York, NY, USA*

The series Lecture Notes in Computer Science (LNCS), including its subseries Lecture Notes in Artificial Intelligence (LNAI) and Lecture Notes in Bioinformatics (LNBI), has established itself as a medium for the publication of new developments in computer science and information technology research, teaching, and education.

LNCS enjoys close cooperation with the computer science R & D community, the series counts many renowned academics among its volume editors and paper authors, and collaborates with prestigious societies. Its mission is to serve this international community by providing an invaluable service, mainly focused on the publication of conference and workshop proceedings and postproceedings. LNCS commenced publication in 1973.

Hirohiko Mori · Yumi Asahi
Editors

Human Interface
and the Management
of Information

Thematic Area, HIMI 2024
Held as Part of the 26th HCI International Conference, HCII 2024
Washington, DC, USA, June 29 – July 4, 2024
Proceedings, Part II

 Springer

Editors
Hirohiko Mori
Tokyo City University
Tokyo, Japan

Yumi Asahi
Tokyo University of Science
Tokyo, Japan

ISSN 0302-9743   ISSN 1611-3349 (electronic)
Lecture Notes in Computer Science
ISBN 978-3-031-60113-2   ISBN 978-3-031-60114-9 (eBook)
https://doi.org/10.1007/978-3-031-60114-9

This Springer imprint is published by the registered company Springer Nature Switzerland AG
The registered company address is: Gewerbestrasse 11, 6330 Cham, Switzerland

If disposing of this product, please recycle the paper.

Foreword

This year we celebrate 40 years since the establishment of the HCI International (HCII) Conference, which has been a hub for presenting groundbreaking research and novel ideas and collaboration for people from all over the world.

The HCII conference was founded in 1984 by Prof. Gavriel Salvendy (Purdue University, USA, Tsinghua University, P.R. China, and University of Central Florida, USA) and the first event of the series, "1st USA-Japan Conference on Human-Computer Interaction", was held in Honolulu, Hawaii, USA, 18–20 August. Since then, HCI International is held jointly with several Thematic Areas and Affiliated Conferences, with each one under the auspices of a distinguished international Program Board and under one management and one registration. Twenty-six HCI International Conferences have been organized so far (every two years until 2013, and annually thereafter).

Over the years, this conference has served as a platform for scholars, researchers, industry experts and students to exchange ideas, connect, and address challenges in the ever-evolving HCI field. Throughout these 40 years, the conference has evolved itself, adapting to new technologies and emerging trends, while staying committed to its core mission of advancing knowledge and driving change.

As we celebrate this milestone anniversary, we reflect on the contributions of its founding members and appreciate the commitment of its current and past Affiliated Conference Program Board Chairs and members. We are also thankful to all past conference attendees who have shaped this community into what it is today.

The 26th International Conference on Human-Computer Interaction, HCI International 2024 (HCII 2024), was held as a 'hybrid' event at the Washington Hilton Hotel, Washington, DC, USA, during 29 June – 4 July 2024. It incorporated the 21 thematic areas and affiliated conferences listed below.

A total of 5108 individuals from academia, research institutes, industry, and government agencies from 85 countries submitted contributions, and 1271 papers and 309 posters were included in the volumes of the proceedings that were published just before the start of the conference, these are listed below. The contributions thoroughly cover the entire field of human-computer interaction, addressing major advances in knowledge and effective use of computers in a variety of application areas. These papers provide academics, researchers, engineers, scientists, practitioners and students with state-of-the-art information on the most recent advances in HCI.

The HCI International (HCII) conference also offers the option of presenting 'Late Breaking Work', and this applies both for papers and posters, with corresponding volumes of proceedings that will be published after the conference. Full papers will be included in the 'HCII 2024 - Late Breaking Papers' volumes of the proceedings to be published in the Springer LNCS series, while 'Poster Extended Abstracts' will be included as short research papers in the 'HCII 2024 - Late Breaking Posters' volumes to be published in the Springer CCIS series.

I would like to thank the Program Board Chairs and the members of the Program Boards of all thematic areas and affiliated conferences for their contribution towards the high scientific quality and overall success of the HCI International 2024 conference. Their manifold support in terms of paper reviewing (single-blind review process, with a minimum of two reviews per submission), session organization and their willingness to act as goodwill ambassadors for the conference is most highly appreciated.

This conference would not have been possible without the continuous and unwavering support and advice of Gavriel Salvendy, founder, General Chair Emeritus, and Scientific Advisor. For his outstanding efforts, I would like to express my sincere appreciation to Abbas Moallem, Communications Chair and Editor of HCI International News.

July 2024   Constantine Stephanidis

HCI International 2024 Thematic Areas
and Affiliated Conferences

- HCI: Human-Computer Interaction Thematic Area
- HIMI: Human Interface and the Management of Information Thematic Area
- EPCE: 21st International Conference on Engineering Psychology and Cognitive Ergonomics
- AC: 18th International Conference on Augmented Cognition
- UAHCI: 18th International Conference on Universal Access in Human-Computer Interaction
- CCD: 16th International Conference on Cross-Cultural Design
- SCSM: 16th International Conference on Social Computing and Social Media
- VAMR: 16th International Conference on Virtual, Augmented and Mixed Reality
- DHM: 15th International Conference on Digital Human Modeling & Applications in Health, Safety, Ergonomics & Risk Management
- DUXU: 13th International Conference on Design, User Experience and Usability
- C&C: 12th International Conference on Culture and Computing
- DAPI: 12th International Conference on Distributed, Ambient and Pervasive Interactions
- HCIBGO: 11th International Conference on HCI in Business, Government and Organizations
- LCT: 11th International Conference on Learning and Collaboration Technologies
- ITAP: 10th International Conference on Human Aspects of IT for the Aged Population
- AIS: 6th International Conference on Adaptive Instructional Systems
- HCI-CPT: 6th International Conference on HCI for Cybersecurity, Privacy and Trust
- HCI-Games: 6th International Conference on HCI in Games
- MobiTAS: 6th International Conference on HCI in Mobility, Transport and Automotive Systems
- AI-HCI: 5th International Conference on Artificial Intelligence in HCI
- MOBILE: 5th International Conference on Human-Centered Design, Operation and Evaluation of Mobile Communications

List of Conference Proceedings Volumes Appearing Before the Conference

1. LNCS 14684, Human-Computer Interaction: Part I, edited by Masaaki Kurosu and Ayako Hashizume
2. LNCS 14685, Human-Computer Interaction: Part II, edited by Masaaki Kurosu and Ayako Hashizume
3. LNCS 14686, Human-Computer Interaction: Part III, edited by Masaaki Kurosu and Ayako Hashizume
4. LNCS 14687, Human-Computer Interaction: Part IV, edited by Masaaki Kurosu and Ayako Hashizume
5. LNCS 14688, Human-Computer Interaction: Part V, edited by Masaaki Kurosu and Ayako Hashizume
6. LNCS 14689, Human Interface and the Management of Information: Part I, edited by Hirohiko Mori and Yumi Asahi
7. LNCS 14690, Human Interface and the Management of Information: Part II, edited by Hirohiko Mori and Yumi Asahi
8. LNCS 14691, Human Interface and the Management of Information: Part III, edited by Hirohiko Mori and Yumi Asahi
9. LNAI 14692, Engineering Psychology and Cognitive Ergonomics: Part I, edited by Don Harris and Wen-Chin Li
10. LNAI 14693, Engineering Psychology and Cognitive Ergonomics: Part II, edited by Don Harris and Wen-Chin Li
11. LNAI 14694, Augmented Cognition, Part I, edited by Dylan D. Schmorrow and Cali M. Fidopiastis
12. LNAI 14695, Augmented Cognition, Part II, edited by Dylan D. Schmorrow and Cali M. Fidopiastis
13. LNCS 14696, Universal Access in Human-Computer Interaction: Part I, edited by Margherita Antona and Constantine Stephanidis
14. LNCS 14697, Universal Access in Human-Computer Interaction: Part II, edited by Margherita Antona and Constantine Stephanidis
15. LNCS 14698, Universal Access in Human-Computer Interaction: Part III, edited by Margherita Antona and Constantine Stephanidis
16. LNCS 14699, Cross-Cultural Design: Part I, edited by Pei-Luen Patrick Rau
17. LNCS 14700, Cross-Cultural Design: Part II, edited by Pei-Luen Patrick Rau
18. LNCS 14701, Cross-Cultural Design: Part III, edited by Pei-Luen Patrick Rau
19. LNCS 14702, Cross-Cultural Design: Part IV, edited by Pei-Luen Patrick Rau
20. LNCS 14703, Social Computing and Social Media: Part I, edited by Adela Coman and Simona Vasilache
21. LNCS 14704, Social Computing and Social Media: Part II, edited by Adela Coman and Simona Vasilache
22. LNCS 14705, Social Computing and Social Media: Part III, edited by Adela Coman and Simona Vasilache

47. LNCS 14730, HCI in Games: Part I, edited by Xiaowen Fang
48. LNCS 14731, HCI in Games: Part II, edited by Xiaowen Fang
49. LNCS 14732, HCI in Mobility, Transport and Automotive Systems: Part I, edited by Heidi Krömker
50. LNCS 14733, HCI in Mobility, Transport and Automotive Systems: Part II, edited by Heidi Krömker
51. LNAI 14734, Artificial Intelligence in HCI: Part I, edited by Helmut Degen and Stavroula Ntoa
52. LNAI 14735, Artificial Intelligence in HCI: Part II, edited by Helmut Degen and Stavroula Ntoa
53. LNAI 14736, Artificial Intelligence in HCI: Part III, edited by Helmut Degen and Stavroula Ntoa
54. LNCS 14737, Design, Operation and Evaluation of Mobile Communications: Part I, edited by June Wei and George Margetis
55. LNCS 14738, Design, Operation and Evaluation of Mobile Communications: Part II, edited by June Wei and George Margetis
56. CCIS 2114, HCI International 2024 Posters - Part I, edited by Constantine Stephanidis, Margherita Antona, Stavroula Ntoa and Gavriel Salvendy
57. CCIS 2115, HCI International 2024 Posters - Part II, edited by Constantine Stephanidis, Margherita Antona, Stavroula Ntoa and Gavriel Salvendy
58. CCIS 2116, HCI International 2024 Posters - Part III, edited by Constantine Stephanidis, Margherita Antona, Stavroula Ntoa and Gavriel Salvendy
59. CCIS 2117, HCI International 2024 Posters - Part IV, edited by Constantine Stephanidis, Margherita Antona, Stavroula Ntoa and Gavriel Salvendy
60. CCIS 2118, HCI International 2024 Posters - Part V, edited by Constantine Stephanidis, Margherita Antona, Stavroula Ntoa and Gavriel Salvendy
61. CCIS 2119, HCI International 2024 Posters - Part VI, edited by Constantine Stephanidis, Margherita Antona, Stavroula Ntoa and Gavriel Salvendy
62. CCIS 2120, HCI International 2024 Posters - Part VII, edited by Constantine Stephanidis, Margherita Antona, Stavroula Ntoa and Gavriel Salvendy

https://2024.hci.international/proceedings

Preface

Human Interface and the Management of Information (HIMI) is a Thematic Area of the International Conference on Human-Computer Interaction (HCII), addressing topics related to information and data design, retrieval, presentation and visualization, management, and evaluation in human computer interaction in a variety of application domains, such as learning, work, decision, collaboration, medical support, and service engineering. This area of research is acquiring rapidly increasing importance towards developing new and more effective types of human interfaces addressing new emerging challenges, and evaluating their effectiveness. The ultimate goal is for information to be provided in such a way as to satisfy human needs and enhance quality of life.

The related topics include, but are not limited to the following:

- *Service Engineering:* Business Integration; Community Computing; E-commerce; E-learning and E-education; Harmonized Work; IoT and Human Behavior; Knowledge Management; Organizational Design and Management; Service Applications; Service Design; Sustainable Design; User Experience Design
- *New HI (Human Interface) and Human QOL (Quality of Life):* Electronics Instrumentation; Evaluating Information; Health Promotion; E-health and Its Application; Human-Centered Organization; Legal Issues in IT; Mobile Networking; Disasters and HCI
- *Information in VR, AR and MR:* Application of VR, AR, and MR in Human Activity; Art with New Technology; Digital Museum; Gesture/Movement Studies; New Haptics and Tactile Interaction; Presentation Information; Multimodal Interaction; Sense of Embodiment (SoE) in VR and HCI
- *AI, Human Performance and Collaboration:* Automatic Driving Vehicles; Collaborative Work; Data Visualization and Big Data; Decision Support Systems; Human AI Collaboration; Human-Robot Interaction; Humanization of Work; Intellectual Property; Intelligent System; Medical Information System and Its Application; Participatory Design

Three volumes of the HCII 2024 proceedings are dedicated to this year's edition of the HIMI Thematic Area. The first focuses on topics related to Information and Multimodality, and Information and Service Design. The second focuses on topics related to Data Visualization, and User Experience Design and Evaluation. Finally, the third focuses on topics related to Information in Learning and Education, Information in Business and eCommerce, and Knowledge Management and Collaborative Work.

The papers in these volumes were accepted for publication after a minimum of two single-blind reviews from the members of the HIMI Program Board or, in some cases, from members of the Program Boards of other affiliated conferences. We would like to thank all of them for their invaluable contribution, support, and efforts.

July 2024

Hirohiko Mori
Yumi Asahi

Human Interface and the Management of Information Thematic Area (HIMI 2024)

Program Board Chairs: **Hirohiko Mori,** *Tokyo City University, Japan* and **Yumi Asahi,** *Tokyo University of Science, Japan*

- Takako Akakura, *Tokyo University of Science, Japan*
- Shin'ichi Fukuzumi, *Riken, Japan*
- Michitaka Hirose, *Tokyo University, Japan*
- Chen Chiung Hsieh, *Tatung University, Taiwan*
- Yen-Yu Kang, *National Kaohsiung Normal University, Taiwan*
- Keiko Kasamatsu, *Tokyo Metropolitan University, Japan*
- Daiji Kobayashi, *Chitose Institute of Science and Technology, Japan*
- Yusuke Kometani, *Kagawa University, Japan*
- Kentaro Kotani, *Kansai University, Japan*
- Masahiro Kuroda, *Okayama University of Science, Japan*
- Yuichi Mori, *Okayama University of Science, Japan*
- Ryosuke Saga, *Osaka Metropolitan University, Japan*
- Katsunori Shimohara, *Doshisha University, Japan*
- Kim-Phuong L. Vu, *California State University, Long Beach, USA*
- Tomio Watanabe, *Okayama Prefectural University, Japan*
- Takehiko Yamaguchi, *Suwa University of Science, Japan*

The full list with the Program Board Chairs and the members of the Program Boards of all thematic areas and affiliated conferences of HCII 2024 is available online at:

http://www.hci.international/board-members-2024.php

HCI International 2025 Conference

The 27th International Conference on Human-Computer Interaction, HCI International 2025, will be held jointly with the affiliated conferences at the Swedish Exhibition & Congress Centre and Gothia Towers Hotel, Gothenburg, Sweden, June 22–27, 2025. It will cover a broad spectrum of themes related to Human-Computer Interaction, including theoretical issues, methods, tools, processes, and case studies in HCI design, as well as novel interaction techniques, interfaces, and applications. The proceedings will be published by Springer. More information will become available on the conference website: https://2025.hci.international/.

General Chair
Prof. Constantine Stephanidis
University of Crete and ICS-FORTH
Heraklion, Crete, Greece
Email: general_chair@2025.hci.international

https://2025.hci.international/

Contents – Part II

User Experience Design and Evaluation

Data Visualization

Bridging Understanding: A Multi-year Study of the Effect of Aesthetics, Usability and User Domain Knowledge on Interpreting Scientific Visualization

Daniel Carruth[1]([⊠]), Julie Baca[1,2], Christopher Lewis[1,2], and Michael Stephens[2]

[1] Center for Advanced Vehicular Systems, Mississippi State University, MS State, Starkville, MS 39759, USA
dwc2@cavs.msstate.edu, julie.a.baca@usace.army.mil, christopher.d.lewis@erdc.dren.mil
[2] Engineering Research and Development Center, 3909 Halls Ferry Road , Vicksburg, MS 39180, USA
michael.m.stephens@usace.army.mil

Abstract. This multi-year study formally evaluated the efficacy of scientific visualization for multiple categories of users, including both domain experts as well as users from the general public. The study was conducted in four phases using two different scientific visualizations and three separate groups of participants. Efficacy was evaluated for understanding, usability, and aesthetic value. Results indicate that aesthetics play a critical role in enhancing and improving user understanding of scientific research by non-expert viewers. Results also suggest that the methods developed in this study provide an approach for evaluation of the efficacy of improvements to scientific visualizations intended to increase user understanding.

Keywords: Visualization · aesthetics · usability · iterative design · evaluation

1 Introduction

The field of scientific visualization first arose from the needs of researchers to analyze the massive amounts of data generated in the dawning era of supercomputing. In addition to the need for data analysis was the need for researchers to communicate results with peers collaborating to solve the same or similar problems. The immense power of visualization to communicate to broader audiences beyond domain experts was recognized early in their inception and continues to be a significant driver in their use and delivery. Modern visualization technologies must fulfill a multi-faceted mission, serving not only the needs of domain experts, but of equal importance, educating and informing broader, "non-expert" audiences about the nature and impact of the research. These audiences may include sponsors and funding agencies, stakeholders, and politicians, as well as other segments of the public. The broad implications and diverse population of viewers have made objectively evaluating the efficacy of scientific visualization a complex and multi-dimensional endeavor.

© The Author(s), under exclusive license to Springer Nature Switzerland AG 2024
H. Mori and Y. Asahi (Eds.): HCII 2024, LNCS 14690, pp. 3–13, 2024.
https://doi.org/10.1007/978-3-031-60114-9_1

Early visualization evaluation research emphasized algorithmic measures and improvements with little to no user involvement in the process. As the technology matured, user-centered reports began to appear but often lacked structured, replicable methods and heavily relied on reports of feedback from expert users during informal demonstrations (Isenberg et al. 2013).

This paper presents the results of the most recent phase of a multi-year study, conducted by our research center, aimed at identifying and better understanding the impact of and complex interaction among several core evaluation issues, particularly those of aesthetics, usability, and user domain knowledge.

The first phase of our study sought to address gaps in user participation by engaging diverse populations of potential users in a formal evaluation of the efficacy of scientific visualization. Our center provides visualization services to scientists who analyze large volumes of complex data in a high-performance computing environment. We assist scientists who use scientific visualization to facilitate collaboration with specialists in their fields and communication with non-specialist sponsors and the public. Therefore, two user groups, categorized as expert and non-expert based primarily on self-reported education and occupation, recruited for participation in this phase. Participants, recruited from among faculty, staff and students at a university research center, were asked to watch videos of a scientific visualization, answer questions about its content, and evaluate its aesthetic quality. They were also asked to rate their perception of the impact of the visualized research on science and the military. The results indicated that viewers' perception of aesthetic quality was a significant predictor of user perception of the significance of research to science. In addition, perception of aesthetic quality affected user understanding of the impact of the research.

In the second phase of the study, a visualization created by the original researcher was directly compared a visualization with an enhanced presentation to determine the contribution of aesthetics to user understanding of the research for engineers compared to non-engineers. For engineers, the enhanced visualization did not significantly improve their understanding of the research. Non-engineers' understanding of the research matched engineer understanding when viewing the enhanced visualization. *However, on the original visualization, non-engineers had a poorer understanding of the research than engineers.* The modifications made to the visualization to improve the aesthetics of the presentation, led to improved understanding in non-engineers that was close to engineer understanding of the research. A drawback of the design of the second study was that participants did not view both visualizations and were unable to directly compare the output.

In the third phase of the study, we address this drawback by asking the participants to view a new set of visualizations, respond to questions about their understanding of the first visualization, rank their perception of the quality of aesthetics of the first visualization, then view the second visualization, rate the perception of the quality of aesthetics of the second visualization, and assess whether the changes in the video affected their understanding or their perception of the research.

In the new design, we replicate the assessment of the effect of the visualization with a new set of visualizations and we introduce the direct comparison of aesthetics and perceived effect on understanding and perception that was not included in the previous work.

Taken together, these studies provide a method for evaluation of the effects of enhancements of visualizations on users' understanding of research, perception of the importance and relevance of the research, and their perception of the aesthetics of the visualizations, including a direct comparison of the original visualization and the enhanced visualization.

2   Background

The US Army Corps of Engineers Engineer Research and Development Center (ERDC) houses the Data Analysis and Assessment Center (DAAC). The DAAC offers visualization services for researchers working within the DoD High Performance Computing Modernization Program (HPCMP). This initiative stemmed from the recognition of the importance of assessing the impact of scientific visualization across potential user viewpoints. Our clients generate and analyze vast data sets using many different techniques in many different application domains from weather simulation to calculating the effects of explosive blasts and to assessing changes to atomization during fuel injection. These scientists come to the DAAC for assistance in, among other things, extracting data and images and applying visualization techniques to help communicate the importance and the results of their work. In most cases, the scientists are communicating to multiple audiences including other scientists with relevant expertise, laboratory management and technical directors, political sponsors, and the general public.

If we consider these audiences as generally belonging to one of two groups, domain experts and non-experts, prior work has shown that their understanding and their perception of the research can be affected in different ways by choices in the presentation of the visualization. This work investigates specifically how differences in aesthetics affects how viewers understand and perceive the research and presents a method for measuring how well DAAC's enhancements to a visualization achieve the team's objectives.

2.1   Related Research

Our research draws on three primary evaluation methods within the field of information visualization:

1.Usability-Centered Evaluations (Nielsen 1980) focus on the viewers ability to interact with the visualizations and understand the displayed information.

2.Aesthetic Evaluation (Purchase et al. 2002), (Hartman 2006) considers the visual appeal of the visualizations and its impact on user engagement and comprehension. These evaluations often rely on principles such as those suggested by Tufte (1990), which advocate for using natural, software color palettes and incorporating organic movements or animations to enhance effectiveness of the informative display.

3.Iterative, Generative Design-Based Evaluations (Jackson et al. 2012) emphasize the ongoing refinement of visualization tools through user feedback and iterative development processes.

These evaluation categories may overlap or be used simultaneously within a study or development process to explore various aspects, such as the interplay between aesthetics and usability, as in (Cawthon and Van de Moere 2007). In our study, we integrate elements from the first two evaluation types to investigate how aesthetics influence viewer understanding of the content and the importance of the research, particularly for different types of viewers.

3 Method: Atomization Spray Visualization

To understand the effects of aesthetics on viewer understanding and perception of the research, we presented participants with two versions of a visualization of fuel atomization in a direct injection fuel delivery system. The original version was independently produced by the Principal Investigator (PI) on the original research effort. The enhanced version was developed by the DAAC in collaboration with the PI.

3.1 Visualization Description

U.S. Army research into heavy fuel engines with direct injection systems led to the creation of a detailed visualization highlighting the atomization spray process, critical for improving fuel conversion efficiency. The PI of this project produced an initial visualization capturing a vrucial moment in the atomization process. Figure 1 shows a key frame from the visualization near the midpoint of the process. Further refining this visualization, our center worked closely with the researcher through an iterative design process. Based on the researcher's suggestions, we focused on illustrating the atomization's breakup features and internal flow structure, opting for a transparent color scheme and introducing camera movements to offer varied perspectives of the spray. This enhanced visualization was developed through repeated reviews and research feedback, culminating in a depiction that met the researcher's objectives. Figure 2 illustrates key moments that effectively convey the dynamics of fuel atomization.

3.2 Research Questions

We had two goals in this initial phase of the study: (1) determine the impact of the enhancements on viewer understanding and perception of the research and (2) assess how engineers and non-engineers were affected differently. We identified three hypotheses for the study:

- **Hypothesis 1**: Understanding of the research will be improved for everyone when viewing the enhanced visualization compared to the original visualization.

Fig. 1. Original visualization of atomization spray.

i. Atomization Spray:
Droplets Begin to Form

ii. Atomization Spray:
Mid-Late Animation

iii. Atomization Spray Droplets:
Final Frame

Fig. 2. Visualization frames: early to final atomization.

- **Hypothesis 2**: Perception of aesthetics will be higher for the enhanced visualization compared to the original visualization.
- **Hypothesis 3**: Non-engineers will have reduced understanding of the research compared to engineers.

3.3 Participants

We recruited participants from among faculty, general staff, and students across multiple disciplines at a university. Participants were asked whether they held or were working towards engineering degrees and to estimate their domain knowledge of the research on a scale of 1–5. Those with a background in engineering or a domain knowledge score equal to or greater than 3 were counted as engineers. All others were counted as non-engineers.

Table 1. Subject Numbers for Fuel Atomization Visualization Study

N	Original Video	Enhanced Video
Engineers	26	36
Non-Engineers	17	37

3.4 Experimental Treatments

Participants viewed either the original or the enhanced visualization of the atomization of the fuel spray. They were given a text description along with the video that described the basic intent of the atomization research. The participants were asked to review the video and answer questions that probed their understanding of the content and their perception of the aesthetics of the visualization. Responses included open-ended answers which were scored by readers on a 3-point scale where 0 indicated an incorrect response, 1 indicated a correct response with little detail, and 2 indicated a correct and detailed response. Each participant's score was the average of the reader's scores. The aesthetics responses included an assessment from "beautiful" to "ugly" on a 100-point scale and open-ended comments.

4   Results: Atomization Spray Visualization

The core quantitative findings from this study have been previously published (Baca et al. 2022) and indicate that, across all participants, there was no statistically significant difference in understanding or aesthetic appreciation between the original and enhanced visualizations. Despite initial expectations, improvements in visualization did not lead to a notable increase in participant comprehension of the central problem, main idea, impact, or aesthetic ratings.

However, a detailed analysis revealed significant differences in perception between engineers and non-engineers when interacting with the original visualization. Non-engineers demonstrated significantly lower accuracy in understanding the central problem and found the original visualization less aesthetically pleasing compared to engineers. In contrast, no significant differences were found between the two groups with the enhanced visualization.

Further, non-engineers showed a markedly better understanding of the main idea and impact, and a higher aesthetic rating for the enhanced visualization compared to the original. This suggests that the enhancements made to the visualization were particularly effective for non-engineer participants, improving both their comprehension and appreciation of the visualization's aesthetics.

In addition to quantitative assessments of understanding and aesthetics, we asked an open-ended question about the presentation of the visualization to the engineers and non-engineers who observed either the original visualization or the modified visualization. In the following section, we examine representative comments from the engineers and non-engineers about the original video and then the enhanced video.

Almost every comment from the engineers was positive. In fact, there was only a single negative comment suggesting that the original video wasn't "nice to look at." In contrast, other engineers reported that the original video, containing a simple green colored representation of the fluid, contained nice colors that were "pleasing to the eyes" and "visually riveting." The engineers also noted that there was a good "level of detail in the computational analysis" that helped them "gain a better understanding." Multiple engineers recognized the effort involved in generating the visualization noting that it was "very professional" and likely "took a long time to run."

The opinions of the non-engineers were more mixed. While some non-engineers noted that the "detail is impressive", others commented that the video was "plain and simple." The visualization was considered "good", "clear", "visually pleasing", and "accurate and useful" by some non-engineers. Another noted that the visualization was "more scientific than artistic" and remarked that "if that's what it looks like, that's what it looks like." One of the non-engineers offered suggestions for how to improve the display. Others noted that the green was a "nasty color" that was "alarming" and "not attractive."

For those engineers that viewed the enhanced visualization, the overall sense of their opinions was mixed. While many engineers noted that the video was a "great visualization" that was "nice to look at" with "vivid colors." Other engineers noted that the colors could be better used to "describe the droplet sizes" and the visualization should "focus more on the process." Some engineers felt that the enhanced video provided "no context" with "nothing on the flow rate." Some engineers felt it was a "good representation" that looked "authentic" while others did not believe that it was realistic and "lacked detail." A number of engineers were frustrated by the changing views and different angles that were "unnecessary" and did not support understanding.

In contrast, the non-engineers were largely positive in their opinion of the enhanced visualization. While some agreed with the engineers that it did not "greatly impact [their] ability to understand," many others felt that the "multiple angles helped visualize" the flow and "see the main focal point" in "cool" ways. There were some comments that suggested that the "resolution [was] too low" in the enhanced visualization. However, most non-engineers found the video to be "aesthetically pleasing" and "visually stimulating" with an "easy to interpret" presentation that "looked very real" and was "well put together."

The qualitative results generally agree with the quantitative results that indicate that the enhancements to the visualization are seen as more aesthetically pleasing by the non-engineers and helped the non-engineers better understand the content of the video. When examining the engineers' comments on the original video and the enhanced video, it does appear that the engineers appreciated some aspects of the enhanced visualization (e.g., the nice to look at colors) while dismissing the value of other aspects (e.g., the use of panning and rotating around the atomizing spray). Considering all the responses and our own perception of the aesthetics of the two videos, we remain somewhat surprised by the engineers' broad support for the original video. In this phase, the participants viewed only one of the visualizations and were not asked to directly compare the aesthetics of the two videos. In the next phase, we give the participants the opportunity to directly compare a different set of visualizations while retaining the between-subjects assessment of understanding and perception of the importance and relevance of the research.

5 Method: Deflagration to Detonation Visualization

In the third and fourth phases of the study, similar to the first two phases, participants evaluated a visualization produced collaboratively with the principal investigator (PI) of the research and our center, as well as the original visualization produced by the PI with no collaboration with our center. However, in the third phase, we address limitations of the earlier phases by asking the participants to view a new set of visualizations, respond to questions about their understanding of the first visualization, rank their perception of the quality of aesthetics of the first visualization, then view the second visualization, rate the perception of the quality of aesthetics of the second visualization, and assess whether the changes in the visualization affected their understanding or their perception of the research.

In the fourth and final phase, we replicate the assessment of the effect of the visualization with a new set of visualizations and we introduce the direct comparison of aesthetics and perceived effect on understanding and perception that was not included in the previous work.

5.1 Visualization Description

Turbulent flames are pervasive both in our daily lives on earth and in the Universe. They provide power for modern energy generation and propulsion systems, such as gas turbines, internal combustion and jet engines. At the same time, they also have tremendous destructive potential being the primary driver of the majority of gaseous explosions. On astronomical scales, thermonuclear turbulent flames are at the core of some of the most powerful explosions in the Universe, knows as Type Ia supernovae. These are crucibles, in which most of the elements around us from oxygen to iron are synthesized, and in the last 15 years they have been used as cosmological distance probes to discover the existence of dark energy.

Despite their ubiquity, turbulent reacting flows remain poorly understood still posing a number of fundamental questions: What is the structure of turbulent flames at different turbulent intensities? What are the main mechanisms controlling the energy release rate (or the flame speed)? What is the stability of such reacting flows and are they susceptible to catastrophic transitions, e.g., formation of a detonation?

The Naval Research Laboratory has conducted a systematic investigation of the dynamics and properties of fast chemical and thermonuclear turbulent flames. The focus of this study is on the model-free, first-principles modeling of the turbulence-flame interaction with the goal of understanding the fundamental physics of this process. A number of surprising phenomena have emerged in the course of this work. These include the ability of highly subsonic reacting turbulence to develop supersonic detonations spontaneously, pulsating instability and self-acceleration of turbulent flames, presence of the inverse energy cascade and strongly anisotropic turbulent transport, etc. These phenomena are unique to the reacting turbulence and are absent in its more traditional, non-reacting counterpart.

In the visualization used for the final phases of our study, the PI was concerned with the overall structure of the flame surface as it was changing toward the ultimate goal of detonation. Figure 3 shows a key frame of original visualization of the produced by the PI.

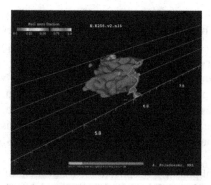

Fig. 3. Original visualization of overall structure of flame surface changing toward the ultimate goal of detonation

Our center created an enhanced visualization of the changes in the flame surface through an iterative design process guided by the PI. Key frames of the enhanced visualization are shown in Fig. 4.

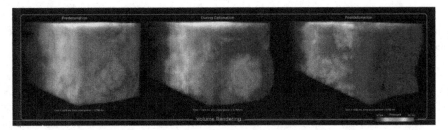

Fig. 4. Key frames of an enhanced visualization of the deflagration to detonation transition

5.2 Research Questions

The third and final phases of the study allowed us to directly compare the original visualization to the enhanced visualization *by the same participant* to determine the contribution of aesthetics to a viewer's understanding of the research. As with the first two phases, hypotheses examined in the third and final phase included:

- **Hypothesis 1**: Understanding of the research will be improved for everyone when viewing the enhanced visualization compared to the original visualization.
- **Hypothesis 2**: Perception of aesthetics will be higher for the enhanced visualization compared to the original visualization.
- **Hypothesis 3**: Non-engineers will have reduced understanding of the research compared to engineers.

5.3 Participants

Participants were again recruited from among faculty, general staff, and students across multiple disciplines at a university. In order to identify participants with relevant knowledge and/or expertise, those who held or were working towards engineering degrees or who rated their domain knowledge of the research at a level of at least 3 on a scale of 1–5 were counted as engineers. All others were counted as non-engineers. Participants were asked to watch videos of the deflagration to detonation visualization, answer questions about its content, and evaluate its aesthetic quality.

5.4 Experimental Treatments

The initial phase of the study progressed in the same way as Phase 1 and 2. Participants viewed a video of either the original or the enhanced visualization deflagration to detonation transition. The participants were asked to answer questions intended to probe their understanding of the content and their perception of the aesthetics of the visualization.

After completing the survey for the initial video, the participants viewed the second video, either the enhanced or the original visualization, whichever they did not already view. The participants were then asked to rate their perception of the aesthetics of the second visualization, allowing us to directly compare their perception of the two videos. In addition, participants were then asked to indicate which of the two videos they preferred, providing a second direct comparison. Participants were also given the opportunity to provide open-ended comments on the aesthetics of the two videos.

The initial responses were scored using the same method as Phase 1 and 2. Participants provided an aesthetic score for the second video, open-ended comments on the second video, and their preference for either the first or second video.

6 Results and Conclusions: Deflagration to Detonation Visualization

While data is currently being gathered for these phases, we expect the results to again show an increase in both understanding and ratings of aesthetic quality for all participants, including engineers and non-engineers for the enhanced visualization. However, we expect the direct comparison of the two videos by the same participant to significantly increase the differences in the ratings and results between the original and enhanced visualizations. We also expect this difference to be of even greater significance for non-engineers than engineers.

Finally, this multi-year study addresses critical gaps in the area of scientific visualization evaluation, both by conducting formal evaluations that directly include a diverse range of users, including both domain and non-domain experts. More specifically, the study presents formal evaluations of visualizations that were enhanced according to guidelines for scientific visualization and through an iterative design process including the original researcher and our center. By engaging multiple categories of potential actual users in the formal comparison, the study highlights the importance of enhanced aesthetics for a large portion of the potential audience, the non-experts.

Longer term we plan to use the results of these studies during design and development to enhance the quality of visualizations provided to researchers, scientists, and the general public. This research will enable a more explicit formulation of a visualization usability process to follow to attain our goal.

Acknowledgements. This paper is based upon work supported by the U.S. Army Engineer Research and Development Center (ERDC) under Contract No. W912HZ-17-C-0015.

References

Isenberg, T., Isenberg, P., Chen, J., Sedlmair, M., Moller, T.: A systematic review on the practice of evaluating visualization. IEE Trans. Visualization Comput. Graph. **19**(12), 2818–2827 (2013)

Nielsen, J.: Usability inspection methods. John Wiley and Sons, New York (1980)

Purchase, H., Allder, J.A., Carrington, D.: Metrics for graphic drawing aesthetics. J. Vis. Lang. Comput.Comput. **13**, 501–516 (2002)

Hartman, J.: Assessing the attractiveness of interactive systems. In: Proceedings of CHI '06 Extended Abstracts on Human Factors in Computing Systems, pp. 1755–1758. ACM Press, Montreal Quebec, Canada (2006)

Jackson, B., et al.: Towards mixed method evaluation of scientific visualizations and design process as an evaluation tool. In: Proceedings of BELIEV 2012, Seattle, Washington, USA (2012)

Cawthon, N., Vande Moere, A.: Qualities of perceived aesthetic in data visualization. In: Proceedings of CHI 2007, pp. 1–11, ACM Press, San Jose, CA, USA (2007)

Cawthon, N., Vande Moere, A.: The effect of aesthetic on the usability of data visualization. In: Proceedings of 11th International Conference on Information Visualization IV'07, pp. 637–648, IEEE Computer Society, Washington D.C., USA (2007)

Tufte, E.: Envisioning Information. Graphics Press, Cheshire, Conn., USA (1990)

Gwet, K.L.: Handbook of inter-rater reliability. Advanced Analytics, LLC, Maryland, USA (2012)

Baca, J., Lewis, C., Stephens, M., Carruth, D.W.: Evidence for Effect of Aesthetic on Interpretation of Visualizations by Engineers and Non-Engineers. Usability and User Experience, 39, pp. 280–287, AHFE International (2022)

Visualization and Interpretation of Latent Space in Deep Learning

Mizuki Dai[1] and Kenya Jin'no[2]([envelope])

[1] Informatics, Graduate School of Integrative Science and Engineering,
Tokyo City University, Tokyo, Japan
`g2381436@tcu.ac.jp`
[2] Department of Intelligent Systems, Faculty of Information Technology,
Tokyo City University, Tokyo, Japan
`kjinno@tcu.ac.jp`

Abstract. Deep learning-based image classification represents a significant advancement in enabling computers to identify the content of images. This process involves a component known as the *feature extractor*, which extracts vital features from images, followed by a *classifier* that uses this information to determine the category to which an image belongs. For enhancing classification accuracy, it is crucial to efficiently extract latent features, which are the hidden information within images.

Despite the high accuracy of some models, the detailed mechanisms through which these latent features are effectively extracted remain insufficiently understood. In this study, we delve into how the feature extractor contributes to information retrieval from images. Specifically, we analyze the nature of feature vectors generated when employing *categorical cross-entropy* and how these vectors aid the classifier's decision-making process.

By representing these feature vectors in two dimensions, we can visually depict them, deepening our understanding of the interplay between feature extractors and classifiers. Through this approach, our goal is to elucidate the underlying mechanisms of high-precision image classification models, bringing us closer to unraveling the complexities behind efficient feature extraction and classification.

Keywords: Deep Learning · Image Classifier · Latent Space · Categorical Cross Entropy

1 Introduction

In recent years, deep learning technologies have garnered significant attention due to their broad applicability. Among various tasks, image classification stands out as a fundamental yet crucial area. In this domain, a variety of models with diverse architectures have been proposed, including convolutional neural networks (CNNs) such as AlexNet [1], VGGNet [2], Inception [3], and ResNet [4], as well as models inspired by successes in natural language processing (NLP),

H. Mori and Y. Asahi (Eds.): HCII 2024, LNCS 14690, pp. 14–23, 2024.
https://doi.org/10.1007/978-3-031-60114-9_2

employing attention mechanisms like the Vision Transformer (ViT) [5] and Swin Transformer [6]. The high classification performance of these models is attributed to their capability to effectively capture latent features within datasets. However, the specifics of this process are not fully understood.

This study aims to enhance the performance of deep learning models in image classification tasks by focusing on the latent variables extracted in the models' final layers. Specifically, we concentrate our analysis on latent variables when represented in two dimensions. Visualizing the two-dimensional latent variable space allows us to analyze the distribution of data within this space, offering insights into how models capture features and perform classification. This approach seeks to deepen our understanding of deep learning models, contributing towards the development of more transparent and interpretable artificial intelligence (AI) systems.

2   Deep Classification Model

Image classification tasks in many deep learning models possess a typical structure, as shown in Fig. 1.

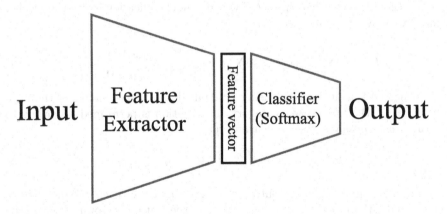

Fig. 1. Typical structure of an image classification system in deep learning models.

In this process, an input image is processed by a "feature extractor," which extracts significant information, or features, contained within the image. Various models have been proposed for this "feature extractor," including AlexNet [1], VGGNet [2], Inception [3], and ResNet [4]. The extracted feature vector, commonly referred to as the latent variable vector, is then utilized by a "classifier" to determine the category to which the input image belongs.

The classifier calculates the dot product between the latent variable vector and a weight vector assigned to each category. Based on these dot product values, the Softmax function is employed to compute the probability of belonging to each category. Eventually, the category with the highest probability is selected as the model's output. If the latent variable vector extracted by the feature extractor is denoted as $\boldsymbol{x}_i \in \mathbb{R}^M$, the weight vector corresponding to the i-th category of the classifier as $\boldsymbol{W}_i \in \mathbb{R}^M$, and the number of categories as N, then the i-th output of the Softmax function, y_i, is defined by the following equation:

$$y_i = \frac{\exp(\boldsymbol{x}\boldsymbol{W}_i)}{\sum_{k=1}^{N} \exp(\boldsymbol{x}\boldsymbol{W}_k)} \tag{1}$$

This output, y_i, is interpreted as the probability that the input image belongs to category i.

3   Learning Dynamics of Feature Extractors and Classifiers

In the context of classifying the categories of input images, the teacher signal representing the probability distribution is denoted by an N-dimensional vector $\boldsymbol{t}$. Both the "feature extractor" and the "classifier" advance their learning using the cross-entropy L_c as the loss function, which is shown in Eq. (2). The cross-entropy reaches its minimum value when the distribution of the model output $\boldsymbol{y}$ matches that of the teacher signal $\boldsymbol{t}$. Typically, in classification tasks, the teacher signal $\boldsymbol{t}$ employs a one-hot vector.

$$L_c = -\sum_i t_i \log y_i = -\sum_i t_i \log \left(\frac{\exp(\boldsymbol{x}\boldsymbol{W}_i)}{\sum_{k=1}^{N} \exp(\boldsymbol{x}\boldsymbol{W}_k)} \right) \tag{2}$$

During the learning process using gradient descent, the update of the classifier's weight $\boldsymbol{W}_i$ for the i-th category classification is performed according to Eq. (3), where η represents the learning rate.

$$\boldsymbol{W}_i \leftarrow \boldsymbol{W}_i - \eta \frac{\partial L_c}{\partial \boldsymbol{W}_i} = \boldsymbol{W}_i - \eta(y_i - t_i)\boldsymbol{x} \tag{3}$$

From this equation, if the output y_i is less than the teacher signal t_i, the weight vector $\boldsymbol{W}_i$ is updated to move closer to the feature vector $\boldsymbol{x}$. Conversely, if y_i is greater than t_i, $\boldsymbol{W}_i$ is updated to move away from $\boldsymbol{x}$. This means, particularly when the teacher signal $\boldsymbol{t}$ is a one-hot vector, if $t_i = 1$, $\boldsymbol{W}_i$ moves closer to $\boldsymbol{x}$, and if $t_i = 0$, it moves away. Figure 2 illustrates this weight vector updating process.

The output of the feature extractor, denoted as $\mathbf{x}$, is updated through gradient descent. The update formula is given by:

$$\boldsymbol{x} \leftarrow \boldsymbol{x} - \eta \frac{\partial L_c}{\partial \boldsymbol{x}} = \boldsymbol{x} - \sum_i \eta(y_i - t_i)\boldsymbol{W}_i \tag{4}$$

As illustrated in Fig. 3, based on Eq. (4), if $y_i < t_i$, $\mathbf{x}$ moves closer to $\mathbf{W}_i$, and if $y_i > t_i$, it moves away from $\mathbf{W}_i$. This implies that, for a one-hot target vector $\mathbf{t}$, $\mathbf{x}$ is updated to approach $\mathbf{W}_i$ if $t_i = 1$, and to diverge if $t_i = 0$.

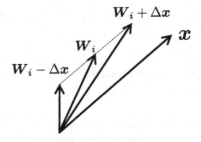

Fig. 2. Updating weights W_i corresponding to the i-th class of the classifier by feature extractor output x based on multi-class cross-entropy loss. W_i is the weight vector for identifying the ith category of the classifier, x is the output of the feature extractor

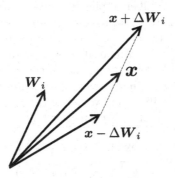

Fig. 3. Updating the output of the feature extractor, $\mathbf{x}$, based on the weights $\mathbf{W}_i$ corresponding to each class in the classifier, utilizing multi-class cross-entropy loss. Here, $\mathbf{W}_i$ represents the weight vector for identifying the i-th category, and $\mathbf{x}$ is the output of the feature extractor.

In deep learning models for image classification tasks, the class corresponding to the maximum inner product of the feature extractor's output $\mathbf{x}$ and the weight vector $\mathbf{W}_i$ for each class is determined. According to the class labels, the model is trained so that $\mathbf{x}$ and $\mathbf{W}_i$ are attracted to each other for the correct label, and repelled for incorrect ones.

Considering a dataset for image classification tasks like CIFAR-10, which involves classification into 10 classes, the classifier's weight vectors must constitute ten distinct direction vectors. Classification is performed using the Softmax function (Eq. (1)), and the loss is calculated using multi-class cross-entropy (Eq. (2)). The multi-class cross-entropy loss is minimized when the Softmax output y_i matches the target signal t_i. Typically, the target signal t_i is one-hot encoded, being either $t_i = 1$ or $t_i = 0$. However, since the Softmax output y_i ranges between $0 < y_i < 1$, the loss function does not reach its minimum value. Consequently, by appropriately adjusting the learning rate according to the epoch, the learning process can be effectively progressed. Through this learning process, the direction of the classifier's weight vector $\mathbf{W}_i$ and the feature extractor's output $\mathbf{x}$ align, and their norms increase.

4 Towards Better Understanding of CNNs: Visualizing the Latent Spaces

In this section, we consider the visualization of the feature extractor's output $\mathbf{x}$ when it is two-dimensional, using the system shown in Fig. 4 as an example. The model depicted in Fig. 4 is the CNN-based classification task model we previously proposed [7]. This model introduces a latent variable space that is reduced to two dimensions before the "Dense + Softmax" layer.

In classification tasks, classifiers typically proceed with learning using a multi-class cross-entropy loss function and a one-hot encoded teacher signal. However, the outputs of the classifier through the Softmax function do not become one-hot encoded, allowing learning to continue. If we set the teacher signal to distribute evenly in the latent variable space using the Softmax function, for instance, we can expect an effect similar to that of using the Center Loss.

Thus, for a 10-class classification, we define the teacher signal vector $\mathbf{t}^m$ for the situation where the m-th class is correct as follows:

$$t_i^m = \frac{\exp\left(\alpha \cos\left(\frac{(m-i)\pi}{5}\right)\right)}{\sum_{k=0}^{9} \exp\left(\alpha \cos\left(\frac{k\pi}{5}\right)\right)} \tag{5}$$

Here, α is a scaling parameter.

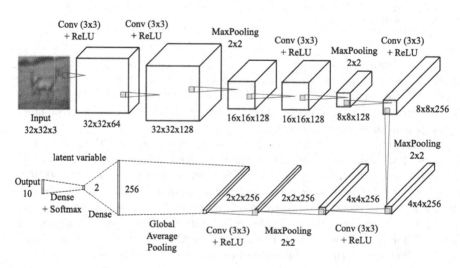

Fig. 4. We modified the Toufu model we proposed in Ref. [7] and inserted a Dense layer that reduces to two dimensions to visualize the latent variables before the output part.

Figure 5 shows how the distribution of teacher signals changes with different values of the scaling parameter α. Figure 5(a) shows the traditional one-hot representation, while (b) $\alpha = 16$, (c) $\alpha = 4$, and (d) $\alpha = 1$ are shown respectively. It is demonstrated that the larger the scaling parameter α, the closer the output approaches a one-hot representation.

We explore the impact of varying the distribution of the teacher signals on the distribution of latent variables, employing the multi-class cross-entropy as the loss function. We utilize the model presented in Fig. 4 and input images from the CIFAR-10 dataset to illustrate the distribution of two-dimensional latent variables for each class, color-coded for clarity.

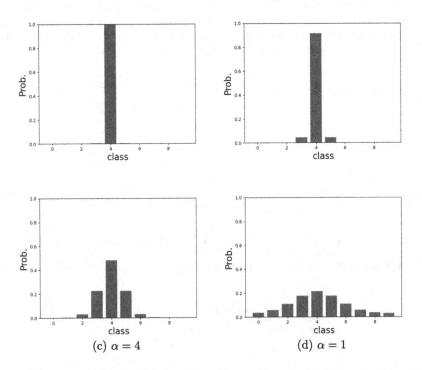

(c) $\alpha = 4$ (d) $\alpha = 1$

Fig. 5. Variation of the distribution of the teacher signal with different values of the scaling parameter α.

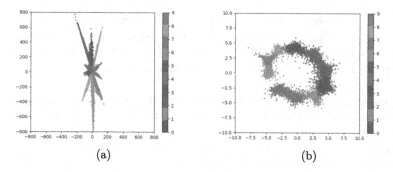

(a)   (b)

Fig. 6. Relationship between the distribution of the teacher signal and the distribution of the latent variable space when multi-class cross-entropy is used in the loss function. (a) When one-hot representation is used for the teacher signal. (b) When the teacher signal is set using the softmax function and given a sort order.

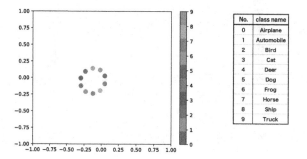

Fig. 7. Distribution of classifier weights W_i when trained in the order of P_1

Table 1. Classification accuracy at training and testing for order P_1 and P_2, respectively

	the order of P_1	the order of P_2
train	0.929	0.963
test	0.788	0.844

Figure 6 demonstrates the effects of different teacher signal distributions on the latent space. Panel (a) of Fig. 6 shows the latent variable distribution when using a one-hot representation as the teacher signal. In contrast, Panel (b) depicts the distribution when employing teacher signals distributed evenly on a unit circle. These experiments were conducted with a constant learning rate, without adjustments for decay over epochs.

In Fig. 6(a), we observe a distribution where latent variables spread outward from the center, indicating a lack of convergence in learning. Conversely, Fig. 6(b) shows a more contained distribution of latent variables, suggesting easier convergence. Notably, the distribution in Fig. 6(a) spans a wider range compared

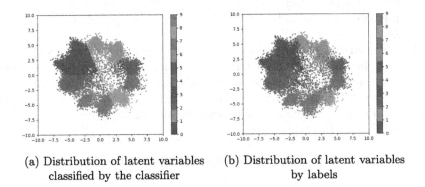

(a) Distribution of latent variables classified by the classifier

(b) Distribution of latent variables by labels

Fig. 8. Distribution of latent variables when the order of P_1 is used as the supervised signal

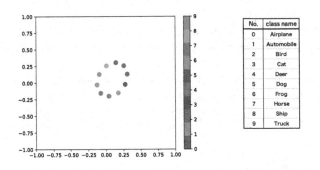

Fig. 9. Distribution of classifier weights W_i when trained in the order of P_2

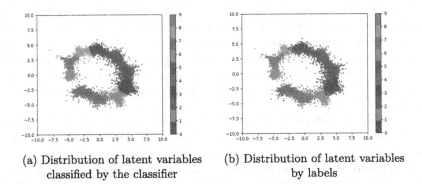

(a) Distribution of latent variables classified by the classifier

(b) Distribution of latent variables by labels

Fig. 10. Distribution of latent variables when the order of P_2 is used as the supervised signal

to Fig. 6(b). This phenomenon can be attributed to an increase in the norm of the feature vector x, gradually aligning the classifier's output closer to a one-hot representation.

When considering the impact of the scale parameter α on classification performance, it becomes evident that the distribution of classifier weight vectors varies significantly with the order in which classes are arranged. In this context, the term "class order" refers to the specific sequence in which classes are organized, represented here by P. We examine the effects of two distinct class orderings, P_1 and P_2, defined as follows:

$$P_1 = [3, 0, 6, 1, 5, 4, 8, 7, 9, 2] \tag{6}$$

$$P_2 = [0, 8, 9, 1, 4, 7, 6, 3, 5, 2] \tag{7}$$

The results from training based on order P_1 are shown in Figs. 7 and 8, while those based on order P_2 are depicted in Figs. 9 and 10. Figures 7 and 9 illustrate the distribution of classifier weight vectors for each ordering, respectively, and Figs. 8 and 10 display the distribution of the latent variables classified by the classifier and by labels. Furthermore, the classification accuracies for images during training and testing phases, corresponding to the orders P_1 and P_2, are presented in Table 1.

These findings reveal that certain distribution patterns, influenced by the class ordering, have a significant impact on classification accuracy. Specifically, in the CIFAR-10 dataset, clusters formed by distinguishing between 'vehicles' and 'animals' classes contribute to improved classification performance.

5   Conclusions

In this article, we conduct an analysis focusing on the distinct roles of feature extractors and classifiers within deep learning-based image classification systems, with a particular emphasis on latent variables. Specifically, our objective is to clarify the distribution of latent variables by conducting experiments within a two-dimensional plane. Through this process, we have elucidated the learning mechanisms employed by classifiers, notably the use of the Softmax function and multi-class cross-entropy. Additionally, our findings suggest characteristics of teacher signals that significantly contribute to the enhancement of classification performance.

The results of our research indicate that the interaction between feature extractors and classifiers has a significant impact on the performance of deep learning-based image classification. This insight underscores the importance of appropriately designed teacher signals in improving classification accuracy. Future research will involve a more detailed analysis of the functionalities of feature extractors. The advancements in this study provide valuable insights into the design and optimization of deep learning-based image classification systems.

Acknowledgement. This work was supported by JSPS KAKENHI Grant-in-Aid for Scientific Research (C) Number: 23K11266, and JSPS KAKENHI Grant-in-Aid for Scientific Research (B) Number: 23H03387. Part of this work was carried out under the Cooperative Research Project Program of the Research Institute of Electrical Communication, Tohoku University. Also, part of this work was carried out under Future Intelligence Research Unit, ARL Research, Tokyo City University.

References

1. Krizhevsky, A., Sutskever, I., Hinton, G.E.: ImageNet Classification with Deep Convolutional Neural Networks. In: Proceedings of NIPS 2012 (2012)
2. Simonyan, K., Zisserman, A.: Very deep convolutional networks for large-scale image recognition. In: Proceedings of ICLR 2015 (2015)
3. Szegedy, C., et al.: Going deeper with convolutions. In: CVPR 2015 (2015)
4. He, K., Zhang, X., Ren, S., Sun, J.: Deep residual learning for image recognition. In: Proceedings of CVPR 2016 (2016)
5. Dosovitskiy, A., et al.: An image is worth 16x16 words: transformers for image recognition at scale. In: Proceedings of ICLR 2021 (2021)
6. Liu, Z., et al.: Swin transformer: hierarchical vision transformer using shifted windows. In: Proceedings of ICCV 2021 (2021)
7. Dai, M., Jin'no, K.: Toward the realization of lightweight CNN. In: Proceedings of IEICE NOLTA 2022, pp. 301–304 (2022). https://doi.org/10.34385/proc.71.B2L-E-04

Events Remembering Support Via Character Relationships' Visualization of Novels

Kosuke Fujishima[1]([✉]), Junjie Shan[2], and Yoko Nishihara[3]

[1] Graduate School of Information Science and Engineering, Ritsumeikan University,
Kyoto, Japan
`is0472ek@ed.ritsumei.ac.jp`
[2] Ritsumeikan Global Innovation Research Organization, Ritsumeikan University,
Kyoto, Japan
`shan@fc.ritsumei.ac.jp`
[3] College of Information Science and Engineering, Ritsumeikan University,
Kyoto, Japan
`nishihara@fc.ritsumei.ac.jp`

Abstract. When people read a long novel, they usually find it difficult to finish it at once. Therefore, people have to repeat the "read-and-pause" step before finishing a story. This would cause a lot of confusion in the reader's memory, especially when they are reading multiple novels at the same time. They tend to forget the events of novels by the time they resume reading, which would make them give up on continuing.

This study proposes an interface to support remembering novels' events by visualizing characters' relationships. The interface shows three types of characters' relationships: positive, negative, and neutral, and visualizes them for each episode. The relationships are displayed in chronological order on the interface.

Experimental results showed that the proposed interface could support the participants in remembering the events of the novel.

Keywords: Support for resuming reading · Visualizing characters' relationships

1 Introduction

The Internet has become a part of people's lives due to the spread of smartphones and computers. The market size of Internet content has expanded. Though the market size of paper books is on the decline. The market size of e-books is on the rise. People do not need to carry heavy paper books if they have e-books. When people choose e-books, they can easily read as many books as they want, e.g., online novels. People can read online novels from their devices such as smartphones through novel posting sites. More than 900,000 novels have been posted on popular novel posting sites. It is expected that the demand for online novels will continue to increase in the future.

H. Mori and Y. Asahi (Eds.): HCII 2024, LNCS 14690, pp. 24–34, 2024.
https://doi.org/10.1007/978-3-031-60114-9_3

The novel posting site "Become a novelist" [6] is popular for its wide range of novels in genres such as fantasy and romance. There are many postings of works in these genres. Popular novels tend to be full-length works with more than 100 episodes, and many of these novels have not yet been completed. Therefore, the following situations often occur among readers of the online novels:

(a) When reading a long novel, people usually find it difficult to finish it in one sitting. Therefore, people have to repeat the "read-and-paus" step before finishing a story.
(b) When the novel people read is still "under serialization," readers have to wait for the author to update the subsequent content. The period of "pause" in reading becomes longer.
(c) People are likely to read multiple novels under the same genre they like simultaneously, due to the ease of accessing a large amount of content on the novel's publishing site.

This will lead people to have faulty memories of each novel, such as forgetting the characters and related stories in the novels. Compared to manga and anime, novels contain only text, so it is difficult to remember the characters by their appearance, such as their faces and clothes. They may forget the characters and the events they were involved in. If they continue reading without remembering what they have already read, it becomes difficult for them to understand the events of the story. People usually have no choice but to repeat the parts they have already read at such time, but that will take extra time for them to finish the novel.

In this paper, the authors propose an interface that supports to remember the events of an online novel by visualizing the relationships between the characters. Characters and their relationships are extracted from the novel. The relationships between characters are visualized by each episode and are presented in chronological order of number of episodes. The visualized relationships and their changes support for readers in recalling the events in the "already-read" parts.

The contributions of this research are as follows. The study proposed an interface that visualizes characters' relationships to support remembering events in the novel. The proposed interface displays three types of characters' relationships for each episode. Users can access three types of information through the proposed interface: (1) characters' relationships for an episode, (2) a transition of the characters' relationships in chronological order, and (3) entrances and exits of characters. Experimental results showed that the proposed interface could support the participants in remembering the events of the novel.

2 Related Work

2.1 Extraction of Characters' Relationships from Texts

The authors introduce existing research on extracting character relationship diagrams from narrative texts. Agarwal et al. extracted a relationship diagram with nodes as characters and edges as events [1]. Elson et al. extracted a relationship diagram by using nodes as characters and edges as the amount of conversation between two characters [2]. Marazzato et al. extracted a relationship diagram with nodes as characters and locations, and edges as interactions between them [3]. Jayakumar et al. extracted a dynamic relationship diagram that changes as the story progresses, with nodes as characters and edges as communications [4] In many online novels, the characters and information related to them are deeply related to the story.

2.2   Support for Understanding Text Content

Some research on supporting the understanding of text content visualizes the chronological sequence of characters and locations [5]. Similar to this research, it targets readers who are reading multiple books at the same time, and supports them to resume reading smoothly. In this research, the authors propose an interface that visualizes the characters' relationships and supports to remember the events of novels.

3   Proposed Interface

In this research, the author proposed an interface that visualizes the relationships between characters that enter in a novel. The proposed interface could help reduce the time spent on re-reading by supporting remembering events in the "already-read" parts. When users use the proposed interface, they can recall the events by the visualization of character relationships without having to re-read the novel once again.

3.1   Overview of the Proposed Interface

Figure 1 shows the entrance of the proposed interface. The interface consists of two main parts. The lower part of the interface visualizes characters' relationships, and the upper part visualizes meta information.

Characters' relationships are visualized using cells and directed edges. Cells represent characters, while edges represent characters' relationships. Characters' relationships are visualized by each episode and arranged horizontally along the time axis. Placing them side by side makes comparing characters' relationships easier before and after the story of interest. For example, the information on characters' entrances/exits and the difference between their relationships can be grasped. Meta information includes the title of the novel and explanations of cells and edges type. The proposed interface was developed using joint.js [7]. The users view it on a web browser. The scroll direction of the screen is horizontal.

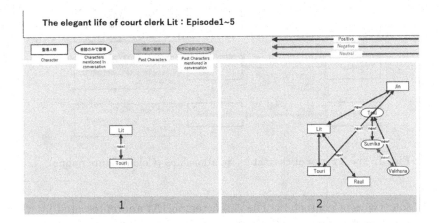

Fig. 1. Appearance of the proposed interface

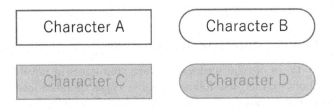

Fig. 2. Visualize 4 types of characters in cells (Colour figure online)

3.2 Characters' Relationships Visualization Procedure

Characters' relationships are extracted from the novel text. A characters' relationships visualization is created for each episode from the extracted characters' relationships. The created character relationships' visualizations are arranged and presented in chronological order by episode number

3.3 Extraction of Characters from a Novel Text

First, the characters are extracted from a novel. In novels, not all characters enter in every episode; some are present, while others have appeared in the past. Some characters act in the episode, while others are only referred to by name in the conversation. In this study, authors extract four types of characters from novel texts for each story.

(A) Characters actually acting in the episode
(B) Characters mentioned in the conversations
(C) Characters who acted in the past episode
(D) Past characters mentioned in the conversations

These four types of characters are distinguished by the shape and color of the cells. Figure 2 shows an example of these differences in the cell representations

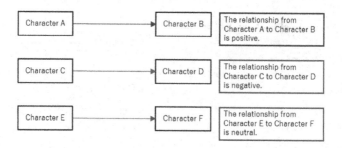

Fig. 3. The 3 types of characters' relationships (Colour figure online)

for the four types of characters. The characters in (A) are represented by white rectangles. The characters of (B) is represented by a white oval. The characters of (C) are represented by gray rectangles. The characters of (D) are represented by gray ovals.

3.4   Extraction of Characters' Relationships

There are many types of relationships between characters in novel text. In this study, the authors extract the following three types of relationships between characters from novel texts.

(a) Positive relationships: allies, friendships, etc.
(b) Negative relationship: hostile relationship, dislike of the other person, etc.
(c) Neutral relationship: Cases where the above does not apply.

The difference between these three types of relationships is expressed by the color of the edges. Figure 3 shows an example of edge display. The relationship of (a) is blue, relationship of (b) is red, and relationship of (c) is green. If Character A shows a positive relationship with Character B, a blue arrow edge is pasted from Character A to Character B.

3.5   Arrangement of Characters

This section explain the arrangement of the characters. Figure 4 shows an example of the arrangement. The main character's cell is placed in the center. The interface links the cells by edges so that they do not overlap the cells. Characters other than the main character are assigned to cells by order of their entrance.

Some characters might change their names as the story progresses because they are called by the name of their status (father, mother, senior, king, etc.). If people forget the story of the novel, they will also forget those calling names that appeared and changed. Even if a character's name has appeared and changed, cells for the same character would be placed in the same location on the visualization.

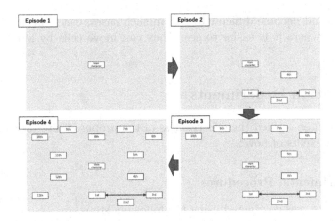

Fig. 4. Arrangement rule of characters

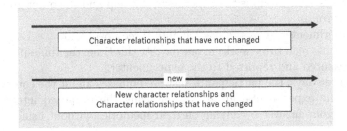

Fig. 5. Add "new" label to the edge for new and changed characters' relationships

The users can see the visualization of characters' relationships in chronological order by episode number. Therefore, they can know the timing of a character's entrance and name change. If a character's entrance and name change is related to an event in the novel, the user can remember the event.

3.6 Functions on the User Interface

Highlighting New and Changed Characters' Relationships. When users view the visualization of characters' relationships in each episode side by side using the proposed interface, they can visually grasp the changes between characters' relationships. Authors developed a function that will highlight the changes in characters' relationships and new characters' relationships. The implemented function is shown in Fig. 5. The changed characters' relationships and new characters' relationships are pasted new labels to the edge of characters' relationship. Adding a new label will highlight it compared to other characters' relationships. The users can see new characters' relationships from the label.

Moving Cells. Visualization of characters' relationships consists of cells and edges, but depending on the relationship between characters, cells and edges may overlap and become difficult to see. In such cases, users can move the cell to a position where it is easier to see. They can move cells by left-clicking on them.

4   Evaluation Experiments

The experimenter verified the effectiveness of the proposed interface to support remembering events of novel.

4.1   Experimental Procedures

The experiment was conducted using the following steps.

(1) The experimenter gathers the participants. Participants are divided into two groups. One group is the experimental group and the other group is the control group.
(2) The experimenter gives the participants three novel texts.
(3) Participants read three works in one day. At this time, the time spent reading was measured and reported to the experimenter.
(4) After three days, the participants answered quizzes about the content of the novel. The experimental group answer using the proposed interface. The control group answer by relying on their memories without using anything.

A total of 28 participants were asked to participate in the experiment, 14 were in the experimental group and 14 were in the control group. Based on the Ebbinghaus forgetting curve [8], the saving rate after two days is 27% and the saving rate after six days is 25%, so Experimenter decided that the period between reading and taking the quizzes would be about three days.

4.2   Used Novel Texts and Prepared Quizzes

Novels. Table 1 shows the genres and titles of the novels used in the experiment. The experiment used two novels from each of the three genres of fantasy, romance, and mystery. Fantasy and romance genres are popular genres on "Become a novelist", a novel posting site. There are many posts for the genres (fantasy is the most while romance is the 2nd most). The structure of texts in the mystery genre was different from romance and fantasy. The mystery novel texts often contain the motive for the crime and foreshadowing. So, the authors chose the mystery genre for the experiment.

The experimenters used episodes of No. 1 to 5 of each novel. The novel posting site "Become a novelist" displays the estimated reading time based on the average reading speed. People often read 500 characters in one minute. The participants can read the novel that is chosen for the experiment in 20 to 30 min. Therefore, the authors decided to ask the participants to read five episodes in this experiment.

Table 1. Genre and title of the novels used in the experiment

	Genre	Title
1	Fantasy	Re:ZERO -Starting Life in Another World
2	Fantasy	The Eminence in Shadow
3	Romance	The Most Heretical Last Boss Queen: From Villainess to Savior
4	Romance	The Fiancée Chosen by the Ring
5	Mystery	The Apothecary Diaries
6	Mystery	The Elegant Life of Royal Clerk Rit

Table 2. Correct rate of interface group and non-interface group

Group	Correct rate
Experimental	0.68
Control	0.43

Quizzes. The experimenter created 72 quizzes. These were three types of quizzes about the episodes of six novels. There were three types of quizzes used in the experiment, including the "flow of the episode", "characters' relationships", and "conversations between characters".

"Flow of the episode" are quizzes regarding information about the flow of events in the episode as a whole and the abstract flow of the novel. Based on the answer to the quizzes, the experimenter investigated whether the proposed interface could supported participants to remember the changes in characters' relationships.

"Characters' relationships" are quizzes about characters' relationships and episodes related to them. Based on the answer to the quizzes, the experimenter investigate whether the proposed interface could supported participants to remember events related to characters' relationships.

"Conversations between characters" are quizzes regarding the content of the conversation between characters. Based on the answers to the quizzes, the experimenter investigate whether the proposed interface could supported participants to remember the content of conversations between characters.

4.3 Evaluation Method

The experimenter calculated the score of the answer data of the participants who took the quizzes. They were calculated using the point addition method. If the answer is correct, add 1 point to score. No points will be added if the answer is incorrect. A two-sample t-test was used to test whether there was a difference in the mean of the two sample tests for experimental group and control group.

4.4   Experimental Results

Table 2 shows the average correct answer rate for experimental group and control group. Table 3 shows the average correct answer rate organized by question type for the experimental group and control group. Table 4 shows the average correct answer rate organized by genre for the experimental group and control group.

Table 3. Correct rate by type of quizzes

Group	Flow of the episode	Characters' relationships	Conversations between characters
Experimental	0.75	0.66	0.63
Control	0.49	0.36	0.45

Table 4. Correct rate by genres

Group	Fantasy	Romance	Mystery
Experimental	0.65	0.70	0.70
Control	0.40	0.53	0.36

5   Discussion

This section discuss the effects on remembering events in novel texts by using the experimental results.

5.1   Consideration of Average Correct Answer Rate by Question Type

The authors discuss events remembering support based on the correct answer rate of quizzes. Table 2 shows the correct answer rates for Experimental and Control group. The correct answer rate was 0.68(Experimental group) and 0.43(Control group).

The correct rate was higher when the participants used the proposed interface. The authors think that participants were able to remember events more easily by viewing the characters' relationships and their changes visualized in the proposed interface about this result.

Next, the authors discuss the correct answer rate for each type of the quizzes. When participants used the proposed interface, quizzes about the flow of the episode had the highest correct answer rate. The flow of the episode is often created by changes in characters' relationships, such as the appearance and departure of characters. For this reason, the authors think that the rate of correct answers regarding the flow of the episode was higher when the proposed interface was used.

On the other hand, when participants used the proposed interface, the quizzes about the conversations between characters had the lowest correct answer rate. When users look at the visualization of the proposed interface, they can tell whether the characters have had a conversation with each other. However, it is difficult to remember the contents like conversation details. For this reason, the authors think when participants used the proposed interface, the correct answer rate for quizzes about the conversations between characters was low.

5.2 Effect of Novel Genre

There were differences in the correct answer rate for quizzes by genre. Table 4 shows the correct answer rate of quizzes organized by genre. The mystery genre had the highest difference in correct answer rates. When the genre was mystery, the correct answer rate were 0.7(Experimental group) and 0.36(Control group). Mystery has more characters than other genres, and their relationships are more complex. Therefore, the number of relationship types is expected to increase. The proposed interface visualizes the characters' relationships, making it easier to remember even when there are many types of events. The authors think this is the reason why the difference in correct answer rates was highest.

6 Conclusion

This study proposed an interface that visualizes characters' relationships to support remembering events in the novel. The proposed interface displays three types of characters' relationships for each episode. They are positive, negative and neutral. Visualizations of characters' relationships were created for each episode. The relationships are displayed in chronological order on the interface. Users can access three types of information through the proposed interface: (1) characters' relationships for an episode, (2) a transition of the characters' relationships in chronological order, and (3) entrances and exits of characters. Experimental results showed that the proposed interface could support the participants in remembering the events of the novel. As a future work, in the proposed interface, as the number of read parts increases, the number of visualizations related to characters will also increase, so if there are many read parts, the number of visualizations to be viewed will increase. To solve this problem, it is necessary to add a function to suppress the increase in the number of visualizations of characters' relationships.

References

1. Agarwal, A., Kotalwar, A., Rambow, O.: Automatic extraction of social networks from literary text: a case study on alice in wonderland. In: Proceedings of the Sixth International Joint Conference on Natural Language Processing, pp. 1202-1208. Asian Federation of Natural Language Processing, Nagoya, Japan, October 2013. https://www.aclweb.org/anthology/I13-1171
2. Elson, D., Dames, N., McKeown, K.: Extracting social networks from literary fiction. In: Proceedings of the 48th Annual Meeting of the Association for Computational Linguistics, pp. 138-147. Association for Computational Linguistics, Uppsala, Sweden, July 2010. https://www.aclweb.org/anthology/P10-101
3. Marazzato, R., Carolina Sparavigna, A.: Extracting networks of characters and places from written works with CHAPLIN (2014). https://arxiv.org/ftp/arxiv/papers/1402/1402.4259.pdf
4. Jayakumar, A., Rao, V., Rohit Kumar, A.S., Banerjee, P., Ravish, R.: Analyzing the development of complex social systems of characters in a work of literary fiction. In: 3rd International Conference for Emerging Technology (INCET). Belgaum, India 2022, pp. 1–7 (2022). https://doi.org/10.1109/INCET54531.2022.9824015
5. Nishihara, Y., Ma, J., Yamanishi, R.: A support interface for remembering events in novels by visualizing time-series information of characters and their existing places. In: Yamamoto, S., Mori, H. (eds.) HCII 2021. LNCS, vol. 12765, pp. 76–87. Springer, Cham (2021). https://doi.org/10.1007/978-3-030-78321-1_7
6. Become a novelist(The site name was translated by the authors.) https://syosetu.com. Access confirmed on January 5th
7. Joint.js. https://www.jointjs.com. Access confirmed on January 5th
8. Forgetting curve. https://en.wikipedia.org/wiki/Forgetting_curve. Access confirmed on January 26th

Generative Artificial Intelligence for the Visualization of Source Code as Comics

David Heidrich[1]([✉])[iD], Andreas Schreiber[2][iD], and Sabine Theis[2][iD]

[1] German Aerospace Center (DLR), Institute for Software Technology,
Münchener Straße 20, 82234 Weßling, Germany
`david.heidrich@dlr.de`

[2] German Aerospace Center (DLR), Institute for Software Technology, Linder Höhe,
51147 Cologne, Germany
`{andreas.schreiber,sabine.theis}@dlr.de`

Abstract. Data comics offer an innovative and accessible approach to visualizing abstract data, like source code. However, creating these comics is very challenging, as it requires an artist who can conceive and draw the comic while having a deep knowledge of the abstract data. This work explores the application of state-of-the art generative AI models, specifically GPT-4 and DALL·E 3, to generate a complete comic using a zero-shot approach with three different prompts. Our experiment focuses on generating comics from Python source code. Through a qualitative evaluation, we observed that chain-of-thought prompting could enhance the quality of the generated comics, showcasing the potential advantages and limitations of current generative AI models in creating comics aimed at software comprehension.

Keywords: Comics · Software Visualization · Software Comprehension · Generative AI

1 Introduction

Visual representations have become essential for making complex information understandable [5,20,36,38]. They can help humans to read, interpret, and understand abstract data, like source code, through a variety of different forms. Among various visualization forms, like graphs [16,17] or virtual environments [14,32], data comics have emerged as a compelling method for storytelling with data [3,9]. Their simplicity and accessibility allow for the effective communication of insights from complex datasets, including networks [2], provenance [42], or interactive data [52]. However, creating engaging comics for abstract datasets, like source code, poses significant challenges. It requires a creator who is not only artistically skilled but also deeply familiar with the underlying data.

Recent technological advancements in generative AI offer promising solutions to these obstacles [13]. Heidrich at al.'s [15] exploration into automating data

© The Author(s), under exclusive license to Springer Nature Switzerland AG 2024
H. Mori and Y. Asahi (Eds.): HCII 2024, LNCS 14690, pp. 35–49, 2024.
https://doi.org/10.1007/978-3-031-60114-9_4

comic creation from source code with AI models, like GPT-4 [33] and Stable Diffusion 1.5 [39], highlights the potential to democratize this process. They used a *text-to-text* model to summarize complex source code and to generate comic frame descriptions. Then, they translated the descriptions to prompts and used the *text-to-image* model to generate the individual comic frames. These tools can simplify summarizing complex code and visualizing it as engaging comics, potentially making technology more accessible to non-experts. Nevertheless, limitations in AI capabilities have previously restricted the efficiency and applicability of these methods, especially for those without technical background. For instance, text-to-text models had no knowledge of text-to-image prompting. Hence, the previous methods required the users to manually convert the comic descriptions to text-to-image prompts. Secondly, the used text-to-image models were not capable of generating a complete data comic. Hence, the users had to individually generate each comic frame and then manually combine them.

This paper builds on the foundation laid by previous research, leveraging the latest advancements in generative AI technology [19] to propose an improved method for generating coherent data comics directly from source code. By employing a zero-shot approach facilitated by an enhanced version of GPT-4 and the text-to-image model DALL·E 3, we aim to significantly reduce the barriers to creating data comics. This research not only addresses the technical limitations encountered by Heidrich et al. [15] but also compares three prompting strategies to elevate the quality and coherence of generated comics. Through this work, we seek to expand the accessibility and applicability of data comics as a powerful tool for data-driven storytelling.

2   Related Work

2.1   Generative AI

Generative AI models and their ability to generate or transform texts to other modalities have enormous implications in various research areas [29]. Among emerging modalities, such as text-to-video or text-to-3D [10], text-to-text models—in form of *large language models* (LLMs) [53]—and *text-to-image models*—in form of *diffusion models* [39]—are already widely adopted.

Due to their ability to *comprehend* abstract data, such as source code, LLMs can significantly increase the productivity of users working with such data. For example, LLMs can increase software developer productivity by supporting architecture-centric design decisions [1], fixing bugs [44], or automatically repairing software systems [8]. Due to the abstract and complex nature of source code, LLMs can have many more applications in the field of software engineering [34], such as source code generation [23], source code understanding [54], or automated unit test writing [41]. In this context, LLMs are also used to help novice learners to write and understand source code [21] or to generate engaging captions for data visualizations [15,24]. Although the interaction with a LLM in the form of a text conversation seems very natural, giving the right instructions to the LLM, i.e., prompting, is not trivial and can significantly affect the quality of the output [27]. For example, proving the LLM with examples of the expected output (few-shot) tends to return better results than a zero-shot approach [6]. Additionally, *chain-of-thought* prompting, i.e., telling the LLM to thing step by step, also tends to increase its performance in a range of arithmetic, common-sense, and symbolic tasks [53], especially in zero-shot approaches [22].

While text-to-image models provide an accessible and cost-effective way to generate images [7], their output quality also depends on the quality of the prompt [26,35]. Although expert users can create high-quality images through specialized prompts and other methods, such as blending concepts [31], non-expert users might struggle to generate specific images. However, recent advances in LLMs enable them to generate specialized text-to-image prompts and even choose an appropriate text-to-image model [37]. This allows a wider range of users to create high-quality images through a LLM conversation, e.g., making it very easy for educators to create images [7].

2.2   Code Comics

Data-driven storytelling through images is a simple and accessible format for communicating data and context [3,9,52]. They are used in many disciplines to make abstract information more understandable [43]. For example, in healthcare, data comics are used to convey factual health information [30] or to enhance the understanding of medical information [40]. In computer science, data comics are commonly used to communicate insights into complex data and concepts, such as networks [2] or provenance [42]. Data comics are also a central part of different tools for teaching and learning programming, such as Coding Strip [49] or CodeToon [46]. Here, data comics provide code-driven storytelling that can help users grasp abstract algorithmic concepts [4,48]. However, comics are also used to facilitate the comprehension process of complex documents, such as user agreements [47,55].

Creating comics for abstract data traditionally requires a creator who is not only artistically skilled but also deeply familiar with the data. While limitations in AI capabilities have previously restricted the efficiency and the capability of automated methods [15], recent advances in text-to-image models have created new possibilities for zero-shot guided creations of coherent images [19].

3   Generation of Comics for Visualizing Source Code

The comic generation process is a task that involves multiple steps [15]: First, the functionality of the source code is summarized. Then, based on that summary, the comic description is created, i.e., we describe (a) the comic character and (b) the individual comic frames. Finally, the descriptions are converted into a text-to-image prompt and used to generate the comic.

Our proposed method uses state-of-the art generative AI models to (1) generate the comic descriptions and the text-to-image prompt with the text-to-text model GPT-4 and to (2) generate the comic with the text-to-image model

DALL·E 3. Due to GPT-4's ability to automatically send the text-to-image prompt to DALL·E 3 and to present the image in the text conversation, the user can generate the comics with a single prompt (see Fig. 1). Optional optimizations or changes can also be performed in this natural conversation.

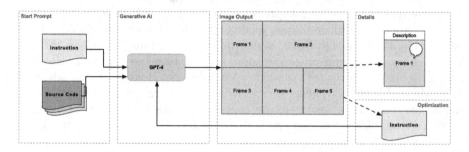

Fig. 1. The described process of generating comics: We start with a prompt that includes the instructions and source code, then GPT-4 generates the comic. Optionally, the user can further optimize the image with instructions or manually add more details, such as speech bubbles or texts.

3.1 Prompt Design

Writing and optimizing LLM prompts is not trivial [27]. Although providing a few examples of inputs and outputs can improve the overall output of the model [56], we opted for a zero-shot prompting approach, as collecting specific examples adds more workload to users [6]. Due to the niche use case of data comics for source code, such examples might not even exist for certain programming languages or concepts. Therefore, we focus on using an optimized zero-shot prompt for a comic creation. As—to the knowledge of the authors—this has not yet been explored in the context of comic generation, this work explores three different prompting methods (see Table 1).

For a baseline, we use a low-quality prompt, where we tell the LLM to generate a data comic without providing any additional information. Here, the only information indicating the task to the LLM is the request for a *creative data comic*. The second prompt is the baseline prompt with chain-of-thought. As described in previous work [22], this can be achieved by adding "Let's think step by step" to the prompt and could potentially increase the quality of the output. For the last prompt, this work explores a high-detailed chain-of-thought prompt. It describes the individual comic creation steps to the LLM and also tells the LLM to follow common "Design Guidelines for Data Comics". This detailed prompt offers the most information to the LLM; therefore, it should produce the best results [27].

3.2 Comics Generation

Following the proposed method, we generated 10 comics with each prompt. All prompts included a Python function from the open-source software project

Table 1. The three different prompts used to generate the comics: The low-quality *Prompt 1*, the low-quality but chain-of-thought *Prompt 2*, and the detailed chain-of-thought *Prompt 3*.

Prompt 1: *Generate a creative data comic that explains the provided source code.*
Prompt 2: *Generate a creative data comic that explains the source code provided. Let's think step by step.*
Prompt 3: *First, create a very short summary of the source code provided. Second, use your "Design Patterns for Data Comics" knowledge to come up with a creative data comic for the summarized code. Finally, use your DALL·E capabilities to generate the comic.*

NetworkX [11,12]. More specifically, they include the `lattice_reference` function (with 74 lines of code) as it uses an advanced algorithm to "untangle" a given graph by swapping edges [28,45].

All prompts produced images that looked like data comics. Although all images contained text, these texts were mainly hallucinated letters (see Fig. 2). Therefore, all images would have needed manual work to insert readable text. But for better comparability of the zero-shot approach, we did not alter the images, nor did we use additional prompting to improve them.

3.3 Study

We conducted interviews with 5 software developers from the German Aerospace Center (DLR). The participants had an average coding experience of 5.75 ($SD = 3.49$) years. None of the participants had used data comics for software comprehension before. Furthermore, none of the participants was familiar with the source code used in this experiment. Hence, all participants had a first-hand experience of understanding a novel piece of source code.

First, the participants went through a preparation phase. Here, participants familiarized themselves with the `lattice_reference` source code. Then, we introduced them to the concept of data comics and presented them our AI-based approach of generating comics from source code. After the preparation phase, we presented our three groups of generated comics to the participants. The order of the groups was randomized. For each comic, the participants first inspected the comic and then the interviewee showed them the GPT-4 output, which included the frame descriptions. After inspecting both outputs, participants rated *image quality* and *story quality* on a 9-point Likert scale [18,25] (from 1 to 10) in terms of how well they facilitate software comprehension for the specific source code. Finally, we asked the participants which comic group, i.e., prompt, they preferred, asked them to generate two additional comics with their preferred prompts, and asked them for an evaluation of the overall comic creation process.

Fig. 2. The highest rated comic (P1-10) with using Prompt 1. The generated description includes 5 frames, which show (1) a programmer who introduces the 'lattice_reference' function, (2) a visual metaphor of the graph and the restrictions on the graph size, (3) a demonstration of the process of picking random edges, (4) the rewiring attempts of the edges, and (5) the resulting modified graph and the satisfied programmer.

3.4 Results

For the generated *text descriptions*, Prompt 1 had the lowest average user rating of 5.08 ($SD = 1.26$), Prompt 2 had an average rating of 5.48 ($SD = 1.30$), and Prompt 3 had the highest average rating of 7.10 ($SD = 1.45$). In the qualitative feedback, *all* participants agreed that prompt 1 produced the worst comic descriptions (see Fig. 3). Participants thought that this was mainly due to the text descriptions being hard to draw for the text-to-image model. For example, P1-10 (see Fig. 2) contained the description: "Frame 2 shows a visual metaphor of the graph and restrictions on the graph size". Additionally, many descriptions did not tell a coherent story across the comic frames. In regards to the other prompts, participants generally liked the generated descriptions with Prompt 2, because they often managed to tell coherent stories across the comic frames and stayed close the source code. However, *all* participants preferred the descriptions generated with Prompt 3. Although no comic descriptions generated with Prompt 1 or 2 received a *perfect* score, four participants gave at least one *perfect* score to comic descriptions generated with Prompt 3. Participants liked the creativity of how the concepts of the source code were translated into comic stories and stated that it produced the most interesting stories.

For the generated *comics*, Prompt 1 had the lowest average user rating of 3.24 ($SD = 1.02$), Prompt 2 had an average rating of 5.14 ($SD = 1.48$), and Prompt 3 had the highest average rating of 5.98 ($SD = 1.10$). In the qualitative feedback, *all* participants agreed that Prompt 1 produced the worst comics

Prompt 1	
P1-1 M=2.00 (SD=0.89)	**P1-2** M=3.20 (SD=0.75)
P1-3 M=2.20 (SD=0.75)	**P1-4** M=3.40 (SD=1.02)
P1-5 M=2.60 (SD=0.49)	**P1-6** M=3.00 (SD=0.00)
P1-7 M=4.60 (SD=0.49)	**P1-8** M=4.00 (SD=0.63)
P1-9 M=1.80 (SD=0.40)	**P1-10** M=2.80 (SD=0.75)

Prompt 2	
P2-1 M=4.80 (SD=1.17)	**P2-2** M=5.20 (SD=2.40)
P2-3 M=2.40 (SD=0.49)	**P2-4** M=5.60 (SD=2.58)
P2-5 M=7.80 (SD=0.75)	**P2-6** M=3.40 (SD=0.49)
P2-7 M=4.20 (SD=0.40)	**P2-8** M=5.40 (SD=2.06)
P2-9 M=3.40 (SD=1.50)	**P2-10** M=7.80 (SD=1.17)

Prompt 3	
P3-1 M=8.60 (SD=1.20)	**P3-2** M=8.20 (SD=3.12)
P3-3 M=5.80 (SD=2.32)	**P3-4** M=6.40 (SD=1.36)
P3-5 M=6.40 (SD=1.74)	**P3-6** M=6.40 (SD=1.36)
P3-7 M=6.00 (SD=0.63)	**P3-8** M=7.20 (SD=1.47)
P3-9 M=7.40 (SD=0.80)	**P3-10** M=8.60 (SD=0.49)

Fig. 3. Comic description quality ratings by the participants for each comic on how well the comic frame descriptions explain the functionality of the source code. Lower ratings are red and higher ratings are green. (Color figure online)

(see Fig. 4). Comics generated with Prompt 1 were not coherent, contained too much unnecessary information, and were too overloaded. *All* participants stated that Prompt 2 and 3 created significantly better comics. These comics were more coherent, contained more useful information, and were easier to understand. Here, four participants favored the comics created with Prompt 3, because they had better image composition and contained only relevant information. But, one participant favored the comics created with the Prompt 2. This was due to personal taste, as Prompt 3 lead to "too creative images"—like a very colorful space setting in P3-3 (see Fig. 6)—while Prompt 2 was more "realistic".

After rating the pre-generated comics and generating comics by themselves, all participants agreed that *all* generated comics had some kind of issue that required additional work to fix it. This includes replacing hallucinated texts with the texts from the generated descriptions and removing frames that were falsely added by the text-to-image model. Additionally, some comics were unusable as they did not follow the text-to-image prompts or they were missing important frames. However, despite these issues, *all* participants agreed that the described comic creation method is very easy to use and that the resulting comics—with additional manual optimization—can help them and other software developers to better understand the source code (Fig. 5).

Prompt 1		Prompt 2		Prompt 3	
P1-1 *M=5.20* *(SD=0.75)*	**P1-2** *M=3.80* *(SD=0.98)*	**P2-1** *M=4.60* *(SD=1.62)*	**P2-2** *M=5.80* *(SD=2.56)*	**P3-1** *M=7.20* *(SD=1.60)*	**P3-2** *M=5.40* *(SD=1.74)*
P1-3 *M=3.80* *(SD=2.23)*	**P1-4** *M=1.40* *(SD=0.49)*	**P2-3** *M=3.40* *(SD=1.85)*	**P2-4** *M=6.40* *(SD=2.58)*	**P3-3** *M=5.80* *(SD=2.32)*	**P3-4** *M=4.60* *(SD=0.49)*
P1-5 *M=4.20* *(SD=0.40)*	**P1-6** *M=3.20* *(SD=0.75)*	**P2-5** *M=3.00* *(SD=0.00)*	**P2-6** *M=5.80* *(SD=1.83)*	**P3-5** *M=4.00* *(SD=1.90)*	**P3-6** *M=4.80* *(SD=0.75)*
P1-7 *M=2.80* *(SD=1.47)*	**P1-8** *M=1.80* *(SD=0.75)*	**P2-7** *M=5.00* *(SD=1.41)*	**P2-8** *M=5.80* *(SD=1.72)*	**P3-7** *M=5.60* *(SD=0.80)*	**P3-8** *M=8.40* *(SD=0.49)*
P1-9 *M=1.00* *(SD=0.00)*	**P1-10** *M=5.20* *(SD=2.40)*	**P2-9** *M=3.40* *(SD=0.49)*	**P2-10** *M=8.20* *(SD=0.75)*	**P3-9** *M=7.40* *(SD=0.49)*	**P3-10** *M=6.60* *(SD=0.49)*

Fig. 4. Comic quality rating by the participants for each generated comic on how well the comics explain the functionality of the source code. Lower ratings are red and higher ratings are green. (Color figure online)

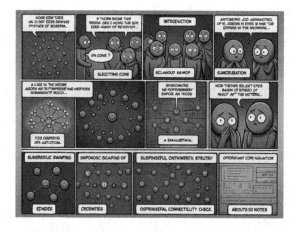

Fig. 5. The highest rated comic (P2-10) using Prompt 2. The generated description includes 8 frames, which show (1) an introduction of the node characters which are connected by edges, (2) the nodes expressing concern if the network is too small, (3) the algorithm initiating the rewiring process, (4) the selection of edges based on probability, (5) the dramatic swapping of edges, (6) a suspenseful connectivity check, (7) the optimized network structure, and (8) the credits.

Fig. 6. The highest rated comic (P3-3) using Prompt 3. The generated description includes 6 frames, which show (1) a galaxy of nodes and edges, (2) a 'Graph Inspector' ensuring it has enough nodes and edges, (3) a 'Node Selector' with a fishing rod randomly picking nodes and a 'Degree Balancer' measuring the edges, (4) a 'Edge Rewirer' swapping connections between nodes aiming for a diagonal pattern in the graph, (5) a dramatic scene where a connection swap almost breaks the graph, and (6) the graph with a lattice structure and the characters celebrating.

4   Discussion

The qualitative study was designed to evaluate our zero-shot approach to generate comics from source code with three different prompts. All participants rated the same collection of pre-generated text descriptions and comics. The prompts differed in their strategy, but all used the same source code. In this way, we investigated the influence of different prompting styles on generated comics in a zero-shot scenario. Additionally, the participants generated comics for themselves with our method. In this way, we investigated the overall acceptance of our comic generation method.

4.1   Code Comic Generation

For the generated text descriptions, the qualitative evaluation indicates qualitative differences between the three prompts. As expected, the low-quality Prompt 1 received the worst feedback, with the lowest rated comic description P1-9 of 1.80 ($SD = 0.40$) and the highest rated comic description P1-4 of 4.60 ($SD = 0.49$). It consistently produced low-quality text descriptions while also providing very short frame descriptions. Hence, especially the fact that GPT-4 did not provide reasoning on why it chose the frame descriptions, made Prompt 1 not suitable for our comic generation process. In this regard, adding chain-of-thought improved this behavior. Prompt 2 and 3 resulted in detailed source code summaries and frame descriptions with explanations. While the qualitative results indicate an overall quality improvement of Prompt 2 compared to

Prompt 1, the quality of the individual comic descriptions differed strongly. For example, prompt 2 resulted in comic descriptions P2-3 with an average user rating of 2.4 ($SD = 0.48$) and also in comic description P2-10 with an average user rating of 7.8 ($SD = 1.16$). Hence, it's inconsistency might reduce the overall usability of our comic generation process, as it requires knowledge by the user to determine the quality of the results and whether they must re-generate the output. However,—based on the user feedback—this inconsistency issue seems to be resolved in the high-detailed Prompt 3. While it received the highest overall user ratings, the individual comic descriptions also received high ratings with the lowest rated comic description P3-3 with 5.8 ($SD = 1.16$) and the two highest rated comic descriptions P3-1 ($SD = 1.20$) and P3-10 ($SD = 0.48$) with an average rating of 8.60. Hence, for data comic text descriptions, our results are in line related work with our detailed chain-of-thought Propmt 3 being preferred by the users.

For the generated comics, the qualitative evaluation also indicated qualitative differences between the three prompts. Notably, two comics of the low-quality Prompt 1 got very low ratings. Comic P1-9 got the lowest possible rating of 1.00 ($SD = 0.00$) and comic P1-4 got an average rating of 1.40 ($SD = 0.49$). In both cases, the text-to-image AI generated a single comic frame with seemingly random content. While some comics generated with Prompt 1 got higher ratings, e.g., the highest average rated comic P1-10 with 5.02 ($SD = 2.2$), Prompt 1 received the worst feedback again. The reason for this might be the bad text description basis, as bad comic descriptions generally might results in worse comics. Interestingly, the differences in average user ratings between Prompt 2 and 3 were very low. For example, the highest rated comic P2-10 with Prompt 2 got an average rating of 8.20 ($SD = 0.75$) and the highest rated comic P3-8 with Prompt 3 got an average rating of 8.40 ($SD = 0.49$). The lowest rated comic P2-5 with prompt 2 got an average rating of 3.00 ($SD = 0.00$) and the lowest rated comic P3-5 with prompt 3 got an average rating of 4.00 ($SD = 1.90$). Hence, while the comics generated with Prompt 3 received the best user feedback, Prompt 2 and Prompt 3 seemed to produce similar text-to-image prompts.

Overall, the qualitative feedback indicates a strong quality improvement for the chain-of-thought prompts in our zero-shot use-case for generating comics. Despite the seemingly small difference between Prompt 1 and Prompt 2, participants clearly favored the results of Prompt 2. Hence, our results are in line with prior LLM research [22] and adds another scenario in which chain-of-thought prompting can potentially improve the quality of the output. Additionally, our results indicate that extending a simple chain-of-thought prompt with additional information, i.e., the required steps needed to solve the task, explicitly mentioning best practices, and mentioning the text-to-image model, seemed to further improve the quality of the output. While we must conduct more user studies, our results indicate that—independent from the comic creation method—the prompt used for the LLM might have a significant impact on the overall quality of the comics. While Prompt 2 and Prompt 3 both received good feedback from our participants, the non-chain-of-thought Prompt 1 seemed to be an inferior prompt for our use case. Especially, as it lacks additional explanations and feedback, which is needed for a good user experience [50].

In addition, the qualitative feedback highlights the potential of the porposed comic generation process to help users to better understand software by presenting complex software systems in an accessible and engaging comic. As the proposed method—especially with Prompt 3—did consistently produce detailed comic descriptions and coherent comics, the potential target group could not only include software developers, but also newcomers to software projects, management, or students who may not have a technical background but still need to understand the software.

4.2   Limitations

Despite the positive qualitative feedback, the proposed method has several limitations:

- We used two cloud-based and closed-source generative AI models (GPT-4 and DALL·E 3) for our comics generation. While this makes it easier for people without the required hardware to run generative AI models, it ultimately makes it harder to reproduce our results. For example, iterative updates to GPT-4 might change it's behavior for certain prompts. Therefore, future work is needed to test our method on different open-source generative AI models, such as LLama [51] and Stable Diffusion [39].
- DALL·E 3 generated non-readable text to every comic. While this will probably be fixed in a future version, this probably had a negative impact on the overall rating of the comics and our methodology. We did not fix the texts by hand to maintain fair comparisons between the prompts. However, showing optimized comics to our participants might have resulted in different ratings.
- Regarding the visualized source code, this work used a single Python function. We chose this function because it was very complex, hence, be a realistic use case where software developers might need help to comprehend the source code. While we only looked at a single Python function to get more comparable results across the different prompts, further work is needed to see if we get similar results for other Python functions or other prograOn the basis of languages. Based on the LLM, results across different programming languages might change.
- Finally, we conducted interviews with a small number of experts. Hence, for a more reliable and valid result, we should increase the number of participants. Additionally, to evaluate the accessibility of out method, we have to conduct additional interviews with non-programmers. That way, we can evaluate whether certain user groups, who cannot write and understand source, might also be able to create data comics.

5   Conclusions and Future Work

This paper explored the capabilities of current state-of-the-art generative AI models to create complete data comic from source code in a zero-shot approach.

In this paper, we presented a comic generation process based on the text-to-text model GPT-4 and the text-to-image model DALL·E 3. We evaluated the proposed method in a qualitative user study with professional software developers and explored three different prompting techniques in regard the generated comic descriptions and the generated comics.

The participants found the overall zero-shot generation process very accessible and helpful for software comprehension. However, all generated comics contained hallucinated components, like text or additional comic frames, that required manual optimizations. In regards to the prompts, participants preferred the generated comic descriptions and comics from the chain-of-thought prompts. In this context, the high-detailed chain-of-thought prompt received the most positive feedback compare to the low-detail chain-of-thought prompt.

Future research is needed to test the proposed method with more participants and different target groups, e.g., non-programmers. Additionally, the proposed method needs to be tested with different programming languages. Another research direction is testing the comic generation method with open-source generative AI models, as this ultimately results in more reproducible results.

References

1. Ahmad, A., Waseem, M., Liang, P., Fahmideh, M., Aktar, M.S., Mikkonen, T.: Towards human-bot collaborative software architecting with ChatGPT. In: Proceedings of the 27th International Conference on Evaluation and Assessment in Software Engineering. pp. 279–285 (2023)
2. Bach, B., Kerracher, N., Hall, K.W., Carpendale, S., Kennedy, J., Henry Riche, N.: Telling stories about dynamic networks with graph comics. In: Proceedings of the 2016 CHI Conference on Human Factors in Computing Systems, pp. 3670–3682 (2016)
3. Bach, B., Riche, N.H., Carpendale, S., Pfister, H.: The emerging genre of data comics. IEEE Comput. Graphics Appl. **37**(3), 6–13 (2017)
4. Bettin, B., Jarvie-Eggart, M., Steelman, K.S., Wallace, C.: Developing a comic-creation assignment and rubric for teaching and assessing algorithmic concepts. In: 2021 IEEE Frontiers in Education Conference (FIE), pp. 1–5. IEEE (2021)
5. Chotisarn, N., Merino, L., Zheng, X., Lonapalawong, S., Zhang, T., Xu, M., Chen, W.: A systematic literature review of modern software visualization. J. Visualization **23**, 539–558 (2020)
6. Dang, H., Goller, S., Lehmann, F., Buschek, D.: Choice over control: how users write with large language models using diegetic and non-diegetic prompting. In: Proceedings of the 2023 CHI Conference on Human Factors in Computing Systems, pp. 1–17 (2023)
7. Dehouche, N., Dehouche, K.: What's in a text-to-image prompt? The potential of stable diffusion in visual arts education. Heliyon (2023)
8. Fan, Z., Gao, X., Mirchev, M., Roychoudhury, A., Tan, S.H.: Automated repair of programs from large language models. In: 2023 IEEE/ACM 45th International Conference on Software Engineering (ICSE), pp. 1469–1481. IEEE (2023)
9. Farmer, L.S.: Information architecture and the comic arts: knowledge structure and access. In: Web Design and Development: Concepts, Methodologies, Tools, and Applications, pp. 569–588. IGI Global (2016)

10. Gozalo-Brizuela, R., Garrido-Merchan, E.C.: ChatGPT is not all you need. a state of the art review of large generative AI models. arXiv preprint arXiv:2301.04655 (2023)
11. Hagberg, A., Schult, D., Swart, P.: NetworkX (2024). https://github.com/networkx/networkx
12. Hagberg, A.A., Schult, D.A., Swart, P.J.: Exploring network structure, dynamics, and function using NetworkX. In: Varoquaux, G., Vaught, T., Millman, J. (eds.) Proceedings of the 7th Python in Science Conference, pp. 11 – 15. Pasadena, CA USA (2008)
13. He, Y., Cao, S., Shi, Y., Chen, Q., Xu, K., Cao, N.: Leveraging large models for crafting narrative visualization: a survey. arXiv preprint arXiv:2401.14010 (2024)
14. Heidrich, D., Meinecke, A., Schreiber, A., Byška, J., Jänicke, S., Schmidt, J.: Towards a collaborative experimental environment for graph visualization research in virtual reality. In: EuroVis 2021-Posters (2021)
15. Heidrich, D., Schreiber, A.: Visualizing source code as comics using generative AI. In: 2023 Working Conference on Software Visualization (VISSOFT), pp. 40–44. IEEE (2023). https://doi.org/10.1109/VISSOFT60811.2023.00014
16. Heidrich, D., Schreiber, A., Oberdörfer, S.: Towards generating labeled property graphs for comprehending c#-based software projects. In: Proceedings of the 37th IEEE/ACM International Conference on Automated Software Engineering, pp. 1–4 (2022)
17. Herman, I., Melançon, G., Marshall, M.S.: Graph visualization and navigation in information visualization: a survey. IEEE Trans. Visual Comput. Graphics 6(1), 24–43 (2000)
18. Jebb, A.T., Ng, V., Tay, L.: A review of key likert scale development advances: 1995–2019. Front. Psychol. 12 (2021). https://doi.org/10.3389/fpsyg.2021.637547
19. Jeong, H., Kwon, G., Ye, J.C.: Zero-shot generation of coherent storybook from plain text story using diffusion models. arXiv preprint arXiv:2302.03900 (2023)
20. Tomihisa, K., Satoru, K.: A general framework for visualizing abstract objects and relations (1991)
21. Kazemitabaar, M., Hou, X., Henley, A., Ericson, B.J., Weintrop, D., Grossman, T.: How novices use llm-based code generators to solve cs1 coding tasks in a self-paced learning environment. arXiv preprint arXiv:2309.14049 (2023)
22. Kojima, T., Gu, S.S., Reid, M., Matsuo, Y., Iwasawa, Y.: Large language models are zero-shot reasoners. Adv. Neural. Inf. Process. Syst. 35, 22199–22213 (2022)
23. Li, R., et al.: Starcoder: may the source be with you! arXiv preprint arXiv:2305.06161 (2023)
24. Liew, A., Mueller, K.: Using large language models to generate engaging captions for data visualizations. arXiv preprint arXiv:2212.14047 (2022)
25. Likert, R.: A technique for the measurement of attitudes. Arch. Psychol. 22, 1–55 (1932)
26. Lin, Y., Xian, X., Shi, Y., Lin, L.: Mirrordiffusion: stabilizing diffusion process in zero-shot image translation by prompts redescription and beyond. IEEE Signal Process. Lett. (2024)
27. Liu, P., Yuan, W., Fu, J., Jiang, Z., Hayashi, H., Neubig, G.: Pre-train, prompt, and predict: a systematic survey of prompting methods in natural language processing. ACM Comput. Surv. 55(9), 1–35 (2023)
28. Maslov, S., Sneppen, K.: Specificity and stability in topology of protein networks. Science 296(5569), 910–913 (2002)

29. McIntosh, T.R., Susnjak, T., Liu, T., Watters, P., Halgamuge, M.N.: From google Gemini to OpenAI q* (q-star): a survey of reshaping the generative artificial intelligence (AI) research landscape (2023)
30. McNicol, S.: The potential of educational comics as a health information medium. Health Inf. Librar. J. **34**(1), 20–31 (2017)
31. Melzi, S., Peñaloza, R., Raganato, A.: Does stable diffusion dream of electric sheep? (2023)
32. Misiak, M., Schreiber, A., Fuhrmann, A., Zur, S., Seider, D., Nafeie, L.: Islandviz: a tool for visualizing modular software systems in virtual reality. In: 2018 IEEE Working Conference on Software Visualization (VISSOFT), pp. 112–116. IEEE (2018)
33. OpenAI: GPT-4 technical report. arxiv 2303.08774 **2**, 13 (2023)
34. Ozkaya, I.: Application of large language models to software engineering tasks: opportunities, risks, and implications. IEEE Softw. **40**(3), 4–8 (2023)
35. Pavlichenko, N., Ustalov, D.: Best prompts for text-to-image models and how to find them. In: Proceedings of the 46th International ACM SIGIR Conference on Research and Development in Information Retrieval, pp. 2067–2071 (2023)
36. al Qaimari, G., Paton, N.W., Kilgour, A.C.: Visualizing advanced data modelling constructs. Inf. Software Technol. **36**(10), 597–605 (1994)
37. Qin, J., et al.: Diffusiongpt: LLM-driven text-to-image generation system. arXiv preprint arXiv:2401.10061 (2024)
38. Raquel Navarro-Prieto, J.C.: Mental representation and imagery in program comprehension. In: Annual Workshop of the Psychology of Programming Interest Group (1999)
39. Rombach, R., Blattmann, A., Lorenz, D., Esser, P., Ommer, B.: High-resolution image synthesis with latent diffusion models. In: Proceedings of the IEEE/CVF Conference on Computer Vision and Pattern Recognition, pp. 10684–10695 (2022)
40. Rothwell, E., Cheek-O'Donnell, S., Johnson, E., Wilson, A., Anderson, R.A., Botkin, J.: Exploring the use of a comic for education about expanded carrier screening among a diverse group of mothers. J. Commun. Healthc. **14**(3), 252–258 (2021)
41. Schäfer, M., Nadi, S., Eghbali, A., Tip, F.: An empirical evaluation of using large language models for automated unit test generation. IEEE Trans. Software Eng. **50**, 85–105 (2023)
42. Schreiber, A., Struminksi, R.: Visualizing the provenance of personal data using comics. Computers **7**(1), 12 (2018)
43. Siregar, H.F., Siregar, Y.H., Melani, M.: Perancangan aplikasi komik hadist berbasis multimedia. (JurTI) Jurnal Teknologi Informasi **2**(2), 113–121 (2018)
44. Sobania, D., Briesch, M., Hanna, C., Petke, J.: An analysis of the automatic bug fixing performance of chatgpt. arXiv preprint arXiv:2301.08653 (2023)
45. Sporns, O., Zwi, J.D.: The small world of the cerebral cortex. Neuroinformatics **2**, 145–162 (2004)
46. Suh, S.: Codetoon: a new visual programming environment using comics for teaching and learning programming. In: Proceedings of the 53rd ACM Technical Symposium on Computer Science Education V. 2. SIGCSE 2022, New York, NY, USA, p. 1177. Association for Computing Machinery (2022). https://doi.org/10.1145/3478432.3499254
47. Suh, S., Lamorea, S., Law, E., Zhang-Kennedy, L.: Privacytoon: concept-driven storytelling with creativity support for privacy concepts. In: Designing Interactive Systems Conference, pp. 41–57 (2022)

48. Suh, S., Latulipe, C., Lee, K.J., Cheng, B., Law, E.: Using comics to introduce and reinforce programming concepts in CS1. In: SIGCSE, pp. 369–375 (2021)
49. Suh, S., Lee, M., Xia, G., law, E.: Coding strip: a pedagogical tool for teaching and learning programming concepts through comics. In: 2020 IEEE Symposium on Visual Languages and Human-Centric Computing (VL/HCC), pp. 1–10 (2020). https://doi.org/10.1109/VL/HCC50065.2020.9127262
50. Theis, S., Jentzsch, S., Deligiannaki, F., Berro, C., Raulf, A.P., Bruder, C.: Requirements for explainability and acceptance of artificial intelligence in collaborative work. In: Degen, H., Ntoa, S. (eds.) HCII 2023. LNCS, vol. 14050, pp. 355–380. Springer, Cham (2023). https://doi.org/10.1007/978-3-031-35891-3_22
51. Touvron, H., et al.: Llama: open and efficient foundation language models. arXiv preprint arXiv:2302.13971 (2023)
52. Wang, Z., Romat, H., Chevalier, F., Riche, N.H., Murray-Rust, D., Bach, B.: Interactive data comics. IEEE Trans. Visual Comput. Graphics **28**(1), 944–954 (2022). https://doi.org/10.1109/TVCG.2021.3114849
53. Wei, J., et al.: Emergent abilities of large language models. arXiv preprint arXiv:2206.07682 (2022)
54. Wong, M.F., Guo, S., Hang, C.N., Ho, S.W., Tan, C.W.: Natural language generation and understanding of big code for AI-assisted programming: a review. Entropy **25**(6), 888 (2023)
55. Yu, H.: Conceptual art or readable contract: the use of comics in technical communication. Tech. Commun. Q. **29**(3), 222–239 (2020)
56. Zhao, Z., Wallace, E., Feng, S., Klein, D., Singh, S.: Calibrate before use: improving few-shot performance of language models. In: International Conference on Machine Learning, pp. 12697–12706. PMLR (2021)

Analysis of Relationships Between Suicide and Time of Life and Lifestyle Behaviors in Japan Before and After the COVID-19 Pandemic and Use of Generative AI for EBPM

Takafumi Kubota(✉) ⓘD

Tama University, 4-1-1 Tama-Shi, Hijirigaoka 206-0022, Japan
kubota@tama.ac.jp

Abstract. This study aims to explore regional trends in metropolitan suicide rates in Tokyo and the metropolitan area around Tokyo before and after the COVID-19 pandemic, using generative AI to provide evidence for policy-making. Data for one municipality in Tokyo in 2016 and 2021, extracted from the Ministry of Health, Labour and Welfare's Basic Data on Suicide in the Region, will be used. The data will include 71 variables, including age, living together, occupation, location, method, time of day, day of the week, reason for suicide and history of suicide attempts.

The survey method visualizes suicide data for the years 2016 and 2021. Then, spatial correlation is detected using suicide data in the metropolitan area. In addition, data on usual health, working conditions and lifestyle behaviors such as volunteering and hobbies are integrated with the suicide data from the living time and lifestyle data. Here, the data is expanded to all municipalities in Japan, and the relationships are tested using linear regression and vector generalized linear models.

Another research approach uses ChatGPT (version 4), a generative AI. Fuchu City, Tokyo, where the author lives, is the focus of this study, comparing annual changes in Fuchu City before and after the COVID-19 pandemic (2016 and 2021) and contrasting data for Tokyo as a whole and Fuchu City in 2021. Here, a comparison of Fuchu City (municipality) and Tokyo (prefecture) averages is prompted into ChatGPT using 71 variables of data, allowing it to detect differences and generate a document summarizing the results; the accuracy of the AI-generated content is assessed to determine its suitability for evidence-based policy-making.

Keywords: Generative AI · Spatial Correlation · Vector Generalized Linear Model

1 Introduction

1.1 Study Motivation

The primary motivation for this study is to understand the impact of the COVID-19 pandemic on suicide rates in Tokyo and its surrounding metropolitan area, with a specific focus on Fuchu City. By leveraging the capabilities of generative AI, specifically

H. Mori and Y. Asahi (Eds.): HCII 2024, LNCS 14690, pp. 50–64, 2024.
https://doi.org/10.1007/978-3-031-60114-9_5

ChatGPT version 4, this research aims to analyze complex and multifaceted data, encompassing 71 variables such as age, occupation, reasons for suicide, and more. The study's goal is to identify patterns and correlations that may not be immediately apparent through traditional analytical methods. This approach is expected to yield insights that can guide effective policy-making, particularly in addressing mental health issues exacerbated by the pandemic. The research also seeks to evaluate the efficacy of AI tools in processing and interpreting large datasets for public health research, potentially setting a precedent for future studies in this domain.

1.2 Previous Studies

The impact of COVID-19 on suicide is discussed in Tanaka et al. (2021) and Koda et al. (2022). Another study conducted linear regression analysis linking with other data is Liu et al. (2024). Examples utilizing generative AI, such as ChatGPT, are discussed in Kubota (2023) and Kubota et al. (2023).

Tanaka et al. (2021) observed that Japan's suicide rate fell 14% early in the COVID-19 pandemic but surged 16% in the second wave, heavily impacting women and youth, attributing initial declines to government aid and reduced work hours but noting increased stress during the pandemic's continuation.

Koda et al. (2022) highlight the rise in suicide rates post-COVID-19, particularly among women, and examine gender-specific causes. It notes that men's suicides were mainly due to economic and workplace issues, while women's were linked to family conflicts and health problems. The findings stress the importance of creating targeted suicide prevention strategies and policies that address these distinct reasons by gender.

Liu et al. (2024) explored how biological rhythm disruptions affect suicidal ideation in 50 Major Depressive Disorder patients and 50 controls using linear regression analysis. The Hamilton Depression Rating Scale and the Beck Scale for Suicide Ideation linked rhythm disturbances with suicidal thought severity. This research underscores the critical role of biological rhythms in understanding and preventing suicide, suggesting that addressing these disruptions could be critical in intervention strategies.

In Kubota (2023), spatial correlations were confirmed in the municipalities of Tokyo, and the potential use of ChatGPT was examined; within one prefecture, Tokyo, a cluster analysis was carried out using many suicide-related variables. Regarding the use of ChatGPT, focusing on one municipality, the study examined whether it would be possible to make appropriate and valuable comparisons between the focused municipality and Tokyo.

Kubota et al. (2023) discussed the possibility of utilizing ChatGPT in many fields. In particular, the validity of the answers to the questions generated by ChatGPT and the processes that lead to the correct answers are also discussed. Furthermore, the paper also proposes a method to improve individual cases in the field of education based on the text generated by ChatGPT.

1.3 Study Aim

Based on the above, the main focus of this study was to A) confirm changes in suicide trends before and after COVID-19 in the Tokyo metropolitan area in the context of visualization and spatial correlation, B) analyze differences in lifestyle behavior and suicide in particular throughout Japan, and C) utilize the generative AI represented by ChatGPT to further these analyses.

2 Data

2.1 Suicide Data

The data covered in this study are data on suicide by a municipality in 2016 and 2021. They are based on the "Basic Data on Suicide in Local Communities" of the statistics on suicide compiled by the Ministry of Health, Labor and Welfare. In addition to the suicide death rate, suicide items include age, cohabitation, occupation, location, means, time, day of the week, specified reason, and whether or not an attempt was made, each of which has multiple items, so that overall, the data includes 71 variables, including region names.

The target areas are one municipality, Fuchu City; one prefecture, Tokyo Prefecture, which consists of several municipalities; the Tokyo metropolitan area, which consists of several prefectures (consisting of. Gunma, Ibaraki, Saitama, Chiba, Tokyo, Kanagawa and Yamanashi prefectures) and the whole of Japan (consisting of. 47 prefectures, about 1400 municipalities).

2.2 Lifestyle Behavior Data and Linear Models

Linear regression analysis and analysis based on a vector generalized linear model were conducted by linking the 2021 Questionnaire A from the Basic Survey of Social Life, including the city-by-municipality activity rate for lifestyle behavior (hereafter simply Questionnaire A), with the suicide data in 2.1.

suicide.rate	Suicide rates in suicide data (2.1)
s.fml,s.hlt,s.eco,s.wrk	Suicide rates by cause motivation (in order: family, health, economy, workplace, from suicide data of 2.1)
badhealth	Questionnaire A: Percentage of respondents who answered 'not well' and 'not so well' out of the 'usual health status' questions
care	Questionnaire A: Percentage of respondents who answered 'no' to the question 'Do you usually care for a family member?'
neet	Questionnaire A: Percentage of respondents who answered 'no' to the question 'Do you usually work?'
lean	Questionnaire A: Percentage of respondents who answered 'yes' to the question 'Do you do learn, self-development and training?'
learn_culture	Questionnaire A: Percentage of respondents whose 'purpose' is 'to improve my education' out of the questions on 'learning, self-development and training.'
learn_seek	Questionnaire A: Percentage of respondents whose 'purpose' is 'to get a job' out of the questions on 'learning, self-development and training.'

(*continued*)

(continued)

suicide.rate	Suicide rates in suicide data (2.1)
learn_skillup	Questionnaire A: Percentage of respondents whose 'purpose' is 'help to my current job' out of the questions on 'learning, self-development and training.'
volunteer	Questionnaire A: Percentage of respondents who answered 'yes' to the question 'Do you have any VOLUNTEER activities?'
sports	Questionnaire A: Percentage of respondents who answered 'yes' to the question 'Do you have any SOPRTS activities?'
hobby	Questionnaire A: Percentage of respondents who answered 'yes' to the question 'Do you have any HOBBIES and pastimes?'
travel	Questionnaire A: Percentage of respondents who answered 'yes' to the question 'Do you have any TRAVEL/excursions?'

Models are as follows:

- Linear model No. 1 (Model 1):

– Objective variable: suicide.rate
– Explanatory variable: badhealth + care + neet + learn + volunteer + sports + hobby + travel

- Linear model No. 2 (Model 2):

– Objective variable: suicide.rate
– Explanatory variables: badhealth + care + neet + learn_culture
   + learn_seek + learn_skillup + volunteer + sports + hobby + travel

- Vector generalized linear model (Model 3):

– Objective variables: (s.fml, s.hlt, s.eco, s.wrk)
   Explanatory variables: badhealth + care + neet + learn + volunteer + sports + hobby + travel.

3   Analysis

3.1   Visualization

This section describes the data visualization: using the suicide data from 2.1, the suicide rate data for the metropolitan area is visualized for 2016 (Fig. 1) and 2021 (Fig. 2) using a choropleth map.

From the two data sets, the following can be said.

- There are 373 entries, suggesting data from numerous cities.
- The average suicide rate in 2016 was about 17.85 per 100,000 people, with a considerable standard deviation of 10.26, indicating significant variability in suicide rates across cities.

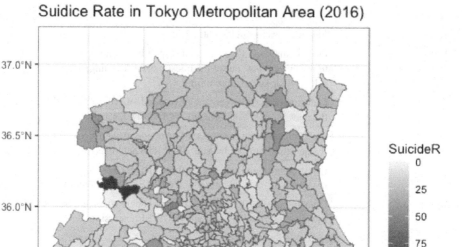

Fig. 1. Choropleth map for Suicide Rate in Tokyo Metropolitan Area in 2016

- In 2021, the average suicide rate slightly decreased to approximately 16.39 per 100,000 people. The standard deviation for 2021 is 9.91, which still reflects substantial variability but suggests a slight overall decrease in suicide rates.
- The minimum suicide rate for both years was 0.00, indicating that there were cities with no recorded suicides in both 2016 and 2021.
- The maximum suicide rate observed increased from 95.33 in 2016 to 99.80 in 2021, showing that the highest recorded suicide rate among the cities increased.
- The 25th, 50th (median), and 75th percentiles all indicate a general decrease in suicide rates from 2016 to 2021 across the dataset.
- This analysis indicates a slight overall decrease in the average suicide rate from 2016 to 2021 across the cities included in the dataset, despite the presence of cities with increases in their suicide rates. The data shows a wide range of suicide rates among cities, highlighting the importance of localized suicide prevention and mental health strategies.

The following two points can be made as a comparison between areas with high and low suicide rates.

In 2016, the city with the highest suicide rate was Kanna-Machi (Gunma Prefecture), with a rate of 95.33 per 100,000 people. Interestingly, this city had a suicide rate of 0.0 per

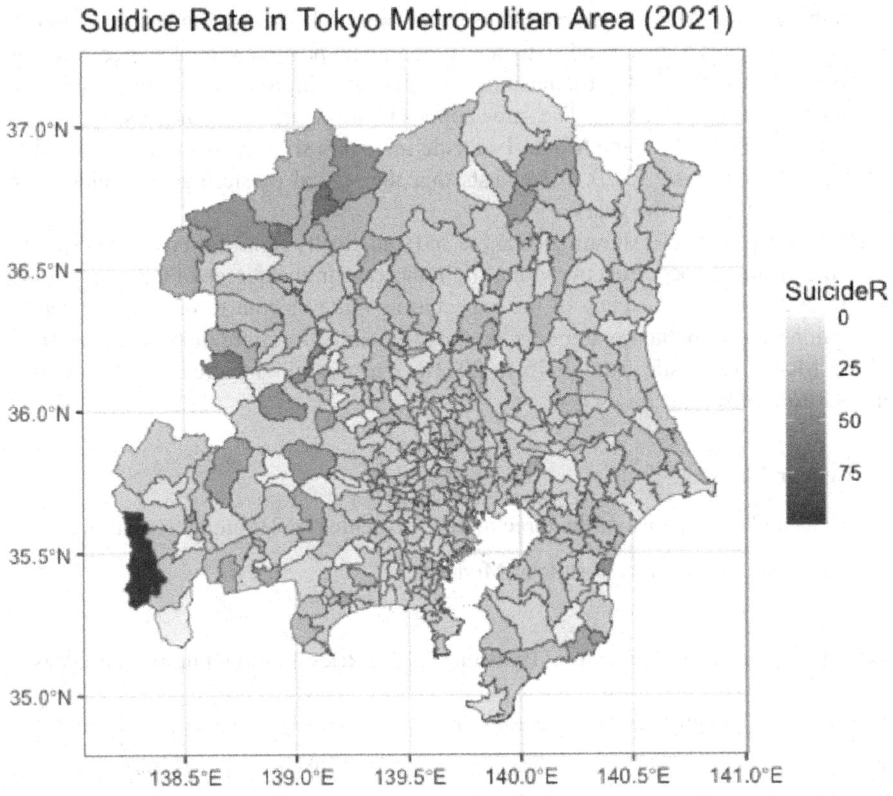

Suidice Rate in Tokyo Metropolitan Area (2021)

Fig. 2. Choropleth map for Suicide Rate in Tokyo Metropolitan Area in 2021

100,000 in 2021, indicating a significant decrease. The city with the lowest suicide rate in 2016, excluding those with a rate of 0, was Hitachi-Omiya-Shi (Ibaraki Prefecture), with a rate of 2.27 per 100,000 people. By 2021, this city's suicide rate increased to 14.78 per 100,000.

Conversely, in 2021, the city with the highest suicide rate was Hayakawa-Cho (Yamanashi Prefecture (, with a rate of 99.80 per 100,000 people, up from 0.0 in 2016, showing a dramatic increase. The city with the lowest suicide rate in 2021, excluding those with a rate of 0, was Inzai-Shi (Chiba Prefecture), with a rate of 0.95 per 100,000 people, down from 8.42 in 2016.

This comparison shows significant variations in suicide rates across different cities from 2016 to 2021, with some cities experiencing dramatic changes in their suicide rates over the five years. These differences highlight the complexity of factors influencing suicide rates and the need for localized approaches to suicide prevention.

Based on these data, i.e. the number of suicides in 373 municipalities in the Tokyo metropolitan area in 2016 and 2021, municipal neighborhood information was further calculated and analyzed for spatial autocorrelation by the Moran test. As a result, spatial autocorrelation was confirmed for both years.

For the result of 2016, the Moran I statistic is around 0.38, with a standard deviation of 12.99, and indicates a strong and statistically significant positive spatial autocorrelation (with p-values less than 2.2e-16), meaning that areas with high suicide numbers are near other areas with high numbers. The same applies to areas with low numbers.

For the result of 2021, the Moran I statistic increases slightly to around 0.390 with a standard deviation of 13.20. It suggests that the spatial clustering of suicides has increased slightly over the years.

In summary, both tests show a substantial and statistically significant pattern of spatial clustering in suicide occurrences, with a slight increase in the degree of clustering from 2016 to 2021. The consistency of the expectation value in both tests indicates stable assumptions about spatial randomness. At the same time, the slight increase in variance and the Moran I statistic from 2016 to 2021 suggest a minor increase in the spatial concentration of suicide cases.

3.2 Lenear Model

The results and discussions of the three models presented in 2.2 are presented in turn.

Model 1. Table 1 shows the results of Model 1.

Table 1. Linear Regression Analysis Predicting Suicide Rates Based on Lifestyle Behaviors

Variable	Coefficient	Std. Error	t value	Pr(>ltl)
Intercept	26.87229	2.86838	9.368	< 0.00001***
badhealth	4.61588	4.57505	1.009	0.31318
care	−0.69402	4.71288	−0.147	0.88295
neet	−7.50064	4.67979	−1.603	0.10921
learn	−8.07637	2.94890	−2.739	0.00624**
volunteer	21.05024	2.67777	7.861	< 0.00001***
sports	−7.63319	3.09025	−2.470	0.01362*
hobby	−6.23442	3.74416	−1.665	0.09611
travel	0.02545	2.30965	0.011	0.99121

Significance codes: 0 '' 0.001 '' 0.01 '' 0.05 '.' 0.1 ' ' 1
Residual standard error: 9.057 on 1416 degrees of freedom
Multiple R-squared: 0.07312, Adjusted R-squared: 0.06788
F-statistic: 13.96 on 8 and 1416 DF, p-value: < 2.2e−16

This linear regression model was developed to predict suicide rates (suicide.rate) using various lifestyle behaviors (badhealth, care, meet, learn, volunteer, sports, hobby, travel) as explanatory variables. The analysis of the model's results provides insights into how these variables might be associated with suicide rates.

The residuals of the model, ranging from −17.195 to 90.735, indicate a broad spread with an exceptionally high maximum value, suggesting the presence of outliers not accounted for by the model. While the median of the residuals is close to zero, and the first and third quartiles (-5.238 and 3.363, respectively) suggest a somewhat symmetric distribution around the center, the presence of extreme outliers indicates potential skewness in the residuals.

The coefficients of the model offer insights into the relationships between lifestyle behaviors and suicide rates. The intercept, estimated at 26.87229, represents the predicted suicide rate when all explanatory variables are zero. Variables such as learn, volunteer, and sports have significant coefficients, with learn and sports showing a negative relationship with suicide rates, indicating that engagement in learning and sports activities might be associated with lower suicide rates. Conversely, volunteer activities have a positive coefficient, suggesting a positive association with suicide rates, although this interpretation requires caution due to the counterintuitive direction of the relationship.

Notably, several variables, including badhealth, care, neet, hobby, and travel, did not show statistically significant effects on suicide rates, as indicated by their p-values. This lack of significance suggests that these variables, within the context of this model, may not have a clear or consistent impact on suicide rates.

The model's overall fit, as indicated by the Multiple R-squared value of 0.07312 and the Adjusted R-squared of 0.06788, suggests that the model explains only a tiny portion of the variance in suicide rates (approximately 7.3%). Although the model is statistically significant, as evidenced by the F-statistic's p-value of less than $2.2e-16$, the relatively low R-squared values highlight the model's limited explanatory power.

In conclusion, this analysis reveals that while certain lifestyle behaviors have significant associations with suicide rates, the overall model captures only a tiny fraction of the variability in suicide rates. The presence of significant outliers and the low R-squared values suggest that there are other factors not included in this model that are influential in determining suicide rates. This analysis underscores the complexity of predicting suicide rates and the need for a more comprehensive approach that includes a broader range of variables.

Model 2. Table 2 shows the results of Model 2.

The revised linear regression analysis (Model 2) introduces a more detailed examination of learning activities by segmenting the learning variable into learn_culture, learn_seek, and learn_skillup, aiming to provide a nuanced understanding of their impact on suicide rates. Despite these adjustments, the overall findings from this model closely mirror those of the initial analysis, both in terms of the statistical significance of various lifestyle behaviors and the model's explanatory power.

The range and quartiles of the residuals in this revised model suggest a distribution around the predicted values similar to the initial model, indicating that the presence of large residuals, and thus outliers, continues to challenge the model's accuracy. This similarity extends to the model's coefficients and their significance levels. Variables such as volunteering and sports maintain their statistically significant relationships with suicide rates, with volunteering associated with an increase and sports with a decrease in suicide rates, reaffirming the findings from the previous model.

The attempt to dissect the learning activities into three distinct categories does not significantly alter the model's insights. Although learn_culture shows a potential negative association with suicide rates, its p-value hovers just above the threshold for statistical

Table 2. Revised Linear Regression Analysis Predicting Suicide Rates Based on Expanded Lifestyle Behaviors

Variable	Coefficient	Std. Error	t value	Pr(>|t|)
Intercept	26.7282	2.8950	9.233	< 0.00001***
badhealth	4.8486	4.5825	1.058	0.2902
care	−0.8768	4.7327	−0.185	0.8531
neet	−7.4781	4.7305	−1.581	0.1141
learn_culture	−7.0781	3.9849	−1.776	0.0759
learn_seek	−6.0831	10.5150	−0.579	0.5630
learn_skillup	−4.5075	5.1655	−0.873	0.3830
volunteer	20.6974	2.6745	7.739	1.9e-14 ***
sports	−7.7534	3.0820	−2.516	0.0120 *
hobby	−6.9764	3.7088	−1.881	0.0602
travel	0.2725	2.3421	0.116	0.9074

Significance codes: 0 '' 0.001 '' 0.01 '' 0.05 '.' 0.1 ' ' 1
Residual standard error: 9.063 on 1414 degrees of freedom
Multiple R-squared: 0.07312, Adjusted R-squared: 0.06656
F-statistic: 11.15 on 10 and 1414 DF, p-value: < 2.2e−16

significance, suggesting a weak relationship at best. The other two learning variables, learn_seek and learn_skillup, do not demonstrate statistically significant effects, underscoring the challenge of pinpointing the impact of specific learning activities on suicide rates.

Regarding the model's fit and predictive power, the nearly identical R-squared values between the two analyses indicate that the additional granularity provided by the breakdown of the learning variable does little to enhance the model's capacity to explain the variance in suicide rates. While indicating the model's overall significance, the F-statistic also reflects the marginal impact of adding more detailed variables concerning learning activities.

Model 3. Table 3 shows the result of Model 3: Vector Generalized Linear Model (VGLM) for effects of Lifestyle Behaviors on Cause-Specific Suicide Rates.

In model 3, the analysis explores the effects of various lifestyle behaviors (badhealth, care, neet, learn, volunteer, sports, hobby, travel) on cause-specific suicide rates, categorically divided into family, health, economic, and workplace reasons. This model enables a detailed understanding of how each lifestyle behavior correlates with different aspects leading to suicide, providing nuanced insights into the complex interplay between lifestyle factors and suicide risks.

The findings from Model 3 necessitate a thorough examination of how explanatory variables influence each cause-specific suicide rate. The significant effect of the care variable on the economic cause of suicide ($p < 0.001$) suggests that the need for care, whether it be for oneself or others, could be associated with economic pressures or

Table 3. Effects of Lifestyle Behaviors on Cause-Specific Suicide Rates Using Vector Generalized Linear Model (VGLM)

	s.fml	s.hlt	s.eco	s.wrk
badhealth	1.0333	2.7504	2.3153**	0.6578
care	1.1380	4.6154	6.6646	0.9207
neet	1.3066	−1.6071	−2.2586	−0.5744
learn	−0.3239	−0.1516	−0.2697	−1.0833
volunteer	−0.0061	0.1913	0.9576	1.2750
sports	−1.9409	1.9255	−0.4461	0.4988
hobby	−0.8383	−3.0041	1.9999	−0.7963
travel	2.5114**	3.6281*	0.7759	1.7058**

Signif. Codes: 0 '***' 0.001 '**' 0.01 '*' 0.05 '.' 0.1 ' ' 1
Log-likelihood: -15856.58 on 11360 degrees of freedom
Number of Fisher scoring iterations: 5

financial stress. This relationship might indicate that the costs or the economic burden associated with care needs could contribute to increased suicide rates related to economic factors. It could suggest that individuals requiring more care might experience increased pressure or stress in the workplace. Furthermore, travel shows a positive impact across all cause-specific suicide rates, suggesting that travel could contribute to stress reduction and an overall increase in well-being, thereby potentially leading to lower suicide rates.

For other variables, the statistical significance of their effects on specific causes of suicide appears limited. This observation suggests the complex causal relationships behind suicide, where a single lifestyle behavior does not directly lead to suicide. For instance, the lack of statistically significant impacts on badhealth, neet, learning, volunteering, sports, and hobbies on specific causes of suicide indicates that these behaviors might interact in complex ways to influence suicide risk.

By evaluating the impact of lifestyle behaviors on cause-specific suicide rates, model 3 provides important insights for designing suicide prevention measures. Understanding the effects of variables like care and travel is particularly valuable in developing suicide prevention programs, such as improving workplace environments or promoting leisure activities.

In conclusion, model 3 offers an effective tool for delving into the complex social and psychological factors underlying suicide by assessing the impact of lifestyle behaviors on cause-specific suicide rates. This approach facilitates the formulation of targeted prevention measures, contributing to the reduction of suicide rates by addressing the multifaceted nature of its causes.

3.3 ChatGPT

The discussion begins with utilizing a generative AI such as ChatGPT in data analysis. Although it cannot replace the entire research process, it can be used to.

1. Raise research questions (to assist in finding research objectives),
2. Review previous research (to assist in selecting research methods),
3. Check statistical data and research results (to assist in discussing research results),
4. Generate evidence from research results for policy decisions (to assist in proposing policies from research results) (Assistance from research results to policy proposals).

Of these, 2) is not mentioned in this paper because it is not limited to ChatGPT but is also possible with conventional websites specializing in web search and article search. It has already been fully incorporated into research in many fields. Also, 4) is not mentioned in this paper because it still needs further study for a helpful measure. This study presents the methods used, particularly for 1) and 3).

Raise Research Questions. In order to confirm the relationship between the given suicide data and the life behavior data from a general perspective, we will consider making use of the findings possessed by the LLM. As the number of suicides is assumed here as the objective variable, we consider narrowing down the explanatory variables for use in linear models from the hundreds of data on lifestyle behavior.

Therefore, by prompting the variables included in the lifestyle behaviors in detail, general causes of suicide are generated as textual results.

The text given as prompting is as follows.

The data on lifestyle behavior includes the following information on the main activities in free time, etc. ('learning/self-development/training', 'volunteering', 'sports', 'hobbies/entertainment' and 'travel/excursions'), by whether the respondents engaged in each type of activity in the past year, the frequency and purpose of the activity and the person with whom the respondent engaged in the activity, as well as the number and percentage of respondents who engaged in the relevant type of activity. The number and percentage of people who have engaged in each type of activity in the past year, by frequency and purpose of the activity, and by the people they were with.

Please consider items related to suicidal behavior.

The results obtained from the ChatGPT are summarized below.

1. Frequency and Type of Activities: Both very high or extremely low frequency of activities could be indicative of mental health states. For example, intense frequent engagement in "Learning, Self-Improvement, or Training" might signal stress or excessive pressure, while minimal activity might indicate social isolation or depressive states.

2. Purpose of Activities: The underlying motives for engaging in activities can reflect an individual's mental health state. Activities pursued for stress relief or social interaction might suggest a healthier lifestyle, whereas activities for escapism or isolation might indicate potential issues.

3. Company in Activities: Spending a lot of time alone or a lack of social support can be indicators of loneliness or social isolation, factors known to be associated with higher suicide risk.

4. Type of Hobbies and Entertainment: Certain hobbies or leisure activities can impact an individual's mood and stress level. Active hobbies (like sports or outdoor activities) generally have a positive impact on mental health, while passive or solitary hobbies might sometimes increase feelings of social isolation or anxiety.

5. Frequency and Nature of Travel and Recreation: Travel and recreational activities are generally associated with positive experiences, but a lack of these activities or excessive frequency could be indicators of stress or dissatisfaction.

The relevant and associated variables were entered as explanatory variables and analyzed in 3.2. However, not all variables were significantly affected.

Aids to the Discussion of Research Results. Comparing many variables in given or visualized data and capturing the characteristics of the data requires much effort (human resources, time and money) when done by humans. By using ChatGPT, results can be obtained more accurately and quickly. For this data comparison between Tokyo and Fuchu City, we first cleaned data by calculating the given data into rates per population. Then, the author used the data for prompting as follows. The latter part of the prompting is simply a copy and paste of the CSV obtained from the data cleaning.

Please explain the difference between the two suicide data sets.

Region Name Suicide death rate Annualized suicide death rate Age under 20 years Age 20.29 years Age 30.39 years Age 40.49 years Age 50.59 years Age 60.69 years Age 70.79 years Age 80 years and over Age Unknown Living together Yes Living together No Living together Unknown Occupation Self-employed . Family employee Occupation employed. Employed Occupation unemployed Occupation student. Student, etc. Occupation unemployed Occupation housewife Occupation unemployed Occupation pension. Unemployed Occupation unemployed Occupation unemployed Occupation unemployed Occupation unemployed Occupation pension. Lake. Rivers, etc. Location Mountains Location Other Location Unknown Hand Hangings Hand Poisoning Hand Charcoal Briquettes, etc. Hand Jumping Hand Diving Hand Other Hand Unknown Time 0.2 hrs Time 2.4 hrs Time 4.6 hrs Time 6.8 hrs Time 8.10 hrs Time 10.12 hrs Time 12.14 hrs Time 14.16 hrs Time 16.18 hrs Time 18.20 hrs Time 20.22 hrs Time 22.24 hrs Time Unknown Sunday Sunday Monday Tuesday Wednesday Thursday Friday Saturday Saturday Unknown Cause Family problems Cause Health problems Cause Economic. Life problems cause Work problems cause Gender problems cause School problems cause Other cause Unknown Attempted Yes No Attempted Unknown

Tokyo 16.25309 16.25309 0.63 2.82 2.17 2.88 2.96 1.65 2.01 1.13 0.01 8.89 7.19 0.17 0.72 5.59 9.43 1.11 8.32 1.01 0.59 1.9 4.83 0.51 9.25 2.3 0.5 0.81 0.22 3.16 0 9 .51 0.44 0.85 3.04 0.71 1.68 0.02 1.86 0.97 1.07 1.12 0.87 0.93 1.18 0.95 1.03 0.93 0.83 0.89 3.63 2.09 2.45 2.27 2.48 2.28 1.99 1.9 0.79 1.63 6.23 1.7 1.18 0.56 0 .3 0.51 7.26 3.12 8.52 4.61

Fuchu, Tokyo 18.44345 18.44345 0 4.61 0.77 3.07 5 1.92 2.31 0.77 0 8.45 9.61 0.38 1.15 6.92 9.99 1.15 8.84 0.77 0 2.69 5.38 0.38 10.37 1.54 1.54 0.77 0 4.23 0 11.91 0.381.15 2.31 0.77 1.92 0 3.07 0.38 1.54 1.54 1.15 2.69 1.54 1.54 0.77

0 0.77 1.92 1.54 2.31 2.31 1.92 4.23 3.07 3.07 1.54 0 1.15 5.38 1.15 1.54 0.77 0
0.38 8.84 3.07 9. 99 5.38

The results obtained are as follows. The results have been checked and found to be valid concerning the content.

I'll explain the differences in the suicide data for Tokyo and Tokyo's Fuchu City in English.

Suicide Mortality Rate: The rate in Tokyo is 16.25309, while in Fuchu City it's 18.44345. This indicates a higher suicide rate in Fuchu City.

Age-wise Suicide Rate: Suicides among those under 20 exist in Tokyo but are absent in Fuchu City. Notably, the rate in the age groups 50-59 and 20-29 are higher in Fuchu City.

Living Situation: Tokyo has a higher rate among those living alone, whereas Fuchu City has a higher rate among those living with someone.

Occupation-wise Suicide Rate: Both regions show a high rate among employed persons and the unemployed. However, the rate is even higher among employed persons in Fuchu City.

Location of Suicide: Suicides at home or similar places are more frequent in Fuchu City. There's also a slight increase in suicides from tall buildings in Fuchu City.

Method of Suicide: Suicides by hanging are more frequent in Fuchu City, while other methods seem similar between the two regions.

Time-wise Suicide Rate: There doesn't appear to be a significant difference between the two regions based on the time of day suicides occur.

Day of the Week: In Fuchu City, the suicide rate is particularly high on Fridays.

Reason for Suicide: Economic and livelihood issues are a major cause of suicides in Fuchu City, while family problems stand out in Tokyo.

Attempted Suicides: Fuchu City has a slightly higher number of attempted suicides.

The differences could be due to a range of factors including the demographic composition of the areas, socio-economic conditions, and mental health status among others.

4 Concluding Remarks and Future Studies

This study evaluates suicide rate changes in the Tokyo Metropolitan Area for 2016 and 2021, using data from 373 cities. It finds a slight decrease in average suicide rates from 17.85 to 16.39 per 100,000 people, despite the highest rates increasing and significant variability across regions. Spatial autocorrelation analysis revealed minor increases in suicide rate clustering, indicating more pronounced spatial concentration over time. The research highlights the challenge of interpreting data from areas with small populations due to potential random fluctuations, underscoring the importance of localized mental health strategies. It suggests the necessity of employing smoothing techniques in future analyses to more accurately represent underlying trends and spatial patterns. By refining analytical methods, future studies aim to provide deeper insights into suicide prevention efforts, emphasizing the complex, varied landscape of suicide rates across the metropolitan area and the need for targeted interventions.

For Linear model regression, Model 1 reveals only a modest portion of the variance in suicide rates can be explained by variables such as learning, volunteering, and sports activities, with a surprising positive association found for volunteering. Despite its statistical significance, the model's explanatory power is limited, as indicated by low R-squared values, suggesting a vast array of unaccounted factors affecting suicide rates.

Further refinement in Model 2, specifically breaking down learning activities into categories (learn_culture, learn_seek, and learn_skillup), does not significantly enhance the model's explanatory power. Although it offers a slightly more detailed view, the impact of these nuanced learning activities on suicide rates remains unclear, with most not reaching statistical significance.

Model 3 shifts focus to cause-specific suicide rates, examining how different lifestyle behaviors influence suicide reasons such as family, health, economic, and workplace issues. This model highlights significant relationships, like the association between the care variable and economic causes of suicide, suggesting nuanced interactions between lifestyle factors and suicide risks. However, many lifestyle behaviors still do not show a significant impact on specific suicide causes, underlining the complexity of factors contributing to suicide.

Collectively, these models underscore the multifaceted nature of suicide, where lifestyle behaviors interact with a broader spectrum of socio-economic and personal factors. While certain activities show potential links to suicide rates, the overall findings stress the need for a comprehensive approach to suicide prevention, incorporating a wide range of variables to fully understand and address the roots of suicide risk.

These analyses have been conducted solely with post-COVID-19 data, highlighting the influence of lifestyle behaviors on suicide rates in the aftermath of the pandemic. However, to gain a more comprehensive understanding of these dynamics, future research will extend to pre-COVID-19 data. This approach will enable a comparison between the periods before and after the pandemic, shedding light on how the global health crisis may have altered the relationship between lifestyle factors and suicide rates. Such comparative analysis is crucial for identifying shifts in suicide risk factors attributable to the pandemic's societal and psychological impacts.

In the analysis conducted using ChatGPT, examples were introduced for two out of four parts, showcasing the potential applications and insights generated through the tool. However, it's crucial to recognize that ChatGPT's utilization does not incorporate expertise from specialists directly, and due to the inherent characteristics of Large Language Models (LLMs), the results obtained are not guaranteed to be accurate. This limitation is particularly noteworthy in the second part, where careful consideration is required to ensure the reliability of the findings.

To address these limitations and improve the quality of analysis, there's a need to develop enhanced LLMs that are trained on the knowledge of experts. Such advancements would allow for a more accurate and nuanced understanding of complex subjects, marking a significant direction for future research.

Furthermore, as of February 2024, ChatGPT (version 4) has become capable of processing data in CSV format, which opens up new possibilities for the utilization of data. This development suggests that the scope for leveraging data in innovative ways through ChatGPT is likely to expand, offering exciting prospects for future applications and research in various fields.

Acknowledgments. This research was a part of the study of the 'Research on the promotion of the use of statistics and other micro-data to contribute to post-colonial suicide prevention' in 'Innovative Research Program on Suicide Countermeasures'.

References

Tanaka, T., Okamoto, S.: Increase in suicide following an initial decline during the COVID-19 pandemic in Japan. Nat. Hum. Behav.Behav. **5**(2), 229–238 (2021)

Koda, M., Harada, N., Eguchi, A., Nomura, S., and Ishida, Y.: Reasons for Suicide During the COVID-19 Pandemic in Japan. JAMA Netw Open, 5(1) (2022)

Liu, D., et al.: Relationship between biological rhythm dysregulation and suicidal ideation in patients with major depressive disorder. BMC Psychiatry **24**, 87 (2024)

Kubota, T.: Analyzing regional suicide patterns in Japan before and after the COVID-19 pandemic and usage of generative AI for EBPM, 23th International Conference on Computational Statistics (COMPSTAT 2018), London (2023)

Kubota, T., Ishikawa, H., Suganuma, M., Yoshimine, N., & Nakamura, S.: Potentials for Application of Generative AI in Basic Education Subjects at Universities. The 12th conference of the Asian Regional Section of the International Association for Statistical Computing (IASC-ARS), Sydney (2023)

The Linked Microposter Plots Family as New Means for the Visualization of Eye Tracking Data

Chunyang Li[1,2] and Jürgen Symanzik[3(✉)]

[1] Division of Epidemiology, University of Utah, Salt Lake City, UT 84108, USA
Catherine.li@utah.edu
[2] George E. Wahlen Veterans Health Administration, Salt Lake City, UT 84148, USA
[3] Department of Mathematics and Statistics, Utah State University,
Logan, UT 84322-3900, USA
juergen.symanzik@usu.edu

Abstract. Eye tracking has been used in many scientific fields, such as education, usability research, sports, psychology, and marketing. Often, visualization plays an important role in the analysis of eye tracking data. In the past, linked micromap plots have been widely used to visualize geographic patterns of regions and subregions. Based on the idea of linked micromap plots, we introduce three different types of linked microposter plots to visualize the eye movement pattern when people are looking at different components (such as headings, tables, figures, and different sections of text) of scientific posters. These types are basic linked microposter plots, linked timeline microposter plots, and linked scanpath microposter plots. When using linked microposter plots, the eye tracking data of people looking at various poster components can be better and more easily interpreted. Linked timeline microposter plots and linked scanpath microposter plots are extensions of basic linked microposter plots. The scanpath time series information is included in the linked scanpath microposter plots visualization. The linked microposter plots and their extensions provide several features that overcome some of the disadvantages of previously existing eye tracking data visualization methods. The linked microposter plots can be created automatically using our **EyeTrackR** R package and can be easily extended to other applications.

Keywords: Eye Tracking Visualizations · Graphics · Scientific Posters

1 Introduction

Eye tracking is the process of measuring where people are looking at with an eye tracker device. Eye trackers were first built in the late 1800s and have been developed rapidly during the past century. [16] provided a comprehensive review on the history of eye trackers as well as on the principles of how they work.

H. Mori and Y. Asahi (Eds.): HCII 2024, LNCS 14690, pp. 65–82, 2024.
https://doi.org/10.1007/978-3-031-60114-9_6

Eye tracking techniques have been applied in a variety of research fields, such as education, usability research, sports, psychology, and marketing. There exist several literature reviews focusing on the application of eye tracking, e.g., [30] provided a comprehensive review on eye tracking for the past twenty years in reading and information processing, and [18] provided a comprehensive review of eye tracking in human-computer interaction and usability research. Software for eye tracking data has been developed for R [29], a freely available language and environment for statistical computing and graphics, in particular the R packages **saccadr** [24], **eyeTrackR** [13], **eyetrackingR** [7,9], **gazeR** [11,12], and **popEye** [31], as well as three additional R packages **eyetracking** [17], **gazepath** [37], and **saccades** [38] that are currently only available in an archived format from the Comprehensive R Archive Network (CRAN). Matlab toolboxes and functions [3,19], Python packages [6,32], and software in other computing environments [15] have also been developed to detect eye movement events, to visualize and model eye tracking data, and to clean raw eye tracking data.

In general, eye tracking technology has become more and more affordable and accessible nowadays [39]. There exists some research on eye tracking for posters and related media. [2] investigated posters in a computer simulated outdoor environment in order to "provide common measurement framework for poster panel visibility across settings and perspectives" with an eye tracking approach. [1] looked at the effect of visual in-store advertisement designing on customers' decisions on purchasing, with participants' eye movement data recorded sitting in front of a computer screen. Using a mobile eye tracker, [10] investigated how people were looking at posters in an indoor environment, but with a focus on academic posters from psychology. However, none of the existing literature on eye tracking for posters has specifically discussed eye tracking visualization or adopted any new visualization techniques. Also, there is only a limited focus on the visualization of eye tracking data in the software packages mentioned above. In this article, we propose three different types of linked microposter plots to visualize eye tracking data of how people are looking at posters, recorded with a mobile eye tracker. These types are basic linked microposter plots, linked timeline microposter plots, and linked scanpath microposter plots. Linked timeline microposter plots and linked scanpath microposter plots are extensions of basic linked micromap plots and are used to visualize the scanpath of the eye tracking data. Therefore, time series information of eye tracking data is included in these two types of linked microposter plots visualizations. Basic linked microposter plots were first introduced in [21]. Software implementations of these three types of linked microposter plots can be found in the **EyeTrackR** R package [20,22]. This article revisits, updates, and extends some of the information from these three references.

The remainder of this article is structured as follows: We will discuss eye tracking data and commonly used eye tracking visualization tools in Sect. 2. The development of linked microposter plots and the construction of linked microposter plots will be discussed in Sects. 3 and 4, respectively. Some resulting plots will be presented and interpreted in Sect. 5. Linked timeline microposter

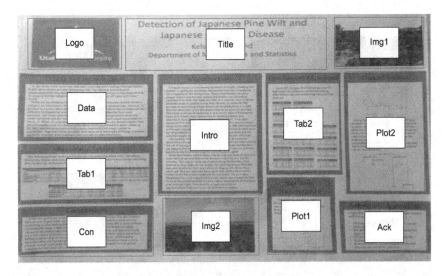

Fig. 1. Poster 1 with twelve AOIs (shown inside the red bounding boxes). The abbreviations Img, Tab, Intro, Con, and Ack refer to the images, tables, introduction, conclusion, and acknowledgement in the poster. (Color figure online)

plots and linked scanpath microposter plots will be introduced and presented in Sect. 6. The **EyeTrackR** R package will be briefly summarized in Sect. 7. We will finish with our conclusion and outline of our future work in Sect. 8.

2 Eye Tracking Data and Visualization

2.1 Data

The two co-authors of this article looked at a series of statistical and other scientific posters, using a 30 Hz mobile eye tracker from ASL that records 30 images per second. For each poster, the areas of interest (AOIs) were defined in advance, such as the title, logos, multiple text areas, images, and tables. For this article, two of the posters, simply called Poster 1 (see Fig. 1) and Poster 2 (see Fig. 2), the resulting videos, and data files have been used. The data for Poster 1 is based on a controlled experiment where the participant was only allowed to look at each AOI for a few seconds. The data for Poster 2 is based on a "free-viewing" experiment where no instructions were given to the participant. Figure 3 shows all the automatically extracted focus points overlaid on Poster 1.

2.2 Visualization

Graphical methods are among the most important tools to explore eye tracking data. Common statistical graphics, such as dot plots, bar charts, and box plots, are frequently used to visualize eye tracking data. Figures 4 and 5 show

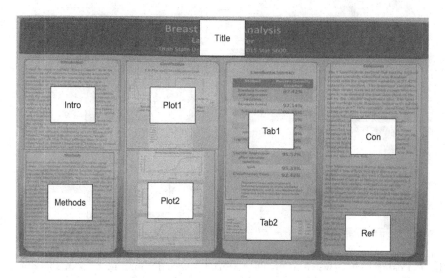

Fig. 2. Poster 2 with nine AOIs (shown inside the red bounding boxes). In addition to the abbreviations already used in Fig. 1, Ref is used to refer to the references in this poster. (Color figure online)

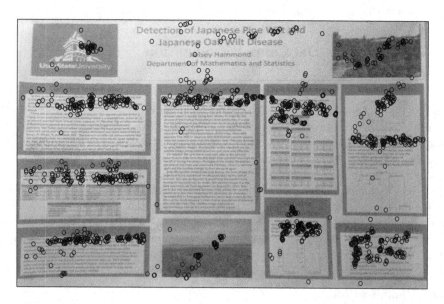

Fig. 3. All extracted focus points overlaid on Poster 1, based on the video frames of the viewing of Poster 1.

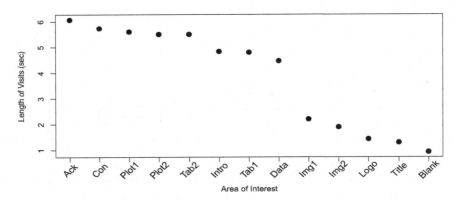

Fig. 4. Dot plot: visualizing the length of visits in each AOI for Poster 1. Blank represents the area between the twelve AOIs.

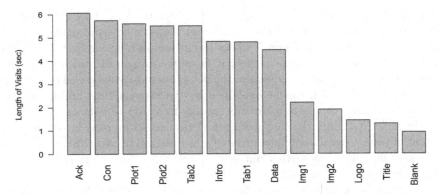

Fig. 5. Bar chart: visualizing the length of visits in each AOI for Poster 1.

examples of using dot plots and bar charts to visualize how much time the participant has spent on each AOI of Poster 1. Figure 6 shows an example of using box plots to visualize the pupil radius in each AOI of Poster 1. The participant's pupil dilated looking at Image 1 and the variation of the pupil radiuses is high looking at the Blank area. Pupil radiuses are measured in pixels on the eye camera and are only comparable within the same experiment with the same calibration. Though it has not been fully established what the changes of pupil radiuses really mean, pupil dilation has been shown to be an indication of changes in light, arousal, cognitive and emotional events, and the difficulty of the task at hand [8]. These three graphs present the eye tracking data statistics, however, they are not overlaid on the scientific poster. Therefore, it is more difficult to obtain further insights of the viewing patterns of the participant in the context of the underlying poster, similarly to looking at summaries of geographic data without looking at a map.

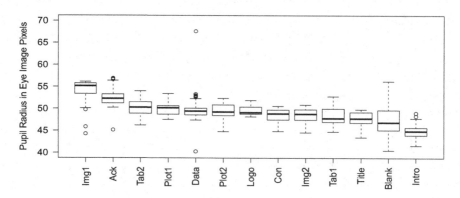

Fig. 6. Box plot: visualizing the pupil radius in each AOI for Poster 1.

Attention maps are also frequently used for eye tracking data visualization [16]. Attention maps are usually based on heat maps or hot spot maps, using a Gaussian kernel function. Figure 7 shows the attention map for Poster 1. With the hot spots overlaid on the poster, it is quite obvious at which areas the participant is looking most frequently: the hot spots mostly appeared on the top part of each AOI, which can be explained by the viewing time limitations for each AOI. Because the participant was reading from top to bottom and left to right in each AOI, only the first few lines of text could be read in the allowed amount of time. Overall, only one variable at a time can be visualized in a single attention map. Also, converting numeric values into a few colors results in an immediate loss of information.

The term "scanpath" was first introduced by [23] to describe the chain of fixations and saccades. A fixation is the state when the eye remains stable for a period of time, and a saccade is the rapid movement of the eye from one fixation to another. In visual representations of scanpaths, circles are typically used to represent fixations and lines are used to represent saccades [14]. The radiuses of the circles indicate the duration of the fixation. Figure 8 shows the scanpath map for Poster 1. Fixations and saccades are identified with the **saccades** R package [38]. The numbers in the circles indicate the sequential order of the fixations. Scanpaths give the sequence of one's eye movements, however, when the viewing patterns become more complex, the crossings and overlaps of scanpaths make it more difficult to perceive the visual patterns.

The AOI timeline for Poster 1 (Fig. 9) shows both the start and end times, as well as the temporal sequence of changes between AOIs. The horizontal axis shows the AOIs and the vertical axis shows the time. We can see from the plot that the participant revisited the data and the title very briefly. The conclusion has been visited twice as well, with a very short visit at the first time. However, an AOI timeline does not present the spatial locations of each AOI from the underlying poster.

There does not exist any type of plot that is specifically designed to visualize how people are looking at posters. To overcome some of the shortcomings of the

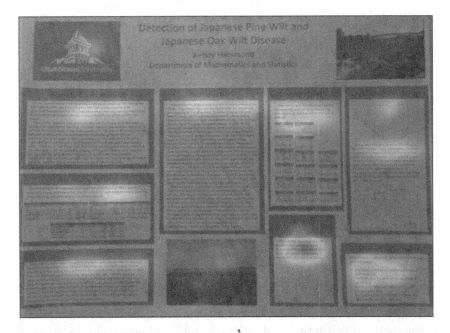

Fig. 7. Attention map: hot spots that attract the participant's attention for Poster 1.

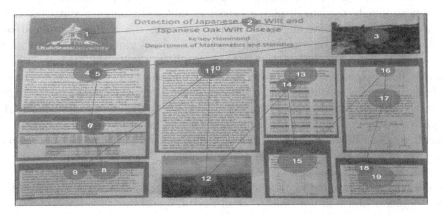

Fig. 8. Scanpath map: the viewing sequences of the participant looking at Poster 1.

commonly used eye tracking data visualization techniques, we introduce linked microposter plots to visualize eye tracking data on posters. Further, linked timeline microposter plots and linked scanpath microposter plots are extensions of basic linked microposter plots that include scanpath and time series information in the plot.

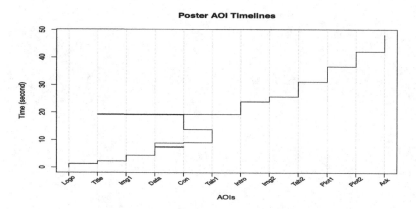

Fig. 9. AOI timelines: the temporal sequence of changes in viewing between AOIs for Poster 1.

3   The Development of Linked Microposter Plots

Linked microposter plots are based on the idea of linked micromap plots, a plot type that was first introduced in 1996 to highlight geographic patterns and associations among the variables in a spatial dataset [5]. Linked micromap plots have been widely used to display geospatially-indexed summary statistics. For some in-depth discussion of linked micromap plots, the reader is referred to [4,35,36], and [34]. According to [4], linked micromap plots can represent any two-dimensional space, not just latitude-longitude on the Earth's surface. Based on this idea, we can think of a poster as a map and the AOIs of the poster as the different countries or states. The AOIs of the posters are the figures, tables, text areas, titles, etc. The length of time spent and the number of times each AOI is visited and pupil radiuses are some of the variables of interest that could be visualized using linked microposter plots. Other variables, such as eye movement speed, could also be visualized using linked microposter plots. Variables can be visualized with different plot types, such as dot plots, bar charts, and box plots, in different statistical data columns of the linked microposter plots, all linked to the original poster and not isolated as in Figs. 4, 5 and 6.

Compared to an attention map, linked microposter plots can be used to explore selected AOIs, instead of simply looking at the hot spots. Rather than focusing on a single detailed poster, there are multiple small posters (microposters) shown in linked microposter plots. The same colors are used to link the areas in the microposters, the names of the AOIs, and the statistical data columns. Providing small microposters on the sides, linked microposter plots reveal the location patterns where one (or multiple) participants look at most on a poster.

4 Linked Microposter Plots Construction

Computer code to construct linked micromap plots has been available since their introduction in 1996, as summarized in [33]. Major R code was provided in 2010 in support of [4]. With the advancement of the R computing environment, more advanced R code for the production of linked micromap plots has been developed. Two R packages, **micromap** [25, 26], and **micromapST** [27, 28], have also been developed to make it easier for non-experts to produce linked micromap plots. However, the **micromapST** R package is primarily focused on linked micromap plots for the United States. The **micromap** R package can be used for any geographic regions, but it requires new geographic shapefiles. Therefore, we developed our R code in the **EyeTrackR** R package for the construction of linked microposter plots based on the original R code for linked micromap plots provided by [4].

The state border data for linked micropmap plots is replaced with the R border data generated by user-defined AOIs. The nation border for linked micromap plots is changed to the border of the whole poster. The poster image is used as the background image in each linked microposter plot. For better showing of the colors that link the various columns, the poster image is changed to a grayscale version.

The variables investigated in our experiments for this article are the length of visits, number of visits to each AOI, and the pupil radius in pixels. Length of visits is how long the participant has spent looking at each AOI. Number of visits is how many times the participant has looked at each AOI.

5 Linked Microposter Plots Interpretation

Figure 10 shows linked microposter plots for Poster 1. The first column shows the microposters, the second column shows the color legend, and the third column shows the AOI names. The last three columns are the statistical columns. The gray shaded AOIs in the first column are the AOIs that are not of interest in the corresponding panel. The light yellow shaded AOIs are the AOIs that have already been investigated in the previous microposters above the current microposter. The rows are sorted in a decreasing order of the length of visits. Each colored dot that represents an AOI is horizontally aligned with its AOI name and linked through color with the AOI of the same color on the microposter. The AOIs are separated into several perceptual groups (three in Fig. 10 and two in Fig. 11). Perceptual groups typically contain between two and five of the AOIs. Such a design helps the reader to focus on the values of a few mapped AOIs at once and allows to quickly identify clusters of mapped AOIs with similar values of the sorting variable [4].

As stated in Sect. 2, the video of Poster 1 was recorded for a controlled experiment where the participant was looking at eight AOIs for about six seconds and at four AOIs for about two seconds. Figure 10 reveals that the length of visits for eight AOIs actually are about four to six seconds and around two seconds

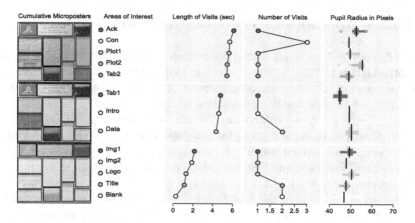

Fig. 10. Linked microposter plots of the eye tracking data for the AOIs for Poster 1.

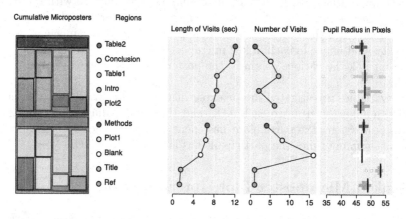

Fig. 11. Linked microposter plots of the eye tracking data for the AOIs for Poster 2.

for the remaining AOIs other than the Blank area. Although all of the AOIs are supposed to be visited only once, several of the number of visits are bigger than one. This is because the participant's visual focus point is moving from one AOI to another and may pass through other AOIs, resulting in an increased number of visits for those AOIs. To take some of these situations into account, if the length of visits is less than a threshold of $1/10$ s, it does not count as a visit. The threshold can be changed by the data analyst. The rightmost statistical column in Fig. 10 shows the pupil radiuses for each AOI visualized via boxplots. The participant's pupil dilated while looking at the acknowledgement and at Image 1 of the poster, possibly because the participant saw someone he knows in the acknowledgement during the six seconds of reading and the image attracted him shortly for the two seconds of looking at it.

Linked microposter plots for Poster 2 are shown in Fig. 11. This figure shows some spatial clusters of the eye tracking data that we would not be able to see in the simpler row-labelled plot designs shown in Figs. 4, 5, and 6. We can see that the top microposter highlights the main content in the center regions of the poster, while the bottom microposter highlights the parts in the corners of the poster. This indicates that the participant has spent most of the time looking at the main content of the poster, i.e., both tables, the introduction, the conclusion, and one of the plots of the poster.

We are able to visualize and compare multiple variables via several statistics columns in linked microposter plots, making it easier to identify the relationship between these variables. In Fig. 11, the number of visits and the length of visits does not seem to have a strong association. In fact, a numerical assessment confirms that the correlation coefficient r is 0.032 between these two variables. Pupil radius seems to be negatively associated with the number of visits and the length of visits, with $r = -0.43$ and -0.64, respectively (r is calculated based on the median pupil radius in each AOI.).

6   Linked Timeline Microposter Plots and Linked Scanpath Microposter Plots

Linked timeline microposter plots and linked scanpath microposter plots are extensions of basic linked microposter plots. Linked microposter plots have many advantages over the commonly used eye tracking visualization techniques, however, the viewing sequences can not be shown in basic linked microposter plots. To overcome this disadvantage, we developed linked timeline microposter plots and linked scanpath microposter plots to visualize the timeline and the scanpath of the eye movement. Linked timeline microposter plots are inspired by the idea of AOI timelines and linked scanpath microposter plots are inspired by the scanpath map.

6.1   Linked Timeline Microposter Plots

Compared with an AOI timeline, linked timeline microposter plots also show the spatial locations of the AOIs. Thus, the spatial clusters of the participant's viewing patterns can be identified. When there are many revisits of the AOIs, an AOI timeline is becoming complicated and confusing. Since linked timeline microposter plots only focus on several AOIs at a time in a microposter, an increased number of visits does not affect the quality of the visualization. Further, with more quantitive variables presented in a single plot, readers are able to explore the relationship among several variables.

Figure 12 shows an example of linked timeline microposter plots sorted by the viewing sequence. The numbers labeled inside the AOIs indicate the viewing sequence. Each of the 13 colors used represents one of the twelve AOIs or the Blank area. We can see from the plot that the participant is looking from the top left to the top right and then from top to bottom, column by column. While it is quite difficult to extract the exact viewing sequence of the AOIs from Fig. 9, the sequential top-down arrangement immediately reveals the viewing sequence

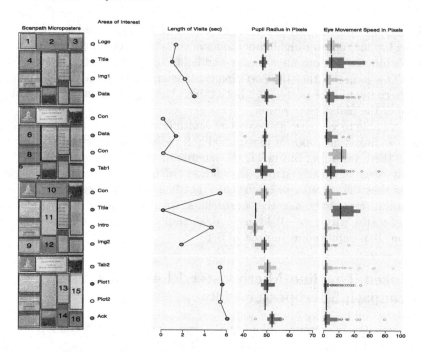

Fig. 12. Linked timeline microposter plots sorted by viewing sequence for Poster 1.

of the AOIs in Fig. 12 respectively. Ideally, each of the AOIs should have a different color, making it easier to identify the revisits of a certain AOI. For example, in Fig. 12, the light red, dark green, and dark blue show up two or three times in the microposters. Therefore, it is apparent that the bottom left AOI (the conclusion section "Con") colored in light red has been visited three times, although the visits number 5 and 7 are just very quick glances. The visits of the "Data" section (colored in dark green) are split into visits 4 and 6, due to the participant's glance at the conclusion section. The participant's eye passed by the "Title" section (colored in dark blue) again while his focus point moved from the first column to the second column of the poster. If the number of AOIs is more than the number of colors used here, the colors could be recycled, i.e., some AOIs could be shaded with the same color, or a color scheme with additional colors could be used.

Linked timeline microposter plots can also be sorted by any of the other variables shown in the statistical columns, such as the length of visits and pupil radius. Therefore, the relationship between the viewing sequence and any other variable can be explored. Figure 13 shows an example of sorting the plot by the median of the pupil radiuses in a descending order. The plot shows that the participant's pupil radius is larger at the beginning and the end of the recording. Since it is a simple test recording, the participant is possibly excited at the beginning and the end of the test, while feeling bored in the middle of the test. The pupil radiuses seem to be slightly negatively correlated with the eye

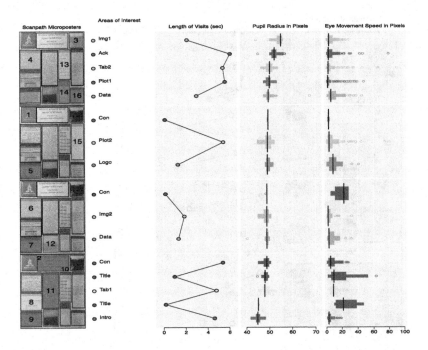

Fig. 13. Linked timeline microposter plots sorted by pupil radius for Poster 1.

movement speed (shown in the third statistical column), with $r = -0.39$. The eye movement speed is calculated by taking the distance between the consecutive locations.

6.2   Linked Scanpath Microposter Plots

Figure 14 shows an example of linked scanpath microposter plots sorted by the fixation sequences. Instead of defining the AOIs, fixations are detected using the **saccades** R package [38]. The statistical columns display the statistical summaries of the fixations, including the duration of the fixations (length of visits) and the pupil radius for each fixation.

Compared with a scanpath map shown in Fig. 8, the linked scanpath microposter plots in Fig. 14 are focusing on a few fixations at a time, instead of presenting the fixations all at once in a single graph. This feature makes even more complicated visual scanpath patterns easier to understand. The scanpath map uses the radius of a circle to indicate the duration of the fixation. When the duration of a fixation is very small or very large, corresponding circles in the scanpath map become unclear or overlapping. Using a dot plot in a separate statistical column to visualize the duration of the fixations and linking to the fixations via color overcomes this issue. The capability of visualizing multiple variables in one single graph also shows the advantage of linked scanpath microposter plots over the commonly used scanpath map.

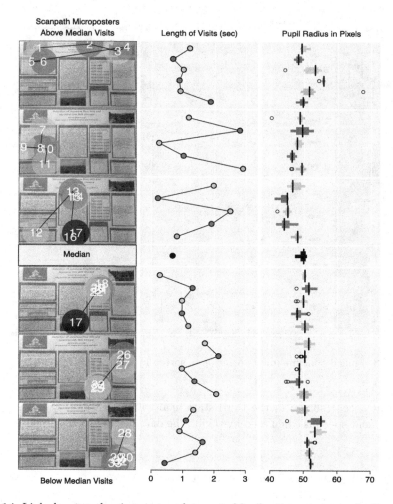

Fig. 14. Linked scanpath microposter plots sorted by fixation sequences for Poster 1.

From Fig. 14, we can see fixation points 8 and 11, labeled in blue and light red, lasted relatively longer than the other fixation points. The corresponding pupil radiuses also look relatively larger. However, there seems to be a weak negative correlation between the median pupil radius and the duration of fixation, with $r = -0.15$.

Table 1. Visualization Functions in the **EyeTrackR** R Package.

Function Name	Visualization Functionality Group
(i) Common Eye Tracking Visualization Tools	
DrawEyeDotplot	Create a dot plot indicating the time spent on each AOI
DrawEyeBoxplot	Create a box plot showing the participant's pupil radiuses in each AOI
DrawEyeBarplot	Create a bar plot indicating the time spent on each AOI
DrawEyeScatterplot	Create a scatter plot showing the participant's focus points
DrawEyeHeatmap	Create a heat map or hot spot map with Gaussian kernel
DrawEyeAOITimelines	Create an AOI timeline plot
DrawEyeScanpathMap	Create a scanpath map
(ii) Linked Microposter Plots Visualizations	
DrawEyeLMPlot	Create linked microposter plots
DrawEyeLTMPlot	Create linked timeline microposter plots
DrawEyeLSMPlot	Create linked scanpath microposter plots

7   Visualization with the EyeTrackR R Package

Commonly used eye tracking visualization techniques and the visualizations from the linked microposter plots family can be used from our **EyeTrackR** R package [20, 22] that is available at https://github.com/ChunyangCLi/EyeTrackR. This R package contains two groups of visualization functions for eye tracking data: (i) common eye tracking visualization tools, and (ii) linked microposter plots visualizations. Common eye tracking visualization tools contain functions that create the commonly used eye tracking visualization techniques such as dot plots, bar charts, attention maps, etc., shown in Figs. 4, 5, 6, 7, 8 and 9. Linked microposter plots visualizations contain three functions that create linked microposter plots, linked timeline microposter plots, and linked scanpath microposter plots, shown in Figs. 10, 11, 12, 13 and 14. Table 1 summarizes the functions and their main functionalities.

8   Conclusion and Future Work

In this article, we proposed the linked microposter plots family as a new means to visualize how people are looking at a poster. We also demonstrated how the linked microposter plots family is able to more effectively visualize eye tracking data, compared to the commonly used eye tracking visualization tools. The linked microposter plots family has overcome several of the disadvantages of the commonly used eye tracking data visualization tools, making it possible to present multiple variables at one single plot accurately as well as their relationships. With the perceptual groupings, readers can quickly identify clusters of mapped AOIs with similar values of the sorting variable. Basic linked microposter plots are able to present the eye tracking statistics together with the spatial information. Linked timeline microposter plots and linked scanpath microposter plots add the time information in the plot, in addition to the eye tracking statistics. They make the tangled visual clusters and their statistics more clearly shown in one plot, compared to the traditionally used AOI timelines and scanpath map.

The **EyeTrackR** R package [20, 22] provides functions to create linked microposter plots, linked timeline microposter plots, and linked scanpath microposter plots, in addition to common eye tracking visualization tools. These three types of linked microposter plots can be extended to visualize how people look at web pages, pages from PowerPoint presentations, photos, etc. Also, simultaneously displaying data for multiple participants via single linked microposter plots and their extensions could be investigated in the future.

Disclosure of Interests. The authors have no competing interests to declare that are relevant to the content of this article.

References

1. Andersson, P.: What is an effective layout for in-store posters? Case: Accent — An accessories chain. Ph.D. thesis, Arcada University of Applied Sciences, Helsinki (2010). https://www.theseus.fi/bitstream/handle/10024/14378/Andersson_Pauliina.pdf?sequence=1
2. Barber, P., Sanderson, M., Dickenson, A.: Postar visibility research: an integrative eye-tracking study of visibility hit rates for poster panels in UK environments. School of Psychology Birkbeck College, London (2008). https://web.archive.org/web/20160531143534/http://www.route.org.uk/document-library/postar-visibility-report-wave-4/postar-visibility-research-paper-2008.pdf
3. Berger, C., Winkels, M., Lischke, A., Höppner, J.: GazeAlyze: a Matlab toolbox for the analysis of eye movement data. Behav. Res. Methods **44**(2), 404–419 (2012). https://doi.org/10.3758/s13428-011-0149-x
4. Carr, D.B., Pickle, L.W.: Visualizing Data Patterns with Micromaps. CRC Press, Boca Raton (2010)
5. Carr, D.B., Pierson, S.M.: Emphasizing statistical summaries and showing spatial context with micromaps. Stat. Comput. Stat. Graphics Newslett. **7**(3), 16–23 (1996)
6. Dalmaijer, E.S., Mathôt, S., Van der Stigchel, S.: PyGaze: an open-source, cross-platform toolbox for minimal-effort programming of eyetracking experiments. Behav. Res. Methods **46**(4), 913–921 (2014). https://doi.org/10.3758/s13428-013-0422-2
7. Dink, J., Ferguson, B.: eyetrackingR: an R library for eye-tracking data analysis. Github (2015). http://www.eyetracking-r.com/
8. Fong, J.: The meaning of pupil dilation. The Scientist (2012). https://www.the-scientist.com/daily-news/the-meaning-of-pupil-dilation-40076
9. Forbes, S., Dink, J., Ferguson, B.: eyetrackingR: eye-tracking data analysis (2023). http://CRAN.R-project.org/package=eyetrackingR, R package version 0.2.1
10. Foulsham, T., Kingstone, A.: Look at my poster! Active gaze, preference and memory during a poster session. Perception **40**(11), 1387–1389 (2011). https://doi.org/10.1068/p7015
11. Geller, J., Winn, M., Mahr, T., Mirman, D.: GazeR: a package to analyze gaze position and pupil size data. Github (2019). https://github.com/dmirman-zz/gazer

12. Geller, J., Winn, M.B., Mahr, T., Mirman, D.: GazeR: a package for processing gaze position and pupil size data. Behav. Res. Methods **52**(5), 2232–2255 (2020). https://doi.org/10.3758/s13428-020-01374-8

13. Godwin, H.: eyeTrackR: organising and analysing eye-tracking data (2020). https://CRAN.R-project.org/package=eyeTrackR, R package version 1.0.1

14. Goldberg, J.H., Helfman, J.I.: Visual scanpath representation. In: ETRA '10: Proceedings of the 2010 Symposium on Eye-Tracking Research & Applications, New York, NY, pp. 203–210. ACM (2010), https://doi.org/10.1145/1743666.1743717

15. Heminghous, J., Duchowski, A.T.: iComp: a tool for scanpath visualization and comparison. In: APGV '06: Proceedings of the 3rd Symposium on Applied Perception in Graphics and Visualization, New York, NY, p. 152. ACM (2006). https://doi.org/10.1145/1140491.1140529

16. Holmqvist, K., Nyström, M., Andersson, R., Dewhurst, R., Jarodzka, H., Van de Weijer, J.: Eye Tracking: A Comprehensive Guide to Methods and Measures. Oxford University Press, Oxford, New York (2011)

17. Hope, R.M.: eyetracking: eyetracking helper functions (2012). http://CRAN.R-project.org/package=eyetracking, R package version 1.1

18. Jacob, R.J.K., Karn, K.S.: Commentary on Section 4. Eye tracking in human-computer interaction and usability research: ready to deliver the promises. In: Deubel, H., Hyönä, J.R. (eds.) The Mind's Eye: Cognitive and Applied Aspects of Eye Movement Research, pp. 573–605. Elsevier Science BV, Oxford (2003). https://doi.org/10.1016/B978-044451020-4/50031-1

19. Krassanakis, V., Filippakopoulou, V., Nakos, B.: EyeMMV toolbox: an eye movement post-analysis tool based on a two-step spatial dispersion threshold for fixation identification. J. Eye Movement Res. **7**(1), 1–10 (2014). https://doi.org/10.16910/jemr.7.1.1

20. Li, C.: Extracting and Visualizing Data from Mobile and Static Eye Trackers in R and Matlab. Ph.D. thesis, Utah State University, Department of Mathematics and Statistics, Logan, Utah (2017). https://doi.org/10.26076/5c8c-d8a5

21. Li, C., Symanzik, J.: The linked microposter plot as a new means for the visualization of eye tracking data. In: 2016 JSM Proceedings, Alexandria, VA. American Statistical Association (2016)

22. Li, C., Symanzik, J.: EyeTrackR: an R package for extraction and visualization of eye tracking data from people looking at posters. In: 2018 JSM Proceedings, Alexandria, VA. American Statistical Association (2017)

23. Noton, D., Stark, L.: Scanpaths in eye movements during pattern perception. Science **171**(3968), 308–311 (1971). https://doi.org/10.1126/science.171.3968.308

24. Pastukhov, A.: saccadr: extract saccades via an ensemble of methods approach (2023). http://CRAN.R-project.org/package=saccadr, R package version 0.1.3

25. Payton, Q., Olsen, T.: micromap: linked micromap plots. R version 1.9.7 (2023). https://CRAN.R-project.org/package=micromap

26. Payton, Q.C., McManus, M.G., Weber, M.H., Olsen, A.R., Kincaid, T.M.: micromap: a package for linked micromaps. J. Stat. Software **63**(2), 1–16 (2015). https://doi.org/10.18637/jss.v063.i02

27. Pearson, J., Carr, D.: micromapST: linked micromap plots for U. S. and other geographic areas. R version 3.0.2 (2024). https://CRAN.R-project.org/package=micromapST

28. Pickle, L.W., Pearson, J.B., Carr, D.B.: micromapST: exploring and communicating geospatial patterns in US state data. J. Stat. Software **63**(3), 1–25 (2015). https://doi.org/10.18637/jss.v063.i03

29. R Core Team: R: A language and environment for statistical computing. Vienna, Austria: R Foundation for Statistical Computing (2023). http://www.R-project. org/

30. Rayner, K.: Eye movements in reading and information processing: 20 years of research. Psychol. Bull. **124**(3), 372–422 (1998). https://doi.org/10.1037/0033-2909.124.3.372

31. Schroeder, S.: popEye: an R package to analyze eye-tracking data from reading experiments. Github (2024). https://github.com/sascha2schroeder/popEye

32. Sogo, H.: GazeParser: an open-source and multiplatform library for low-cost eye tracking and analysis. Behav. Res. Methods **45**(3), 684–695 (2013). https://doi. org/10.3758/s13428-012-0286-x

33. Symanzik, J., Carr, D.B.: Linked micromap plots in R. In: Cho, S.H. (ed.) Asian Regional Section of the IASC. Proceedings of IASC-Satellite Conference for the 59th ISI WSC & The 8th Conference of IASC-ARS, pp. 213–218 (2013)

34. Symanzik, J., Carr, D.B., McManus, M.G., Weber, M.H.: Micromaps. Wiley StatsRef: Statistics Reference Online, pp. 1–11 (2017). https://doi.org/10.1002/9781118445112.stat07938

35. Symanzik, J., Dai, X., Weber, M.H., Payton, Q., McManus, M.G.: Linked micromap plots for South America—General design considerations and specific adjustments. Revista Colombiana de Estadística: Current Topics Stat. Graphics **37**(2), 451–469 (2014). https://doi.org/10.15446/rce.v37n2spe.47949

36. Symanzik, J., Carr, D.B.: Interactive linked micromap plots for the display of geographically referenced statistical data. In: Chen, C., Härdle, W., Unwin, A. (eds.) Handbook of Data Visualization, pp. 267–294. Springer, Heidelberg (2008). https://doi.org/10.1007/978-3-540-33037-0_12

37. van Renswoude, D., Visser, I.: gazepath: Parse eye-tracking data into fixations (2020). http://CRAN.R-project.org/package=gazepath, R package version 1.3

38. von der Malsburg, T.: saccades: detection of fixations in eye-tracking data (2015). http://CRAN.R-project.org/package=saccades. R package version 0.1-1

39. Zolna, J., Gould, N.: Eye tracking and web usability: a good fit? UX Magazine (509) (2010). https://uxmag.com/articles/eye-tracking-and-web-usability-a-good-fit

Visualization of ESG-Related Information in Integrated Reports Using Text Mining and Usefulness as Teaching Material

Mizuki Nakamura[1]([envelope]) and Takako Akakura[2]

[1] Graduate School of Engineering, Tokyo University of Science,
6-3-1 Niijuku,Katsushika-ku, Tokyo 125-8585, Japan
`nakamura.mizuki.tus@gmail.com`

[2] Faculty of Engineering, Tokyo University of Science, 6-3-1 Niijuku, Katsushika-ku,
Tokyo 125-8585, Japan

Abstract. Recently, there has been a rapid increase in environmental, social, and governance (ESG) investments. According to the Global Sustainable Investment Alliance, during 2016–2020, the global level of ESG investments increased 1.5 times to approximately 1,364 trillion yen; in Japan, it surged six-fold to approximately 264 trillion yen. This surge has led to a growing interest in ESG-related information disclosed by companies. However, studies on visualizing and combining integrated reports of multiple companies are scarce. Therefore, this study visualized and examined the type of ESG-related information emphasized in integrated reports of the banking sector and identified future focal points and challenges. In addition, a questionnaire survey was conducted to validate the usefulness of the visualization. The results confirmed the possibility of efficient and rapid understanding of the focus areas of the entire industry using a large amount of textual data, such as integrated reports. Furthermore, the visualization results provide an opportunity to learn about specific methods for incorporating ESG into management and its strategic significance.

Keywords: ESG · Integrated Reports · Text Mining

1 Introduction

ESG investment refers to the investments in the following three elements in corporate analysis and evaluation:

- "E" : Environment
- "S" : Social
- "G" : Governance

ESG investments have increased in recent years. According to the Global Sustainable Investment Alliance, which compiles data on the global balance of ESG

H. Mori and Y. Asahi (Eds.): HCII 2024, LNCS 14690, pp. 83–94, 2024.
https://doi.org/10.1007/978-3-031-60114-9_7

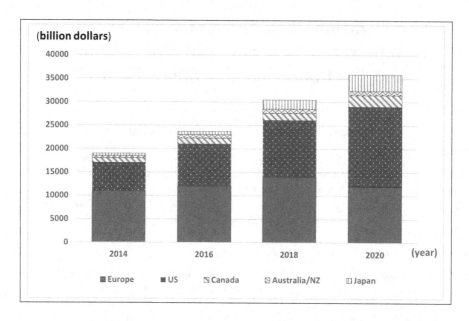

Fig. 1. Growth of the global ESG investment balance [1]

investments, the balance of ESG investments in five major countries/regions (Japan, the United States, Europe, Canada, and Australia/NZ) was approximately $35.3 trillion as of 2020 (Fig. 1).

In particular, the investment balance in Japan increased six-fold from 2016 to 2020. Moreover, because Japan accounts for 8% of the global ESG investment, interest in ESG investment within the country has been growing significantly. Consequently, efforts have been made to institutionalize and mandate the disclosure of ESG-related information, which has been primarily disclosed on a voluntary basis. Japan requires the disclosure of ESG-related information in securities and corporate governance reports [2]. In particular, "integrated reports," which convey important financial information about a company's sustainable value creation and non-financial information including ESG in a single medium, has garnered significant attention. According to a survey by Edge International, Inc., 716 companies published integrated reports in 2021, compared to 599 in 2020 (an increase of 117) (Fig. 2) [3]. Consequently, there has been a growing interest in the analysis of integrated reports.

This study focused on the banking industry owing to the following reasons. Financial institutions have a significant social impact, rendering their engagement with ESG very important. Banks have strong relationships with many stakeholders; hence, there is a high demand for ESG information. Furthermore, this industry is advancing toward institutionalizing and mandating the disclosure of ESG-related information; thus, it among the few sectors with readily available integrated report data.

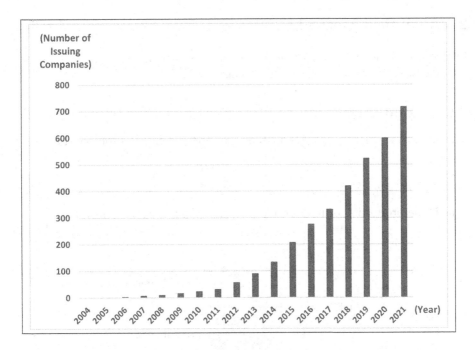

Fig. 2. Increase in the number of companies publishing integrated Reports [3]

Tazawa et al. [4] analyzed the integrated reports of universities, indicating their potential as valuable resources for new indicators in university evaluations. Kagami et al. [5] analyzed transitions based on information such as words and their frequency in the integrated reports of a company. They examined the change in corporate challenges with societal changes. However, to date, no research has visualized and compared the integrated reports of multiple companies. Although integrated reports have garnered attention, incorporating such information presents new challenges. Non-financial ESG-related information is often published as textual rather than numerical data. Moreover, integrated reports typically comprise dozens of pages per company, necessitating a considerable amount of time to read documents from multiple companies to understand overall industry trends. Therefore, this study attempted to understand the overall trends in integrated reports in a specific industry efficiently and visually using text mining. Focusing on the banking sector, this study reviewed the publication status of their integrated reports. Furthermore, co-occurrence network diagrams were used to visualize the ESG-related information emphasized upon by different banks and examine future focal points and challenges in investment. The visualization results are easy to understand by beginners in management studies and can potentially serve as educational materials. Consequently, this study explored the possibility of utilizing these findings in management and economics education through a survey.

2   Analytical Method

In this study, the Jaccard coefficient was used to calculate co-occurrence in the creation of co-occurrence network diagrams.

2.1   Jaccard Coefficient

The Jaccard coefficient J(A, B) for sets A and B is defined as follows (Fig. 3).

$$J(A, B) = \frac{|A \cap B|}{|A \cup B|} \tag{1}$$

This is the proportion of intersection of a pair of terms with their unions.

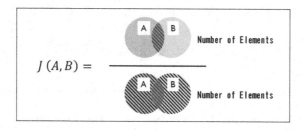

Fig. 3. Jaccard Coefficient

Therefore, the Jaccard coefficient represents the proportion of elements wherein both specific terms are used among all elements that use either or both terms; the average value of the Jaccard coefficient is in the range of 0–1. A higher value indicates a greater proportion of elements using both terms, signifying a higher similarity between the two sets of terms used in the text. This study considered the Jaccard coefficient because it is calculated by dividing the number of common elements between two sets by the total number of elements in both sets (excluding duplicates). Thus, this coefficient, which does not consider duplicates between sets, is suitable for a co-occurrence analysis. Moreover, when handling large datasets in the analysis, the Jaccard coefficient was chosen because it can effectively clarify the relationships between different items. The Jaccard coefficient has several other advantages, including its ease of interpretation, generality, suitability to different types of data, and ability to fairly assess the overlap between two sets.

2.2   Tools Used in Analysis

Table 1 lists the tools used in this study.

Table 1. Tools Used for Analysis

Language	Python3
Morphological Analysis	MeCab [6], Neologd [7]
Network Visualization	Cytoscape [8]

2.3 Preprocessing

In text mining, preprocessing, such as morphological analysis, handling of stop words, and unification of notation variations, is necessary. These processes are described in detail as follows.

Morphological Analysis. Morphological analysis is a part of natural language processing. It involves breaking down the words (natural language) that we use daily into "morphemes" (the smallest units of meaningful expression) and classifying them according to their parts of speech. This is a string-extraction method for categorizing these elements.

Stop Words and Unification of Notation Variations. Stop words are generally excluded from natural language processing because they are common and not useful. In the unification of notation variations, processing such as standardizing the character type of words and absorbing spelling and notation variations is performed by replacing the words.

3 Analysis Procedure

3.1 Analysis Data

This study aimed to elucidate the trends in specific industries based on integrated reports. Therefore, integrated reports issued for 2016 and 2021 were selected to understand and analyze the differences in content over the years. Herein, 2016 was chosen as the analysis target as it represents a time before the increase in the number of companies issuing integrated reports and the balance of ESG investments, and before the outbreak of the COVID-19 pandemic. On the contrary, 2021 was chosen because the pandemic was present during this period, and thus it was of interest to analyze the different aspects focused upon by companies in their integrated reports. This study analyzed 74 banks/groups in 2016 and 87 banks/groups in 2021. These banks were divided into three categories: city banks, first-tier regional banks (local banks), and second-tier regional banks. A breakdown of the sample numbers is presented in Table 2.

Banks that had provided integrated reports or "Disclosure Magazines" in PDF format on their websites were considered for analysis.

Table 2. Breakdown of sample numbers

2016	City Banks	4
	First Regional Banks	46
	Second Regional Banks	24
2021	City Banks	4
	First Regional Banks	53
	Second Regional Banks	30

3.2 Analysis Process

The general outline of the analysis comprised four stages: 1) data collection, 2) data preparation, 3) visualization, and 4) analysis. This process is illustrated in Fig. 4.

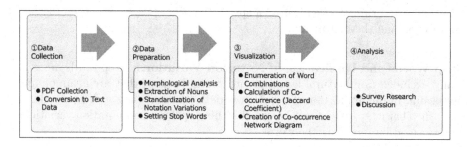

Fig. 4. Analysis process employed in this study

Data Collection. PDF files of integrated reports or disclosure magazines were collected from the website of each bank and converted into textual data.

Data Preparation. Morphological analysis was conducted sentence-by-sentence on the converted text data using MeCab and NEologd. The text was divided into words, and only nouns were extracted. Different notations for the same noun were unified in the standard form. Common words, symbols, and accounting terms deemed unnecessary for analysis were excluded as stop words.

3.3 Visualization/Analysis

In the co-occurrence network diagram, if a pair of words was included in one sentence, it was considered a co-occurrence. Therefore, we searched for combinations of words that appeared in the same sentence. This was achieved by enumerating the combinations using Cartesian products. The degree of co-occurrence was calculated using the Jaccard coefficient. Jaccard coefficient values of 0.1 and 0.2 indicated relevance and strong relevance, respectively, as a guideline. A co-occurrence network diagram was prepared using the following three steps:

1. Addition of words as nodes in the graph.
2. Addition of only edges where the Jaccard coefficient exceeded the threshold.
3. Removal of nodes that were isolated and not connected to any other nodes.

The color of the nodes is presented in Table 3.

Table 3. Color coding of the co-occurrence network diagram

Category	Color
Environmental Related	Green
Social Related	Pink
Governance Related	Purple
Business Related	Blue
Financial Related	Yellow
COVID-19 Related	Orange
Digital Related	Red
Position Related	Light Blue
Other	Gray

In addition, words that appeared more frequently were depicted with larger circles.

4   Results

The visualization results are shown in Figs. 5, 6, 7, 8, 9 and 10.

The diagrams of the created co-occurrence networks show that each bank had its own approach to the ESG fields and management strategies. Moreover, there were notable differences in awareness. Specifically, city banks strongly focused on environmental issues among ESG-related matters and emphasized on digital transformation. In the first group of regional banks, characteristics such as consciousness of contributing to local communities and economies were observed (Fig. 5, 6, 8 and 9), whereas in the second group of regional banks, a lower frequency of ESG-related words compared to other groups and a lack of digitation-related words were noted, which suggested a delay in digitalization efforts (Fig. 7 and 10).

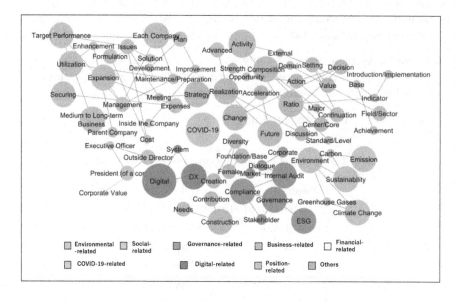

Fig. 5. City banks in 2021

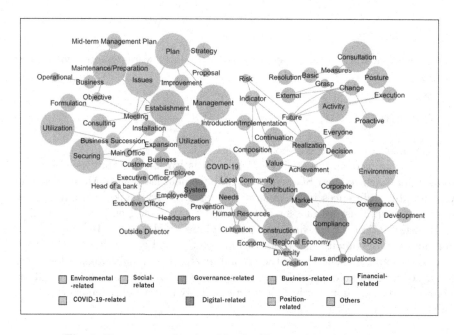

Fig. 6. First group of regional banks (Regional Banks) in 2021

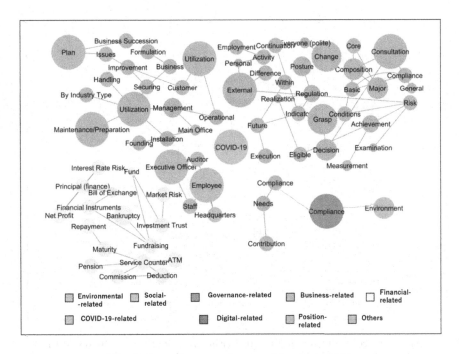

Fig. 7. Second group of regional banks in 2021

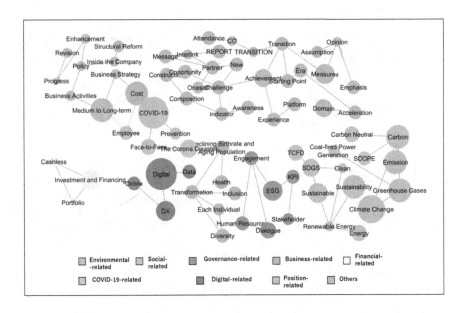

Fig. 8. Words Increased Compared to 2016 (City Banks)

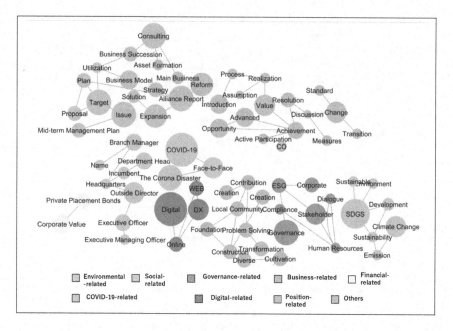

Fig. 9. Words Increased Compared to 2016 (First Regional Banks (Regional Banks))

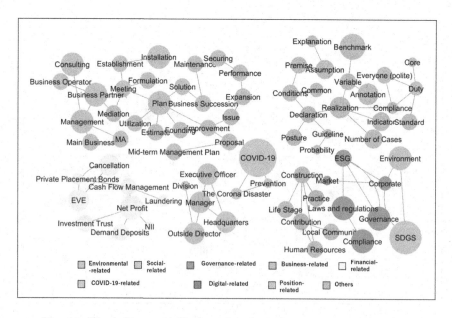

Fig. 10. Words Increased Compared to 2016 (Second Regional Banks)

5 Survey

The visualization results are easy to understand, even by beginners in management studies, and they could be used as teaching materials for novices. Therefore, a survey was conducted with 10 students and bank employees from the Faculty of Management and Economics. The survey examined the visibility of the visualization results, comparisons between groups, and the educational utility. The survey results are summarized in Table 4.

Table 4. Survey Results

Question Item [5-point scale (positive evaluation at 5)]	Average	Standard Deviation
How helpful is it in understanding ESG-related information?	4.3	0.41
Does the co-occurrence network diagram render it easier to learn about sustainable management strategies?	4.2	0.43
Is the visualization helpful in understanding trends and issues in the banking industry?	4.1	0.45
Does analyzing the approach to ESG provide hints for thinking about sustainable management strategies?	4.0	0.44

Based on these results, we can conclude that the overall evaluation was intuitive. In particular, the question on how helpful it was in understanding the ESG-related information received the highest average rating of 4.3 with a standard deviation of 0.41, indicating a very positive assessment. This suggests that ESG-related information is easier to understand following the conversion of vast textual data in integrated reports into co-occurrence network diagrams. Moreover, the average rating of 4.2 and a standard deviation of 0.43 for the question on whether the co-occurrence network diagram rendered it easier to learn about sustainable management strategies indicated that these visualization results could be used as teaching materials for beginners in management studies.

6 Conclusion and Future Works

This study visualized integrated reports in the banking industry using co-occurrence network diagrams to analyze ESG-related issues in the industry. Furthermore, based on the analysis results, we considered these materials as potential teaching materials for beginners and conducted a survey. The results confirmed the possibility of efficient and quick understanding of the focus areas of the industry as a whole from the vast amount of textual data in integrated reports. Moreover, the visualization results can provide guidelines related to management strategies and can be used as suitable teaching materials for beginners in management strategies. Future challenges in this field include the expansion of the categories for a more detailed analysis and the consideration of how to reflect the quality of integrated reports in the visualization.

Acknowledgements. This research was partially supported by a Grant-in-Aid for Scientific Research (B) (#20H01730; Principal Investigator: Takako Akakura) from Japan Society for the Promotion of Science (JSPS).

References

1. The Japan Research Institute, Limited. https://www.jri.co.jp/page.jsp?id=39388. Accessed 20 Nov 2023
2. FSA. https://www.fsa.go.jp/news/r4/sonota/20221107/20221107.html. Accessed 20 Nov 2023
3. CVRL. https://cvrl-jp.com/archive/pdf/list2021_J.pdf. Accessed 20 Nov 2023
4. Tazawa, S., Furukawa,T., Miura, T., Hirano, Y., Harada, J., Hashimoto, T.: Text mining analysis of university integrated reports. In: DEIM 2022 (2022). (in Japanese)
5. Kagami, S., Kawasaki,R., Sakurai, S., Uemura, H., Mazidofu, T., Hashimoto, T.: Exploration of the evolution and key issues in corporate integrated reporting. In: DEIM 2022 (2022). (in Japanese)
6. MeCab. https://taku910.github.io/mecab/. Accessed 20 Nov 2023
7. mecab-ipadic-NEologd. https://github.com/neologd/mecab-ipadic-neologd. Accessed 20 Nov 2023
8. Cytoscape Consortium. https://cytoscape.org/. Accessed 20 Nov 2023

Analysis of Feedback in Error Visualization Systems Using Thinking Aloud Protocol

Yukito Nakamura[1]($\boxtimes$), Nonoka Aikawa[2], and Takahito Tomoto[3]

[1] Graduate School of Information and Computer Science, Chiba Institute of Technology, Narashino, Chiba, Japan
s2381034hr@s.chibakoudai.jp
[2] Graduate School of Engineering, Tokyo Polytechnic University, Atsugi, Kanagawa, Japan
[3] Faculty of Information and Computer Science, Chiba Institute of Technology, Narashino, Chiba, Japan

Abstract. When learning, visualizing one's answers can encourage reflection. However, the visualization of errors requires elements such as visibility, reliability, and suggestiveness. In this study, we analyze whether feedback provided by a learning support system using error visualization was properly conveyed to the learner. Specifically, we propose a method for analyzing the learner's speech while using the system by performing thinking-aloud protocol analysis. The results showed that some of the feedback contents were not properly recognized by the learners.

Keywords: Error Visualization · Thinking-Aloud Protocol · Error-based Simulation

1 Introduction

In learning, it is important for the learner to reflect on his or her incorrect answers. By doing so, learners can realize why their answers were incorrect, thereby leading to a better understanding of the problem.

One method for encouraging learners to reflect on their answers is error visualization, which is a way to make learners aware of their own errors by showing them the consequences that result from their errors. One approach to error visualization is error-based simulation (EBS) [1]. EBS presents to the learner a simulation of what happens when their (incorrect) answer is assumed to be correct. The difference between the presented simulation and the actual behavior allows the learner to recognize the error.

For the EBS to lead a learner who answered incorrectly to the correct solution, it is important that the feedback presented to the learner be correctly conveyed to the learner. If the feedback is not properly communicated to the learner, it may lead to further confusion.

In this study, we investigated whether the feedback provided by a learning support system using error visualization was correctly conveyed to the learner. We previously proposed a method involving thinking-aloud protocol analysis for evaluating the learner's

H. Mori and Y. Asahi (Eds.): HCII 2024, LNCS 14690, pp. 95–110, 2024.
https://doi.org/10.1007/978-3-031-60114-9_8

utterances while using the system [2]. The thinking-aloud protocol analysis is a method of analyzing the content of speech by voicing what comes to mind as it comes to mind.

The results of the analysis indicated that some feedback content was not correctly recognized by the learners. Therefore, we investigated the reasons why learners may not have been able to accurately perceive the feedback. Furthermore, we proposed a new method of adding a phase to the error visualization system in which the learner is made aware of the connection between the feedback and their answer.

2   Error Visualization

Error visualization is a supportive method aimed at internally prompting learners to recognize errors in their answers. The conventional method of a teacher instructing a large group of students may lead to passive learning, where the correct answers are simply memorized. However, error visualization allows active learning, such as understanding what is incorrect in one's answers, by having the learner realize the errors themselves. For learners who give incorrect answers, the results based on the learner's answers are affirmed in order to make the learner aware of the error. Error visualization has been achieved through experimental exercises.

EBS is an error-visualization method in which the learner is presented with a funny simulation based on their incorrect answer, showing them what would result if their input was assumed to be correct. An example is shown in Fig. 1. This figure shows an example of EBS visualizing an error in the "object is stationary on the floor" problem. When the correct gravitational and vertical reaction forces are entered, the system will simulate the correct situation in which the object is at rest on the floor. In contrast, if only the gravitational force is input, the system simulates the unrealistic phenomenon of an object sinking into the floor. Thus, by presenting simulations based on learners' answers, EBS encourages learners to recognize the errors in their answers. EBS is effective at illustrating errors because it presents learners with simulations of phenomena that cannot occur, such as "object sinks into the floor."

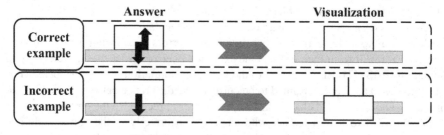

Fig. 1. Examples of error visualization

A model for visualizing EBS errors is shown in Fig. 2. To achieve error visualization, EBS uses three key elements for simulation: visibility, reliability, and suggestiveness [1].

The term "visibility" indicates the degree of difference between the simulation generated by EBS and the correct behavior. If the difference between the simulation and the correct behavior is not noticeable to the learner, it may lead to learner confusion. Therefore, feedback that is highly "manifest" is important.

Next, "reliability" indicates trust in the validity of the generated simulations. When the feedback provided by the EBS is not valid, it will not be understood as being based on the learner's own answers. In such a case, no matter how much feedback is presented, the learner may not trust it, and thus it may not lead to correction. Therefore, it is necessary to ensure that the feedback is visualized in a reliable manner by the learner.

Finally, "suggestiveness" indicates whether the errors manifested by the EBS adequately suggest what the learner should correct. If the feedback provided by the EBS does not adequately guide the learner to the correct answer, there is a risk that the learner will not reach the correct answer and will not be able to make corrections. Therefore, feedback with high suggestiveness is important. Feedback with a high degree of visibility, reliability, and suggestiveness, will help learners to correct their mistakes.

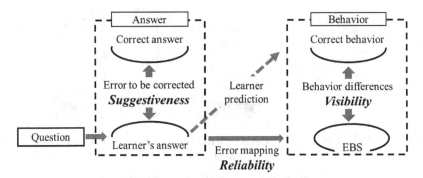

Fig. 2. EBS visualization model

3   Proposed Analysis Method

3.1   Thinking-Aloud Protocol

In this study, we propose a method for analyzing how feedback from the error visualization system is conveyed to learners, using the thinking-aloud protocol. In the thinking-aloud protocol, the learner is instructed to immediately utter the words and thoughts that come to their mind while performing a task, and this is recorded on video or by other means [5]. In the speech protocol analysis, the participants are asked to touch the system while voicing out loud what comes to mind or what they are thinking, and an analysis is performed to determine what can be learned from the content of their speech.

An example of thinking-aloud protocol analysis is shown in Fig. 3. In the figure, the learner's utterances are displayed in the visualization system when they give an incorrect answer. For example, in the case where a person uttered, "What is it? My answer and the correct behavior are different. That means something is wrong..." The part of the utterance "My answer and the correct behavior are different" Indicates that the learner is aware that their answer is incorrect, while the utterance "That means something is wrong" indicates that they do not know where their error lies. In this way, we can determine what we can learn from the learner's utterances.

There are two reasons for using the thinking-aloud protocol analysis in this study. First, we can see what the learner is thinking as they use the system. Second, the content of the experiment can be confirmed by recording speech. It is important that the observer not be involved in the learner's thinking or give hints to the learner when their utterances are being recorded. Furthermore, the observer should not record their own thoughts about the learner and consider instead only what can actually be known based on the protocol and the behavior at that time. This paper proposes an analysis method to categorize learners' recorded utterances and to evaluate their perceptions of "visibility, reliability, and suggestiveness.

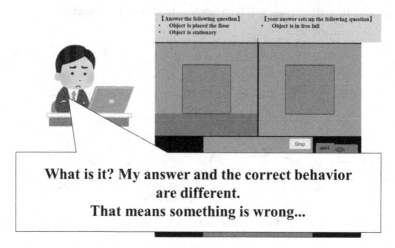

Fig. 3. Examples of thinking-aloud protocol analysis

3.2 Speech-Based Analysis Methods

An overview of the analysis based on the acquired utterances is shown in Fig. 4. This analysis is based on the following four steps.

1. Collecting utterances after feedback.
2. Assigning attributes to collected utterances.
3. Classifying the utterances into three categories based on the combination of attributes assigned: visibility, reliability, and suggestiveness.
4. Evaluating whether an utterance is correct or incorrect in terms of visibility, reliability, and suggestiveness.

This study aims to elucidate error visualization feedback, so we focused on step (1) collecting utterances after feedback. Although it is assumed that utterances before feedback are also useful for analysis, we did not include them in the analysis because of their complexity.

Next, we followed step (2) assigning attributes to the collected utterances. The flow of the learner's solution is as follows: (I) answer the question, (II) understand the feedback given, (III) compare the feedback with the correct behavior, and (IV) revise the solution. Then, four attributes are assigned, corresponding to (I) through (IV), as follows: (I) feedback, (II) my solution, (III) correct behavior, and (IV) correction.

Then, we followed step (3), classifying the utterances into three categories based on the combination of attributes assigned: visibility, reliability, and suggestiveness. Figure 5 shows four attributes adapted to the error visualization model. Visibility is the difference between the behavior generated based on the incorrect answer (feedback) and the correct behavior. Therefore, utterances with the two attributes "feedback" and "correct behavior" are "visibility" utterances. Moreover, reliability is the validity of "feedback" based on "my solution." Therefore, an utterance that has the two attributes "my solution" and "feedback" is an utterance with "reliability." Finally, suggestiveness is the insight into the difference between "my solution" and modification toward the correct solution. Therefore, an utterance that has the two attributes "my solution" and "correction" is a "suggestiveness" utterance.

Here we give some specific examples to illustrate the process. For the problem "Enter the force when at rest on the floor." The correct solution is to input the gravitational and vertical reaction forces, but we assume that the learner gives an incorrect answer, such as entering only the gravitational force. Feedback is given that shows the object break through the floor, and the user says, "It fell through the floor when there was only a downward force. It is strange that it breaks through the floor, so let's try to cancel out the downward force." In this case, the "feedback" utterances include those that refer to feedback such as "it fell through the ground." The "my solution" attribute includes utterances that refer to one's own answer, such as "only downward force." The "correct behavior" attribute includes utterances that refer to the correctness or incorrectness of the system-generated behavior, such as "it is strange that it breaks through the floor." The "correction" attribute includes utterances that refer to how the solution should be made, such as "let's try to cancel out the downward force."

As shown in Fig. 4, in step (2), the collected utterances that correspond to the above attributes are detected and assigned attributes. Then, in step (3), the utterances related to visibility, reliability, and suggestiveness are collected from the combination of utterances with those attributes. For example, utterance (A) is assigned the attribute "feedback," and utterance (B) is assigned the attribute "correct behavior," and if the two utterances refer to the same feedback, they are considered to be related to "visibility." Similarly, for "reliability" and "suggestiveness," if the two utterances refer to the same feedback, such as "feedback" and "my solution" or "correct behavior," then they are considered to be related to "reliability" and "suggestiveness."

Finally, in step (4), we evaluate the correctness or incorrectness of utterances classified into the three categories visibility, reliability, and suggestiveness. The evaluation method is determined by whether the learner's utterances are in line with the intended content of the system's visualization.

With the above procedure, it is possible to classify each feedback for visibility, reliability, and suggestiveness as "correct," "incorrect," or "no mention." For these classifications, the visualization method is expected to be problematic for feedback that often results in "no mention" or "incorrect" results for any of the three indicators based on the analysis of several learners' utterances.

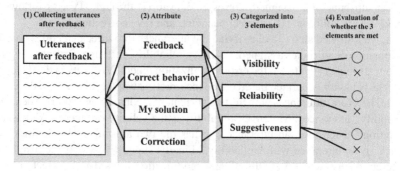

Fig. 4. Overview of Thinking Aloud Protocol Analysis

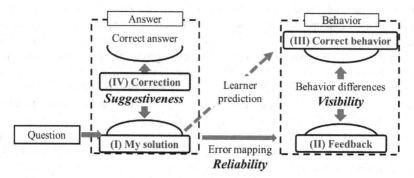

Fig. 5. Error visualization model adapting four attributes

4   Evaluation Experiment

4.1   Evaluation Experimental Method

In this experiment, 11 engineering students were surveyed, and the learners were divided into two groups: group A (6 students) and group B (5 students). We analyzed how the feedback of the system under investigation was conveyed to the learners, based on the speech of the two groups. In particular, we analyzed how the feedback from the system was communicated to the learner when they gave incorrect answers while using the system. In addition, we evaluated the visibility, reliability, and suggestiveness of the system's feedback. The experiments were conducted with the above objectives in mind.

In the experiment, the Permutations and Combinations System [4] and the Error-based Problem Posing (EBPP) system [3], which are learning support systems that use error visualization, were used by the engineering students. This paper analyzes only the EBPP system.

Group A recorded utterances using the thinking-aloud protocol in the order of the Permutations and Combinations system → EBPP system, while in Group B the order was reversed. This was done because there is a risk that the amount of speech produced by learners who are new to the thinking-aloud protocol method will be biased between the systems if the order is fixed, and that the effects of the first system will affect the second system. By having two groups with different orders, we thought it would be possible to infer whether a given result was due to the system feedback or the order.

4.2 EBPP System

The EBPP system is an application of error visualization that presents another question as feedback for an incorrect answer entered by the learner: "The solution you have entered is not correct for the question presented; you actually solved this question."

An example of feedback from the EBPP system is shown in Fig. 6. If the forces entered by the learner are correct, the system gives the learner the same problem set as the one presented as feedback. In contrast, if the learner inputs an incorrect force, the system gives the learner a situation different from the original problem setup as feedback (Fig. 6).

Figure 7 shows a specific example. Figure 7 shows the feedback given when the learner inputs an incorrect force, such as an upward force, for the "object is at rest on the floor" problem. The correct solution in this problem is to input the gravitational and vertical reaction forces. However, in the case of the incorrect answer shown in Fig. 7, the problem setting is presented differently from the "pulled by a string" or "pulled by a magnet" problem. This feedback based on the learner's answers helps them to recognize the errors in their answers. Depending on the force input by the learner, the system generates problems such as "being pushed against one wall" or "being in a gravity-free space" and gives them to the learner as feedback.

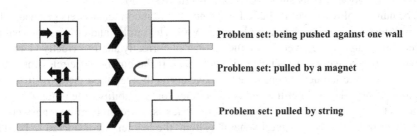

Fig. 6. Problem setting and feedback response

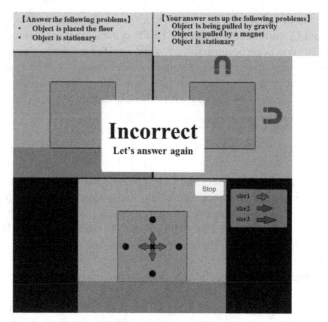

Fig. 7. Example of EBPP system feedback

5 Analysis Results

5.1 Feedback Analysis Results

Table 1 shows the analysis results for the EBPP system, especially for Problem 2, which had the highest feedback number. Problem 2 asks the learner to input what forces act on an object in motion at constant velocity on a frictionless floor.

The number of responses in Table 1 is the number of incorrect answers given and the feedback received for Problem 2 by learners A–G. The circles and crosses for visibility, reliability, and suggestiveness are the number of correctly and incorrectly identified utterances, respectively, for each of these elements. If the number of circles for "visibility" is high, the learner is considered to have correctly identified the error from the system feedback. The greater the number of circles for "reliability," the more likely the learner is to be convinced that the system's feedback is based on their own answers. If the number of circles for "suggestiveness" is high, the learner is considered to be able to infer the correct solution from the system's feedback.

Table 1 shows that the total number of circles for "visibility" was 16 and the total number of crosses was 8. However, the number of crosses was higher for "reliability" and especially for "suggestiveness," with a total of 33 crosses compared with a total of 3 circles. This suggests that the participants can recognize errors from the feedback (high visibility) but are not convinced by them (low reliability) and do not know how to correct them (low suggestiveness).

Below are the results of the analysis for each feedback. Figure 8 shows the feedback given to learners B–G. This is a constant-velocity motion problem, but this is the feedback

Table 1. Results of the analysis of utterances in question 2 (overall)

Learner		A	B	C	D	E	F	G	total
Number of responses		8	8	4	2	6	-	12	
Visibility	○	6	3	1	0	5		1	16
	×	3	0	1	0	1		3	8
Reliability	○	1	2	0	0	4		1	8
	×	3	3	0	1	1		2	10
Suggestiveness	○	1	0	0	0	1		1	3
	×	6	7	3	1	6		10	33

that is presented when a solution applies a force in the direction of motion. Table 2 shows the results of the analysis of utterances made in response to this. The table shows that every learner who saw this feedback produced utterances in which "suggestiveness" was inappropriate. Looking at the utterances, the learner, when given this feedback, made an erroneous correction to the other rightward force because the presented and generated problem settings had "people are moving to the right" in common.

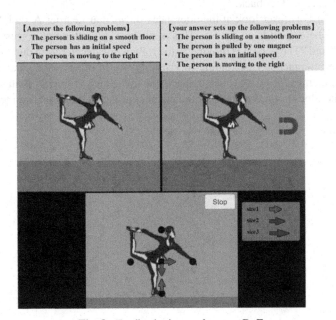

Fig. 8. Feedback given to learners B–F

Table 2. Results of the analysis of utterances in Fig. 8

Learner		A	B	C	D	E	F	G	total
Number of responses		-	1	1	1	1	-	1	
Visibility	○		1	0	0	1		0	2
	×		0	1	0	0		0	1
Reliability	○		0	0	0	1		0	1
	×		1	0	0	1		1	3
Suggestiveness	○		0	0	0	0		0	0
	×		1	1	1	1		1	1

Figure 9 shows the feedback given to learner A. This is the feedback that is presented when the learner does not describe the gravitational and vertical reaction forces and instead inputs rightward and leftward forces. Table 3 shows the results of the analysis of utterances made in response to this.

In Table 3, the authors focused on "visibility." The result was that Learner A made both appropriate and inappropriate utterances about "visibility" despite the utterances being about the same feedback.

In this regard, a closer look at the utterances shows that Learner A said, "A person is in a space where there is no gravity. This is strange." (an utterance corresponding to visibility ○)" and "The person is moving to the right while decelerating due to the initial velocity." (an utterance corresponding to visibility ×). In other words, learner A may think that the element of going to outer space due to the lack of gravity in this feedback is incorrect but does not recognize that the element of decelerating is also incorrect.

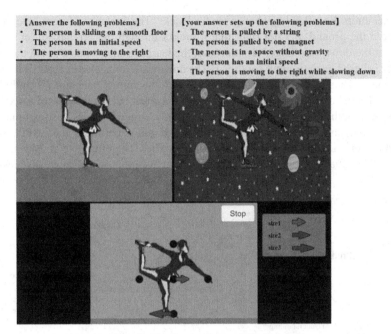

Fig. 9. Feedback given to learner A

Table 3. Results of the analysis of utterances in Fig. 9

Learner		A	B	C	D	E	F	G	total
Number of responses		-	1	1	1	1	-	1	
Visibility	○		1	0	0	1		0	1
	×		0	1	0	0		0	1
Reliability	○		0	0	0	1		0	1
	×		1	0	0	1		1	0
Suggestiveness	○		0	0	0	0		0	0
	×		1	1	1	1		1	1

5.2 Consideration of the Causes of the Results

Based on the analysis of the learners' utterances, the EBPP system has high visibility but low reliability and suggestiveness. Therefore, it is important to increase both the reliability and suggestiveness of the system.

We believe that there is a connection in the way we perceive visibility, reliability, and suggestiveness. Figure 10 shows the sequence of solutions generated by EBS. Suppose the learner utters the following when given feedback: "The downward force alone caused it to fall to the ground. It's not right that it breaks through the ground, so let's try to cancel out the downward force." In this case, the learner understands that (1) the given feedback is based on their input solution ("The downward force alone caused it to fall to the ground"). Then, (2) compare the feedback with the correct behavior ("It fell to the ground"). Then, based on (1) and (2) ("Let's try to cancel out the downward force") (3) examine and modify the differential. In other words, suggestiveness is something that must be accompanied by visibility and reliability. In this experiment, the EBPP system performed well in terms of visibility but not reliability. Therefore, we considered that increasing the reliability of the EBPP system might also improve its suggestiveness.

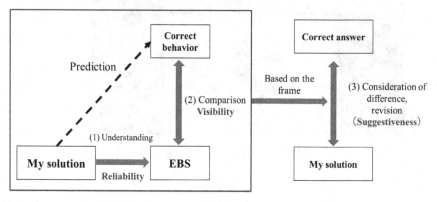

Fig. 10. Sequence of solutions generated by EBS

6 Proposed Method

As mentioned in the previous section, to increase the suggestiveness of the EBPP system, it is necessary to increase its reliability, we proposed adding a phase to the EBPP system for this purpose.

To increase the reliability, it is necessary to make the learner aware of the connection between their answer and the feedback.

A conventional EBPP presents the problem setup with a figure and problem text in response to the learner's input. Learners using the EBPP see the presented information, notice errors, and make corrections. In the conventional EBPP, the graph and the problem text are associated with the answers entered by the learner. The EBPP proposed in this study will incorporate methods that explicitly require the learner to manipulate shapes, a method has been used in error visualization in mathematical vectors [6]. In addition to presenting the problem set with a graph and a problem text, the system includes a new phase in which the system presents part of the graph and the problem text and asks the learner to select the corresponding arrow.

An example is shown in Fig. 11. In the figure, the learner is presented with the problems "The object is sliding on a smooth floor," "The object has an initial velocity," and "The object is moving to the right." The learner's answer is "gravity," "vertical reaction force," "right from the center," and "right from the right-side face of the object." As feedback, the learner is given the following problem setup: "The object is sliding on a smooth floor," "The object has an initial velocity," "The object is being pulled by one magnet," "The object is being pulled by one string," and "The object is moving to the right."

After this, the learner is asked which of their answers corresponds to the force arrow shown in the problem setup "The object is being pulled by one magnet." Then, the correctness of the learner's answers is given as feedback. Feedback is generated based on the point of action and direction of the force input by the learner.

In the example in Fig. 11, the learner's solution has the correct direction of the force but the point of action is incorrect. Therefore, the sentence "The direction of the force is correct, but the magnet is a force from inside the object" is given to the learner as feedback.

Thus, in the newly added phase, the learner is asked to answer how his or her answer corresponds to the problem setting. This allows the learner to understand how his or her answer corresponds to the feedback (problem set). We considered that adding a new phase to the EBPP system in this way would increase the reliability of the EBPP system.

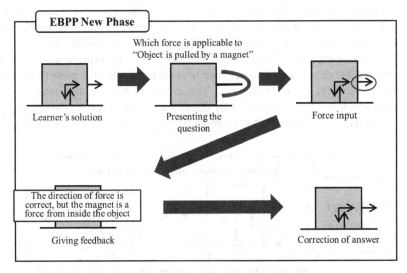

Fig. 11. Example of EBPP New Phase

7 Related Research on EBS

7.1 Research on Reliability

Research on EBS has been conducted for some time. According to Horiguchi et al., the factors that characterize the effectiveness of EBS are showing errors with an emphasis on reliability and showing errors with emphasis on visibility [10]. When focusing on reliability, we used a method of minimizing to the extent possible the changes in the parameters of the feedback presented to the learner. In placing emphasis on visibility, we used a method that increases the difference between the feedback presented to the learner and the correct behavior. For the two perspectives, it is necessary to use them differently based on educational aims. However, in the proposed method, instead of changing parameters and using different simulations to present feedback, a new phase in which the learner is asked to answer where their answer corresponds to the feedback is added to the conventional EBS with the aim of improving reliability.

7.2 Research on Suggestiveness

Horiguchi et al. introduced a method for changing the parameters of EBS simulations to improve suggestiveness [7]. This method solves the problem in which a simulation that suggests errors may suggest an unintended one. The parameters of the EBS are manipulated to make appropriate suggestions.

As an example, consider the problem "Enter the equation of motion for a block of mass m2 connected by a string to a cart of mass m1 subjected to an external force F and moving in the right direction" (Fig. 12). The correct answers to this question are $m1a = F - T$ and $m2a = T - \mu m2g$ but suppose there is an incorrect answer $m2a = T + \mu m2g$ (where μ is the coefficient of friction and g is the acceleration due to Earth's gravity). In this case, we would like to present a simulation in which the block moves closer and closer to the cart to suggest that the direction of friction is different, but it may suggest something other than what we had intended—that the string is getting shorter and shorter. In this case, a parameter change is made to increase the mass of the block in order to achieve the desired simulation. This results in an unnatural increase in the speed of the block as its mass increases. By manipulating the parameters in this way, the system correctly suggests the error to be corrected and improves suggestiveness.

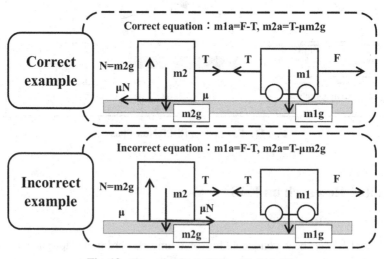

Fig. 12. Examples from Horiguchi et al. [7].

As a difference from the proposed method, Horiguchi et al. manipulated parameters to increase the suggestibility of EBS. However, the proposed method asks the learner to answer where their answer is related to the feedback in order to increase suggestiveness. In addition, Horiguchi et al. attempted to improve suggestiveness by devising the feedback content, but some changes in feedback may affect reliability. The proposed method adds a phase that requires the learner to perform operations, thereby improving suggestiveness by increasing reliability.

Nishioka et al. also introduced a method in which learners assemble concept maps before and after EBS simulations in order to eliminate "motion implies force" misconceptions [8], referring to erroneous notions of physics derived from everyday life, such as "an object in motion has a force acting on it in the direction of motion." By adding a phase in which concept maps are created before and after learning by EBS, the learner's understanding can be known at the concept-map level. In addition, by having the learner create a concept map, it is possible to measure whether the EBS has eliminated such misconceptions. In this way, it can be determined whether the EBS has suggestiveness. In contrast to the proposed method, Nishioka et al. introduced concept maps to measure the correction of misconceptions, but this did not improve suggestiveness. Therefore, to increase suggestiveness, the proposed method connects the learner's answers and the feedback.

Kuze et al. introduced a method of presenting learners with concept maps in addition to the EBS simulation results [9]. This technique helps the learner to make a correct answer and use the concept map to compare the concept maps of each answer up to the correct answer. The learner is then able to understand what the revised solution looks like by connecting their solution with the part of the solution that changed their mind. This method is also considered effective for improving suggestiveness because it uses a technique in which the learner's answers are transcribed onto a concept map and the changes in the answers are compared on the concept map. However, in the study by Kuze et al., to promote metacognition, the system automatically generates and presents a concept map corresponding to each answer after the learner correctly answers a question in the EBS. Therefore, to improve suggestiveness toward that goal, it is necessary to have learners compare the concept maps of their previous and subsequent answers for each problem.

8   Conclusion

In this paper, we developed and evaluated a method based on thinking-aloud protocol analysis that analyzes error visualization feedback. The results revealed low suggestiveness in some feedback and in some issues.

In this paper, visibility, reliability, and suggestiveness were determined for each feedback, some examples of which were appropriate, while others were not. Therefore, in the future it will be necessary to aggregate feedback by its components. In future work, we will analyze other learners and systems that could not be analyzed in this paper, and investigate the factors involved in how learners perceive feedback. Furthermore, we will implement the proposed method in an actual system and conduct evaluation experiments to verify whether the proposed method contributes to the improvement of learners' abilities.

References

1. Hirashima, T., Horiguchi, T., Kashihara, A., Toyoda, J.: Error-based simulation for error-visualization and its management. Int. J. Artif. Intell. Educ. **9**(1–2), 17–31 (1998)
2. Nakamura, Y., Tomoto, T.: Thinking aloud protocol analysis and considerations for feedback of error-visualization system. In: Japanese Society for Information and Systems in Education (JSiSE) 2022 Special Paper Workshop, vol. 37, no. 7, pp. 122–127 (2023). (in Japanese)
3. Aikawa, N., Saito, K., Koike, K., Tomoto, T.: Development of an error-based problem posing system in mechanics based on learner's errors. IEICE Trans. Inf. Syst. (Jpn. Ed.) **106**(2), 144–155 (2023). (in Japanese)
4. Shiroto, S., Tomoto, T.: A support system for learning permutations and combinations by visualizing problem solving process. IEICE Trans. Inf. Syst. (Jpn. Ed.) **121**(406), 25–30 (2022). (in Japanese)
5. Kato, R.: Cognitive Interface, Ohm Publishing House (2002)
6. Jumonji, T., Aikawa, N., Tomoto, T.: Development of a semi-active learning support system with operation index for the mathematics of vectors. In: Workshop Proceedings of the International Conference on Computers in Education ICCE 2023, pp. 333–342 (2023)
7. Horiguchi, T., Hirashima, T.: Simulation-based learning environment for assisting error-correction management of error-based simulation considering the cause of errors. Jpn. Soc. Artif. Intell. J. **17**(4), 462–472 (2002). (in Japanese)
8. Nishioka, Y., Shimoji, K., Hayashi, Y., Hirashima, T.: Observation of correction effect of error-based simulation for MIF misconception using concept map. Jpn. Soc. Inf. Syst. Educ. (JSiSE) Res. Rep. **35**(3), 77–84 (2020). (in Japanese)
9. Kuze, T., Tomoto, T.: Using error-based simulation (EBS) and concept maps development and evaluation of a system to promote abstraction operations in metacognitive activities. Jpn. Soc. Inf. Syst. Educ. (JSiSE) Res. Rep. **34**(6), 199–204 (2020). (in Japanese)
10. Horiguchi, T., Hirashima, T.: Simulation-based learning environment for assisting error-awareness management of error-based simulation considering the expressiveness and effectiveness. Jpn. Soc. Artif. Intell. J. **18**(3–4), 364–376 (2001). (in Japanese)

Predicting the Risk of Bicycle Theft Occurrence Considering Routine Activity Theory and Spatial Correlation

Moe Nishisako[✉] and Tomokazu Fujino

Fukuoka Women's University, 1-1-1, Kasumigaoka, Higashi-ku, Fukuoka, Japan
19ue043@fwu.jp, fujino@fwu.ac.jp

Abstract. The purpose of this study is to predict the risk of bicycle theft with high accuracy. We hypothesized that a model that takes into account spatial correlations would improve prediction accuracy by allowing the model to reflect near repeat victimization, one of the phenomena of crime. We employed the Poisson CAR (conditional autoregressive) model as a model that takes spatial correlation into account and conducted forecasting. For performance comparison, we also used the Poisson regression model, which does not take spatial correlation into account, to make predictions. As a result, the Poisson CAR model had higher prediction accuracy than the ordinary Poisson regression model.

Keywords: Bycycle Theft · Poisson CAR model · near repeat victimization

1 Background

In May 2021, the Ministry of Land, Infrastructure, Transport and Tourism (MLIT) in Japan approved the Second Bicycle Utilization Promotion Plan [5] by Cabinet decision in order to further promote the use of bicycles toward the realization of a sustainable society. In addition, local governments across Japan are also formulating "local versions of bicycle utilization promotion plans" according to the actual conditions of each region. As the momentum to expand bicycle use grows in Japanese society, bicycle theft is a major concern, accounting for 27.9% of all thefts in Japan in 2021, or approximately 100,000 cases. On the other hand, the arrest rate for bicycle theft was about 8%. Since the arrest rate for criminal offenses is 46.6%, bicycle theft can be said to be a crime with a low arrest rate. In addition, citizens' opinions were expressed in a questionnaire and public comments on the framework of the Second Bicycle Utilization Promotion Plan, calling for measures to prevent bicycle theft. Based on the above, it is considered necessary to address bicycle theft in order to promote bicycle use in Japan.

Many studies that have analyzed factors contributing to crimes of opportunity have analyzed what characteristics of urban spaces influence the occurrence

H. Mori and Y. Asahi (Eds.): HCII 2024, LNCS 14690, pp. 111–120, 2024.
https://doi.org/10.1007/978-3-031-60114-9_9

of crimes. The main basis for these studies is the routine activity theory, one of the theories of criminology. The daily activity theory states that crime occurs when the following three factors coincide in time and space.

1. Motivated offender
2. Suitable target
3. Absence of a suitable guardian

Studies that have analyzed factors contributing to bicycle theft on the basis of the routine activity theory include Mburu et al. (2016) [8] and Levy et al. (2018) [7]. These studies used negative binomial regression with explanatory variables chosen based on the routine activity theory as a predictive model. Conventional geographical crime prediction studies have employed generalized linear models such as negative binomial regression and Poisson regression as forecasting models. However, the use of generalized linear models that take spatial correlation into account may improve the prediction accuracy of crime occurrence risk. The basis for this is proximity repetitive victimization, which is known as a crime phenomenon. Proximity repetitive victimization is a phenomenon in which once a crime occurs, similar damage occurs repeatedly in the surrounding area. We hypothesized that a model that takes into account spatial correlations would be able to predict the risk of occurrence with high accuracy by reflecting the near repeat victimization.

Vomfell et al. (2018) [16] predicted the number of crimes using a model that considered spatial correlation, but did not mention proximity repetitive victimization. In addition, the prediction target in this study is the violent and property crimes in New York city, and it is not appropriate to use the results of this study in predicting bicycle theft in Japan, where social conditions are different.

Studies conducted on bicycle theft in Japan include Sugiura et al. [15] and Hashimoto et al. [4]. However, these studies analyzed the impact of urban components on the occurrence of bicycle theft and did not predict the risk of occurrence.

Table 1. Literature overview

Study	Crime type	City	Methods	Explanatory	Predictive	Spatial correlation
Mburu et al. [8]	Bicycle theft	Inner London	Negative binomial regression	✓	×	×
Levy et al. [7]	Bicycle theft	Washington DC	Negative binomial Regression	✓	×	×
Vomefell et al. [16]	Violent and property crime	New York	Linear models, count models and machine learning	✓	✓	✓
Sugiura et al. [15]	Bicycle theft	Tokyo	Negative binomial Regression	✓	×	×
Hashimoto et al. [4]	Bicycle theft	Okayama and Kurashiki, JPN	Kernel density estimation and multiple regression	✓	×	×
This study	Bicycle theft	Fukuoka, JPN	Poisson regression and poisson CAR	✓	✓	✓

This study is novel in that it uses a model that considers spatial correlation to predict the risk of bicycle theft in Japan. Table 1 summarizes the characteristics of the existing studies and this study.

2   Methods

In this study, we fit ordinary and spatial generalized linear models to the data and compare their performance in order to confirm the effectiveness of considering spatial correlation. Since the objective variable is count data, Poisson regression is used. Poisson regression model is described by the following equation

$$y_i \sim \text{Poisson}(\theta_i) \qquad \theta_i = \exp\left(\sum_{k=1}^{K} x_{i,k}\beta_k\right) \tag{1}$$

where y_i is the number of bicycle thefts in the i-th subregion and is distributed according to a Poisson distribution with mean θ_i. The $x_{i,k}$ is the kth explanatory variable in the ith subregion. β_k is the kth regression coefficient. On the other hand, the Poisson CAR (conditional auto-regressive) model [6], which is a spatial generalized linear model, is described by the following equation

$$y_i \sim \text{Poisson}(\theta_i) \qquad \theta_i = \exp\left(\sum_{k=1}^{K} x_{i,k}\beta_k + z_i\right) \tag{2}$$

where z_i is a variable to capture spatial correlations and is assumed to follow the CAR model. In this study, the Leroux model, which is one of the CAR models, is used and is represented by the following equation.

$$z_i|z_{j\neq i} \sim N\left(\frac{\rho\sum_j c_{ij}z_j}{\rho\sum_j c_{ij} + 1 - \rho}, \frac{\tau^2}{\rho\sum_j c_{ij} + 1 - \rho}\right) \tag{3}$$

where ρ is a parameter related to spatial correlation.

These models were fitted to the data using the CARBayes package in R. MCMC methods are used to estimate the parameters of the CAR models.

3   Materials

The data used in this study covered 1136 subregions of Fukuoka City. The objective variable in the regression analysis is the number of bicycle thefts in each subregion in 2019. The data used was open data published by the Fukuoka Prefectural Police [9].

The explanatory variables used in the regression model are as shown in Table 2, where column "corr" means correlation coefficients between each variable and bicycle theft. In order to make comparisons with studies modeling crime in Japan, the explanatory variables were grouped as shown in Table 3 for a total of five models. The correspondence between each group and the explanatory variables and the details of each explanatory variable are as follows.

Table 2. Summary statistics for the data set

variable	mean	s.d.	min	median	max	corr
Bicycle theft	3.9	7.1	0	1	70	–
Population density	9600	7200	0	8700	50200	0.25
Number of households	673	552	0	569	3791	0.45
Headcount per capita	2.0	0.7	0	2.2	3.9	−0.22
Percentage of one-person household	0.402	0.229	0	0.363	1	0.45
Percentage of rented homes	0.140	0.278	0	0	1	0.21
Percentage of non-working households	0.356	0.135	0	0.368	0.852	0.34
Station	0.087	0.282	0	0	1	0.35
Police facilities	0.06	0.24	0	0	1	0.19
School	0.206	0.40	0	0	1	0.04
Population of stay	19833	20470	264	14518	218432	0.58
Passengers	1550	8452	0	0	148166	0.55

3.1   Households

Population Density. The data was obtained from e-Stat's 2015 Census Boundary Data by Town, Street, Character, etc. [2]. This data summarizes the area, population, and number of households for each subregion. The variable Population density is defined here as the population of a subregion divided by its area.

Number of Housholds. The data was obtained from e-Stat's 2015 Census Boundary Data by Town, Street, Character, etc. [2]. This data summarizes the area, population, and number of households for each subregion. The variable Number of households is used here to indicate how many households are located in a subregion.

Headcount per Capita. The data was obtained from e-Stat's 2015 Census subregional aggregate data on population and other basic aggregates [13]. This data summarizes the number of persons in general households and persons per household for each subregion. The variable that represents the average number of persons per household in the general households within the subregion is Headcount per capita.

Percentage of One-Person Household. The data was obtained from e-Stat's 2015 Census subregional aggregate data on population and other basic aggregates [13]. This data summarizes the number of persons in general households and persons per household for each subregion. The variable Percentage of one-person households is used here to represent the percentage of one-person households in the subregion.

Table 3. Settings of variables

Features	Settings				
	1	2	3	4	5
Households	✓			✓	✓
Nearby facilities		✓		✓	✓
Human dynamics			✓		✓

Percentage of Rented Homes. The data was obtained from e-Stat's 2015 Census subregional aggregate data on basic aggregates such as population [14]. This data summarizes the types of housing for each subregion. The variable Percentage of rented homes is the sum of the number of public and private rented homes in the subregion, divided by the total number of households in the general population.

Percentage of Non-working Households. The data was obtained from e-Stat's 2015 Census subregional aggregate data on basic aggregation of household structure and other data [12]. This data summarizes the number of general households by economic composition of households in each subregion. The variable used here is Percentage of non-working households, which represents the percentage of non-working households among the general households in the subregion.

3.2   Nearby Facilities

Station. Data on the number of passengers by station from the National Land Information Download Site [11]. This data is a compilation of railroad stations and the number of passengers at those stations throughout Japan. Four railroad operators operate in Fukuoka City: Kyushu Railway, West Japan Railway, Nishi-Nippon Railroad, and Fukuoka City Subway. The variable used here is Station, which represents the number of railroad stations within the subregion.

Police Facilities. The data was obtained from the Digital National Land Information Download Site's police station data [10]. This data is point data for police headquarters, police stations, branch offices, police boxes, police stations, police dispatch centers, police academies, community safety centers, liaison offices, and so on. The variable that represents how many of these facilities are located in the subregion is defined here as Police facilities.

School. The data was obtained from School Data [1] on the Digital National Land Information Download Site. This data is point data for kindergartens, certified kindergartens, elementary schools, junior high schools, compulsory education schools, high schools, secondary education schools, special support schools, universities, technical colleges, special training schools as stipulated in Article 124 of the School Education Law, and various schools as stipulated in Article 134 of the same law. Here, School is the variable that indicates how many of these facilities are located in the subregion.

3.3 Human Dynamics

Population of Stay. The data was obtained from the G-Spatial Information Center's National Human Flow Open Data [3]. This data was compiled for each month from January 2019 to December 2021 and contains when and how many people stayed in each 1 km mesh. In accordance with the methodology used in this study, the values from January 2019 to December 2019 were summed to obtain a value during 2019, and a value per subregion was estimated from the 1km mesh value by prorating the area. This value is used as the variable of the resident population.

Passengers. The data was obtained from the Digital National Land Information Download Site's data on the number of passengers by station [11]. This data is a compilation of railroad stations and the number of passengers at those stations throughout Japan. Four railroad operators operate in Fukuoka City: Kyushu Railway, West Japan Railway, Nishi-Nippon Railroad, and Fukuoka City Subway. Here, the variable Passengers is the sum of the number of passengers at all railroad stations in the subregion.

4   Results

After running the model, the obtained DIC(Deviance Information Criterion) and mean squared error are shown in Table 4 and Table 5, respectively. For all combinations of explanatory variables, the Poisson CAR model was a better fit than the usual Poisson regression. In addition, Setting 5 with all explanatory variables was the best fit.

Setting 5, which was the best fit, is discussed below. Table 6 summarizes the regression coefficients for the Poisson regression model and the Poisson CAR model for Setting 5. 95% credit intervals include 0, which confirms that the population staying and Passengers have no significant effect.

Figure 1 and Fig. 2 plot the residuals of the regular Poisson regression model and Poisson CAR, respectively, on the map. It can be seen that the number of subregions with large residuals is much smaller in the Poisson CAR than in the ordinary Poisson regression. With the normal Poisson regression model, the fit in the urban centers is significantly worse. It can be inferred that urban centers are more susceptible to neighborhoods because of the concentration of small subregions with smaller areas compared to suburban areas.

Table 4. DIC

Features	Settings				
	1	2	3	4	5
Poisson	7381	9482	8560	7148	6076
Poisson CAR	4017	4074	4076	3989	3979

Table 5. Mean Squared Error

Features	Settings				
	1	2	3	4	5
Poisson	33.8	41.0	42.7	23.4	24.2
Poisson CAR	0.85	0.71	0.71	0.92	0.91

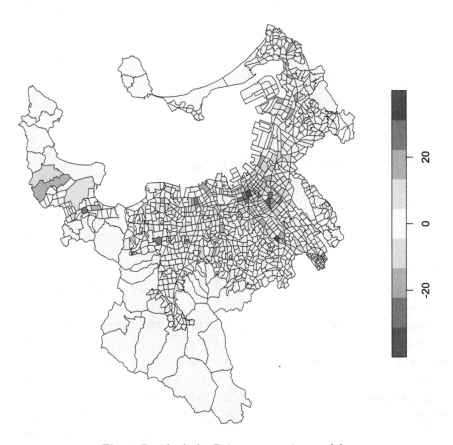

Fig. 1. Residuals for Poisson regression model

Fig. 2. Residuals for Poisson CAR model

Table 6. Results of setting 5

Variable	Poisson			Poisson CAR		
	mean	2.5%	97.5%	mean	2.5%	97.5%
Intercept	−0.40	−0.66	−0.16	−1.35	−1.90	−0.85
Population density	0.00	−0.00	0.00	0.00	0.00	0.00
Number of households	0.0006	0.0005	0.0007	0.0007	0.0006	0.0010
Headcount per capita	−0.07	−0.16	0.02	0.09	−0.09	0.28
Percentage of one-person household	2.00	1.72	2.30	2.49	1.81	3.19
Percentage of rented homes	−0.15	−0.24	−0.06	−0.07	−0.28	0.15
Percentage of non-working households	0.14	−0.29	0.56	−0.90	−1.83	−0.02
Station	0.46	0.37	0.54	0.60	0.34	0.84
Police facilities	0.21	0.11	0.30	0.23	−0.03	0.53
School	0.26	0.18	0.33	0.21	0.05	0.37
Population of stay	0.00	0.00	0.00	0.00	0.00	0.00
Passengers	0.00	0.00	0.00	0.00	0.00	0.00

5   Discussion

With the goal of predicting the risk of bicycle theft, this study fitted several models to data on bicycle theft in each subregion and compared the results. The results showed that the Poisson CAR model, which considered spatial correlation with all explanatory variables, was the best fit. This may be because the model was able to reflect proximity repetition damage. Although the Poisson CAR model is a model that takes into account the spatial correlation of the objective variable, a model that takes into account the spatial correlation of the explanatory variables is not addressed in this study. Comparative studies with these models are needed in the future. In addition, this study assumed that the number of bicycle thefts is distributed according to a Poisson distribution, but the data used in this study were overdispersed, with the number of bicycle thefts being zero in many areas, so a CAR with a zero-inflated Poisson distribution should be considered in the future.

References

1. National land numerical information | school data. https://nlftp.mlit.go.jp/ksj/gml/datalist/KsjTmplt-P29-v2_0.html. Accessed 02 Feb 2024
2. Statistical geographic information system data download | comprehensive portal for government statistics. https://www.e-stat.go.jp/gis/statmap-search?page=1&type=2&aggregateUnitForBoundary=A&toukeiCode=00200521&toukeiYear=2015&serveyId=A002005212015&prefCode=40&coordsys=1&format=shape&datum=2011. Accessed 02 Feb 2024
3. Center, G.S.I.: Nationwide human flow open data (1km mesh, by origin for cities, wards, towns, and villages). https://www.geospatial.jp/ckan/dataset/mlit-1km-fromto. Accessed 02 Feb 2024
4. Hashimoto, S., Yata, A., Kudo, H., Unno, H., Higuchi, T.: Considerations on the construction of a predictive model for high bicycle theft areas. Proc. Res. Traffic Eng. **42**, 759–766 (2022)
5. Ministry of Land, Infrastructure, T., of Japan, T.: Cabinet decision on the second bicycle utilization promotion plan. https://www.mlit.go.jp/road/bicycleuse/torikumi.html. Accessed 11 May 2023
6. Lee, D., Rushworth, A., Napier, G.: Spatio-temporal areal unit modeling in r with conditional autoregressive priors using the carbayesst package. Journal of Statistical Software **84** (2018). https://doi.org/10.18637/jss.v084.i09, https://www.jstatsoft.org/article/view/v084i09
7. Levy, J.M., Irvin-Erickson, Y., Vigne, N.L.: A case study of bicycle theft on the washington dc metrorail system using a routine activities and crime pattern theory framework. Secur. J. **31**, 226–246 (2018)
8. Mburu, L.W., Helbich, M.: Environmental risk factors influencing bicycle theft: a spatial analysis in London, UK. PLoS ONE **11**, e0163354 (2016)
9. Police, F.P.: Fukuoka prefectural police, statistics corner. https://www.police.pref.fukuoka.jp/tokei/index.html. Accessed 03 Feb 2024
10. Site, N.L.N.I.D.: National land numerical information | police station data. https://nlftp.mlit.go.jp/ksj/gml/datalist/KsjTmplt-P18.html. Accessed 02 Feb 2024

11. Site, N.L.N.I.D.: National land numerical information | station passenger numbers data. https://nlftp.mlit.go.jp/ksj/gml/datalist/KsjTmplt-S12-v3_0.html. Accessed 02 Feb 2024

12. e Stat: National census 2015 small area aggregation for fukuoka prefecture: Basic aggregation on household economic composition (12 divisions) - towns, streets, etc. https://www.e-stat.go.jp/stat-search/files?page=1&layout=datalist&toukei=00200521&tstat=000001080615&cycle=0&tclass1=000001094495&tclass2=000001094539&stat_infid=000031642688&tclass3val=0. Accessed 02 Feb 2024

13. e Stat: National census 2015 small area aggregation for fukuoka prefecture: Basic aggregation on population etc. for household types (2 divisions), household members (7 divisions), general households, household members, per household member, facility households and facility household members - towns, streets, etc. https://www.e-stat.go.jp/stat-search/files?page=1&layout=datalist&toukei=00200521&tstat=000001080615&cycle=0&tclass1=000001094495&tclass2=000001094539&stat_infid=000031522267&tclass3val=0. Accessed 02 Feb 2024

14. e Stat: National census 2015 small area aggregation for fukuoka prefecture: Basic aggregation on population etc. for types of dwellings & housing ownership (6 divisions) - towns, streets, etc. https://www.e-stat.go.jp/stat-search/files?page=1&layout=datalist&toukei=00200521&tstat=000001080615&cycle=0&tclass1=000001094495&tclass2=000001094539&stat_infid=000031522269&tclass3val=0. Accessed 02 Feb 2024

15. Sugiura, K., Hino, K., Asami, Y., Yamada, I.: The relationship between environmental factors and bicycle theft occurrences around railway stations. J. Archit. Inst. Jpn. Plann. Ser. **87**, 123–132 (2022). https://doi.org/10.3130/AIJA.87.123

16. Vomfell, L., Hardle, W.K., Lessmann, S.: Improving crime count forecasts using twitter and taxi data. Decision Support Systems **113**, 73–85 (2018). https://doi.org/10.1016/j.dss.2018.07.003, https://www.sciencedirect.com/science/article/pii/S0167923618301209

Visualization of Software Development Provenance

Andreas Schreiber[1]([✉]) [iD], Lynn von Kurnatowski[2] [iD], Annika Meinecke[1] [iD],
and Claas de Boer[3] [iD]

[1] Institute for Software Technology, German Aerospace Center (DLR), Linder Höhe,
51147 Cologne, Germany
andreas.schreiber@dlr.de
[2] Institute for Software Technology, German Aerospace Center (DLR),
Münchener Straße 20, 82234 Weßling, Germany
[3] Institute for Software Technology, German Aerospace Center (DLR),
Rutherfordstr. 2, 12489 Berlin, Germany

Abstract. Software development is a complex process that involves
many people and development tools and their interactions; during development, many data is generated or modified, such as source code, documents or software artifacts, and information such as issues, discussions,
or code analysis. To obtain better information about the quality, reliability, and trustworthiness of software, it is useful to analyze the software
development process in addition to analyzing and visualizing software
systems. To gain insight and knowledge about software development
processes, we extract the provenance of development processes, especially from version control systems for Git-based software projects, and
visualize the provenance information using graph visualization, metrics
representation, and development timelines, including integration of these
methods into a web-based dashboard. Using visual provenance representations, project managers can gain insight into development progress,
the effects of process changes, and interactions among developers and
with external contributors.

Keywords: Provenance · Software visualization · Software
development processes · Visual analytics · Graph visualization

1 Introduction

Software is an important innovation factor and a crucial part of modern research
and development. However, the process of software development is complex and
is becoming increasingly so. To cope with this complexity, more and more software development tools are being developed and used. These tools produce various types of data during the development process, in particular source code,
documentation, or software artifacts (e.g., releases). The individual steps of the
process are performed by humans–with AIs increasingly taking over the roles
of humans–who interact with the tools or with each other. To understand the

H. Mori and Y. Asahi (Eds.): HCII 2024, LNCS 14690, pp. 121–139, 2024.
https://doi.org/10.1007/978-3-031-60114-9_10

software development process and thus make better assertions about the quality, reliability, and trustworthiness of the resulting software product, one can record and analyze the *provenance* [32] of the process or the resulting artifacts.

Today, provenance recording and analysis helps in many research areas in verifying data products and understanding the processes that led to them. In general, provenance helps to make statements about the quality, reliability, and trustworthiness of data or to verify compliance with the process by which it was created. Complete provenance ideally includes information on all sources, all dependencies, and all contextual information that entered and influenced the process.

Although we focus on the provenance of software development processes and software artifacts, provenance can be captured and analyzed at many levels, for example, in the execution of scripts, of code, of machine learning pipelines, or of entire distributed and decentralized workflows. In some of these application areas, provenance recording and analysis has many relationships with corresponding methods for runtime logs, DevOps data, or project dependencies (i.e., multi-project analysis).

One way to analyze provenance information and thereby gain insight into the process under investigation is through visual analytics, using methods such as graph visualization or visual representation of provenance metrics. We contribute with *visual analysis methods for retrospective provenance of software development processes*, which we retrieve by repository mining from code hosting environments based on the version control system *git*.

The necessary background information and our contributions are structured as follows:

- We give an overview and some basics about provenance (Sect. 2).
- We describe our method and tools for retrospectively extracting provenance from the code hosting platforms GitHub and GitLab. In particular, we show examples of what provenance looks like, after extracting it from GitLab using our tool GITLAB2PROV (Sect. 3).
- We show our visualizations of the provenance of the software development process, in particular graph visualization, visualization of different metrics, and their combination in interactive web-based interfaces (Sect. 4).
- Finally, we summarize related work, in particular provenance visualization, visualization of software development processes, and visualization of software evolution (Sect. 5).

It is beyond the scope of this paper to perform a comprehensive evaluation with a user study or a case study and a detailed analysis of a specific development process.

2   Provenance

The definition of *provenance* is: *"Provenance is a record that describes the people, institutions, entities, and activities involved in producing, influencing, or delivering a piece of data or a thing [34]"*.

Provenance can be expressed in many different ways. We use the W3C specification PROV [33], which defines the provenance data model PROV-DM [34] and an ontology PROV-O [25], among others. PROV was inspired by several different approaches [31] that are adaptable to any domain.

The core structure of PROV-DM is based on the definition of the model class elements *entities* (Entity), *activities* (Activity), and *agents* (Agent) that are involved in the creation of a piece of data or an artifact, and the definition of *relations* to relate these class elements, such as *wasGeneratedBy*, *wasAssociatedWith*, *wasAttributedTo*, and *used* (Fig. 1). Entities represent physical (e.g., sensors or medical devices), digital (e.g., datasets), conceptual (e.g., a workflow description), or other types of objects. An activity is a process that uses or generates entities and can be associated with an agent, meaning that the agent is responsible for the activity. Each of the class elements and relations can have *additional attributes*.

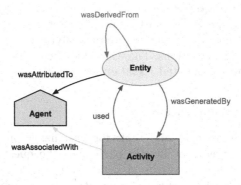

Fig. 1. Overview of the PROV model concepts: class elements *entities*, *activities*, and *agents* with relations.

To use provenance in your own applications, first define the questions you want to answer with provenance information. Then a provenance data model is modeled with PROV-DM. The provenance information is then either captured by the applications at run-time or later extracted from available data (e.g., files, repositories, or databases) and stored as files or in databases.

Several serialization formats with human-readable syntax to store provenance information as text representation in files, in particular the provenance notation format PROV-N[1], PROV-JSON, PROV-RDF, and PROV-XML. A public repository for storing provenance files is PROVSTORE [18].

Provenance can be represented as a graph termed a *provenance graph*. The recorded or generated provenance of an entity (i.e., a file, a dataset, or any other type of artifact) is a *directed acyclic graph* (DAG), which can be stored in graph databases as a *labeled property graph* [1].

---

[1] https://www.w3.org/TR/2013/REC-prov-n-20130430/.

Since all the nodes and edges of the provenance graph have a defined semantics, the provenance graph is a specific knowledge graph. This means that for specific uses of PROV-DM, each class element (i.e., entity, activity, and agent) has at least one specialization with a particular semantics. For example, to model knowledge for software development processes using `git` [47], we consider the semantics and an ontology for `git` [22].

2.1 Using and Analyzing Provenance

The provenance graphs grow over time as the runtime of the process progresses (see also Sect. 3). The derived relation *wasDerivedFrom* represents progress over time. Entities and activities have a lifetime bounded by two events; entities begin to exist after a generation event and end with an invalidation event, and activities begin with a start event and end with an end event [33].

Because provenance graphs can quickly become very large and complex in real-world applications, it is difficult to manually interpret, understand, or verify the information they contain. There are several analytical and visual methods for analyzing large provenance graphs. These are in particular *network analysis* [17], *graph summarization* [30,50], and *visual exploration* [52].

2.2 Provenance Visualization

There are several approaches and tools for visualizing provenance that differ in their user requirements and, in particular, the questions that need to be answered. The questions can be classified in terms of origin, inheritance, participation, dependencies, progress, or quality [56]. Examples are PROV-O-VIZ [15], VISTRAILS [4], Provenance Explorer [9], Provenance Viewer [21], AVOCADO [48], or ProvViz [54]; the PROVSTORE [18] also has some visualizations such as Sankey, Wheel, Hive, and Gantt charts.

In many graph visualizations, the provenance graph is sorted topologically from left to right or top to bottom. Similarly to a family tree, the "oldest" data can then be seen on the left or top, and the "youngest," most recent data on the right or bottom. The default visualization is a graph using the recommended PROV graph layout conventions[2].

Because provenance graphs can grow to enormous sizes, even experts have a hard time understanding them. The span of immediate memory is limited to 7 ± 2 entities at a time [29]. Therefore, graphs containing more than five to nine entities become gradually harder to interpret as each new item is added. However, 7 ± 2 is a value that is easily reached and exceeded even by simple examples of provenance graphs. The larger the graphs become, the more difficult it is to draw conclusions and derive new insights from the provenance data. Instead, the visualization should be simple, self-explanatory, and familiar enough so that end users can read and understand it almost effortlessly.

---

[2] https://www.w3.org/2011/prov/wiki/Diagrams.

3   Provenance of Software Development Processes

Due to the complexity and diversity of today's software systems, numerous software development processes and associated development tools have emerged. A typical tool suite consists of at least an integrated development environment (IDE), a version control system, an issue tracker, a continuous integration and deployment infrastructure, and a documentation system. With this tool suite, the actual software artifacts are initially created, modified, and further artifacts are derived from them. In addition, there are connections through interactions between developers, between tools and developers, and-sometimes automatically-between tools. For example, developers discuss feature requests (*developer ↔ developer*), developers document requirements in the issue tracking system (*developer ↔ tool*), or the version control system automatically starts code checks after a commit (*tool ↔ tool*). Based on previous work [53], with PROV we are progressively developing a general and extensible provenance model for software development processes, which currently includes issue tracking, version control management, continuous integration, and releases. The general model can and must be specialized for concrete processes and tools used [43], such as the git-based version control systems GitHub and GitLab.

3.1   Provenance for git Repositories

For software development processes based on git repositories, we extract *retrospective provenance* [28] with data mining on the repositories; in the case of GitHub and GitLab, this includes provenance information from the respective issue trackers and release systems. The resulting provenance data then includes all modeled activities (e.g., commits, issue changes, releases), the generated or modified entities (e.g., source code files or issues), and the involved agents (e.g., developers, testers, or users) along with their relationships. For git-only repositories, GIT2PROV [11] extracts provenance using the git command line tool. GITHUB2PROV [39] extends GIT2PROV and additionally extracts information from the GitHub issue tracker using the GitHub API. Our tool GITLAB2PROV [44] uses only the GitLab API. All three tools generate the provenance information in the form of the text representation PROV-JSON, which is converted to other formats for further analysis and visualization, and imported as a property graph into the graph database Neo4j (Fig. 2). In particular, for graph visualization, we use the three tools GEPHI [2], MATHEMATICA, and Python with the libraries NETWORKX and PLOTLY; in addition to the graph visualization feature of Neo4j.

3.2   GITLAB2PROV Example

To show how the PROV graph evolves with a GitLab project and to illustrate its growth with each activity performed, we performed sample steps on a newly created GitLab project.

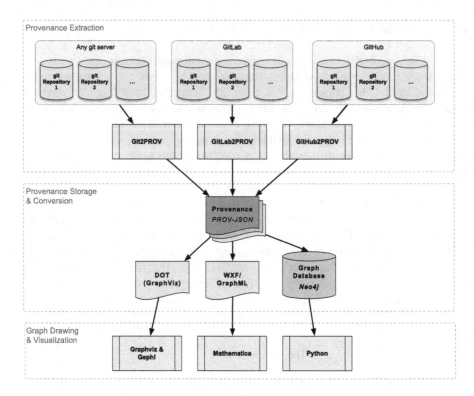

Fig. 2. Extracting provenance from projects hosted on git repositories on standalone servers, on GitLab, or on GitHub (i.e., git repositories, issues, releases, etc.) to PROV documents (i.e., files in PROV-JSON format), storing in the graph database Neo4j, converting to graph file formats for visualization with tools such as Gephi, Graphviz, or Mathematica.

Example Steps of Three Devolopers in GitLab

(1) Developer A [Agent] creates the file README.md [Entity] .

(2) Developer B [Agent] creates a new issue #1 [Entity] .

(3) Developer A [Agent] assigns issue #1 [Entity] to herself.

(4) Developer A [Agent] comments issue #1 [Entity] .

(5) Developer A [Agent] changes README.md [Entity] and references issue #1 [Entity] in the commit message.

(6) Developer B [Agent] likes the comment of developer A [Agent] in issue #1 [Entity] with an "Rocket Emoji."

(7) Developer A [Agent] creates a release with release tag "v0.1."

(8) Developer C [Agent] comments the commit from Developer A [Agent] .

After eight steps, the PROV graph already contains 34 nodes and 75 edges[3] (Fig. 3). The evolution of each PROV graph with each successive step shows how

---

[3] The PROV document is available at the PROVSTORE: https://openprovenance.org/store/documents/4243.

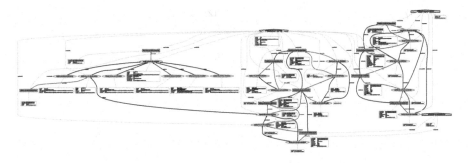

Fig. 3. Provenance graph for the example GitLab project after step (8). The graph was drawn with GRAPHVIZ.

the corresponding nodes and edges are added for each step (Fig. 4). Due to the underlying provenance model, several nodes are added for each step: usually at least one activity (i.e., the action performed) and one entity (i.e., the file or issue added or modified). Sometimes, subgraphs are not connected, for example, in step (2), where "Developer B" has created a new issue; this activity is at this point completely independent of the activities of "Developer A" regarding the new file from step (1). The connection then comes in step (3), where "Developer A" assigns the issue to herself; then both subgraphs are at least connected to the agent "Developer A."

4   Visualizations of Software Engineering Provenance

Information from the provenance graph can be visually represented in many different ways. Visualizations are derived from questions that developers, project managers, or other stakeholders have about the development process. The goal is always to obtain *insights* [3] into the development process that are not provided directly by the development tools. The goal is to extract and visualize the knowledge contained in the provenance graph about the activities performed by the developers, the files and issues created or modified, or the responsibilities of the developers.

Queries and visualizations can be related to a single project or a group of projects, depending on the question. This can be scaled up, for example, to do repository mining on many projects (e.g., all projects in an organization, or all projects with certain characteristics) to identify differences or common patterns.

Currently, our provenance dataset only contains the provenance information extracted with GITLAB2PROV. In particular, this means that there is no information on the semantics and content of the individual entities (i.e., the source code files and the text in issues and commit messages). It also does not include information about modules, packages, or the architecture of the software system.

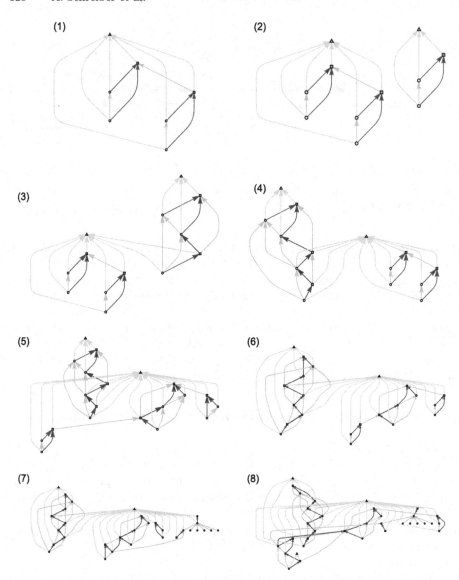

Fig. 4. Evolution of provenance graphs for the example GitLab project. The eight steps that the three developers involved performed on GitLab are arranged line by line from top to bottom. The graphs were drawn with MATHEMATICA; for better clarity, all labels are omitted.

Depending on the question and the intended visual representation, we define appropriate CYPHER queries on the provenance information stored in the Neo4j database. The principle is always the same: First, we define whether information about the PROV class elements Entities, Activities, or Agents is needed. Then, we further narrow the query by specifying relationships (i.e., the structure in which the PROV class elements are related) and by restricting the query to certain attributes (e.g., time periods, types, or names).

An example of a query on the provenance graph is the following CYPHER query, which returns a list of all files created or modified by at least two developers during development:

```
MATCH
  (d1:Agent)-[:wasAttributedTo]-(:Entity)
    -[:specializationOf]
    -(file:Entity {`prov:type`: 'file'})
    -[:specializationOf]-(:Entity)
    -[:wasAttributedTo]-(d2:Agent)
WHERE
  d1.user_name <> d2.user_name AND ID(d1) < ID(d2)
RETURN
  COLLECT(DISTINCT file.file_path_at_addition),
  d1.user_name, d2.user_name
```

To visually represent the provenance information (i.e., the results of the CYPHER queries), we use various visualizations, such as graph visualizations, metric visualizations (e.g., bar charts), time-oriented visualizations (e.g., Sankey charts), task- and work process-oriented visualizations (e.g., Gantt charts), or hierarchy-oriented visualizations (e.g., treemap charts).

To provide more interactivity and to deliver the visualizations in the form of a web application, we can combine individual visualizations into a dashboard or a computational notebook (Sect. 4.5).

To implement the visualizations, we use Python with the libraries PLOTLY and NETWORKX. In addition, we use the basic libraries PY2NEO to query the Neo4j database and PANDAS to store the query results and prepare the data.

4.1   Graph Visualization

The obvious visualization of the provenance graph is to draw the graph using graph-drawing tools. This can be helpful for identifying visual patterns—especially when compared to the provenance graphs of other projects—to find errors in the PROV model, and for communication and presentation purposes.

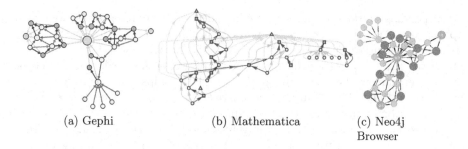

(a) Gephi   (b) Mathematica   (c) Neo4j
                                                                   Browser

Fig. 5. Comparison of three graph visualization tools: Gephi (using the layout algorithm of Yifan Hu [16]), Mathematica (using the `LayeredGraphPlot` function), and Neo4j Browser (using the force-directed layout of the underlying D3 library [6]).

Since complete provenance graphs can become very large and continue to grow as the development process progresses, they are primarily useful for providing a general visual impression of the complexity of the development process. It is often useful to draw subgraphs based on queries, for example, to show local dependencies. For example, we use this to visually illustrate the files on which individual developers have worked. For graph drawings, there are many different ways to design their style and layout (Fig. 5). Basically, layouts can be classified into force-directed layouts, force-directed layouts for large graphs, multidimensional scaling, and layouts that incorporate knowledge of the graph topology [16,35]. For example, we use Yifan Hu's algorithm [16] for graph drawing with GEPHI (Figs. 5a and 7), layered graph drawing or hierarchical graph drawing [49] for graph drawing with MATHEMATICA (Fig. 5b), and the force-directed layout of the underlying D3 library [6] with Neo4j (Fig. 5c). For the *agent-entity relationship diagram*[4] (Fig. 6), where we visually represent how many files the developers made changes to, we use the "NEATO" layout algorithm from NetworkX, which is based on an approach by Kamada and Kawai [20].

For small graphs, the different provenance graphs of different development processes can be directly compared visually. However, for graphs of this structure (DAGs), it is still a subject of current research to determine how perception of people can recognize and perceive similarities and differences [51].

For very large graphs, there are various strategies to improve readability, such as edge bundling, edge concentration, or confluent drawing. This is helpful for certain tasks, but the graph drawing may no longer be faithful [35,36]. Other strategies include topology compression, semantic abstraction, interactive exploration, or view transformation [16].

---

[4] The entity-relationship diagram is basically a *node-link diagram* [7].

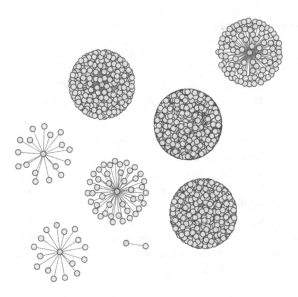

Fig. 6. Agent-entity relationship diagram, which shows agents (◍) such as developers making changes to entities (i.e., files and issues) ( )

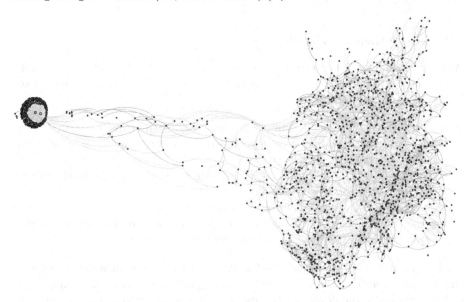

Fig. 7. Graph visualization of the provenance graph for the `lucaapp/android` project: entities (i.e., files and issues) ( ), agents (◍), and activities (i.e., commit, issue changes, etc.) (●). Visualization tool: GEPHI. Layout algorithm: Yifan Hu (relative strength 0.2)

4.2   Metrics Visualization

Provenance graph metrics are basic network metrics that characterize the topological properties of graphs in general, which are partially adapted to the type information of provenance graphs. They are independent of the application domain, so these metrics can be compared with those of the provenance graphs of other applications [17].

- The general network metric *number of nodes*, which indicates the total number of provenance elements in the graph, results in the provenance-specific metrics *number of entities*, *number of activities*, and *number of agents*.
- The *number of edges* network metric provides the number of provenance relationships in the graph.
- The *graph diameter* is the longest distance in the graph, where the distance between two nodes is the length of the shortest path between those nodes. A corresponding provenance-specific metric is the *maximum finite distance* (MFD), which describes the longest chain of influence in the provenance graph.

To visualize metrics (i.e., numerical numbers), we use charts such as *bar charts*, *line charts*, *pie charts*, or even *tables*.

4.3   Time-Oriented Visualization

As the software development process progresses over time, the provenance graph grows and contains some temporal information that can be retrieved directly or indirectly (via graph queries).

- Entities Entity have a lifetime that starts with a time specification at the *wasGeneratedBy* events and ends with a time specification at the *wasInvalidatedBy* events.
- Activities Activity have a lifetime that is specified by time in the form of their *startTime* and *endTime* attributes.
- For Agents Agent, you can determine an activity time in the process by querying the time between the start time of the first associated activity and the completion time of the last associated activity.

To visualize the time-oriented information of the provenance graph, we use timeline and Gantt charts. To visualize individual events with additional color coding to indicate the developer, we use a scatter plot with one axis as the time axis.

4.4   Task-Oriented, Work Process-Oriented, and Hierarchy-Oriented Visualization

During the software development process, developers contribute to the creation of software or projects through their activities (i.e., commits, issues changes, releases, etc.). Activities performed (i.e., tasks) create dependencies between developers and projects or entities of projects.

To visualize dependencies and contributions, we use Sankey diagrams (e.g., for mapping developers to projects) and treemaps (e.g., for a hierarchical view of all files that a developer has changed). Other possible visualizations include tree graphs, circular hierarchical edge-bundling diagrams [19], or developer rivers [8].

4.5   Interactive Interfaces

To enhance the usability and interaction of the described visualizations, they can be integrated into web-based user interfaces. There are two common approaches: *computational notebooks* and *dashboards*.

Computational Notebooks. Computational notebooks [24] have become an ubiquitous medium for much data science work. At their best, computational notebooks enable Knuth's concept of literate programming [5] with their ability to weave code, text, and outputs such as visuals into a computational narrative. These notebooks support incremental and iterative analysis, explanation of an analyst's thoughts and processes, and sharing of code, text, and visuals in a single document. Computational notebook interfaces such as Jupyter [14,38] are well suited for exploratory, flexible data analysis, and interactive data visualization [38].

Dashboards. Dashboards [12] provide a more rigid but interactive web-based interface that aims to provide an overview of information (similar to reports). We build dashboards using the Python framework DASH[5]. Visualizations created with the Python library PLOTLY can be integrated into interactive web-based applications; in particular, it is possible to add interaction elements such as menus, radio buttons, or input fields. Individual charts benefit from PLOTLY's basic features[6], such as zoom, responsiveness, compare data on hover, selection and cross-filtering, and custom controls.

The interactive web-based dashboard contains a selection of possible visualizations integrated with interactive controls [45]. In the "PROV Metrics" section, one can select the projects whose metrics will be displayed. In the "Event Timeline" one can select only one project. The "Entities Timeline" refers to all projects, since it concerns the development activities over time; here one can select the resampling frequency to display, for example, daily, weekly or quarterly activities. In the "Agent-Entity Relations" area, the left pane shows the individual developers and the files they have worked on; if you select one of the developers, the treemap in the right pane shows the changed files in a hierarchical view.

Currently, the layout and built-in visualizations are defined in Python code, and the connected Neo4j database is fixed [45].

---

[5] https://dash.plotly.com/.

[6] https://plotly.com/python/plotly-fundamentals/.

5   Related Work

There is much related work in the relevant research areas of provenance analytics, provenance visualization, development process visualization, and software evolution visualization.

Provenance Analytics. Ragan et al. [42] provide an overview, based on a literature review, of the types of provenance information and the uses of provenance. To summarize provenance graphs, Moreau [30] used an aggregation of provenance types using edge labels. Huynh et al. [17] and Marzagão et al. [27] defined and used provenance network metrics and provenance graph kernels to classify provenance graphs. Pimentel et al. [40] analyze the evolution of provenance from scripts.

Provenance Visualization. There are numerous approaches to visualizing provenance information; many of them are based on graph visualization and originate from applications studying the provenance of scientific workflows: *Prov Viewer* [21] is a graph-based visualization tool for visual exploration of PROV graphs, *Provenance Map Orbiter* [26] focuses on interactive exploration of large provenance graphs, *AVOCADO* [48] visualizes provenance based on data flows in biomedical research, and *PROV-O-Viz* [15] is a web-based PROV visualization tool that uses Sankey diagrams and adds a number of provenance-specific features. *ProvViz* [54] is a web-based PROV editor and visualizer. It supports loading, modifying, visualizing, and exporting PROV documents.

Visualization of Development Processes and Software Evolution. In software visualization and repository mining research, there are numerous approaches and visualization tools whose visual concepts can be applied to the visualization of provenance information. However, many approaches focus on metrics and visualizations of source code, for example, by Nuzrath et al. [37] or by Pinzger et al. [41]. Similar to our work is the work of Grabner et al. [13], who extract data from version control, issue tracking, and CI systems, store it in a database, and present it in interactive web-based visualizations.

Also very similar is the work of Curt et al. [10], who collect software traces from version control and issue tracking systems to build a provenance graph that helps to understand software releases.

To understand development activity in large software systems, Burch et al. [8] introduced Developer Rivers as a visualization method that combines a hierarchy view with a river view to visualize time-dependent activities of developers.

6   Conclusion and Future Work

We have described how we visualize provenance information from `git`-based software development projects; specifically, projects hosted at GitLab. We do this by extracting the provenance using the GITLAB2PROV tool, storing the provenance graph in the Neo4j graph database, and querying for relevant information using CYPHER to generate visualizations for questions of interest.

In contrast to other related work on analysis and visualization of development processes, we use the standardized data model PROV-DM. Using this standardized format allows us to combine provenance information with that of other applications (e.g., the provenance of the execution of the developed software or of the data generated by the software).

Our visualizations and evaluations are based solely on provenance information. The content and information about the semantics of the project, the source code files, or the problems are not considered. However, such data can be linked to the provenance graph depending on the question, for example, information about the development team, results of code analysis, or information about the software structure and architecture.

Our current and future work will focus on the following areas:

- Include additional data sources beyond GitLab or GitHub, particularly the provenance of the use of local tools on the developer's development system, such as IDEs.
- Analyze provenance graphs using network analysis and machine learning methods. We focus on comparing network metrics to identify peculiarities and differences in the development process of different software projects.
- Conceptualize and develop new approaches to visualize the provenance of software development in conjunction with other data to analyze software quality metrics such as security, performance, usability, or maintainability— For example, a dashboard for visual analysis of security vulnerabilities added during development [46].
- Improve and evolve dashboards, especially with respect to their visual design, interaction patterns, and usage scenarios, based on the needs and interests of software developers [23] and subsequent user studies [55]).

References

1. Angles, R., Gutierrez, C.: Survey of graph database models. ACM Comput. Surv. **40**(1), 1–39 (2008). https://doi.org/10.1145/1322432.1322433
2. Bastian, M., Heymann, S., Jacomy, M.: Gephi: an open source software for exploring and manipulating networks. In: Proceedings of the International AAAI Conference on Web and Social Media, vol. 3 (2009). https://doi.org/10.1609/icwsm. v3i1.13937. http://www.aaai.org/ocs/index.php/ICWSM/09/paper/view/154
3. Battle, L., Ottley, A.: What do we mean when we say "insight"? A formal synthesis of existing theory. IEEE Trans. Vis. Comput. Graph. (01), 1–14 (2023). https:// doi.org/10.1109/TVCG.2023.3326698

4. Bavoil, L., Callahan, S.P., Crossno, P.J., Freire, J., Vo, H.T.: VisTrails: enabling interactive multiple-view visualizations, pp. 135–142. IEEE (2005). https://doi.org/10.1109/VISUAL.2005.1532788

5. Bentley, J., Knuth, D., McIlroy, D.: Programming pearls: a literate program. Commun. ACM **29**(6), 471–483 (1986). https://doi.org/10.1145/5948.315654

6. Bostock, M., Ogievetsky, V., Heer, J.: D^3 data-driven documents. IEEE Trans. Visual Comput. Graph. **17**(12), 2301–2309 (2011). https://doi.org/10.1109/TVCG.2011.185

7. Burch, M., ten Brinke, K.B., Castella, A., Peters, G.K.S., Shteriyanov, V., Vlasvinkel, R.: Dynamic graph exploration by interactively linked node-link diagrams and matrix visualizations. Visual Comput. Ind. Biomed. Art **4**(1), 23 (2021)

8. Burch, M., Munz, T., Beck, F., Weiskopf, D.: Visualizing work processes in software engineering with developer rivers. In: 2015 IEEE 3rd Working Conference on Software Visualization (VISSOFT), pp. 116–124 (2015). https://doi.org/10.1109/VISSOFT.2015.7332421

9. Cheung, K., Hunter, J.: Provenance explorer – customized provenance views using semantic inferencing. In: Cruz, I., et al. (eds.) ISWC 2006. LNCS, vol. 4273, pp. 215–227. Springer, Heidelberg (2006). https://doi.org/10.1007/11926078_16

10. Curty, F., Kohwalter, T.C., Braganholo, V., Murta, L.: An infrastructure for software release analysis through provenance graphs. CoRR abs/1809.10265 (2018). http://arxiv.org/abs/1809.10265

11. De Nies, T., et al.: Git2PROV: exposing version control system content as W3C PROV. In: Proceedings of the 12th International Semantic Web Conference (Posters and Demonstrations Track), ISWC-PD 2013, vol. 1035, pp. 125–128. CEUR-WS.org (2013)

12. Few, S.: Information Dashboard Design: The Effective Visual Communication of Data. O'Reilly Media Inc., Sebastopol (2006)

13. Grabner, J., Decker, R., Artner, T., Bernhart, M., Grechenig, T.: Combining and visualizing time-oriented data from the software engineering toolset. In: 2018 IEEE Working Conference on Software Visualization (VISSOFT), Los Alamitos, CA, USA, pp. 76–86. IEEE Computer Society, September 2018. https://doi.org/10.1109/VISSOFT.2018.00016. https://doi.ieeecomputersociety.org/10.1109/VISSOFT.2018.00016

14. Granger, B.E., Perez, F.: Jupyter: thinking and storytelling with code and data. Comput. Sci. Eng. **23**(02), 7–14 (2021). https://doi.org/10.1109/MCSE.2021.3059263

15. Hoekstra, R., Groth, P.: PROV-O-Viz - understanding the role of activities in provenance. In: Ludäscher, B., Plale, B. (eds.) IPAW 2014. LNCS, vol. 8628, pp. 215–220. Springer, Cham (2015). https://doi.org/10.1007/978-3-319-16462-5_18

16. Hu, Y., Shi, L.: Visualizing large graphs. WIREs Comput. Stat. **7**(2), 115–136 (2015). https://onlinelibrary.wiley.com/doi/abs/10.1002/wics.1343

17. Huynh, T.D., Ebden, M., Fischer, J., Roberts, S., Moreau, L.: Provenance network analytics. Data Min. Knowl. Disc. **32**(3), 708–735 (2018)

18. Huynh, T.D., Moreau, L.: ProvStore: a public provenance repository. In: Ludäscher, B., Plale, B. (eds.) IPAW 2014. LNCS, vol. 8628, pp. 275–277. Springer, Cham (2015). https://doi.org/10.1007/978-3-319-16462-5_32

19. Illescas, S., Lopez-Herrejon, R.E., Egyed, A.: Towards visualization of feature interactions in software product lines. In: 2016 IEEE Working Conference on Software Visualization (VISSOFT), pp. 46–50 (2016). https://doi.org/10.1109/VISSOFT.2016.16

20. Kamada, T., Kawai, S.: An algorithm for drawing general undirected graphs. Inf. Process. Lett. **31**(1), 7–15 (1989)
21. Kohwalter, T., Oliveira, T., Freire, J., Clua, E., Murta, L.: Prov viewer: a graph-based visualization tool for interactive exploration of provenance data. In: Mattoso, M., Glavic, B. (eds.) IPAW 2016. LNCS, vol. 9672, pp. 71–82. Springer, Cham (2016). https://doi.org/10.1007/978-3-319-40593-3_6
22. Kubitza, D.O., Böckmann, M., Graux, D.: Towards semantically structuring GitHub. In: Proceedings of the ISWC 2019 Satellite Tracks (Posters & Demonstrations, Industry, and Outrageous Ideas) Co-located with 18th International Semantic Web Conference (ISWC 2019), Auckland, New Zealand, 26–30 October 2019, pp. 141–144 (2019). http://ceur-ws.org/Vol-2456/paper37.pdf
23. von Kurnatowski, L., Meinecke, A., Rieger, A.: Towards using focus groups to identify software developer's interests regarding their development process. In: 2022 IEEE International Conference on Software Analysis, Evolution and Reengineering (SANER), pp. 1266–1269 (2022). https://doi.org/10.1109/SANER53432.2022.00151
24. Lau, S., Drosos, I., Markel, J.M., Guo, P.J.: The design space of computational notebooks: an analysis of 60 systems in academia and industry. In: 2020 IEEE Symposium on Visual Languages and Human-Centric Computing (VL/HCC), pp. 1–11 (2020). https://doi.org/10.1109/VL/HCC50065.2020.9127201
25. Lebo, T., et al.: PROV-O: the PROV ontology, 30 April 2013 (2013). http://www.w3.org/TR/2013/REC-prov-o-20130430/
26. Macko, P., Seltzer, M.: Provenance map orbiter: interactive exploration of large provenance graphs. In: 3rd USENIX Workshop on the Theory and Practice of Provenance (TaPP 2011), Heraklion, Crete Greece. USENIX Association, June 2011. https://www.usenix.org/conference/tapp11/provenance-map-orbiter-interactive-exploration-large-provenance-graphs
27. Marzagão, D.K., Huynh, T.D., Helal, A., Moreau, L.: Provenance graph kernel, October 2020
28. McPhillips, T., Bowers, S., Belhajjame, K., Ludäscher, B.: Retrospective provenance without a runtime provenance recorder. In: Proceedings of the 7th USENIX Conference on Theory and Practice of Provenance, TaPP 2015, USA. USENIX Association (2015)
29. Miller, G.A.: The magical number seven, plus or minus two: some limits on our capacity for processing information. Psychol. Rev. **63**(2), 81–97 (1956). https://doi.org/10.1037/h0043158
30. Moreau, L.: Aggregation by provenance types: a technique for summarising provenance graphs. Electron. Proc. Theor. Comput. Sci. **181**, 129–144 (2015). https://doi.org/10.4204/eptcs.181.9
31. Moreau, L., Groth, P., Cheney, J., Lebo, T., Miles, S.: The rationale of PROV. Web Semant. **35**(P4), 235–257 (2015)
32. Moreau, L., et al.: The provenance of electronic data. Commun. ACM **51**(4), 52–58 (2008)
33. Moreau, L., Groth, P.T.: Provenance: An Introduction to PROV. Synthesis Lectures on the Semantic Web: Theory and Technology. Morgan & Claypool Publishers (2013). https://doi.org/10.2200/S00528ED1V01Y201308WBE007
34. Moreau, L., et al.: PROV-DM: the PROV data model, 30 April 2013 (2013). http://www.w3.org/TR/2013/REC-prov-dm-20130430/
35. Nguyen, Q., Eades, P., Hong, S.-H.: On the faithfulness of graph visualizations. In: Didimo, W., Patrignani, M. (eds.) GD 2012. LNCS, vol. 7704, pp. 566–568. Springer, Heidelberg (2013). https://doi.org/10.1007/978-3-642-36763-2_55

36. Nguyen, Q.H., Eades, P.: Towards faithful graph visualizations (2018)
37. Nuzrath, S., Amarasinghe, N.H., Liyanage, K.T., Suriyawansa, K., Madanayake, D.P., Kodagoda, N.: gCodex: a tool to analyze software repositories over time (visualization). In: 2019 International Conference on Advancements in Computing (ICAC), pp. 174–179 (2019). https://doi.org/10.1109/ICAC49085.2019.9103390
38. Ono, J.P., Freire, J., Silva, C.T.: Interactive data visualization in Jupyter notebooks. Comput. Sci. Eng. **23**(02), 99–106 (2021). https://doi.org/10.1109/MCSE.2021.3052619
39. Packer, H.S., Chapman, A., Carr, L.: GitHub2PROV: provenance for supporting software project management. In: Proceedings of the 11th USENIX Conference on Theory and Practice of Provenance, TAPP 2019, USA. USENIX Association (2019)
40. Pimentel, J.F., Freire, J., Braganholo, V., Murta, L.: Tracking and analyzing the evolution of provenance from scripts. In: Mattoso, M., Glavic, B. (eds.) IPAW 2016. LNCS, vol. 9672, pp. 16–28. Springer, Cham (2016). https://doi.org/10.1007/978-3-319-40593-3_2
41. Pinzger, M., Gall, H., Fischer, M., Lanza, M.: Visualizing multiple evolution metrics. In: Proceedings of the 2005 ACM Symposium on Software Visualization, SoftVis 2005, New York, NY, USA, pp. 67–75. Association for Computing Machinery (2005). https://doi.org/10.1145/1056018.1056027
42. Ragan, E.D., Endert, A., Sanyal, J., Chen, J.: Characterizing provenance in visualization and data analysis: an organizational framework of provenance types and purposes. IEEE Trans. Visual Comput. Graph. **22**(1), 31–40 (2016). https://doi.org/10.1109/TVCG.2015.2467551
43. Schreiber, A., de Boer, C.: Modelling knowledge about software processes using provenance graphs and its application to Git-based version control systems. In: 42nd International Conference on Software Engineering Workshops, Seoul, Republic of Korea. IEEE/ACM, May 2020
44. Schreiber, A., de Boer, C., von Kurnatowski, L.: GitLab2PROV—provenance of software projects hosted on GitLab. In: 13th International Workshop on Theory and Practice of Provenance (TaPP 2021). USENIX Association, July 2021. https://www.usenix.org/conference/tapp2021/presentation/schreiber
45. Schreiber, A., von Kurnatowski, L., Meinecke, A., de Boer, C.: An interactive dashboard for visualizing the provenance of software development processes. In: 2021 Working Conference on Software Visualization (VISSOFT), pp. 100–104 (2021). https://doi.org/10.1109/VISSOFT52517.2021.00019
46. Schreiber, A., Sonnekalb, T., von Kurnatowski, L.: Towards visual analytics dashboards for provenance-driven static application security testing. In: 2021 IEEE Symposium on Visualization for Cyber Security (VizSec), pp. 42–46 (2021). https://doi.org/10.1109/VizSec53666.2021.00010
47. Spinellis, D.: Git. IEEE Softw. **29**(3), 100–101 (2012)
48. Stitz, H., Luger, S., Streit, M., Gehlenborg, N.: AVOCADO: visualization of workflow-derived data provenance for reproducible biomedical research. Comput. Graph. Forum **35**(3), 481–490 (2016)
49. Sugiyama, K., Tagawa, S., Toda, M.: Methods for visual understanding of hierarchical system structures. IEEE Trans. Syst. Man Cybern. **11**(2), 109–125 (1981). https://doi.org/10.1109/TSMC.1981.4308636
50. Tian, Y., Hankins, R.A., Patel, J.M.: Efficient aggregation for graph summarization. In: Proceedings of the 2008 ACM SIGMOD International Conference on Management of Data, SIGMOD 2008, New York, NY, USA, pp. 567–580. Association for Computing Machinery (2008). https://doi.org/10.1145/1376616.1376675

51. Wallner, G., Pohl, M., von Landesberger, T., Ballweg, K.: Perception of differences in directed acyclic graphs: influence factors & cognitive strategies. In: Proceedings of the 31st European Conference on Cognitive Ergonomics, ECCE 2019, New York, NY, USA, pp. 57–64. Association for Computing Machinery (2019). https://doi. org/10.1145/3335082.3335083

52. Wattenberg, M.: Visual exploration of multivariate graphs. In: Proceedings of the SIGCHI Conference on Human Factors in Computing Systems, CHI 2006, New York, NY, USA, pp. 811–819. Association for Computing Machinery (2006). https://doi.org/10.1145/1124772.1124891

53. Wendel, H., Kunde, M., Schreiber, A.: Provenance of software development processes. In: McGuinness, D.L., Michaelis, J.R., Moreau, L. (eds.) IPAW 2010. LNCS, vol. 6378, pp. 59–63. Springer, Heidelberg (2010). https://doi.org/10.1007/978-3-642-17819-1_7

54. Werner, B., Moreau, L.: ProvViz: an intuitive Prov editor and visualiser. In: Glavic, B., Braganholo, V., Koop, D. (eds.) IPAW 2020-2021. LNCS, vol. 12839, pp. 231–236. Springer, Cham (2021). https://doi.org/10.1007/978-3-030-80960-7_18

55. Yazici, I.M., Aktas, M.S.: A usability study on data provenance visualization approaches. In: 2021 15th Turkish National Software Engineering Symposium (UYMS), pp. 1–6 (2021). https://doi.org/10.1109/UYMS54260.2021.9659779

56. Yazici, I.M., Aktas, M.S.: A systematic literature review on data provenance visualization. In: García Márquez, F.P., Jamil, A., Eken, S., Hameed, A.A. (eds.) ICCIDA 2022. LNCS, vol. 643, pp. 479–493. Springer, Cham (2023). https://doi.org/10.1007/978-3-031-27099-4_37

Escaping Flatland: Graphics, Dimensionality, and Human Perception

Susan Vanderplas(✉) [ID], Erin Blankenship [ID], and Tyler Wiederich [ID]

Statistics Department,University of Nebraska Lincoln, 340 Hardin Hall North Wing, 3310 Holdrege Street, Lincoln, NE 68503, USA
susan.vanderplas@unl.edu

Abstract. Almost 40 years ago, Cleveland and McGill published the first of 3 papers detailing experiments assessing the accuracy of numerical perception using different types of charts. This study is often cited as a reason to avoid the use of extraneous dimensions in data visualization: 2D bar charts produced more accurate estimates than 3D bar charts; in addition, lines (length) produced more accurate estimates than circles (area). Graphics have changed fairly significantly in the last 40 years: where we once had fixed 3D perspective charts, we now can rotate 3D renderings in digital space and even 3D print our charts to examine physically. Many optical illusions result from perceptual mismatches of 3D visual heuristics and 2D, planar, data representations; more realistic renderings available with modern tools might change the outcome of Cleveland and McGill's experimental comparison of 2D vs. 3D accuracy. In this paper, we present several experiments which replicate the bar chart portion of Cleveland and McGill's original study, comparing 2D, 3D fixed perspective, 3D rendered, and 3D printed charts. We discuss the findings and the importance of replicating classic experiments using modern technology, as well as the benefits of incorporating hands-on research in introductory classes as experiential learning activities.

Keywords: teaching · graphics · user-study · perception · accuracy

Almost 40 years ago, Cleveland & McGill published the first of 3 papers detailing experiments assessing the accuracy of numerical perception using different types of charts. This study is often used to justify aesthetic advice [10,11,18,20,21] to avoid extraneous dimensions in data visualization, though it never reports experimental results for 3D comparisons. Cleveland and McGill [6] create a hierarchy of elementary perceptual tasks, claiming that 2D bars should be more accurately perceived than 3D bars; in addition, lines (length) produced more accurate estimates than circles (area). To support these claims, they ran a series of experiments described over multiple papers [4–6] assessing the accuracy of participant estimations when making comparisons between elements of different types of charts. While estimation precision is not (and should not be) the only goal in statistical graphics [1], the advice to avoid 3D charts persists, even

© The Author(s), under exclusive license to Springer Nature Switzerland AG 2024
H. Mori and Y. Asahi (Eds.): HCII 2024, LNCS 14690, pp. 140–156, 2024.
https://doi.org/10.1007/978-3-031-60114-9_11

though the charts tested in Cleveland and McGill [6] are an extremely limited version of the different types of 3D charts which we can generate today.

Technological Innovation

While 3D computer graphics have existed since Sketchpad was created in 1963 [17], and home computer software has existed since 1978 [13], there were significant developments in 3D software in the 1980s (AutoCAD) [23]. In the 1990s, 3D charts were introduced in MS Excel 3.0 [22], and though this might not be considered an overall improvement, it certainly represented an innovation in the graphical rendering features available to the average user. What is undeniable, however, is that since the 1990s, the pace of 3D graphics rendering software (and the hardware to support ever-increasing detail) has only accelerated. Two important (and related) software innovations worth mentioning for statistical graphics are the development of OpenGL [2], which is still used in packages such as `rgl` [15] and `moderngl` [8] and WebGL, which made these graphics available for publication in web browsers [7,16].

While Cleveland & McGill did directly examine volume comparisons in any of their experiments [4–6], it seems reasonable to conclude that the capabilities to create and interact with rendered 3D graphics have moved well beyond the simple image shown in Fig. 1a; even the full realism of modern interactive 3D representations is not possible to show in PDF form; a screenshot of one such chart is shown in Fig. 1b.

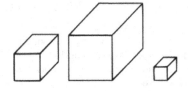

(a) Volume chart recreated from Cleveland and McGill [6]. Stimuli used in the experiment were printed and provided to participants on paper.

(b) Screenshot of a WebGL rendered 3D bar chart. The WebGL context allows this chart to be manipulated by the user; rendered shadows, lighting, and other effects contribute to the realism of the 3D effect.

Fig. 1. A comparison of 3D data renderings from 1984 and 2024.

Moreover, we now have the capability to easily create physical objects from digital renderings using 3D printers. While 3D printing is typically not fast enough to be used for exploratory data analysis (the chart in Fig. 1b takes 5 h to print even at relatively low quality), it does provide a few advantages over digital renderings: tactile experience, accessibility for those with visual impairments, and (for the moment) novelty. More importantly, if we are interested in comparing realistic 3D renderings to the 3D renderings in Cleveland and McGill [6] (or 3D perspective charts more generally), it is useful to assess both the physical objects and the digitally rendered images when comparing to the fixed perspectives used in Fig. 1a.

Perception of Graphics

Because the visual context of 3D graphical renderings has changed so significantly in the past 40 years, it is important to reassess the common guidance to avoid using the third dimension in data visualization in light of new technological capabilities. It is common for artists to intentionally leverage our 3D visual system to create illusions in two dimensions that give a three-dimensional effect, as in Fig. 2a; unfortunately, similar misperceptions can be unintentionally triggered by common charts: stream graphs, candlestick charts, and even confidence interval bands.

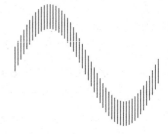

(a) Sidewalk art by Zebit in Liverpool which leverages visual heuristics to provide the illusion of depth. Image by Bill Hunt.

(b) An illustration of the sine illusion [19], also known as the line-width illusion. All vertical lines are the same length, but the lines in the middle of the curve appear to be much shorter.

Fig. 2. Two dimensional situations which create the illusion of three dimensions, either intentionally (a) or unintentionally (b).

A simple example of this phenomenon is shown in Fig. 2b; evenly spaced line segments are shown following a sine curve; even though each line segment is the same length, it appears that the segments along the inflection point are much shorter than the segments at the minimum and maximum of the curve. This illusion results from misapplied depth perception; the perceived length of the lines corresponds instead to the width of the line tangent to the sine curve - that is, the entire series of lines is instead perceived as a single object that exists in 3 dimensions, and the heuristics which would normally determine depth are applied to the stimuli, providing an erroneous estimate of the length of the line. Providing visual stimuli which are rendered using 3D shading and perspective alleviates the effects of the sine illusion and allows viewers to estimate line length properly [19, Fig. 3].

It stands to reason, then, that more realistic renderings of three-dimensional chart objects may alleviate the decreased precision of quantitative estimates found in Cleveland and McGill [6].

Motivation

In this paper, we present the results from several experiments designed to mimic Cleveland and McGill [6]'s exploration of different types of grouped bar charts, with the goal of exploring perception of 2D and 3D charts. We describe the process used to recreate the stimuli from the original experiment, using 2D, 3D fixed perspective, 3D rendered, and 3D printed charts to assess estimation accuracy in a population of undergraduate statistics students. Finally, we discuss the results of our experiment and the importance of replicating classic experiments using modern technology. We also describe the benefits of incorporating hands-on research in introductory classes as experiential learning activities.

Methodology

Participant Recruitment and Experimental Context

Participants were recruited from online and in-person sections of introductory (non-calculus based) statistics courses taught at University of Nebraska Lincoln during the Summer and Fall of 2023; overall, students from sections led by 3 different instructors took part in the experiment. The experiment was integrated into the course as an experiential learning activity accompanied by several written reflections. The stages of the experiential learning activity were as follows:

1. Informed consent - on the LMS during the first 2 weeks of the semester.
2. Pre-study reflection - on the LMS prior to experiment participation. Asks participants to write 3–5 sentences about how scientific investigations happen.
3. Experiment participation - code from experiment entered into the LMS
4. Post experiment reflection - on the LMS after experiment participation. Asks participants to guess at the purpose of the experiment, what the hypothesis under investigation might have been, potential sources of error, what variables were examined, and whether they thought there were elements of randomization or experimental control.
5. Abstract - Students read a 2-page extended abstract written for a scientific conference and reflect on how the information presented differed from their experience of participating in the experiment.
6. Presentation - Students watch a 15-minute conference presentation about the experiment and results and reflect on how the information presented differed from the information in the abstract.

During step 3, experiment participation, students were provided with an additional informed consent for the perceptual experiment. Students were able to opt-out, which prevented their data from being saved, but were required to at least participate in the process of the experiment to receive course credit, which ensured that they would be able to reflect on that experience during the later stages of the experiential learning activity.

Replicating Cleveland & McGill

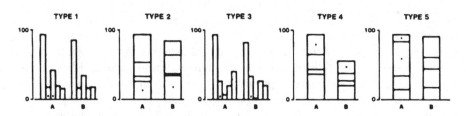

Fig. 3. Types of judgments used in Cleveland and McGill [6].

We decided to only examine the Type 1 and Type 3 comparisons (e.g. those corresponding to grouped bar charts) because multi-color 3D printing was not supported by equipment we had available, and it was easier to mark the bars used for comparison if we did not attempt to segment bars vertically.

Cleveland & McGill asked participants in the position-length experiment (described in [6]) to evaluate marked bars, first indicating which bar was smaller, and then estimating "what percent the smaller is of the larger". The values involved in the judgments were $s_i = 10 \times 10^{(i-1)/12}, i = 1, ..., 10$, that is, $s_i = \{10, 12.12, 14.68, 17.78, 21.54, 26.1, 31.62, 38.31, 46.42, 56.23\}$. Participants judged "10 pairs of values with ratios ranging from 0.18 to 0.83". There are 9 ratios available, as available bar lengths are equally spaced on the log scale; of these, the study examined 7, replicating 3 ratios twice, presumably to provide some estimate of within-participant error. Examining the graphical results in Cleveland and McGill [6], it seems that the values used were 17.8, 26.1, 38.3, 46.4 (twice), 56.2, 68.1 (twice), and 82.5 (twice). The exact bar lengths corresponding to these ratios were not disclosed, but we added the additional constraint that no bar length was used more than twice in the creation of the data sets which would be rendered in 4 different chart types. Bar heights which were not to be compared were chosen "at random, but subject to certain constraints"; these constraints applied to the stacked bar charts, but not the grouped bar charts. To mimic this, we used a scaled Beta(2, 2) distribution to define the size of the other 8 bars not used for comparison.

Experiment Design

We created 7 sets of data containing 10 bars lengths, one for each selected ratio used in Cleveland and McGill [6]. These data sets were assigned colors within chart type (so red in a 3D fixed bar chart represents a different ratio than red in a 3D printed bar chart), primarily to facilitate visually checking that combinations of 3D printed charts in a kit were all of different ratios. Each data set was rendered in 4 different chart types, with two different bar arrangements corresponding to Type 1 and Type 3 comparisons. Thus, the experiment involves $7 \times 2 \times 4 = 42$ different charts.

Each participant evaluated either 15 or 20 different charts, with a charts of each display type shown for each of 5 ratios, allocated according to Fig. 4.

Whether participants were shown adjacent (Type 1) or separated (Type 2) comparisons was randomly determined. Participants recruited from online sections of introductory statistics were shown 2D, 3D fixed, and 3D rendered charts; participants recruited from in-person sections were shown 2D, 3D rendered, and 3D printed charts. Due to an application configuration error, some in-person participants were initially shown 2D, 3D fixed, 3D rendered, and 3D printed charts, for a total of 20 trials. This error was fixed after the first 2023 summer session. Figure 5 provides example stimuli from each different display type. The order of trials for each participant was randomly determined by the data collection app, and in the case of 3D printed chart trials, by the participant themselves.

In order to facilitate the data collection process, we 3D printed sufficient charts to create 21 different kits of 5 physical charts each. Participants in the in-person condition participated in the experiment during office hours: each participant selected a kit from a bin of available options and participated in the experiment via the online app in a quiet study carrel before returning the kit to the bin. The app asked for a kit ID from in-person participants; this ID was used to select digital charts which had the same ratios as those in the kit of 3D printed charts. Each day, an instructor would shuffle the kits within the bin to ensure that each kit had a reasonably equal selection probability.

Stimulus Creation

This experiment uses 4 different presentations of grouped bar charts, shown in Fig. 5.

It is relatively simple to create an all-digital experiment and keep track of the different stimuli (or render them during the experiment based on the parameters used to create them). With physical stimuli, this experiment was slightly more complicated, and as a result, we used slightly different methods to create the 3D files used for both prints and digital renderings. In particular, we wanted to ensure that each chart had a label which could not easily fall off or be removed in order to ensure the ability to audit kit composition reliably. This meant that

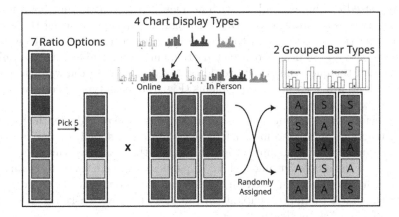

Fig. 4. Schematic showing how trials were determined for each participant.

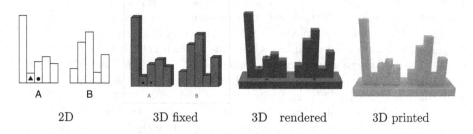

| 2D | 3D fixed | 3D rendered | 3D printed |

Fig. 5. Rendering types used in this experiment. All charts show the same data.

the direct plot-to-STL pipeline provided by `rgl` [15] and `rayshader` [14] was not sufficient. Instead, we inscribed an ID code ("data/pilot/Set85/id-xx/Typexx-Rep01") on the bottom of the base of the charts by creating an OpenSCAD [12] template for a grouped bar chart in OpenSCAD and populated the template with values for each chart using an R script. The ID code was designed to be informative for the experimenters but not the participants, as numerical IDs were randomly assigned to ratio; the use of comparison type in the ID did not provide any information that would not also be available looking at the top of the chart.

2D bar charts were created using `ggplot2` [24] with an extremely minimalist theme. 3D fixed bar charts were created using Microsoft Excel in order to most accurately represent the angle used in these sorts of charts 'in the wild'. While we could have created these using some sort of snapshot of the RGL rendering from a fixed angle, we felt using the same tool used in industry would increase external validity.

App Design

Data were collected using a Shiny app [3]. The app first asked participants for informed consent and basic demographic information: age range, gender identity, and highest education level, along with an identifier ("what is your favorite zoo animal") used as an additional way to distinguish participants using the applet at the same time. Participants then were given three practice problems with 2D charts; these were designed to get participants comfortable with the online interface and the questions which would be asked, similar to the way Cleveland and McGill [6] provided practice problems (Fig. 6) of each type of comparison in their two experiments.

Just before the experiment started, participants were provided with the basic trial instructions and asked for a Kit ID (one option was 'online'). Participants who were online were randomly assigned a kit ID that was used throughout the remainder of the study. During each trial, participants were asked to evaluate a chart which was either displayed on the screen or randomly chosen from the kit of physical charts by the participant (in this case, they were asked to select the chart ID from a list, as shown in Fig. 7).

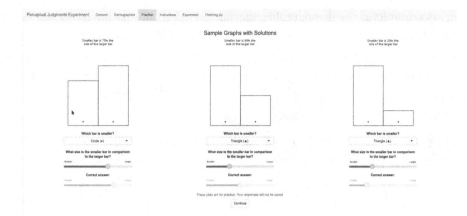

Fig. 6. Practice screen providing participants with guidelines for how to use the sliders and identify the smaller bar.

Fig. 7. Screen showing the app process when a 3D printed chart was randomly selected

Participants first identified which bar was smaller, and then used a slider with no numerical information to show the ratio of the smaller bar to the larger bar. This differs from the numerical estimation procedure in Cleveland and McGill [6], in that it does not require participants to estimate the number from the size ratio, but this difference was intentional - we wanted to reduce participant cognitive load as much as possible; follow up studies may be necessary to determine how much of an impact this design decision has on the results.

At the conclusion of the experiment, participants were provided with a participation code which could be entered into the learning management system to receive credit for experiment participation. This code was provided regardless of whether participants consented to their data being saved for research purposes.

Results

Demographics
Overall, approximately 118 participants met the inclusion criteria (above the age of majority and a student in the class). This number is approximate because we recorded data anonymously, and can thus only track unique sessions where par-

ticipants completed the demographic information - this information intentionally cannot be linked to responses for privacy purposes (Fig. 8).

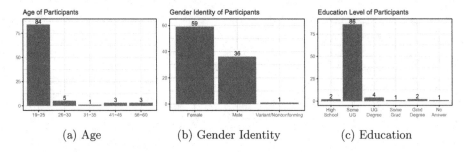

(a) Age   (b) Gender Identity   (c) Education

Fig. 8. Participant Demographics. As participants were recruited from undergraduate statistics classes, imbalances in age, gender, and education level are to be expected.

Of these students, there were 100 participants who completed at least 10 trials.

Data Cleaning
In studies where participants are asked to perform a task, it is typically important to utilize both attention checks (semi-obvious answers that check whether the participant is paying attention) and to be aware of participants who try to submit the study as quickly as possible without completing the task as directed. In this study, we asked participants to identify the smaller marked bar, as in the original study. Of the 1422 trials completed by the 100 participants with at least 10 trials, 92.28% identified the correct bar. Trials where this attention check was not answered correctly have been excluded from the study with the rationale that the ratio between the smaller and larger bar (which is limited to a range of 0–100%) is nonsensical if the smaller bar is not identified correctly.

In addition, we noticed that 15.12% of the trials completed had a response of exactly 50% (the default value of the slider). In particular, 13 participants completed at least 50% of trials with a response of exactly 50%; these participants have been excluded from the study on the grounds that they were clearly not engaging with the purpose of the experiment.

After applying these basic criteria for inclusion in the data analysis, we have 1276 trials completed by 87 participants remaining for further analysis.

Summary Statistics
There are far fewer trials of 3D printed charts, largely because only online sections were offered during the summer, and relatively few in-person sections participated in this experiment during the fall (Fig. 9). As a result, we will exclude the 3D printed charts from further analysis in this study.

Examining participant responses in Fig. 10, it is clear why Cleveland and McGill [6] worked with the midmeans of the responses - there is quite a bit of variability in the estimates created by participants, sometimes in ways that do not make much sense.

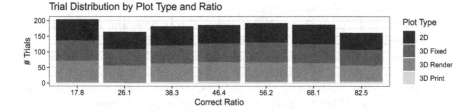

Fig. 9. Number of trials across ratio and plot display type.

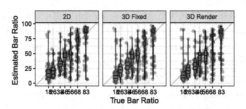

Fig. 10. Violin plots of responses relative to true ratio values. It is clear that some participants misunderstood the estimation task, while others simply did not move the slider from 50%. Nonetheless, there is a general relationship between the true ratio and the central values of the distribution of estimates. Note that 3D printed plots have been removed from this chart because there were too few responses to estimate a distribution.

Midmeans Analysis

If we repeat the analysis performed in Cleveland and McGill [6], examining a 25% trimmed mean of the log absolute error (with a correction),

$$\log_2 \left(|\text{Estimated Percent} - \text{True Percent}| + {}^1/_8 \right),$$

we find that there are very few differences across plot types. Comparing to the actual values reported in Cleveland & McGill, however, we find that errors are much higher in this population under the web-based protocol we are using for data collection than similar midmeans and intervals reported in Cleveland and McGill [6]. Our errors are also larger than those reported in Heer and Bostock [9], which used an online sample but otherwise followed essentially the same procedures using similar stimuli to Cleveland and McGill [6]. It is possible that introductory statistics students do not estimate as accurately as academics and their wives [6] or paid participants through Amazon Mechanical Turk [9]; certainly, the number of participants removed for answering 50% for all trials suggests that at least some participants did not take the task seriously. Another potential explanation is that some of these issues stem from the measures we took to minimize cognitive load while avoiding rounding and clustering of responses around benchmark values. In this study, we used a slider with endpoints marked 0 and 100, but no other numerical feedback was provided - no tick marks, no value of the current estimate. While our goal was to remove rounding tendencies, it is entirely possible that we instead introduced higher error values because participants could not do the spatial mapping operation without going through numeric values; then, participants had to invert this process and map back onto a spatial dimension without any visual aids. Further studies will be necessary to distinguish between these two issues. It may also be helpful to provide feedback on a few demo trials before participating in the experiment in order to ensure that everyone is comfortable with the input mechanisms; the current demo may not provide enough active feedback to really get participants familiar with the interface.

Student Responses
Part of the goal of using this experiment as an experiential learning activity was to introduce the idea that not all charts are equally effective to introductory statistics students. In addition, we hoped to reinforce concepts taught in class, such as randomization, experimental control, blocking, and interpretation of results, using experiential learning to help students make the connection between theoretical concepts and how these concepts play out in real life.

In Fall 2023, this project was offered to students in a 75-person section of online introductory statistics as extra credit. About 40 students both participated and consented to having their responses shared across the 6 different parts of the experiment; only 4 of these components have meaningful responses beyond the question of providing informed consent or a completion code for the experiment, and of these, we will briefly consider questions from the post-experiment reflection, abstract presentation, and presentation. The pre-experiment reflection, which asked students to think about how scientific experimentation works, is less specific to this experiment and will thus be omitted.

In the next 3 subsections, we will provide some brief excerpts from student responses which provide some insight into student learning and engagement with the experiment. Text files with all student responses for each question are available on github.

Post-experiment Reflection. Students were asked to complete a reflection activity 1–2 weeks after completing the experiment, with questions designed to encourage them to assess how material from the course applied to their experience.

What hypotheses might the experimenter have been testing?

– "Students will get progressively less accurate as questions were asked"
– "Do students change their answers when asked the same question over and over?"
– "3D printed bar charts will lead to more accurate ratio judgments compared to 2D or 3D digital charts."
– "That 2d is preferred over 3d. It cleans up the data presentation."
– "The public can more accurately understand data when it is provided to them in a 2-D graph format."

While some of these hypotheses are not correct (and even amusing), over half of the students made some mention of the use of different types or different dimensionality of graph presentations in their answers, and several more provided reasonable hypotheses about e.g. the use of adjacent bars vs. separated bars in comparisons.

What sources of error are involved in this experiment?

- "Fatigue effect over the course of making many judgments, learning patterns from seeing the same ratios multiple times, possibly difference in eyesight among participants."
- "There are no line values to help measure it when there is a small difference between the graphs."
- "People that are guessing"
- "People in the sample misunderstanding directions."

Here, it is clear that students were capable of identifying many of the same sources of error that we have identified when considering the large variability in our results relative to previous studies.

When asked which variables the experimenter examined and whether these variables were quantitative or categorical, students overwhelmingly (37/41) indicated at least some understanding of the response variables (smaller/larger, % of smaller to larger), and many participants also identified manipulated variables (chart type) and demographic variables (age, gender identity, education level) that may have also been of interest.

What elements of experimental design, such as randomization or the use of a control group, do you think were present in the experiment? Why?

- "I believe every graph was randomized for every student. I also believe the practice was meant to be a bit of the control group."
- "Randomization was used as participants all received different sets of graphs to examine. A person wasn't assigned to a certain set of graphs and it was up to random chance on which set of graphs they received."
- "I think that there is randomization but not a control group in my opinion, because there isn't one group that is left alone or not studied...."
- "Randomization was not used because it was offered as an extra credit assignment in class."

These responses indicate that participants were actively considering how their experience of the experimental design matched terms used in class. While the final excerpt represents a misunderstanding of the difference between randomization and random sampling, it is clear from these comments that students are using their experience and considering the terms they've learned in class based on those experiences.

Abstract Reflection. A few weeks after the post-experiment reflection, students were provided with a 2-page extended abstract that described the experiment in a style which was consistent with submission to a conference. Students were asked only a single question, which was **What components of the experiment are clearer now than they were as a participant? What questions do you still have for the experimenter?**

- "I believed that one of the components was the dimension of the graph. However I also thought that the color was the main component and that was not true. The angle was an obvious component I felt, but then again I wondered if it looked that way because I was using my phone."[1]
- "The exam was about perceptual judgement, using the difference between 2D and 3D graphics. This is a different approach than just deciding how much bigger or smaller something is as the participant. A question I have is why we think 3D graphs are harder to perceive than a 2D graph. This seems a bit confusing to me, because they seem to be about the same for me. I also would like to know about the difference between 2D rendered charts compared to a 3D printed chart. Perhaps this is because I took this course online."
- "The scientific question is more clear after reading the extended abstract. I now understand that they wanted to compare differences between 2-dimension, 3-dimension, and printed 3-dimension. They were testing not the correctness, but the perceptual judgment. There was also a formula that they provided for judging how the participant analyzed the bar graphs, and if they were correct provided the formula. The random distribution of ratios also makes sense in that there were 21 different combinations of bar graphs amongst different participants."
- "After reading on the study, I can better understand the reasoning behind it and the purpose of the experiment. I enjoyed that they tried using similar tactics as that of Cleveland and McGill. I thought it was unique that they had strategically planned out the distance between the two bars that were being assessed throughout the study, as I didn't think it was possible to be that in depth and in such detail. Overall, I am impressed by the experiment."
- "After reading the abstract, I was surprised to learn that the subject of the study wasn't the hypothesis I thought it was. Now it's very clear that there's a discrepancy between interpreting 3D and 2D graphs/visuals. I am still curious after reading this what the results of the study are based on students feedback. I also want to know if the student results were different then what was expected based on Cleveland/ McGill's study."

Generalizing beyond the excerpts included here, almost all of the students seemed to enjoy finding out what the experiment was about, and came up with reasonable and cogent questions about the experiment beyond what was in the abstract.

Presentation Reflection. As a final component of this experiment, participants were asked to watch a 15 min conference-style presentation of the results

---

[1] Note that students were explicitly instructed to use a laptop (and one was available for their use); it isn't surprising that this student had a hard time using a device with a much smaller screen.

and reflect on the experiment and information present in the abstract vs. the presentation.

If you had to hear about this study using only the extended abstract or only the presentation, which one would you prefer? Which one would be better for determining whether the experiment was well designed?

- "Again I like the presentation better mostly because it adds a more personal touch! The abstract is probably really the best was to understand the design of the experiment. However I struggle reading that kind of material. So for a participant, the video presentation was the best."
- "I would prefer the presentation. I think that maybe the abstract would be better for determining whether the design of the experiment was better because of the fact that it strictly lays out the experiment and some of what math was involved, whereas even though the presentation did that, it went more in depth about the results as well instead of just the design."
- "I would prefer hearing about the study using the abstract. I believe it provides more detail on the setup of the experiment, which is better for determining if it was well designed."
- "If I had to hear about this study using only one source, I would prefer the video presentation. This may be because I am a visual and auditory learner, but I also had a hard time understanding what the researchers wanted us to get out of the abstract because it was so complex. With the presentation, I was able to understand step by step how the study was conducted."

While participants were decidedly mixed on their preferred information transfer method, most agreed that the extended abstract was preferable for understanding design details, while the presentation was more engaging.

One goal of the introductory statistics class at UNL is to create informed consumers of statistical information. As part of that goal, we asked participants to reflect on what information was available to them at each stage of this project.

How did the information you gained from the components of this project (participation, post-study reflection, extended abstract, presentation) differ?

- "Participation gathers real-time, subjective feedback. Post-study reflection provides deeper insights. The extended abstract offers a formal summary, while the presentation conveys findings to a broader audience. Each component serves a unique role in understanding perceptual judgments on 3D printed bars."
- "The experiment itself didn't make it obvious that 2D presentation of a graph distorts the data, which is an interesting perspective to carry when reading different charts, especially bar graphs. I learned this through the extended abstract and presentation, which drastically changed my thought process when reflecting on why each type of graph led me to believe it had that specific ratio on the slider tool."

- "I think that with each module, we gained more and more insight into the study and its purpose. It was almost like this video was the last part of a scavenger hunt to find the purpose and idea behind the study and the other components were like little puzzle pieces."
- "As a participant in the study, having no idea what the purpose was at first, I truly enjoyed the experiment. I felt like I was doing a self-challenge to try and accurately determine how much smaller the smaller graph was. Next, I read the extended abstract and appreciated the purpose of the experiment, its history behind it, and the strategies used within the experiment. When doing the post-study reflection, I feel like I got to tie everything together that I had learned so far. Finishing off with the presentation, I feel like everything became full circle and I found interest in the additional information that was given that wasn't in the extended abstract."
- "I did not realize the depth of thought that goes into experimental design. As a participant, I had no idea of the depth of the research for this data. Also as I moved through this process it gave me a clearer understanding of the study and its implications. This experiment also helped give me experience in understanding the experiment design process."

Many participants expressed a feeling that information was gradually uncovered over time; the sequential unveiling of information seems to have provided an ongoing engagement and even investment in the study's results, for those who responded. Interestingly, several participants mentioned that the post-study reflection was key for their understanding of the experiment - as no additional information was provided in this reflection, this suggests that the explicit direction to consider how concepts learned in class related to the experiment was a useful exercise for students.

Discussion

While this experiment lacked the precision necessary to provide useful insight into visualization design, the process of incorporating these experiments into introductory statistics classes seems to be a valuable tool for motivating student learning. It is possible that we may be able to reduce response variance in future iterations of this experiment by providing numerical feedback, strictly numerical estimation methods, or otherwise manipulating how students interact with the study. One of the potential explanations for differences between our study and Cleveland and McGill [6] is that we used numerical sliders; however, another explanation is that students did not estimate ratios with the same amount of care as participants in previous studies. Certainly, it is possible to read some of the student reflections and come to the conclusion that some students simply did not read the instructions or participate in good faith.

A much more valuable outcome of this experiment is that participants seemed to enjoy the overall process of participation in the study and reflection upon the experience during the course of their introductory statistics class. While we did not collect information which allows us to assess whether participation increased student learning, we can see from their reflections that most students were able to make connections between participation in the study and concepts in class when prompted to think about these topics. Moreover, students seem to enjoy the "reveal" moments when reading the abstract and watching the presentation. The sense of completing a puzzle was evident in many of the written responses, and it seems likely that the experience of questioning, forming a hypothesis, and having the hypothesis either supported or rejected through new information may stick with them after the concepts in the course are forgotten. In that sense, this experiment was a success, and embedding basic research and experiential learning in statistics courses may prove to be a valuable pedagogical tool.

References

1. Bertini, E., Correll, M., Franconeri, S.: Why shouldn't all charts be scatter plots? beyond precision-driven visualizations. In: 2020 IEEE Visualization Conference (VIS). 2020 IEEE Visualization Conference (VIS), pp. 206–210 (Oct 2020). https://doi.org/10.1109/VIS47514.2020.00048
2. Buss, S.R.: 3D Computer Graphics: A Mathematical Introduction with OpenGL. Google-Books-ID: 1CspAwAAQBAJ. Cambridge University Press, p. 397 (May 19 2003) ISBN: 978-1-139-44038-7
3. Chang, W., et al.: Shiny: Web Application Framework for R. R package version 1.7.5.1 (2023). https://CRAN.R-project.org/package=shiny
4. Cleveland, W.S., McGill, R.: Graphical perception and graphical methods for analyzing scientific data. Science **229**(4716), 828–833 (1985). https://doi.org/10.1126/science.229.4716.828. https://www.jstor.org/stable/1695272. ISSN: 0036-8075 (Accessed 26 Dec 2022)
5. Cleveland, W.S., McGill, R.: Graphical perception: the visual decoding of quantitative information on graphical displays of data. Journal Royal Stat. Soc. Series A (General) **150**(3), 192 (1987). https://doi.org/10.2307/2981473. JSTOR: 2981473. ISSN: 00359238 (Accessed 30 Dec 2022)
6. Cleveland, W.S., McGill, R.: Graphical perception: theory, experimentation, and application to the development of graphical methods. J. Am. Stat. Assoc. **79**(387), 531–554 (1984). https://doi.org/10.1080/01621459.1984.10478080
7. Deits, R.: meshcat-dev/meshcat-python. original-date: 2018-02-19T21:40:59Z (2024). https://github.com/meshcat-dev/meshcat-python (Accessed 26 Jan 2024)
8. Dombi, S., Forselv, E.: ModernGL. Version 5.10.0. 2024. https://moderngl.readthedocs.io/en/5.10.0/ (Accessed 26 Jan 2024)
9. Heer, J., Bostock, M.: Crowdsourcing graphical perception: using mechanical turk to assess visualization design'. In: Proceedings of the SIGCHI Conference on Human Factors in Computing Systems, pp. 203–212. ACM, Atlanta Georgia USA (2010). https://doi.org/10.1145/1753326.1753357. ISBN: 978-1-60558-929-9. Accessed 31 July 2023
10. Kosslyn, S.M.: Graph Design for the Eye and Mind, p. 303. Oxford University Press (2006). ISBN: 978-0-19-530662-0
11. Kosslyn, S.M.: Graphics and human information processing: a review of five books. J. Am. Stat. Assoc. **80**(391), 499–512 (1985). https://www.tandfonline.com/doi/pdf/10.1080/01621459.1985.10478147, https://doi.org/10.1080/01621459.1985.10478147. ISSN: 0162-1459 (Accessed 26 Jan 2024)

12. Kintel, M.: OpenSCAD Documentation. OpenSCAD. tex.ids= kintelOpen-
    SCAD2023 (May 27 2023). https://openscad.org/documentation.html (Accessed
    29 May 2023)
13. Miyazawa, K.: 3D ART GRAPHICS, Tokyo, Japan (June 1978). https://www.
    brutaldeluxe.fr/projects/cassettes/japan/
14. Morgan-Wall, T.: rayshader: Create Maps and Visualize Data in 2D and 3D. R
    package version 0.35.7 (2023). https://CRAN.R-project.org/package=rayshader
15. Murdoch, D., Adler, D.: rgl: 3D Visualization Using OpenGL. R package version
    1.2.1. (2023). https://CRAN.R-project.org/package=rgl
16. Parisi, T.: WebGL: Up and Running. Google-Books-ID: uYnyaBClb3IC. "O'Reilly
    Media, Inc., p. 232 (Aug 15 2012). ISBN: 978-1-4493-2357-8
17. Sutherland, I.E.: Sketchpad: a man-machine graphical communication system. In:
    Proceedings of the May 21-23, 1963, spring joint computer conference. AFIPS 1963
    (Spring), pp. 329–346. Association for Computing Machinery, New York (May
    21 1963) . https://doi.org/10.1145/1461551.1461591, https://dl.acm.org/doi/10.
    1145/1461551.1461591. ISBN: 978-1-4503-7880-2 (Accessed 26 Jan 2024)
18. Tufte, E.: The visual display of quantitative information, 2nd ed., p. 200. Graphics
    Press (Feb 14 2001). ISBN: 1-930824-13-0
19. VanderPlas, S., Hofmann, H.: Signs of the sine illusion-why we need to care. J.
    Compu. Graph. Stat. 24(4), 1170–1190 (2015). https://doi.org/10.1080/10618600.
    2014.951547. ISSN: 1061-8600 (Accessed 12 Dec 2018)
20. Wainer, H.: How to display data badly. In: The American Statistician. Taylor
    & Francis Group (May 1 1984). https://www.tandfonline.com/doi/abs/10.1080/
    00031305.1984.10483186 (Accessed 26 Jan 2024)
21. Wainer, H.: Picturing the Uncertain World: How to Understand, Communicate,
    and Control Uncertainty through Graphical Display. Princeton University Press
    (2009). https://doi.org/10.2307/j.ctv1jk0jwv. ISBN: 978-0-691-13759-9 (Accessed
    June 10 2023)
22. Walkenbach, J.: Versions of Excel Explained. The Spreadsheet Page (2021).
    https://spreadsheetpage.com/excel-version-history/ (Accessed 26 Jan 2024)
23. Walker, J.: The Autodesk File. Fourmilab (2017). https://www.fourmilab.ch/
    autofile/ (Accessed 26 Jan 2024)
24. Wickham, H.: ggplot2: Elegant Graphics for Data Analysis. Springer-Verlag New
    York (2016). https://ggplot2.tidyverse.org. ISBN: 978-3-319-24277-4

Before and After COVID-19 Outbreak Using Variance Representation Comparative Analysis of Newspaper Articles on the Travel Hotel Industry

Yeqing Yang[✉] and Yumi Asahi

Graduate School of Management, Department of Management,
Tokyo University of Science, 1-11-2, Fujimi,
Chiyoda-Ku 102-0071, Tokyo, Japan
8623518@ed.tus.ac.jp, asahi@rs.tus.ac.jp

Abstract. This study explores the impact of COVID-19 on Japan's travel industry by analyzing differences before and after the pandemic through articles from the Nihon Keizai Shimbun. It employs text mining techniques like Latent Semantic Analysis (LSA) and BERT (a natural language model) to process and categorize information from newspaper titles. The analysis involves extracting nouns using MeCab, creating a frequency matrix, decomposing it with NMF for clustering, and setting topics. BERT is used for text classification, focusing on token attention weights and variance representation. The data includes articles from Nikkei Morning News pre- and post-COVID-19, specifically tagged with "Travel & Hotel," totaling 792 articles. Analysis revealed ten topics such as vaccines, business structures, and financial results. Hierarchical clustering grouped these topics across eight clusters. Findings indicate a shift in topics post-COVID-19 towards financial impacts and business activities, highlighting tokens related to company activities and keywords associated with the pandemic. Future work aims at improving classification accuracy and leveraging data insights.

Keywords: COVID-19 · Travel Hotel Industry of Japan · BERT Text Classification

1 Introduction

The new coronavirus has had a major negative impact on Japan's travel industry. In this study, we aim to use text mining techniques to analyze the effects of articles in the Nihon Keizai Shimbun newspaper as information sources. Latent Semantic Analysis (LSA), which has traditionally been used for text mining, can represent documents and their topics as vectors that quantify their relationships with words. On the other hand, BERT uses natural language analysis that is excellent for analyzing short sentences. It is a model that can take text as input

© The Author(s), under exclusive license to Springer Nature Switzerland AG 2024
H. Mori and Y. Asahi (Eds.): HCII 2024, LNCS 14690, pp. 157–174, 2024.
https://doi.org/10.1007/978-3-031-60114-9_12

and classify it into categories. BERT is a model that makes predictions based on vector distributed representations of tokens and their weighted sums. In this research, the trained BERT model uses the titles of newspaper articles published before and after the coronavirus pandemic as input, and analyzes the tokens that have a strong influence on predictions and their distribution in vector space to understand the differences between before and after.

2   Principle

2.1   NMF Latent Semantic Analysis

NMF (Non-Negative Matrix Factorization) is a text analysis based on multivariate analysis and linear algebra techniques, which takes a word frequency matrix M as input data and decomposes it into the product of two low-rank matrices represents the NMF basis, and the matrix H represents the related coefficients (weights). The algorithm iteratively changes the values of W and H so that their product approaches M with the constraint that both the NMF basis and the weights are non-negative. A low-rank matrix with small errors retains much of the original data structure.

The algorithm terminates when the approximation error converges or the specified number of iterations is reached. The NMF algorithm relies on initial values and requires iteration. It can be used as a preprocessing step to reduce the number of dimensions in tasks such as NMF clustering. Expresses the topic of a text as the weight of words that are likely to appear. You can understand what kind of themes they are and extract meaning from text data.

2.2   Hierarchical Clustering

Hierarchical clustering is a method of classifying data hierarchically. The purpose of this is to visualize the relationship between the data by classifying the data into multiple clusters. Hierarchical clustering is a very easy-to-understand method of clustering, and by visualizing it, it is possible to intuitively understand the relationship between data. In addition, it is also effective when the number of features in the data is small or the dimension of the features in the data is large, so it is widely used in data mining and natural language processing.

2.3   BERT Text Classification

BERT [1] is an abbreviation for Bidirectional Encoder Representations from Transformers, which is a pretrained model widely used in natural language processing tasks. BERT has a high level of natural language comprehension by learning vector representations of sentences using a bidirectional encoder by Transformer. By using BERT, the titles of newspaper articles and press releases can be acquired into distributed representations that are more suitable for those categories by classification learning [2], and text classification with higher accuracy can be performed.

$$Attention(Q, K, V) = softmax_k \left(\frac{QK^T}{\sqrt{d_k}} \right) V \tag{1}$$

Consider the key matrix K and the value matrix V of the statement referencing the output vector corresponding to the input (query) vector $Q = (q_1, q_2, \ldots, q_n)$. It is regarded as a function to be considered and sought, and is expressed by the above equation. K,V is the key vector of the i word in the reference sentence. It is a matrix in which k_i and the value vector v_i are arranged.

$$K = \begin{pmatrix} k_1 \\ \vdots \\ k_n \end{pmatrix}, V = \begin{pmatrix} v_1 \\ \vdots \\ v_n \end{pmatrix} \tag{2}$$

3   Analytical Methods

In this study, we extracted newspaper articles about the travel industry by specifying the time period and tags. U sing the word occurrence frequency matrix in the article as input, latent semantic analysis and cluster analysis were performed using NMF. In addition, we performed discriminant learning using the BERT model and analyzed the correlation and importance of keywords based on distributed representation and attention weights.

3.1   NMF Latent Semantic Analysis and Hierarchical Clustering Are Performed by the Following Procedure

- Morphological analysis is performed using MeCab to extract only nouns, but numbers and symbols are excluded. Occurrence of extracted words, The numbers are aggregated and the frequency matrix is N.
- Matrix decompose with NMF with SVD of N as the initial value. The vectors of the sentence were clustered.
- The number of topics is set to 10 by NMF, and the top 20 words in relevance of each topic are extracted.
- Hierarchical clustering analyzes the strong topics of each cluster.

3.2   BERT Text Classification

Perform discriminant learning based on training data (x, y). where x is a document, and $y \in \{BC, AC\}$. BC was before the Corona disaster.AC is post-COVID. The prediction model outputs $P(y|x)$ for input x.

Here's how to do it:

- Split documents into tokens by tokenizer.

- Using the trained model, the following three types of analysis are performed.
- (1)Visualize the attention weight of the token.
- (2)Calculate the aggregate average of the attention weights of each word for each label.
- (3)Embedding of distributed representation in a method of embedding in the low dimension of t-SNE.

4   Experiment

4.1   Data Summary

The data used in this experiment are articles published in the Nikkei morning edition in the year 2019 before the coronavirus pandemic by Nikkei Telecon, and articles published in the Nikkei morning newspaper from April 30, 2021 to April 30, 2022 after the coronavirus pandemic. A s a result of extracting articles with the industry code "travel and hotels", a total of 392 and 400 articles were found before and after the Corona disaster, respectively. In addition, the number of training and test data was 634 and 158, respectively.

4.2   NMF Latent Semantic Analysis

1 to 10 show 10 topics extracted from the article by NMF. I n a word cloud, the size of a word reflects the size of its weight. Figure 1 shows vaccines, Fig. 2 shows business structure, Fig. 3 shows profit and loss, Fig. 4 shows stocks, Fig. 5 shows accommodation, Fig. 6 shows financial results, Fig. 7 shows human resources, Fig. 8 shows business, Fig. 9 shows farewell parties, and Fig. 10 shows hotel topics.

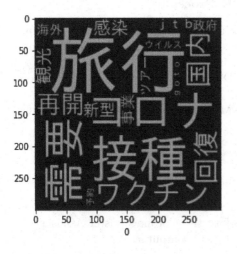

Fig. 1. Word Cloud Topic 0

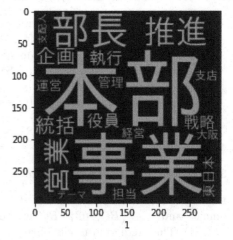

Fig. 2. Word Cloud Topic 1

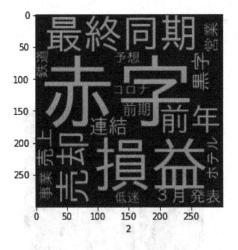

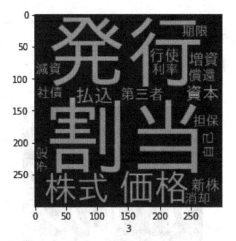

Fig. 3. Word Cloud Topic 2   **Fig. 4.** Word Cloud Topic 3

4.3 Hierarchical Clustering

Figure 11 shows the topic strength of each cluster. T he numbers on the horizontal axis correspond to the topics in Figs. 1, 2, 3, 4, 5, 6, 7, 8, 9 and 10. The box plot shows the distribution of weights of articles belonging to a cluster.

Cluster 0 has articles on business structure and personnel, Cluster 1 has articles on vaccines and accommodation, Cluster 2 has articles on stocks, Cluster 3 has articles on profit and loss and accommodation, Cluster 4 has articles on farewell parties, Cluster 5 has articles on financial results, Cluster 6 has articles on business, and Cluster 7 has articles on hotels are gathering.

4.4 Result

4.4.1 Analysis of Attention Weights Using the learned prediction model, we extract sentences with a high probability of being titles before and after the coronavirus pandemic, and the attention weight of tokens in a sentence is expressed and visualized by color density.

Example sentences with high P_{AC} after the coronavirus pandemic

K ##N ##T － CT 、 最終 赤字 130 億 円 、 今 ##期 、 受託 事業 で 縮小 。

In other sentences: electricity, environment, zero, sale, previous term, business, major, profitability, closure, funds, government, new, billion, investigation, rent, rental, recovery, support, stimulus, deficit, reduction, vaccine, and postal savings have a large weight.

The characteristics of these tokens are economic and medical terms after the coronavirus pandemic.

Next, an example sentence before the coronavirus pandemic and with a high P_{AC} is shown below.

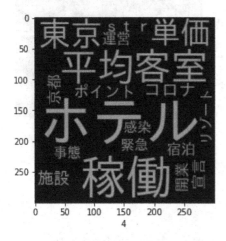

Fig. 5. Word Cloud Topic 4

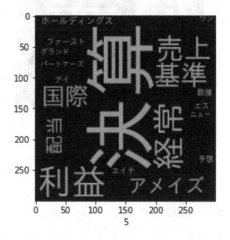

Fig. 6. Word Cloud Topic 5

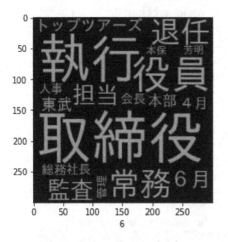

Fig. 7. Word Cloud Topic 6

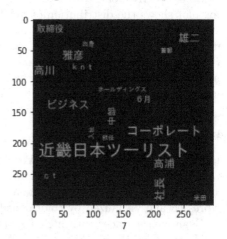

Fig. 8. Word Cloud Topic 7

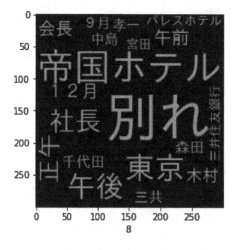

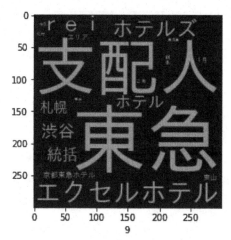

Fig. 9. Word Cloud Topic 8   **Fig. 10.** Word Cloud Topic 9

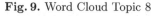
消費 増税 実現 後 の 課題 (中) 西山 由 ##美 ・ 明治 ##学院大学 教授 —— 複数 税率 が 生む 問題 解消 を (経済 教室)

In other sentences: tax increase, meiji, tax rate, hotel, president, seibu, foreign, pass, surplus, recovery, acquisition, revival, tour, service, safety, sale, ryokan, closure, etc. Many of the characteristics related to these tokens are related to Japan's society and economy, which represent the impact of the corona disaster. This is thought to be the reason why it was incorrectly judged as a 2022 article.

Example sentences before the corona disaster and with high P_{BC}

ロイヤル HD 、 2 割 減 ##益 、 ホテル 出店 費用 かさ ##む 、 1 6 月 ##経 常 。

In other sentences: farewell, royal, gym, hotel, world, domestic, Russia, wine, domestic, sales, Toyoko, China, Overseas, Club, Renaissance have a large weight. Many of the features related to these tokens are about pre-pandemic travel and hotels.

Next, example sentences with high P_{BC} after the Corona disaster

リゾート 会員 権 15 ％ 高 、 9 月 、 海外 旅行 の 代替 で 買い 旺盛 、 高 価格 商品 が 押し ##上げ 。

In other sentences: Japanese music, member, overseas, Ichiro, whiskey, palace, golf, Singapore, first semester, Nikkei, Keihan, man, scenery, visit to Japan, guest, Kintetsu, travel, domestic, virgin, net, etc. The characteristics of these tokens are post-pandemic articles, but they represent topics before the negative impact of the pandemic, so they may be the cause of the erroneous judgment of 2019.

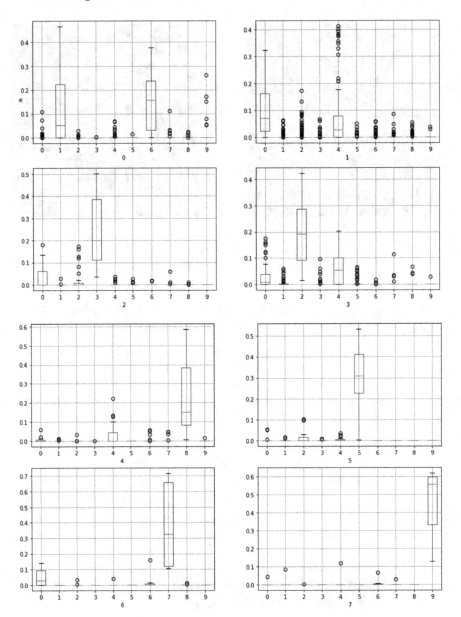

Fig. 11. Hierarchical Clustering

4.4.2 Attention Aggregation Results Table 1 shows the words with the highest attention weights in AC and BC in descending order. Words with a large number of times are: "Japan" and 'Special Feature". Words with a lot of times are more common words. In addition, the words that are only in the 2019 table are "China", "Visit Japan", "Book", "Major", "Real estate", "Profit", "Rice", "Tokyo", "Japan", and "Ryokan", and in the 2022 table, "Deficit", "Recovery", and "Selling".

There are "removal," "chairman," "resumption," "corona," "deceased," "GO," "CT," and "consumption." These tokens are underlined in Table 1. This can be explained by the fact that "China" and "Visit Japan" are more important due to inbound tourism before the coronavirus outbreak, while "GO" and "Resuming" are more important due to requests after the coronavirus outbreak.

4.4.3 Token Vector Extraction and Embedding Figure 20 is Token vector extraction and low-order embedding map. Figure 12, 13, 14, 15, 16, 17, 18 and 19 show enlarged views in from top to bottom and from left to right in Fig. 20. Red is *AC*, blue is *BC*, and these are tokens with high weight. By displaying tokens at the embedded coordinates of the distributed representation, we analyze how tokens belonging to the same category are related to each class. Table 2 summarizes the categories of tokens featured in the expanded map.

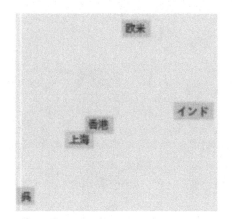

Fig. 12. Lower-order MAP enlarged view-(1)

Fig. 13. Lower-order MAP enlarged view-(2)

Figure 12 shows that (1) There were a lot of political conflicts in Hong Kong and a lot of coronavirus policies in Shanghai.

Figure 13 shows that (2) In relation to the political situation in Myanmar, the word culture is used as a travel term, and the word culture is close to the national language.

Figure 14 shows that (3) After Corona, the impact of business liquidation at the Seibu Group.

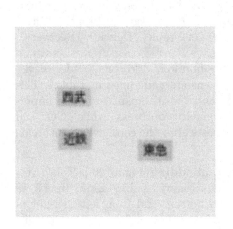

Fig. 14. Lower-order MAP enlarged view-(3)

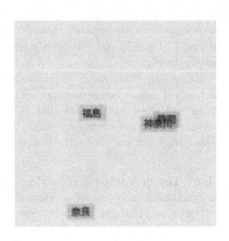

Fig. 15. Lower-order MAP enlarged view-(4)

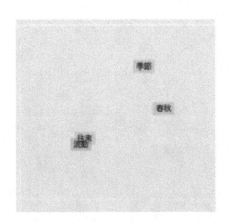

Fig. 16. Lower-order MAP enlarged view-(5)

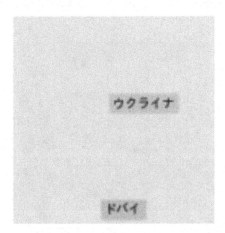

Fig. 17. Lower-order MAP enlarged view-(6)

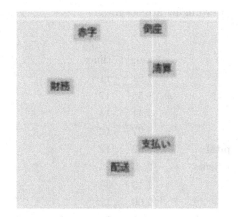

Fig. 18. Lower-order MAP enlarged view-(7)

Fig. 19. Lower-order MAP enlarged view-(8)

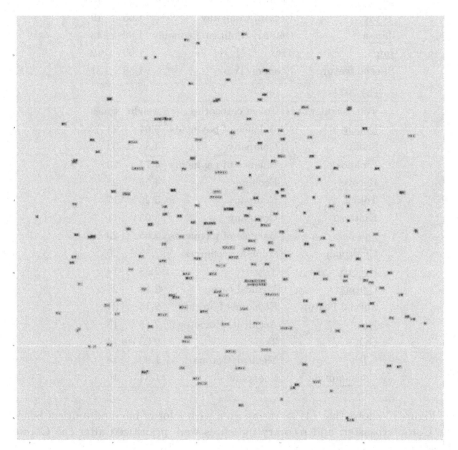

Fig. 20. Token vector extraction and low-order embedding map (Color figure online)

Table 1. Comparison of top words by attention

(a) 2019

Top weight words	Token categories	weight	times
Kintetsu	Company	7.91	11
Tokyu	Company	5.55	17
China	Travel/Politics	3.41	14
Visit to Japan	Trip	3.27	18
Hon	Personnel, Capital	2.89	12
Finance	Balance of Payments	2.33	23
Seibu	Company	2.13	33
Major	Company	2.00	12
Real Estate	Company/Economy	1.96	12
Profit	Balance of Payments	1.88	16
Bei	Country/America/Politics	1.85	16
Tokyo	Region, Company	1.65	19
Japan	Country/Politics/Economy	1.62	43
Inn	Trip	1.60	12
Special feature	EconomyTrip	1.58	31

(b) 2022

Top weight words	Token categories	weight	times
Deficit	Balance of payments	6.04	24
Seibu	Company	4.88	33
Finance	Balance of payments	4.74	23
Recovery	Economy	4.55	21
Tokyu	Company	3.26	17
Kintetsu	Company	3.05	11
Sale	Balance of payments	2.65	20
Chairman	Human Resources	2.55	20
Restart	Trip	2.53	14
Corona	Medical care	2.18	25
Special Feature	Economic Forecast	2.15	31
Ko	Accident, Hometown	2.15	15
GO	Trip	2.00	14
CT	Medical/Corona	1.90	14
Consumption	Economy	1.84	15

Figure 15 shows that (4) It was an area with a lot of inbound tourism before the Corona disaster, and recovery measures were prioritized after the Corona disaster.

Figure 16 shows that (5) After Corona, there was less travel, so another term called "traffic" came to be used.

Table 2. Words closely embedded in map

Category	(1) City	(2) Country and region	(3) Company name
2019	Hong Kong	Culture	Kintetsu, Tokyu
2022	Shanghai	Myanmar,○○Asia	Seibu
Category	(4) Prefecture	(5) Move	(6) Country
2019	Kanagawa, Shizuoka, Nara	flow	Dubai
2022	Fukushima	Coming and going	Ukraine
Category	(7)Country	(8) Employment	
2019	payment	find work	
2022	Delivery, Liquidation, Finance, Deficit, Bankruptcy	Employment	

Figure 17 shows that (6) The invasion of Ukraine and inbound from Dubai.

Figure 18 shows that (7) The number of terms related to restructuring, such as business liquidation and deficits, has increased.

Figure 19 shows that (8) In 2019, new hires were hired, and in 2022, the main topic shifted to maintaining or decreasing employment.

5   In Conclusion

In this study, we analyzed newspaper article data on the Japan travel hotel industry before and after the outbreak of the coronavirus pandemic using pre-processing and distributed representation by NMF latent semantic analysis and hierarchical clustering. The experiment classified the topics of newspaper articles published after the outbreak of the coronavirus pandemic. In addition, by extracting tokens that represent the characteristics before and after the Corona disaster by using BERT text classification, there are many themes related to income and expenses. The company name token finds a company that has done a lot of liquidation. Keywords related to corona, such as GO to, can be extracted, and there is a surprising event of a title that the model incorrectly identified. As a future issue, we will also consider how to improve the accuracy of text classification and how to utilize the data.

Appendix 1: Data Code List

- **Code related to title data analysis**
  https://colab.research.google.com/drive/
  14kVhJuJSRHV0m7zCKCuPuOM0DkPcgKHQ
- **2019 Nikkei morning edition article data**
  https://tus.app.box.com/file/998437276219?
  s=e7hx3pyypf06ekyjjignhpc8b725sdd1
- **2022 Nikkei morning edition article data**
  https://tus.app.box.com/file/947471044518?
  s=bs8c424lfrckgm6o5k8bbh8vuf81axru
- **Weighted word list - positive**
  https://tus.box.com/s/53hksp6tk3o1bjnzbwfkgvxywij7ido6
- **Weighted word list-negative**
  https://tus.box.com/s/stsfk4khv7sa7ihvarnwudeudtraeyjb

Appendix 2: Attention Weight Visualization Example

In English, it is easy because only the alphabet and each word is separated, but in Japanese, kanji, hiragana, katakana, emoji and other words are connected, so it is difficult to judge where to cut. So, since the data used this time is all in Japanese, the analysis results are also attached in Japanese as is. Thank you for your understanding.

Example sentences after the coronavirus pandemic and with high P_{AC}

(1) 電力 シェア ##リング 、 環境 配慮 の ツアー 、 移動 中 の CO 2 実質 ゼロ 。

(2) 小田急 、 「 ハイ ##アット 東京 」 売却 へ 、 1000 億 円 規模 で 。

(3) 日本 ハウス 、 純 利益 2 倍 、 前期 、 住宅 事業 の 工 ##期 短縮 。

(4) 酒 提供 禁止 、 徹底 に 限界 、 大手 は 採算 見 ##込め ず 休業 、 中小 は 資金 ##繰り 悪化 不満 。

(5) 「 行政 デジタル 化 を 」 7 割 、 政権 に 求める 規制 緩和 、 再生 エ ##ネ ・ 遠隔 診療 も (社長 100 人 アンケート)

(6) 西武 HD 、 30 施設 売却 、 ホテル や スキー 場 、 シンガポール 系 に 1500 億 円 規模 。

(7) 小売 ##り や 外 ##食 、 「 脱 プラ 」 対応 、 スタ ##バ は 蓋 なし 提供 、 4 月 の 新 ##法 施行 受け 。

(8) 京都 ホテル 、 10 億 円 調達 、 優先 ##株 発行 、 財務 基盤 を 強化 。

(9) JT ##B 、 福 ##利 厚生 会社 売却 、 ベネ ##・ ##ワン に 150 億 円 で 。

(10) ヒュー リック 、 純 利益 8 ％ 増 、 今 ##期 、 オフィス 賃貸 堅 ##調 。

(11) コロナ 下 の 地価 回復 (下) 海外 勢 「 安い ニッポン 」 物 ##色 、 低 金利 で 円 安 、 投資 妙 ##味 。

(12) JT ##B 、 資本 増強 300 億 円 、 政 投 銀 や 3 メガ 銀 が 支援 。

(13) 日 証 金 、 サン ##ヨー H 株 、 W ##T ##I 原油 受 ##益 証券 、 ヤマ ##ウラ 株 、 植木 ##組 株 、 まんだらけ 株 、 他 の 貸 ##借 取引 で 注意 喚起 。

(14) HI ##S 、 本社 フロア 売却 、 東京 ・ 虎 ##ノ ##門 、 325 億 円 、 資金 確保 。

(15) 飲食 ・ 宿泊 支援 、 2 カ月 で 3000 億 円 、 政 投 銀 に 申請 。

(16) 11 4 月 最大 、 海外 旅行 の 回復 見 ##通 ##せ ず 、 HI ##S 、 最終 赤字 232 億 円 、 政 投 銀 に 資本 支援 要請 。

(17) K ##N ##TC ##T 、 赤字 幅 縮小 、 今 ##期 最終 、 ワクチン 受託 伸びる 。

(18) 環境 債 100 億 円 、 西武 HD 発行 へ 、 省 ##エ ##ネ 車両 導入 。

(19) 日本 郵政 、 かん ##ぽ の 宿 事業 売却 、 32 施設 88 億 円 で 。

Example sentences before the coronavirus pandemic and with high
P_{AC}

(1) ホテル ##オー ##クラ (会社 人事)

(2) 阪急 阪神 ホテル ##ズ (会社 人事)

(3) ホテル 、 ニュー グランド (会社 人事)

(4) JT ##B 高橋 社長 (ニュース 一言)

(5) 西武 ホールディングス 後藤 社長 (ニュース 一言)

(6) 西武 ホールディングス 社長 後藤 高 ##志 氏 (上) 融資 合戦 から 距離 置く (私 の 課長 時代)

(7) 宿泊 業 分野 で 初 、 外国 人 280 人 合格 、 「 特定 技能 」 試験 。

(8) JT ##B 、 4 9 月 44 億 円 最終 黒字 。

(9) 決算 予想 (10 月 ##本 決算) HI ##S 、 ホテル 事業 回復 。

(10) 菊池 製作所 、 信越 ##化学 ##工業 、 三 ##谷 ##セ ##キサ ##ン 、 ベスト ##ワン ##ド ##ット ##コム 、 東京 ##コス ##モス ##電機 、 T ##K ##C (自社 株 取得 枠 設定)

(11) FU ##T ##UR ##EC ##ITY 市 ##来 勇 ##人 代表 取締役 —— 雲 ##仙 温泉 に 復活 の 兆し 、 夏 フェス 来場 者 、 前年 上回る (みちし ##る べ)

(12) 経営 権 争奪 、 正面 対決 に 、 伊藤忠 ・ デ ##サント など 敵対 的 提案 、 今年 6 件 、 事業 会社 、 相次ぎ 動く 。

(13) 星野 ##リゾート 、 来 ##年 ハワイ に 、 開業 海外 3 カ所 目 。

(14) 観光 庁 、 HI ##S を 行政 指導 、 ツアー 中止 で 。

(15) 情報 銀行 、 データ 保護 が 要 、 サービス 本格 開始 へ 、 取得 や 提供 、 問われる 安全 。

(16) ホテル 流動 化 40 億 円 、 共 ##立 メン ##テ 、 利益 計上 へ 、 4 年間 で 。

(17) 不動産 事業 、 22 年 2 月 期 メド 、 松竹 、 営業 益 50 億 円 に 。

(18) 沢田 HD 、 広 ##済 ##堂 株 売却 、 保有 する 全 12 ％ 分 、 月末 に 。

(19) 旅館 「 休業 日 」 広がる 、 人 ##手 不足 が 深刻 、 低 稼働 率 の 日 、 経費 抑制 狙う 。

Example sentences before the coronavirus pandemic and with high
P_{BC}

(1)故 吉田 淑 則 氏 (元 JS ##R 社長) の お 別れ の 会 。

(2)ロイヤル HD 、 10 期 ぶり 減 ##益 、 前期 経 ##常 。

(3)秋 ##篠 ##宮 ご 夫妻 、 鹿児島 に 。

(4)ルネサンス 、 一転 減 ##益 、 前期 営業 益 6 ％ 減 、 小型 ジム 台頭 。

(5)世界 的 ホテル 、 国内 に 50 カ所 、 官房 長官 表明 、 財政 投 ##融 ##資 を 活用 。

(6)ホテル ##オー ##クラ 、 ロシア に 22 年 進出 、 運営 受託 。

(7)富裕 層 厚み 、 高額 品 攻勢 、 資産 1 億 円 世帯 26 ％ 増 、 L ##V ##M ##H 、 EP ##A でも ワイン 高く 、 阪急 ##交通 ##社 、 国内 バス ツアー 98 万円 。

(8)ヒュー リック 、 1 割 増 ##益 、 1 9月 営業 、 新 物件 の 賃貸 収益 増 。

(9)故 米 ##山 稔 氏 (ヨ ##ネック ##ス 創業 者) の お 別れ の 会 。

(10)NHK 受信 料 支払い 確定 、 最高裁 、 東横 イン に 。

(11)グリーン ##ズ (会社 人事)

(12)NI ##K ##KE ##IT ##he ##ST ##Y ##LE —— もて ##なし 変わら ぬ 姿 で 、 幻 の 五輪 や 戦 ##禍 、 歴史 乗り越え 。

(13)中国 、 かす ##む 国慶節 商 ##戦 、 節約 志向 、 小売 ##り や ホテル ため ##息 、 買い物 「 独身 の 日 」 待ち 。

(14)人 ##手 不足 、 M ＆ A で 防衛 、 小田急 、 人材 会社 を 買収 、 IT 各社 は 海外 拠点 新設 も 。

(15)健康 志向 の 若者 つか ##む 、 スポーツ クラブ の ルネサンス 、 4 9月 営業 益 3 ％ 増 。

(16)公立 はこだて 未来 大学 、 ホテル と AI 活用 の 共同 研究 (ダイジェスト)

(17)阪急 阪神 ビジネス トラベル 、 木村 貞則 氏 (新 社長)

(18)孫 氏 「 AI 後進 国 」 脱却 訴え 、 「 日本 企業 に 投資 したい 」 。

(19)ホテル ##オー ##クラ 、 新 本館 を 公開 。

Example sentences after the coronavirus pandemic and with high
P_{BC}

(1) 故 中島 靖 ##子 さん (邦楽 家) の お 別れ の 会 。

(2) NI ##K ##KE ##IT ##he ##ST ##Y ##LE —— 「 イチロー ##ズ ##モル ##ト 」 の 限定 ウイスキー (洗練 逸 ##品)

(3) 旅行 各社 、 人員 つなぎ ##とめ 、 近 ツー 、 営業 職 に 成果 型 報酬 、 JT ##B 系 は IT 人材 に ジョ ##ブ 型 。

(4) HI ##S 、 国内 鉄道 ツアー に 参入 。

(5) 若者 向け 旅行 、 ネット 専売 、 日本 旅行 ・ 旅 工房 が 新 会社 。

(6) シンガポール 航空 、 前期 最終 赤字 3500 億 円 。

(7) 日経 カルチャー 、 年内 で 営業 終了 。

(8) T ##K ##P 、 ホテル 宴 会場 を 運営 、 京阪 系 から 受託 。

(9) エル ##メス 純 利益 77 ％ 増 、 前期 、 コロナ 前 上回る 、 「 バー キン 」 人気 。

(10) NI ##K ##KE ##IT ##he ##ST ##Y ##LE —— ホテル マン の 原 風景 、 LA 、 定 保 英 ##弥 。

(11) AN ##A ##HD 、 富裕 訪日 客 対応 の 人材 育成

(12) 京王 ##プラザ ##ホテル (会社 人事)

(13) 近鉄 ・ 都 ホテル ##ズ (会社 人事)

(14) パレス ##ホテル (会社 人事)

(15) ゴルフ 会員 権 2 . 7 ％ 高 、 8 月 関東 圏 。

(16) ヴァージン 創業 者 、 有人 飛行 、 近づく 宇宙 旅行 時代 、 超 高速 航空 への 応用 期待 。

(17) レッド ・ プラ ##ネット ## ・ ##ジャパン (会社 人事)

(18) 旅行 大手 、 店舗 3 割 削減 、 JT ##B など 10 社 、 ネット 専業 台頭 、 コロナ 追い ##打ち 。

(19) 近畿日本 ##ツー ##リスト 首都 圏 (会社 人事)

References

1. Devlin, J., Chang, M.-W., Lee, K., Toutanova, K.: BERT: pre-training of deep bidirectional transformers for language understanding. CoRR, abs/1810.04805 (2018)
2. Le, Q., Mikolov, T.: Distributed representations of sentences and documents. In: Xing, E.P., Jebara, T. (eds.) Proceedings of the 31st International Conference on Machine Learning, Proceedings of Machine Learning Research, vol. 32 , pp. 1188–1196, Beijing, China, June 2014. PMLR (2014)

Research on the Effects of Multi-visual Coding in Geographic Information Visualization

Jing Zhang[1]([✉]), Xingcheng Di[1], Lijuan Zhao[2], Xiaoke Li[2], and Wei Xu[1]

[1] College of Furnishings and Industrial Design, Nanjing Forestry University, NO.159 Longpan Road, Xuanwu District, Nanjing, China
zhangjing1026@njfu.edu.cn

[2] Dehua TB New Decoration Material Co., Ltd., Huzhou 313200, China

Abstract. The visual attributes such as shape, color, size have been considered as the most basic form of information encoded in geographic information visualization interface; however, the optimal multi-visual coding forms and reasonable quantity are not well defined, nor has it been determined whether the advantage of one-attribute coding is maintained across different multi-visual coding. In this study, we choose four typical visual attributes (text, shape, color, size) in geographic information visualization and argue that the effects of multi-visual coding are affected by the coding forms and the levels of quantity. Our experiment used a within-subjects design, with independent variables of four visual attributes (text, shape, size, color) and the number (1, 2, 3, 4) of visual attributes in multi-visual coding forms. The results support the effects of multi-visual coding in geographic information visualization are modulated not only by the coding characteristics of each visual attribute, but also by the forms and the number of visual attributes in the coding forms.

Keywords: Multiple visual coding · Geographic information visualization · Visual attribute · Visualization interface

1 Introduction

With the rapid development of intelligent interaction technology, the hierarchical relationship and information structure in the geographic information visualization become more and more complex. The visual attributes such as shape, color, size have been considered as the most basic form of information encoded in geographic information visualization interface, and users interpret information through the differences in encoding of these visual attributes, e.g., the shape-coding can represent different types of coordinates, the size-coding can represent the amount of information, and the color-coding can represent the division of different areas. Replacing large amounts of textual information with these different visually coded forms can enhance the aesthetics and readability of geographic information visualization. However, in the process of practical design, one-attribute visual coding such as color has been difficult to meet the complex geographic information visualization needs, designers need to integrating multiple visual attributes

H. Mori and Y. Asahi (Eds.): HCII 2024, LNCS 14690, pp. 175–186, 2024.
https://doi.org/10.1007/978-3-031-60114-9_13

in coding to visualize the complex relationships such as qualitative, ordinal, categorical, and distance in data. Among different kinds of multi-visual coding forms, how to find the most reasonable coding forms to guide users quickly understand the intrinsic information relationship is the key in visualization design. Although abundant studies have conducted some comparative research on the effects and the perceptual differences of typical one-attribute visual coding such as shape [1, 2], color [3–5], size [6], etc., these studies have mainly focused on one or two visual attribute coding, and no research has been carried out on multi-visual coding of more than two visual attributes in the geographic information visualization. For example, Danacia and Cinbisa argued that while the supervised deep features are effective, using them in combination with low-level features can lead to significant improvements in attribute recognition performance [7]. Buetti and Xu found that the brain must compute distinctiveness scores independently for each visual attribute before summing them into the overall score that directs human attention [8].

Although those studies did not explicitly manipulate the coding forms and quantity of those visual attributes, their results suggest that the effects of multi-visual coding might be moderated by the different forms and the number of visual attributes in the coding forms. In addition, the optimal multi-visual coding forms and reasonable quantity are not well defined, nor has it been determined whether the advantage of one-attribute coding is maintained across different multi-visual coding.

The experiments in this article are intended to test the hypothesis that the effects of multi-visual coding are affected by the coding forms and the levels of quantity. Here, we choose four typical visual attributes (text, shape, color, size) in geographic information visualization and compare the performance of subjects on four typical visual attributes in fifteen multi-visual coding forms and four levels of quantity.

2 Method

2.1 Subjects

Eighteen college students participated in experiment for ¥5 and an additional bonus up to ¥5, depending on performance (accuracy) on the task. They ranged in age from 21 to 29 years, with a mean age of 25 years. They had no colorblindness or hemochromatosis, with the corrected visual acuity over 1.0. They were required to practice and train to know the experimental procedure and operation requirements. Each subject sat in a comfortable chair in a soft light and sound-proofed room, and eyes gazed at the center of the screen. A 21.5-in. CRT monitor with a 1920 *1080-pixel resolution was used in the experiment. The distance between subject eyes and the screen was approximately 60 cm, while the horizontal and vertical picture viewing angle was within 2.3° [9]. Two subject was dropped from the experiment because his/her performance was at chance and 2 standard deviations below the mean of the remaining subjects, leaving 16 subjects.

2.2 Design and Materials

This experiment used a within-subjects design, with independent variables of four visual attributes (text, shape, size, color) and the number of visual attributes in multi-visual coding (1, 2, 3, 4). The stimuli were novel geographic information visualizations generated by the online visualization software (SaCa DataVis) based on a Chinese company's sales data, which contains 481 pieces of data such as product sales, product type, city district and locations of stores. The output geographic information visualizations were then processed through Adobe Illustrate software. Based on the correspondences between data structures and four visual attributes, the visual coding rules of each one-attribute in the experimental material were as follows: text-coding represents the store location, shape-coding represents the different types of products, size-coding represents the sales amount of product, and color-coding represents the division of different city districts (see Fig. 1).

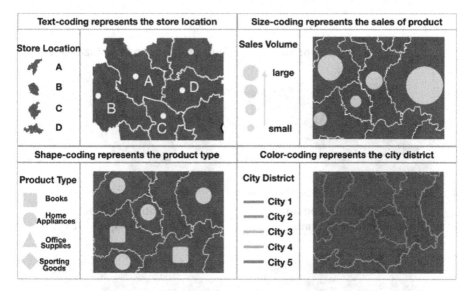

Fig. 1. The visual coding example of each one-attribute

The design involved a total of 15 coding forms, including 4 one-attribute coding forms,6 two-attribute coding forms,4 three-attribute coding forms and 1 four-attribute coding forms (see Table 1). Figure 2 is an example of experimental materials for four multi-visual coding forms containing one to four visual attributes.

2.3 Procedure

Participants performed a two-target visual search task for two sessions. Each session consisted of 30 trials. The 15 coding forms were repeated exactly twice in different geographic information visualization in each session. Trials began with a fixation presented in the center of the screen, and subjects had to press a button to continue (see Fig. 3). On each trial, subjects saw a randomly selected geographic information visualization and a question about two targets in different visual coding above the visualization. Subjects had to make a comparative judgment between the two targets' coding forms. There was no time limit for responses, and after subjects pressed a button, they received auditory feedback that indicated whether their response was correct or not. The reaction

Table 1. The 15 coding forms of four visual attributes.

Classification	The combined coding forms
one-attribute coding forms	Text, Shape, Size, Color
two-attribute coding forms	Text + Shape, Text + Size, Text + Color, Shape + Size, Shape + Color, Size + Color
three-attribute coding forms	Text + Shape + Size, Text + Shape + Color, Text + Size + Color, Shape + Size + Color
four-attribute coding forms	Text + Shape + Size + Color

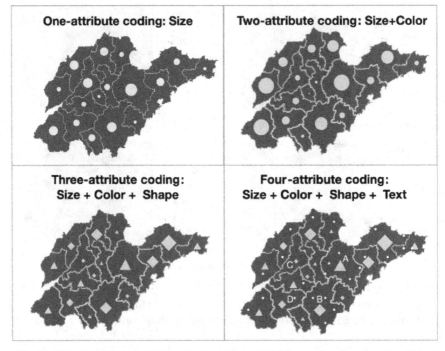

Fig. 2. Example of four multi-visual coding forms containing one to four visual attributes

time and accuracy rate were recorded for data analysis. The entire experiment lasted approximately twenty-five minutes.

3   Results

We analyzed the accuracy data via logistic mixed-effects regressions and reaction times via linear mixed-effects regressions [10, 11]. For the RT analyses, we considered only trials with correct responses and excluded from the analyses cases with RTs more than 3 median absolute deviations above or below the median RT (6.27%).

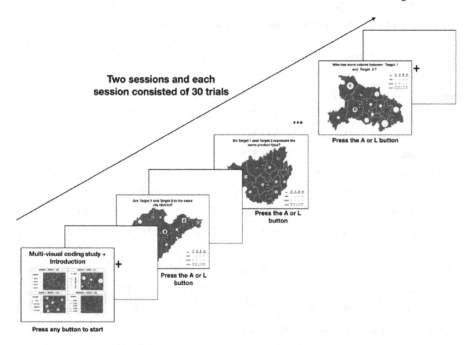

Fig. 3. Example of the procedure in the experiment

3.1 The Quantity in Multi-Visual Coding

As expected, there was a significant interaction between the quantity and the forms of the multi-visual coding on accuracy, $\Delta AIC = 10.95$, LLR χ^2 (1) = 14.946, p < .001, and a significant interaction between the quantity and four visual attributes, $\Delta AIC =$ 284, LLR χ^2 (1) = 302.379, p < .001, such that subject showed a significant difference in RT on recognizing the four visual attributes. Considering the simplicity of the experimental design and the accuracy data of all subjects were above 90%, subjects did not show significant differences among the different quantity containing one to four visual attributes, $\Delta AIC = 1.37$, LLR χ^2 (1) = 4.6273, p = .20, but the RT results showed a significant main effect of quantity in multi-visual coding forms, $\Delta AIC = -21$, LLR $\chi^2(1) = 27.01$, p < .001, such that as the number of visual attributes increase, the complexity of the multi-visual coding form also directly affects the user's cognition, and the cognitive resource requirements increase.

3.2 One-Attribute Coding Forms

The RT results on one-attribute coding forms showed a significant main effect of the kinds of visual attributes, $\Delta AIC = -15.2$, LLR χ^2 (1) = 21.135, p < .001, and an LSD post-test multiple comparison test was performed on the reaction time and the results are shown in Table 2. These results indicated that among the four one-attribute coding forms, the reaction time for subjects to recognize the text-coding and the color-coding was significantly less than the size-coding.

Table 2. Multiple comparisons on RT results of one-attribute coding.

(I)	(J)	Mean Difference (I-J)	Std. Error	Sig.	95% Confidence Interval	
					Lower Bound	Upper Bound
shape	Text	498.923	539.7235	0.36	−588.818	1586.665
	size	−825.534	539.7235	0.133	−1913.276	262.207
	color	618.7292	539.7235	0.258	−469.012	1706.47
Text	shape	−98.923	539.7235	0.36	−1586.665	588.818
	size	−1324.458*	539.7235	0.018	−2412.2	−236.717
	color	119.805	539.7235	0.825	−967.936	1207.547
size	shape	825.534	539.7235	0.133	−262.207	1913.276
	Text	1324.458*	539.7235	0.018	236.717	2412.2
	color	1444.263**	539.7235	0.01	356.523	2532.005
color	shape	−618.729	539.7235	0.258	−1706.47	469.012
	Text	−119.805	539.7235	0.825	−1207.547	967.936
	size	−1444.263**	539.7235	0.01	−2532.005	−356.523

*The mean difference is significant at the 0.05 level

3.3 Two-Attribute Coding Forms

Figure 4 plots the accuracy and reaction time on recognizing targets' four attribute coding forms among six two-attribute coding forms. The results showed a significant difference in accuracy on recognizing the four visual attributes, $\Delta AIC = -12.93$, LLR χ^2 (1) = 18.924, p < .001, and in RT, $\Delta AIC = -136.8$, LLR χ^2 (1) = 142.87, p < .001, such that the reaction time for subjects to recognize the text-coding was significantly less than other three. The results of LSD post-test multiple comparison test on accuracy data and the reaction time are shown in Table 3 and Table 4. These results indicated that among the six two-attribute coding forms, subjects recognized the text-coding significantly better than the shape-coding and the color-coding, and they recognize the size-coding significantly better than the color-coding.

3.4 Three-Attribute Coding Forms

Figure 5 plots the accuracy and reaction time on recognizing targets' four attribute coding forms among four three-attribute coding forms. Consistent with the results of two-attribute coding forms, the results showed a significant difference in accuracy on recognizing the four visual attributes, $\Delta AIC = -14.78$, LLR χ^2 (1) = 20.788, p < .001, such that and in RT, $\Delta AIC = -103$, LLR χ^2 (1) = 108.65, p < .001. The results of LSD post-test multiple comparison test on accuracy data and the reaction time are shown in Table 5 and Table 6. The result indicated that among the four three-attribute coding forms, subjects performed best in recognizing text-coding and worst in recognizing color-coding. In addition, subjects performed significant better on shape-coding than color-coding.

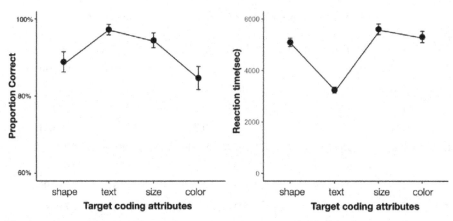

Fig. 4. Mean performance of subjects on recognizing targets' four attribute coding forms in Two-attribute coding forms. Left panel plots accuracy and right panel plots RT. Error bars represent 95% confidence intervals.

Table 3. Multiple comparisons on accuracy of two-attribute coding.

(I)	(J)	Mean Difference (I-J)	Std. Error	Sig.	95% Confidence Interval	
					Lower Bound	Upper Bound
shape	Text	−.0833*	0.0377	0.029	−0.158	−0.009
	size	−0.0556	0.0377	0.143	−0.13	0.019
	color	−.0417	0.0377	0.271	−0.033	0.116
Text	shape	.0833*	0.0377	0.029	0.009	0.158
	size	0.0278	0.0377	0.462	−0.047	0.102
	color	.1250**	0.0377	0.001	0.051	0.199
size	shape	0.0556	0.0377	0.143	0.019	0.13
	Text	−0.0278	0.0377	0.462	−0.102	0.047
	color	.0972*	0.0377	0.011	0.023	0.172
color	shape	−0.0417	0.0377	0.271	−0.116	0.033
	Text	−.1250**	0.0377	0.001	−0.199	−0.051
	size	−.0972*	0.0377	0.011	−0.172	−0.023

*The mean difference is significant at the 0.05 level

3.5 Four-Attribute Coding Forms

Figure 6 plots the accuracy and reaction time on recognizing targets' four attribute coding forms in four-attribute coding forms. Although subjects did not differ significantly in correct rate of four coding attributes, the RT results showed a significant difference, ΔAIC = −56.4, LLR χ^2 (1) = 62.403, p < .001. The results of LSD post-test multiple

Table 4. Multiple comparisons on RT results of two-attribute coding.

(I)	(J)	Mean Difference (I-J)	Std. Error	Sig.	95% Confidence Interval	
					Lower Bound	Upper Bound
shape	Text	1955.681***	371.3657	0.000	1221.471	2689.891
	size	−406.0394	371.3657	0.276	−1140.249	328.171
	color	−98.4954	371.3657	0.791	−832.705	635.715
Text	shape	−1955.681***	371.3657	0.000	−2689.891	−1221.471
	size	−2361.719***	371.3657	0.000	−3095.93	−1627.51
	color	−2054.176***	371.3657	0.000	−2788.386	−1319.966
size	shape	406.0394	371.3657	0.276	−328.171	1140.249
	Text	2361.719***	371.3657	0.000	1627.51	3095.93
	color	307.544	371.3657	0.409	−426.666	1041.754
color	shape	98.4954	371.3657	0.791	−635.715	832.705
	Text	2054.1759***	371.3657	0.000	1319.966	2788.386
	size	−307.544	371.3657	0.409	−1041.754	426.666

*The mean difference is significant at the 0.05 level

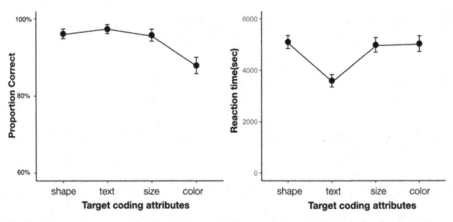

Fig. 5. Mean performance of subjects on recognizing targets' four attribute coding forms in Three-attribute coding forms. Left panel plots accuracy and right panel plots RT. Error bars represent 95% confidence intervals.

comparison test on reaction time are shown in Table 7. Consistent with the results of two-attribute and tree-attribute coding forms, there were significant differences in response times between recognizing text-coding information and other three coding information in the four-attribute coding forms.

Table 5. Multiple comparisons on accuracy of three-attribute coding.

(I)	(J)	Mean Difference (I-J)	Std. Error	Sig.	95% Confidence Interval	
					Lower Bound	Upper Bound
shape	Text	−0.0139	0.0287	0.629	−0.071	0.043
	size	0.0035	0.0287	0.904	−0.053	0.06
	color	.0972*	0.0287	0.001	0.04	0.154
Text	shape	0.0139	0.0287	0.629	−0.043	0.071
	size	0.0174	0.0287	0.546	−0.039	0.074
	color	.1111*	0.0287	0.000	0.054	0.168
size	shape	−0.0035	0.0287	0.904	−0.06	0.053
	Text	−0.0174	0.0287	0.546	−0.074	0.039
	color	.0938*	0.0287	0.001	0.037	0.151
color	shape	−.0972*	0.0287	0.001	−0.154	−0.04
	Text	−.1111*	0.0287	0.000	−0.168	−0.054
	size	−.0938*	0.0287	0.001	−0.151	−0.037

*The mean difference is significant at the 0.05 level

Table 6. Multiple comparisons on RT results of three-attribute coding.

(I)	(J)	Mean Difference(I-J)	Std. Error	Sig.	95% Confidence Interval	
					Lower Bound	Upper Bound
shape	Text	1391.8811***	329.358	0.000	740.723	2043.04
	size	−77.4113	329.358	0.815	−728.57	573.747
	color	−25.9946	329.358	0.937	−677.153	625.164
Text	shape	−1391.881***	329.358	0.000	−2043.04	−740.723
	size	−1469.292***	329.358	0.000	−2120.451	−818.134
	color	−1417.875***	329.358	0.000	−2069.034	−766.717
size	shape	77.4113	329.358	0.815	−573.747	728.57
	Text	1469.2924***	329.358	0.000	818.134	2120.451
	color	51.4166	329.358	0.876	−599.742	702.575
color	shape	25.9946	329.358	0.937	−625.164	677.153
	Text	1417.8758***	329.358	0.000	766.717	2069.034
	size	−51.4166	329.358	0.876	−702.575	599.742

*The mean difference is significant at the 0.05 level

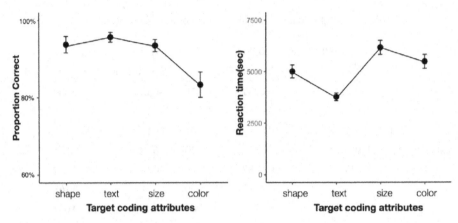

Fig. 6. Mean performance of subjects on recognizing targets' four attribute coding forms in four-attribute coding forms. Left panel plots accuracy and right panel plots RT. Error bars represent 95% confidence intervals.

Table 7. Multiple comparisons on RT results of four-attribute coding.

(I)	(J)	Mean Difference (I-J)	Std. Error	Sig.	95% Confidence Interval	
					Lower Bound	Upper Bound
shape	Text	1559.8171*	764.8507	0.047	18.362	3101.272
	size	−1024.8934	764.8507	0.187	−2566.349	516.562
	color	−320.7222	764.8507	0.677	−1862.178	1220.733
Text	shape	−1559.8171*	764.8507	0.047	−3101.272	−18.362
	size	−2584.710**	764.8507	0.002	−4126.166	−1043.255
	color	−1880.5393*	764.8507	0.018	−3421.995	−339.084
size	shape	1024.8934	764.8507	0.187	−516.562	2566.349
	Text	2584.7104**	764.8507	0.002	1043.255	4126.166
	color	704.1711	764.8507	0.362	−837.284	2245.626
color	shape	320.7222	764.8507	0.677	−1220.733	1862.178
	Text	1880.5393*	764.8507	0.018	339.084	3421.995
	size	−704.1711	764.8507	0.362	−2245.626	837.284

*The mean difference is significant at the 0.05 level

4 Discussion

This study tested the hypothesis that the effects of multi-visual coding in geographic information visualization are modulated not only by the coding characteristics of each visual attribute, but also by the forms and the number of visual attributes in the coding forms. We found evidence that there is a significant interaction between the quantity and the forms of the multi-visual coding on accuracy. Specifically, subjects' performance was affected by the complexity of multi-visual coding forms. As the number of visual attributes in multi-visual coding increases from 1 to 4, there was a significant increase in response time, indicating that the complexity of multi-visual coding does affect the user's cognition. In one-attribute coding condition, there was a significant difference between four visual attributes and subjects performed significantly better in text-coding form, and the benefit of text-coding form was not affected among four multi-visual coding forms containing one to four visual attributes. Two-attribute coding condition replicated the results of one-attribute coding condition. Three-attribute coding forms provided a demonstration that subjects performed significant better on shape-coding than color-coding. However, the benefit of shape-coding was not observed in other three condition. In four-attribute coding condition, subjects still performed best in recognizing text-coding target coding attributes. That is, the advantage of text-coding was maintained across different multi-visual coding, but the advantage of color was not. One explanation for the advantage of text-coding is that the text attribute is more easily and automatically coded as visual cues [12], while color is a perceptual attribute that can be abstracted from an object and by itself lacks functional significance [13].

It is validated that there was a significant interaction between four visual attributes (text, shape, size, color) and the number of visual attributes in multi-visual coding. One explanation for the results is the multi-visual coding forms were closely related to the complexity of the data structure, and as the complexity increases, the difficulty for the user to interpret the geographic visual informatics rises accordingly. The core of optimizing the geographic information visualization interface is to establish a match between the visual coding attributes and the multi-visual coding forms, thus helping the user to quickly establish a semantic correspondence from information to visualization.

This paper contains two limitations, one is that due to time constraints, the multi-visual coding forms only involves one to four visual attributes, the subject's behavior towards more complex coding forms than four need to be further verified by a subsequent research as an excessive number of visual attributes in the multi-visual coding forms may exceed human perceptual limits and affect cognitive performance; Second, the four typical visual attributes (text, shape, color, and size) in the multi-visual coding design here are relatively simple, and the subjects' correctness rates were very high, and this possible confounding factor need to be further eliminated in the future by optimizing the experimental design.

In summary, the current study provides evidence that the effects of multi-visual coding in geographic information visualization are modulated by the coding characteristics of each visual attribute, the number of visual attributes in the coding and the coding forms. The data analysis and conclusion of this thesis can provide a novel and valuable efficiency guidance for geographic information visualization design. All the multi-visual coding design should be based on the advantages and disadvantages of each visual attribute in different combined coding forms.

Acknowledgments. This paper was supported by the National Nature Science Foundation of China Grant (No. 72201128), the China Postdoctoral Science Foundation (No. 2023M730483) and the Collaborative Education Program of the Chinese Education Ministry (No. 202102298009).

Disclosure of Interests. The authors have no competing interests relevant to the content of this article.

References

1. Corbetta, M., et al.: Attentional modulation of neural processing of shape, color, and velocity in humans. Sci. New Ser. **248**(4962), 1556–1559 (1990)
2. Jing, L., Shulan, Y., Xiaoli, W.: Effects of shape character encodings in the human-computer interface on visual cognitive performance. J. Comput.-Aided Des. Comput. Graph. **1**(30), 163–172 (2018)
3. Aginsky, V., University, B., Tarr, M.J.: How are different properties of a scene encoded in visual memory?. Vis. Cogn. **7**(1–3), 147–162 (2000)
4. Beauchemin, M.: Unsupervised colour coding for visualization of categorical maps. Remote Sens. Lett. **10**(1), 77–85 (2019)
5. Van Laar, D.L.: Psychological and cartographic principles for the production of visual layering effects in computer displays. Displays **22**(4), 125–135 (2001)
6. Niu, Y., et al.: Improving accuracy of gaze-control tools: design recommendations for optimum position, sizes, and spacing of interactive objects. Hum. Factors Ergon. Manuf. Serv. Industr. **31**(3), 249–269 (2021)
7. Danaci, E.G., Ikizler-Cinbis, N.: Low-level features for visual attribute recognition: an evaluation. Pattern Recogn. Lett. **84**, 185–191 (2016)
8. Buetti, S., Xu, J., Lleras, A.: Predicting how color and shape combine in the human visual system to direct attention. Sci. Rep. **9**(1), 20258 (2019)
9. Zhang, J., Xue, C., Shen, Z., Chen, X., Shao, J., Zhou, L., Zhou, X.: Study on the effects of semantic memory on icon complexity in cognitive domain. In: Harris, D. (ed.) EPCE 2016. LNCS (LNAI), vol. 9736, pp. 147–157. Springer, Cham (2016). https://doi.org/10.1007/978-3-319-40030-3_16
10. Baayen, R.H., Davidson, D.J., Bates, D.M.: Mixed-effects modeling with crossed random effects for subjects and items. J. Mem. Lang. **59**(4), 390–412 (2008)
11. Jaeger, T.F.: Categorical data analysis: away from ANOVAs (transformation or not) and towards logit mixed models. J. Mem. Lang. **59**(4), 434–446 (2008)
12. Chen, H., Wyble, B.: The location but not the attributes of visual cues are automatically encoded into working memory. Vision. Res. **107**, 76–85 (2015)
13. Pitchford, N.J., Mullen, K.T.: Conceptualization of perceptual attributes: a special case for color? J. Exp. Child Psychol. **80**(3), 289–314 (2001)

User Experience Design and Evaluation

Exploring the Behavior of Users "Training" Douyin's Personalized Recommendation Algorithm System in China

Yunna Cai$^{(\boxtimes)}$ ⓘ and Fan Wang ⓘ

Wuhan University, Wuhan 430072, Hubei, China
caiyunna1106@whu.edu.cn

Abstract. This study investigates a novel form of human-algorithm interaction where users "train" TikTok's recommendation algorithm. Through observations and interviews with 22 self-reported algorithm trainers, researchers identified the motivations, methods, and perceptual influencing factors underlying this behavior. The findings reveal that users employ various strategies, such as adjusting the functions of the recommendation algorithm system. Motivated by the pursuit of values and risk avoidance, this behavior is influenced by users' algorithmic literacy, satisfaction with recommendations, and perceived benefits and costs. The research significantly contributes to our understanding of how individuals positively perceive and engage with algorithmic systems, shedding light on previously overlooked aspects. It introduces a novel strategy on addressing algorithmic risks from the user's standpoint by advocating cooperation with algorithms.

Keywords: TikTok · Information Behavior · Algorithms · Personalized Recommendation Algorithm System · Algorithm awareness · Human algorithm interaction

1 Introduction

TikTok is a globally popular social media platform for creating and sharing short-form video content [25]. The platform's powerful personalized recommendation algorithm utilizes user interaction data, such as "likes," to infer individual preferences and offer tailored video content [27]. However, in light of the potential risks associated with TikTok's recommendation algorithm, such as identity discrimination, there has been a growing resistance among users towards the algorithm, which has recently gained the attention of academics [19].

Recently, a novel phenomenon has been observed on the Chinese version of TikTok, whereby some users have reported undertaking the behavior of training TikTok's personalized recommendation algorithm. For example, if a user wants TikTok to recommend videos of a certain celebrity, he will deliberately click to like every video he encounters about that celebrity, even if some of them are not very interesting to him, in order to train the algorithm system to recommend more videos about that celebrity to him. This

© The Author(s), under exclusive license to Springer Nature Switzerland AG 2024
H. Mori and Y. Asahi (Eds.): HCII 2024, LNCS 14690, pp. 189–208, 2024.
https://doi.org/10.1007/978-3-031-60114-9_14

is called training a personalized recommendation algorithm, which uses various actions to make the algorithm recommend videos that satisfy the user. This process, referred to as training TikTok personalized recommendation algorithm system (hereinafter called TPRA training), involves a range of user actions designed to guide the algorithm in recommending videos that align with the user's preferences.

Instead of engaging in algorithmic resistance, users who engage in TPRA training opt to embrace the algorithm to enhance their individual user experiences. The user perception of the algorithm as a tool rather than a foe may imply their self-efficacy in managing the algorithm's tradeoffs and leveraging it to their benefit. Examining their behavior in training TPRA may provide strategic insights into how individuals can adapt to the algorithmic era and contribute to the theoretical development of algorithmic literacy. However, scholarly inquiry into user training TikTok's algorithm behavior remains limited [32].

To explore users' algorithm training behavior, we asked the following questions:

1. What are the motivations behind users' training TikTok personalized recommendation algorithm behavior in China?
2. What means do users use to train TikTok's personalized recommendation algorithm in China?
3. What perpetual factors influence users' training TikTok personalized recommendation algorithm training behavior in China?

To answer these questions, this study conducted on-site observations and semi-structured interviews to collect data from 22 users who reported algorithm training behaviors on the Chinese version of TikTok and analyzed the data by thematic analysis. This study formally introduces algorithm training behavior, expanding our understanding of how users perceive and interact with algorithmic systems. It provides a creative and positive insight into strategies for addressing algorithmic risks. By cooperating with the algorithm instead of resisting it, we may enhance the benefits of algorithms and mitigate associated risks.

2 Literature Review

It is vital to understand how users interact with algorithms. Humans have experienced the influence of algorithms through their interactions with them, which can lead to both positive and negative outcomes [13]. Algorithms have increasingly become deeply embedded in societal norms and even in establishing regulations, presenting various risks such as unfairness and disseminating misinformation [34, 39]. To mitigate these risks and promote harmony between humans and algorithms, it is crucial to gain insight into user interactions with algorithms [20].

However, there remains a lack of clarity regarding the precise nature of human interactions with algorithms [30]. In order to improve human welfare in the era of algorithms, understanding how users perceive and interact with algorithms has become the primary concern for scholars.

Algorithm awareness influences the interaction between users and algorithms.

Algorithms pose difficulty in being recognized by users for being hidden behind the interface of products. Therefore, how users perceive algorithms becomes a crucial factor shaping their interaction. The prevailing research commonly employs the concept of algorithm awareness to explore how users mentally approach and engage with algorithms. Algorithm awareness is not static, but a process of continuous development and change [8]. As research progresses, the conceptual scope of algorithm consciousness has broadened, now encompassing people's knowledge, attitudes, and personal understanding of algorithms [32]. More concepts are created to describe the user's cognitive process of algorithms, such as algorithm literacy, algorithm folk theory, algorithm imagination, etc.

Initial research found that users were rarely aware of the existence of algorithms [9]. At this stage, most interactions with algorithms occur without conscious awareness on the part of the user. Recent studies have found that users' awareness of algorithms is constantly increasing: more and more users are aware of the existence of algorithms and are trying to understand how algorithms work [30].

Research shows that people's understanding of algorithms comes from different sources of information, which guide users' algorithmic interaction. Some users learn from official algorithm knowledge, such as algorithm companies. However, even if the users grasp the company's public available knowledge about the algorithmic system, it is still hard to understand the overall details of the algorithm's operation due to its black-box mechanism. Therefore, people will intuitively develop their own theories to explain the principles of algorithm operation to help them understand the process of algorithm operation [7]. Some researchers summarize this user's unofficial understanding of algorithms as "algorithm folk theory", and some researchers summarize it as "algorithm imagination" [28].

It is worth noting that algorithmic literacy refers to users' abilities to utilize algorithms, including "being aware of the use of algorithms in online applications, platforms, and services, knowing how algorithms work, being able to critically evaluate algorithmic decision-making as well as having the skills to cope with or even influence algorithmic operations" [8]. Different types of interaction with algorithms reflects different levels of algorithmic literacy.

With the change in algorithm awareness, the interaction behavior of users with algorithms takes on more complex forms [32]. Thus, algorithmic resistance behavior is proposed.

2.1 Research on the Behavior of Algorithm Resistance

With the harm of algorithms, users gradually realize the existence of algorithms and begin to resist algorithms. Algorithmic resistance behavior is distributed across numerous platforms [7]. Among them, the existing research on user resistance to the TikTok algorithm primarily centers on the risks faced by specific user groups when they resist the algorithm's impact on their social identity.

The focus of algorithm resistance research is to understand how these users' beliefs and perceptions about algorithms, known as algorithm folk theory, shape their behavior of resistance. Lee [21] focuses on cross-domain identity groups to resist the Tik-Tok algorithm's violation of LGBT and other LGBT identities to resist the algorithm's marginalization of their social identity. Jones [17] found that some users tried to influence TikTok's algorithm to express their political views, resisting TikTok's algorithm surveillance and treating them as audience goods.

In terms of interactions, Simpson and Semaan [33] found that they reposted content that had been deleted by the system, reconstructed the "for you" page through hashtags to interact with engaging content, and so on. Karizat et al. [19] found that these users deliberately clicked on the content they were not interested in, followed more bloggers with cross-domain identities, and posted videos that matched their real social identity.

However, the limitations of existing research are that current algorithmic resistance behavior research only focuses on the motivations to deal with risks. However, the purposes of algorithmic resistance behavior are diverse and essentially "complicity". That is to say, the purpose of users using algorithms is not only to resist risks, but also to recognize the power of algorithms and enjoy the services of algorithms. Investigating the algorithm training behavior may be able to reveal the different motivations of the interaction behavior and expand the research on algorithm resistance.

2.2 Research on the Behavior of Training Algorithms

The behavior of users training the algorithm, although not specifically explored, has been noticed in the field of algorithmic interaction. According to current research, users claim that they train the algorithm to "Make the algorithm work in my favor" [32]. Due to the opaque nature of algorithms, it is difficult to determine the exact effects of users' "training" behavior [24]. Therefore, the word "training" might be not rigorous. In order to facilitate reading and understanding, this study uses the expression of "training" the algorithm to describe the behavior that users take different measures to influence the results of algorithms and make it cater more precisely to their needs.

Some methods of users training the algorithm has been found in the interview records of some user resistance behavior studies. Simpson [33] interviewed how the LGBT community interacted with the algorithm and found that some interviewers used the word "train" to describe their interaction with the algorithm. Simpson believes that this reflects the strong confidence of users in understanding and managing algorithms. Siles et al. [32] also discovered the behavior of users training TikTok algorithms, and based on users' comments, summarized the main points of training algorithms as follows: "Make the algorithm work in my favor". They squandered the methods that users employ to train algorithms, including retrieving specific keywords. Through in-depth interviews with 18 interviewees, Leong [22] found that they deliberately added strangers as friends to increase the flow of information on the Facebook homepage. Simpson [31] also found in interviews that users perform operations to tell TikTok who they are, training TikTok accounts to present the identity they want their TikTok account to present. However, a detailed exploration of this behavior is still lacking, particularly the perceptual process of this behavior.

Different from the algorithm resistance behavior, the behavior of training the algorithm shows that users start to embrace and collaborate with algorithms, which shows users' higher algorithm literacy [18]. Exploring this behavior could enhance the understanding of interactions with high algorithm literacy users. To our knowledge, research in exploring this behavior remains limited.

2.3 TikTok as a Case Study

Considering TikTok's popularity around the world, the platform presents an intriguing context for studying how users interact with algorithms [2]. Researchers generally agree that TikTok's algorithm is recognized as the most aggressive and addictive among various social media platforms [32]. Unlike Instagram, Snapchat, Vine and many other entertainment products embedded with algorithm recommendation services, the content of TikTok's "for you" interface is completely controlled by the algorithm [31]. TikTok's recommendation algorithm takes into account users' past behavior and personal information, such as their video browsing habits, preferences, commenting and sharing activities, and location data [10, 12]. Utilizing these details, the algorithm aims to offer video content on the user's "recommendation" interface that caters to their inferred preferences, rather than relying solely on content specifically chosen by the user [1]. Kang and Lou [18] elaborate "TikTok's algorithm is so powerful and aggressive that it can learn the vulnerabilities and interests of a user in less than 40 min. (p. 4)". On the one hand, this feature increases the visibility of new content encountered by users and enriches the user's experience; On the other hand, it affects the user's power to control their own information source [31]. In addition, due to the large number of users, the interaction behavior of users with the TikTok algorithm is extensive.

Based on the characteristics and popularity of the TikTok algorithm, the risk of the TikTok recommendation algorithm may be more obvious than other recommendation algorithm services. TikTok admits that it suppresses the dissemination of videos created by people with disabilities, transgender and obesity [5]. Other scholars have pointed out that TikTok uses algorithms to monitor users' social interactions and harvest the fruits of people's labor [17].

Therefore, increasing research focuses on the interactions between users and TikTok's algorithm. For example, researchers closely examine how different user groups, such as the LGBT community and advocates for women's rights, resist the algorithm risks that could violate their social identity [35]. In interviews, scholars also found the expression "train" in the user's speech, but did not delve into the behavior of training the TikTok algorithm [33].

In addition, unlike TikTok, Douyin (the Chinese version of TikTok) cedes more power to users in configuring algorithmic recommendation settings. In response to many recommendation service risks, on March 1, 2022, China's Provisions on the Administration of Internet Information Service Algorithm Recommendation was officially implemented, which put forward specific rectification requirements for apps that use recommendation algorithms [6]. In response to government requirements, Douyin launched the function of turning off personalized recommended content, added the function of "not interested", and the "content preferences", allowing users to change the weight of content recommendations independently [26]. Although the flow of information on the homepage of Douyin's recommendation homepage is still determined by the algorithm, these functions provide users with more possibilities to intervene in the operation of the algorithm. This distinctive feature of Douyin contributes to a unique behavior among users, specifically the practice of training algorithms.

To our knowledge, there is no research focused on the behavior of users training Douyin algorithms, especially around the Chinese version of the Douyin algorithm after rectification. This behavior indicates users' strong ability to influence the algorithms and positive feelings towards algorithms, which differs from the existing research about resistance behavior. Exploring this behavior may enrich our understanding of algorithm interaction and inspire innovative approaches to addressing algorithmic risks. Accordingly, this paper studies the behavior of users training TikTok's algorithms in China.

3   Research Methods

To explore an emerging information behavior, we can refer to previous research to explore the motivation, means and influencing factors of this behavior [11]. Since the user's perception process of the algorithm has great influence on the interaction behavior between users and algorithms, the influencing factors at the perception level need to be focused on. Based on this, three research questions for this paper are identified:

1. What means do users use to train TikTok personalized recommendation algorithm in China?
2. What are the motivations behind users' training TikTok personalized recommendation algorithm behavior in China?
3. What perpetual factors influence users' training TikTok personalized recommendation algorithm training behavior in China?

Interviews are the most widely used method in the study of user-algorithm interaction, great for understanding what users think. However, almost all current user-algorithm interaction studies use this self-report method to collect user behavior data, which may have the problem of bias between recall and facts, which hinders the disclosure and research of information behavior. Some scholars are calling for some new methods of studying algorithms [22]. Bucher [3] recommend observing user interaction with the software.

In this context, this study collects data by onsite observations and semi-structured interviews and analyzes the data using thematic analysis. The method of onsite observation is conducive to understanding the user's actual behavior and reducing the possibility of user recall deviation from facts [37]. After, by conducting semi-structured interviews, it is conducive to understanding the underlying cognitive process. The thematic analysis method is a common method of analyzing qualitative data, and suits for answering the research questions in this paper.

3.1   Recruiting Respondents

The recruitment process consists of two stages: issuing notifications and screening applicants. First, researchers issued a recruitment notice on the Chinese public internet platform "WeChat" and "DouBan", providing 30 RMB to the participants. Respondents obtained recruitment information through browsing public Internet platforms and word of mouth and voluntarily came to participate in the experiment. The recruitment notice requires respondents to meet the following requirements:

1. basic algorithmic awareness.
2. previous experience with TPRA training.

The reason why users are required to have basic algorithm awareness is that training Douyin algorithm behavior requires users to understand the existence of algorithms [30]. They need to have basic algorithmic awareness, including knowledge, so the training behavior is reliable rather than just imagination. In this case, having basic algorithm awareness is a prerequisite for implementing algorithm training behavior. Since this

Table 1. The TikTok's Algorithmic Media Content Awareness Scale with All the Final Items

Dimensions	Items	Response categories
Please indicate to which extent you are aware of the following statements about TikTok's algorithms in media content		
Content filtering	Fil1: algorithms are used to recommend videos to me on TikTok	1 = not at all aware 5 = completely aware
	Fil2: algorithms are used to prioritize certain videos above others on TikTok	
	Fil3: algorithms are used to tailor certain videos to me on TikTok	
	Fil4: algorithms are used to show someone else see different videos than I get to see on TikTok	
Automated decision-making	Adm1: algorithms are used to show me videos on TikTok based on automated decisions	1 = not at all aware 5 = completely aware
	Adm2: algorithms do not require human judgments in deciding which videos to show me on TikTok	
	Adm3: algorithms make automated decisions on what videos I get to see on TikTok	
Human-algorithm interplay	Hai1: the videos that algorithms recommend to me on TikTok depend on my online behavior on TikTok	1 = not at all aware 5 = completely aware
	Hai2: the videos that algorithms recommend to me on TikTok depend on my online behavioral data	
	Hai3: the videos that algorithms recommend to me on TikTok depend on the data that I make available online	
Ethical considerations	Eth1: it is not always transparent why algorithms decide to show me certain videos on TikTok	1 = not at all aware 5 = completely aware

(continued)

Table 1. (*continued*)

Dimensions	Items	Response categories
	Eth2: the videos that algorithms recommend to me on TikTok can be subjected to human biases such as prejudices and stereotypes	
	Eth3: algorithms use my personal data to recommend certain videos on TikTok, and this has consequences for my online privacy	

study uses the Douyin algorithm as an example, respondents need to have rich experience in using the Douyin platform and self-report that they have had training experience.

For the respondents who came to register, this study further tested and screened through the algorithm awareness scale and the method of asking users about their experience of using Douyin. In this study, Zaroual's algorithmic media content awareness scale (AMCA-scale) was used to measure participants' awareness of TikTok's personalized recommendation algorithm (see Table 1) [40], because the scale has been tested for validity and been proven to be a good measure of user awareness of algorithm usage and results on media platforms. Users who pass the scale test (higher than 60 points after the 100-point scale is passed) and can briefly answer their personal experience of training the TikTok algorithm pass the screening. After users pass the Douyin algorithm test, this study will ask participants "How long have you used Douyin every day", and "Can you briefly describe your previous experience of training the Douyin algorithm?" Respondents who have been using more than half a year and can briefly answer the algorithm's experience are screened.

The study went through two rounds of recruitment. The first round of recruitment was announced on May 13, 2023, through the platform "WeChat". The respondents screened in the first round were all students from the same university, which may bring homogeneity issues due to the similar sample identities. To increase the diversity of the samples' identities, researchers conducted the second round of recruitment on July 1, 2023, through the platform "DouBan" for working groups. During this period, recruitment was done in parallel with thematic coding. The saturation requirement is that no new themes emerge when analyzing the new respondent's information [38]. When the results of coding achieve the saturation requirement, the recruitment ends.

In the end, 22 respondents were screened and participated in this study. No new themes emerged when analyzing the 22nd respondents' statistics, therefore the coding results reached saturation and the recruitment ended. Detailed information about respondents is shown in Table 2.

3.2 Participants

The number of participants is 22, which is appropriate for this study for two reasons. First, considering that the number of participants in previous research about interactions

Table 2. Basic Information About Respondents

Number	Gender	Age	Education background	AA score	Occupation
1	Male	18–25	Undergraduate	86.12	Students
2	Female	18–25	Master's degree in progress	80	Students
3	Female	26–30	Undergraduate	87.7	Students
4	Female	18–25	Master degree	90.77	Academic Assistants
5	Female	18–25	Current master student	87.69	Students
6	Female	18–25	Current master student	96.92	Students
7	Female	26–30	Current master student	76.92	Students
8	Female	26–30	Current PhD	90.77	Students
9	Female	18–25	Undergraduate	80	Students
10	Female	18–25	Current master student	84.62	Students
11	Male	18–25	Undergraduate	81.5	Students
12	Male	18–25	Current PhD	87.69	Students
13	Female	18–25	Current master student	87.69	Students
14	Male	26–30	Master degree	83.08	Students
15	Female	18–25	Current master student	81.54	Students
16	Female	18–25	Current master student	100	Students
17	Male	26–30	Bachelor	90.77	Engineers
18	Male	18–25	Bachelor	89.23	Party workers
19	Male	18–25	Bachelor	86.15	Programmers
20	Male	18–25	Bachelor	87.7	Hotel managers
21	Male	18–25	Bachelor	87.7	Designers
22	Male	26–30	Bachelor	84.61	Consultants

with algorithm range from 15 to 20, 22 participants are in line with the sample size of studies in this field. Besides, this study follows the Saturation Test Standard. It ends recruitment when the 22nd participant did not generate new themes.

These samples are diverse and typical, which are suitable to symbolize the users training Tiktok algorithm behavior due to the following factors. First, the samples are a result of random selection, with respondents voluntarily signing up to participate. Besides, their educational backgrounds and careers are diverse, encompassing individuals with bachelor's, master's, and Ph.D. degrees in various fields. Additionally, their professions include students, engineers, designers, and party workers. Moreover, The sample was in the young group of 18–30 and had been using TikTok for a long time. The majority of them use TikTok for more than 2 h a day, and all of them use TikTok for more than 3 h a week. Therefore, they belong to the representative user group of

Douyin, and their interaction with Douyin is also representative. Details are shown in Table 2.

In addition, all participants have been evaluated by researchers on algorithm awareness, proving that they do have the basis for training algorithms, not just out of fantasy. They all claimed to have performed algorithm-training behavior. Therefore, observing and interviewing these users can obtain valuable information about the user's algorithm training behavior.

3.3 Collecting Data

To collect behavioral data that is as realistic as possible, this study used on-site observation and semi-structured interviews for data collection. Data was collected from April 2023 to May 2023. The specific procedures refer to [22, 37], shown as follows.

Initially, participants were informed of the process of collecting data and privacy protection measures. After the user's informed consent. The experiment started.

First, respondents were asked to train the Douyin accounts provided by the researchers according to their daily habits, trying to replicate their usual algorithm training behavior. The training process lasted a maximum of 15 min. During this period, the researchers recorded the interaction behavior on the spot and recorded the screen using the "Tencent Meeting" software. The reason for training accounts provided by researchers rather than respondents' own is to protect user privacy. The training duration is determined based on the pre-experiment. It took 5 pre-trial participants 10–15 min to train the TikTok algorithm. The pre-trial participants decided that they had used enough training tools and did not need to repeat the operation. Therefore, the formal experiment was determined to be 15 min in this study.

Immediately after the training activities, the researchers asked participants to watch videos of their experiments and asked them about the purpose, reason, and feelings of the different behaviors. Specific questions include, "Do you think you're training the algorithm/TikTok at this time?" "What is the purpose of your act?" "Why do you think this move will help you achieve your goals?" "What were you thinking when you performed this act?". In addition, the researchers will supplement questions according to the specific situation of the respondents, such as "Your later training behavior is different from the previous one, why?". The interviews lasted between 15 and 25 min. The recordings were transcribed at the end of each interview.

After removing irrelevant information, this study collected a total of 34,613 words of interview transcripts and field observations.

3.4 Analyzing Data

Our research adopted a thematic analysis approach to analyzing the qualitative material, through a combination of bottom-up and top-down approaches [14]. Two researchers with coding experience were involved in the data analysis and used the software named "Nvivo" to conduct coding. The process of data analysis was as follows:

1. The researchers familiarized themselves with field observation notes and interview notes, by transcribing and reading data.

1. The researchers generated initial codes by coding interesting features of the data systematically.
2. The initial codes were then grouped into different levels of the coding system relevant to the research question.
3. During this process, the researchers continually compared the coded content, merged similar content, and reduced the number of codes.
4. The coding was completed until the two researchers agreed on the coding results.
5. Ultimately, we created 9 themes, 24 sub-themes, and 58 codes.

3.5 Ethics Consideration

This study secured consent from participants, and all privacy data were deleted. The procedures for data collection and analysis were transparent to the participants. Focused on the interaction between humans and algorithms, our study is expected to present no ethical concerns.

4 Results

4.1 RQ1: Motivations for Users Training TikTok Recommendation Algorithm

The coding results indicate that the needs for users training TikTok recommendation algorithm are to have the TikTok "for you" interface recommend content that meets their personalized needs, both in terms of values pursuit and risk avoidance (Table 3).

Table 3. Motivations for Users Training TikTok Personalized Recommendation Algorithm

Theme	Sub-theme	Codes	Post
Pursuit of values	Pursuit of entertainment value	Pursue information that matched personal interests	P1,P5,P6,P7,P10,P12,P14,P15
	Pursuit of utility value	Pursue information that meets practical needs	P2,P3,P4,P12,P18,P20
Avoidance of risks	Avoidance of privacy breaches	Avoid private information recommended by TikTok's algorithm	P3,P4,P5,P13,P22
	Avoidance of information cocoons	Avoid homogenous information recommended by TikTok's algorithm	P3,P8,P13,P21
	Avoidance of luring consumption	Avoid advertisements recommended by TikTok's algorithm	P4,P16,P19,P22

On the one hand, users seek the value of TikTok's algorithmic personalized service. Users are committed to training TPRA to provide interesting or practical information for them automatically. For example, respondents said, "I use TikTok for relaxation and entertainment, so I only watch videos that I like". Other respondents said, "I wish the TikTok algorithm recommends content about news and life tips that might be useful to me."

On the other hand, users avoid the risks of the TikTok recommendation algorithm. Considering the risk of privacy breaches, information cocoons and luring consumption, users tend to avoid private, homogenous or commercial information recommended by TPRA. For example, respondents said "I don't want the TikTok algorithm to keep recommending me things that I am only interested in, which leads me into an information cocoon" (P13), and "I feel like I am leaking my privacy when I see videos recommended by TikTok at my own address, so I want the algorithm not to recommend these to me" (P4), and "I hate advertisements and try my best to avoid them" (P22).

4.2   RQ2: Means of Users Training TikTok Personalized Recommendation Algorithm

The means of users training TPRA were classified to four types: deliberate adjustment of recommendation algorithm system functions, deliberate change of the TikTok usage behavior, deliberate change of personal information with the TikTok account, deliberate reduction of the TikTok algorithm use (see Table 4). By different means to influence the algorithm, they check the training results through the content of the "for you" page.

Deliberate adjustment of recommendation algorithm system functions refers to use of system functions that can directly affect the mechanism of TikTok's recommendation algorithm. TikTok's content preference is a characteristic feature that the Chinese version of TikTok provides for users to adjust the personalized recommended algorithm. Users can choose their own preferred content tags and adjust tags' recommendation weights. This feature gives users the power to manage their own personalized recommended algorithm, regarded as the most effective means of training TikTok recommendation algorithm by users. When users click on the "not interested" feature of a video, the TikTok recommendation system would directly identify the negative feedback from users and promise to reduce relevant recommendations.

Users deliberately change their TikTok usage behavior, thus influencing the results of the TikTok algorithm's guessing of user preferences based on their usage behavior. As users believe that the TikTok algorithm collects behavioral data such as users' search terms, browsing records, follow lists, and video interaction operations to analyze user preferences, users will deliberately engage in TikTok usage behaviors such as video interaction, search, browsing, and following to guide the algorithm in determining their own preference types, thus training the TikTok algorithm to recommend the information they want.

Changing personal information means that users increase or decrease the provision of personal information to TikTok, thus influencing the algorithm's guesses of user preferences based on personal information. Some users avoid filling in private information in their personal information and disabling their mobile phone system's authorization for TikTok to access their location, thus preventing the algorithm from recommending content related to their address. However, some respondents said, "I want to see videos of people I know, so I turn on access to my contacts in my address book" (P14).

In addition, users alter the algorithm's recommendations by reducing their use of the TikTok's algorithm. When TikTok's algorithmic recommendations become homogeneous, some users use TikTok without logging in to their accounts or just stop using TikTok. They learned from their using experience: "When I use TikTok again after a while, the recommendations will be different" (P8).

Table 4. Means of Users Training TikTok Personalized Recommendation Algorithm

Theme	Sub-theme	Codes	Posts
Deliberate adjustment of recommendation algorithm system functions	Adjust the content preference	Select the content tags you are interested in and adjust its recommendation weights	P9,P12,P10
	Click "not interested"	Click on the video action "Not interested" and fill in the reason	P1,P3,P5,P8,P9
Deliberate change of the TikTok usage behavior	Deliberately interact with the video	like, comment, collect, share	P3,P4,P11,P14,P15
	Deliberately search	Retrieve information in the TikTok search bar	P9,P11,P8,P14
	Deliberately browse	Browse hot lists, content watched by friends, other videos on the account's homepage	P3,P8,P4,P13
	Deliberately follow	Follow, unfollow or report, block the account	P6,P4,P11
Deliberate change of personal information with the TikTok account	Deliberately reduce the provision of personal information	Avoid fill in privacy, Cancel authorization to obtain location	P5,P13
	Deliberately increase the provision of personal information	Turn on TikTok's permission to access contacts	P14
Deliberate reduction of the TikTok algorithm use	Turn off the personalized recommended algorithm	Turn off the personalized recommended algorithm	P2,P6,P8

(*continued*)

Table 4. (*continued*)

Theme	Sub-theme	Codes	Posts
	Change the settings of TikTok accounts	Log out of the account, register a new account	P8,P13,P7
	Stop the use of TikTok	Exit the TikTok interface, uninstall TikTok	P8,P15

4.3 RQ3: Perceptual Influencing Factors for Users Training TikTok Personalized Recommendation Algorithm

It is found that algorithmic literacy, recommendations satisfaction, and perceived benefits and costs of training means influence the TPRA training behavior (see Table 5).

Algorithmic literacy refers to the ability of individuals to be aware that online platforms and services use algorithms and to know how algorithms work [8]. The coding results indicate that users' awareness of the existence of the TikTok recommendation algorithm and knowledge of how it works are prerequisites for users to implement algorithm training behaviors. Therefore, algorithmic awareness is the key influencing factor for TPRA training behaviors.

Recommendations satisfaction influences users' algorithm training behavior. When the satisfaction of TikTok's algorithmic recommendations to a high or low degree, users tend to train the TikTok algorithm to increase or decrease such information recommendations. When the satisfaction of TikTok's algorithmic recommendations to a moderate degree, users tend not to train the algorithm.

Perceived benefits and costs of training means to influence their choice of different algorithm training means. Although the TikTok platform has published the basic operating mechanism of the recommendation algorithm, it has not published the specific effect of each user operation on the recommendation algorithm. For users, the internal details of TikTok's recommendation algorithm are still in a "black box" state. As a result, different users make assumptions about the benefits of training algorithm operations based on their own using experiences. For example, some respondents thought that "Likes and favorites have the same training effect on the system" (P13), while others thought that "for me, the positive feedback effect of the three operations - likes, comments, and favorites - on videos is gradually increasing" (P12). The perceived cost of time and effort in training the TikTok algorithm also influenced users' choice of different algorithm training operations.

Table 5. Influencing Factors for Users Training TikTok Personalized Recommendation Algorithm

Theme	Sub-theme	Original records
Algorithmic literacy	The user's awareness of the existence of the TikTok recommendation algorithm affects the user's algorithm training behavior	I sometimes get so addicted to video content that I overlook the TikTok algorithm and forget the purpose of training the algorithm (P4)
	The user's knowledge of the TikTok recommendation algorithm mechanism affects the user algorithm training behavior	I have read the article on popular science about TikTok recommendation algorithm, so I know that the TikTok algorithm collects user behavior data (P12)
Recommendations satisfaction	The high satisfaction of TikTok's algorithmic recommendations influence users to train the algorithm to increase such recommendations	Photography is one of those things that I don't normally swipe to. I find it interesting, I like it, and the subsequent algorithm may recommend it (P12)
	The moderate satisfaction of TikTok's algorithmic recommendations influence users to train the algorithm not to train TikTok algorithm	When I come across videos that are somewhat interesting, but also dispensable, I don't train the algorithm (P6)
		I don't bother to click on "not interested" when I encounter a video that I'm generally not interested in, so I just scroll up (P13)
	The low satisfaction of TikTok's algorithmic recommendations influence users to train the algorithm to reduce such recommendations	Always swiping to ads. I'm angry and want to change it (P9)
Perceived benefits and costs of training means	Perceived benefits of the training means influence users' choice of different training means	I think it's useless to block the account, and it's more effective to click on the way you don't like it (P6)
	Perceived costs of the training means influence users' choice of different training means	I won't do too complex behavior to influence the algorithm because I want to save time (P10)

5 Discussion

This study collected data by observation and interviews, using the thematic analysis method to extract the needs, means and perpetual influencing factors of TPRA training behavior. It is found that the TPRA training behavior is motivated by users' pursuit of values and avoidance of risks. Users influence the results of TikTok's recommendation algorithm by changing personal information and usage behavior, adjusting the algorithm system function, and reducing the use of TikTok's algorithm. Also, they check the training effects through the content of the "for you" page. The influencing factors of TPRA training behavior include users' algorithmic literacy, recommendations satisfaction, and perceived benefits and costs of training means.

A new kind of interaction with the algorithm system, users "training" the algorithm system, was revealed. The motivations, means and perpetual influencing factors of this behavior differ from these of the algorithm resistance behavior, showing a positive behavior pattern of users, which has been less discussed before.

This discovery advances our comprehension of algorithmic system interactions by introducing novel motivations, measures, and influencing factors. It provides valuable insights into addressing algorithmic risks. Besides, the behavior of users training TikTok algorithm system resonate with measures that users take to on different platforms [11, 22], bringing implications of this research beyond the TikTok platform in China.

5.1 Theoretical Implications

Motivations Showing User Appreciation for Algorithms. Compared with previous research on resistance behavior, which focus only on resistance risk, this paper finds that the motivation of users training the algorithm includes two categories: access to services and resistance risk [39]. This indicates that some users appreciate algorithms rather than just alertness and aversion [24].

Innovative and Efficacious "Training" Measures. It is found that the means employed by users to train TikTok's algorithm system can indeed affect the personalized recommendation results [15, 36], according to the principle of the personalized recommendation algorithm disclosed by TikTok in China [4]. For example, TikTok's personalized recommendation algorithm will predict user preferences based on user behavior information, including likes, follow, browsing and other behavioral information, which echoes the means by which users deliberately change their usage behavior.

Besides, this study finds that users "train" the algorithm system through temporary algorithmic isolation, directly adjusting content preferences and clicking on disinterest, which was rarely discussed before [23]. This helps to understand the various means of human-algorithm interaction.

Novel Perceptual Influencing Factors. This paper finds that the user's knowledge of the algorithm directly affects the user's interaction behavior with the algorithm, which was rarely noticed before, showing a better grasp of how algorithms work. Previously, algorithmic knowledge and algorithmic folk theories were discussed in a mixed way, and the latter was discussed more [33]. Therefore, the role of algorithm knowledge has not been paid enough attention. Algorithmic folk theory is highly subjective and unofficial, while algorithmic knowledge is objective and official [28]. The use of algorithmic knowledge rather than algorithmic folk power can more effectively achieve the user's goals.

Besides, user perceptions of the benefits and costs of training algorithm means have been less considered as an influencing factor in user-algorithm interaction behavior in previous research, which may expand the perspective of the research on human-algorithm interaction behavior.

5.2 Methodological Implications

Unlike the previous approach of primarily relying on interviews for data collection [33], this study adopts on-site observation and semi-structured interviews to gather user behavior data. This approach allows for a more detailed exploration, capturing insights that might have been missed by relying solely on user reports. By utilizing a different data collection method, the study bolsters the reliability of its findings.

5.3 Practical Implications

The goal of studying algorithmic interaction behavior is to comprehend the underlying principles guiding user interactions with algorithms, in order to establish a harmonious relationship between humans and algorithm [16]. The research identified a positive pattern of "training" algorithm system by avoiding negativity and emphasizing the positive side. This approach may prove beneficial in managing algorithmic risks. By studying positive mindsets and effective training measures, prioritizing algorithm knowledge education, we can potentially reduce algorithmic risks [29].

5.4 Limitations and Future Work

This study has the following shortcomings. This research exclusively concentrates on training algorithms for Chinese users on the Douyin platform. It is imperative to conduct further investigations into user behavior on other platforms.

In addition, this paper explored the interaction behavior of users and algorithms at the same time, lacking consideration of the time's impact on the interaction behavior. Therefore, it fails to deeply explore the effectiveness of user training algorithms. In the future, longitudinal research should be added to further analyze the difference between users' long-term training behavior and ordinary use behavior on the algorithm recommendation results.

6 Conclusion

This study explores the behavior of users training TikTok algorithms, including motivations, means and perceptual influencing factors. The motivations, means and perpetual influencing factors of this behavior diverge from these of the algorithm resistance behavior, showing a positive and innovative behavior pattern of human-algorithm interaction.

These findings deepen our understanding of human-algorithm interactions and offer important insights into mitigating algorithmic risks from a positive user perspective. Collaborating with algorithms enables users to leverage their services, enjoy benefits, and proactively avoid potential risks.

Disclosure of Interests. The authors have no competing interests.

References

1. Anderson, K.E.: Getting acquainted with social networks and apps: it is time to talk about TikTok. Library hi tech news **37**(4), 7–12 (2020). https://doi.org/10.1108/LHTN-01-2020-0001
2. Bhandari, A., Bimo, S.: Why's everyone on TikTok now? the algorithmized self and the future of self-making on social media. Social Media+Society **8**(1) (2022). https://doi.org/10.1177/20563051221086241
3. Bucher, T.: The algorithmic imaginary: Exploring the ordinary affects of Facebook algorithms. Inf. Commun. Soc. **20**(1), 30–44 (2016). https://doi.org/10.1080/1369118X.2016.1154086
4. Chinese national internet information office: Beian management system (2022). https://beian.cac.gov.cn/
5. Choi, D., Lee, U., Hong, H.: "It's not wrong, but I'm quite disappointed": toward an inclusive algorithmic experience for content creators with disabilities. In: Proceedings of the 2022 CHI Conference on Human Factors in Computing System, USA, 593, pp. 1–19 (2022). https://doi.org/10.1145/3491102.3517574
6. Creemers, R., Webster, G., Toner, H.: Translation: Internet information service algorithmic recommendation management provisions–effective March 1, 2022. January, 10, 22 (2022). https://digichina.stanford.edu/work/translation-internet-information-service-algorithmic-recommendation-management-provisions-effective-march-1-2022/
7. DeVito, M.A.: How transfeminine TikTok creators navigate the algorithmic trap of visibility via folk theorization. Proc. ACM Hum.-Comput. Interact. **6**(CSCW2), 1–31 (2022). https://doi.org/10.1145/3555105
8. Dogruel, L., Masur, P., Joeckel, S.: Development and validation of an algorithm literacy scale for internet users. Commun. Methods Meas. **16**(2), 115–133 (2022). https://doi.org/10.1080/19312458.2021.1968361
9. Eslami, M., et al.: "I always assumed that I wasn't really that close to [her]": reasoning about Invisible algorithms in news feeds. In: Proceedings of the 33rd Annual ACM Conference on Human Factors in Computing Systems, pp. 153–162 (2015). https://doi.org/10.1145/2702123.2702556
10. Feldkamp, J.: The rise of TikTok: the evolution of a social media platform during COVID-19. In: Hovestadt, C., Recker, J., Richter, J., Werder, K. (eds.) Digital Responses to Covid-19. SIS, pp. 73–85. Springer, Cham (2021). https://doi.org/10.1007/978-3-030-66611-8_6
11. Fu, S., Jiang, T. Motivations, purposes, and means of creating information cocoons intentionally for oneself: looking on the bright side. In International Conference on Information, pp. 23–130 (2023). https://doi.org/10.1007/978-3-031-28032-0_10
12. Guinaudeau, B., Munger, K., Votta, F.: Fifteen seconds of fame: TikTok and the supply side of social video. Comput. Commun. Res. **4**(2), 463–485 (2022). https://doi.org/10.5117/CCR2022.2.004.GUIN

13. Hazrati, N., Ricci, F.: Recommender systems effect on the evolution of users' choices distribution. Inform. Proc. Manage. **59**(1), 102766 (2022). https://doi.org/10.1016/j.ipm.2021.102766

14. Hu, X., Chen, J., Wang, Y.H.: University students' use of music for learning and well-being: a qualitative study and design implications. Inform. Proc. Manage. **58**(1), 102409 (2021). https://doi.org/10.1016/j.ipm.2020.102409

15. Huang, J.J., et al.: Negative can be positive: signed graph neural networks for recommendation. Inform. Proc. Manage. **60**(4) (2023). https://doi.org/10.1016/j.ipm.2023.103403

16. Jiang, Q., Zhang, Y., Pian, W.: ChatBot as an emergency exist: mediated empathy for resilience via human-AI interaction during the COVID-19 pandemic. Inform. Proc. Manage. **59**(6), 103074 (2022). https://doi.org/10.1016/j.ipm.2022.103074

17. Jones, C.: How to train your algorithm: the struggle for public control over private audience commodities on TikTok. Media, Cult. Soc. **6**, 1192–1209 (2023) https://doi.org/10.1177/01634437231159555

18. Kang, H., Lou, C.: AI agency vs. human agency: understanding human–AI interactions on TikTok and their implications for user engagement. J. Comput.-Mediated Commun. **27**(5), zmac014 (2022). https://doi.org/10.1093/jcmc/zmac014

19. Karizat, N., Delmonaco, D., Eslami, M., Andalibi, N.: Algorithmic folk theories and identity: how TikTok users co-produce knowledge of identity and engage in algorithmic resistance. Proc. ACM Hum.-Comput. Interact. **5**(CSCW2), 1–44 (2021). https://doi.org/10.1145/3476046

20. Klug, D., Qin, Y., Evans, M., Kaufman, G.: Trick and please: a mixed-method study on user assumptions about the TikTok algorithm. In: Proceedings of the 13th ACM Web Science Conference 2021 (WebSci 2021), USA, pp. 84–92(2021). https://doi.org/10.1145/3447535.3462512

21. Lee, A.Y., et al.: The algorithmic crystal: conceptualizing the self through algorithmic personalization on TikTok. Proc. ACM Hum.-Comput. Interact. **6**(CSCW2), 1–22 (2022). https://doi.org/10.1145/3555601

22. Leong, L.: Domesticating algorithms: an exploratory study of Facebook users in Myanmar. Inf. Soc. **36**(2), 97–108 (2020). https://doi.org/10.1080/01972243.2019.1709930

23. Lu, X., Lu, Z., Liu, C.: Exploring TikTok use and non-use practices and experiences in China. In: Meiselwitz, G. (ed.) HCII 2020. LNCS, vol. 12195, pp. 57–70. Springer, Cham (2020). https://doi.org/10.1007/978-3-030-49576-3_5

24. Oeldorf-Hirsch, A., Neubaum, G.: What do we know about algorithmic literacy? The status quo and a research agenda for a growing field. New Media Soc., 14614448231182662 (2023). https://doi.org/10.1177/14614448231182662

25. Omnicore.: TikTok by the numbers: stats, demographics & fun facts (2021, January 4). https://www.omnicoreagency.com/tiktok-statistics/

26. PingWest.: Chinese apps give power back to users by adding "turn off recommendation" buttons (2021). https://en.pingwest.com/a/9945

27. Rach, M., Peter, M.K.: How TikTok's algorithm beats Facebook & Co. for attention under the theory of escapism: a network sample analysis of Austrian, German and Swiss users. In: Martínez-López, F.J., López López, D. (eds.) DMEC 2021. SPBE, pp. 137–143. Springer, Cham (2021). https://doi.org/10.1007/978-3-030-76520-0_15

28. Schellewald, A.: On getting carried away by the TikTok algorithm. AoIR Sel. Pap. Internet Res. **2021**, 13–16 (2021). https://doi.org/10.5210/spir.v2021i0.12039

29. Shin, D.: How do users interact with algorithm recommender systems? The interaction of users, algorithms, and performance. Comput. Hum. Behav. **109**, 106344 (2020). https://doi.org/10.1016/j.chb.2020.106344

30. Shin, D., Kee, K.F., Shin, E.Y.: Algorithm awareness: why user awareness is critical for personal privacy in the adoption of algorithmic platforms? Int. J. Inf. Manage. **65**, 102494 (2022). https://doi.org/10.1016/j.ijinfomgt.2022.102494

31. Simpson, E., Hamann, A., Semaan, B.: How to tame" your" algorithm: LGBTQ+ Users' domestication of TikTok. Proc. ACM Hum.-Comput. Interact. 6(GROUP), 1–27 (2022). https://doi.org/10.1145/3492841

32. Siles, I., Valerio-Alfaro, L., Meléndez-Moran, A.: Learning to like TikTok. . . and not: algorithm awareness as process. New Media Soc., 14614448221138973 (2022). https://doi.org/10.1177/14614448221138973

33. Simpson, E., Semaan, B.: For you, or for "you"? everyday LGBTQ+ encounters with TikTok. Proc. ACM Hum.-Comput. Interact. **4**(CSCW3), 1–34 (2021). https://doi.org/10.1145/3432951

34. Song, G., Wang, Y.: Mainstream value information push strategy on Chinese aggregation news platform: evolution, modelling and analysis. Sustainability, **13**(19), 11121 (2021). https://doi.org/10.3390/su131911121

35. Sued, G.E., et al.: Vernacular visibility and algorithmic resistance in the public expression of Latin American feminism. Media Int. Australia **183**(1), 60–76 (2022). https://doi.org/10.1177/1329878X211067571

36. Swart, J.: Experiencing algorithms: how young people understand, feel about, and engage with algorithmic news selection on social media. Social Media+Society **7**(2), 20563051211008828 (2021). https://doi.org/10.1177/20563051211008828

37. Tanner, S.A., McCarthy, M.B., O'Reilly, S.J.: Exploring the roles of motivation and cognition in label-usage using a combined eye-tracking and retrospective think aloud approach. Appetite **135**, 146–158 (2019). https://doi.org/10.1016/j.appet.2018.11.015

38. Ye, E.M., et al.: Understanding roles in collaborative information behavior: a case of Chinese group travelling. Inform. Process. Manage. **58**(4), 102581 (2021). https://doi.org/10.1016/j.ipm.2021.102581

39. Velkova, J., Kaun, A.: Algorithmic resistance: media practices and the politics of repair. Inf. Commun. Soc. **24**(4), 523–540 (2021). https://doi.org/10.1080/1369118X.2019.1657162

40. Zarouali, B., Boerman, S.C., de Vreese, C.H.: Is this recommended by an algorithm? The development and validation of the algorithmic media content awareness scale (AMCA-scale). Telematics Inform. **62**, 101607 (2021). https://doi.org/10.1016/j.tele.2021.101607

Structural Equation Modeling for the Effect of Involvement on Consumer Engagement

Masahiro Kuroda[✉] and Akira Oyabu

Okayama University of Science, 1-1 Ridai-cho, Kita-ku, Okayama 700-0005, Japan
{kuroda,ohyabu}@ous.ac.jp

Abstract. Consumer engagement (CE) refers to the interaction between a customer and an organization, such as company or brand, through various online or offline channels. Our study concerned the interplay among CEs with multiple objects in a fashion consumption context. In our qualitative research, CE was defined as Cognitive, Emotional and Behavioral investments made by consumers in fashion-related interactions. We identified the focal objects of CE, such as Fashion, Brand and Sales assistant. Moreover, we investigate the effect of involvement on CE. The involvement is focused on the commitment to the same three objects as CE. Then, we develop conceptual models associated with CEs and involvements and employ structural equation modeling (SEM) to examine their interplay. The quantitative research collected data for measuring CEs and involvements with Likert scale. When observed Likert scale data are not approximately normally distributed, we propose quantifying the data. Nonlinear principal component analysis (NPCA) obtains optimally scaled data by quantifying Likert scale data and computes principal component scores of the optimally scaled data. SEM combined with NPCA is referred to as NPCA-SEM. In the analysis of our research data, we compare the goodness of fit of conceptual models obtained from NPCA-SEM with that from ordinal SEM and examine the performance of NPCA-SEM.

Keywords: Structural equation modeling · Consumer engagement · Involvement · Consumer's fashion context · Optimal scaling · Nonlinear principal component analysis

1 Introduction

Consumer engagement (CE) refers to the interaction between a customer and an organization, such as company or brand, through various online or offline channels (Hollebeek et al. [4]). Early research on CE focused on online contexts, such as online brand communities. Recent studies on CE have been conducted in a variety of both offline and online settings. These studies are primarily conceptual and address how consumers engage with a single engagement object. However,

H. Mori and Y. Asahi (Eds.): HCII 2024, LNCS 14690, pp. 209–223, 2024.
https://doi.org/10.1007/978-3-031-60114-9_15

there is limited understanding regarding CEs involving multiple engagement objects (Heinonen [3]).

We investigated how consumers engage with multiple objects in a fashion consumption context. Then, CE was defined as Cognitive, Emotional and Behavioral investments made by consumers in fashion-related interactions. From this CE perspective, qualitative and quantitative research was conducted. The qualitative research involved semi-structured interviews with consumers who have an affinity for fashion. We identified the focal objects of CE, such as Fashion, Brand and Sales assistant. Moreover, we focus on the interplay between CE and involvement. Involvement is a motivational variable in consumer behavior and explains the degree to which consumers perceive the relevance of an object based on their inherent needs, values and interests (Zaichkowsky [12]). Involvement is defined as the commitment to the same three focal objects as CE, namely, Fashion, Brand and Sales assistant. We develop hypotheses and conceptual models associated with CEs and involvements. The quantitative research collected survey data on multiple objects of CE and involvement. The data are measured with five levels Likert scale. Structural equation modeling (SEM) is employed to investigate the effect of involvement on CE.

SEM assumes that Likert scale data are approximately normal distributed, whereas they may not have a normal distribution. We propose to quantify Likert scale data. Optimal scaling is a quantification technique that assigns numerical values to Likert scale levels and nonlinearly transforms qualitative data into quantitative data. When using the optimal scaling in nonlinear principal component analysis (NPCA) of Young et al. [11], optimally scaled data are obtained by quantifying Likert scale data, and principal component scores are computed from the optimally scaled data. Thus, this approach replaces factor analysis with NPCA in the measurement equation model and treats the scores as observed data instead of Likert scale data. Kuroda et al. [8] referred to SEM combining NPCA as NPCA-SEM. In the analysis of our research data, we compare the goodness of fit of conceptual models obtained from NPCA-SEM with that from ordinal SEM and examine the performance of NPCA-SEM.

This paper is organized as follows: Sect. 2 develops hypotheses and conceptual models describing the interplay between CEs and involvements. Section 3 gives second-order SEM and NPCA-SEM for the conceptual models. Section 4 shows the results of data analysis using SEM and NPCA-SEM. Section 5 presents our concluding remarks.

2   Development of Hypotheses and Conceptual Models

In recent research, Chandler and Lusch [1] and Naumann et al. [9] have focused on CE with multiple focal objects. They also suggested that CE with one object influences their engagement with other object.

Our study concerned the interplay among CEs with multiple objects in a fashion consumption context. Then, we defined CE as Cognitive, Emotional and Behavioral investments into fashion-related interactions. From this CE perspective, qualitative and quantitative research was conducted. In the qualitative research, semi-structured interviews were carried out with 18 consumers interested in fashion in February 2017. The interviewees were asked to talk about their experiences of fashion in everyday life over the past few decades. The analysis focuses on examining what objects consumers engage with, and how multiple CEs are related to each other.

From the interviews, three focal objects were extracted: Fashion, Brand and Sales assistant. Brand is a specific name that distinguishes a product from others. Examples include Louis Vuitton and UNIQLO, which are the names of clothing stores. Many of the respondents were involved with a particular brand. Fashion is also about dressing up and being fashionable. Consumers who engage with fashion do not focus solely on brands but rather on styles that suit them, comfort and balance, which is different from the brand focus mentioned above. This distinction from brand focus is notable. A sales assistant is a person who works on the sales floor in clothing shops. Some respondents imitated the fashion of a particular staff member or engaged in fashion discussions or non-fashion small talk with their favorite staff member.

The respondents also stated that the more interested they were in fashion, the more attached they became to the brand. At the same time, it has been noted that engagement with a company or brand has a positive impact on direct interactions with the company and customer satisfaction (e.g., Jaakkola and Alexander [5]). In particular, in the context of fashion, customers who engage with brands tend to emphasize on the conversations and close relationships with sales assistants. Therefore, the following hypotheses are given:

- $H1$: CE with Fashion influences CE with Brand.
- $H2$: CE with Brand influences CE with Sales assistant.

The conceptual model for hypothesis $\{H1, H2\}$ is presented in the path diagram of Fig. 1.

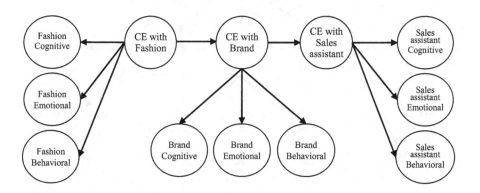

Fig. 1. The conceptual model for hypothesis $\{H1, H2\}$.

The involvement is focused on the commitment to the same three focal objects as CE, namely, Fashion, Brand and Sales assistant. For the interplay among objects of involvement, we hypothesize as follows:

- $H3$: Involvement with Fashion influences involvement with Brand.
- $H4$: Involvement with Brand influences involvement with Sales assistant.

Figure 2 is the diagram of the conceptual model for hypothesis $\{H3, H4\}$.

Fig. 2. The conceptual model for hypothesis $\{H3, H4\}$.

We investigate the interplay between CE and involvement. Then, we propose the following hypothesis:

- $H5$: Involvement has a direct effect on CE.

The diagram in Fig. 3 represents the conceptual model for hypothesis $\{H1, H2, H5\}$.

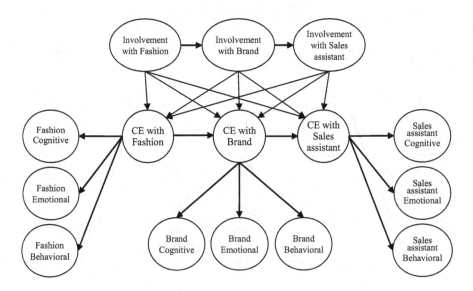

Fig. 3. The conceptual model for hypothesis $\{H1, H2, H5\}$.

3   Structural Equation Modeling for the Effect of Involvement on Consumer Engagement

Structural equation modeling (SEM) is used to study the effect of involvement on CE. SEM integrates the measurement equation model and the structural equation model into a path analytic framework. The measurement equation model is just a factor analysis model. The structural equation model is a path analysis model with latent factors. A latent factor is not measured directly and then is measured by using several observed variables as indicator of the factor. In the structural equation model, we specify the dependencies among latent factors.

3.1   Second-Order Structural Equation Modeling

Table 1 gives observed variables and latent factors with engagement in each focal object. Cognitive is measured with three items, Emotional is with four items, and Behavioral is with four or five items.

Table 1. Observed variables and latent factors with engagement.

Object	Engagement	Factor	Observed variables
Fashion	Cognitive	f_{FC}	$\mathbf{X}_{FC} = (X_{FC1}, X_{FC2}, X_{FC3})$
	Emotional	f_{FE}	$\mathbf{X}_{FE} = (X_{FE1}, X_{FE2}, X_{FE3}, X_{FE4})$
	Behavioral	f_{FB}	$\mathbf{X}_{FB} = (X_{FB1}, X_{FB2}, X_{FB3}, X_{FB4})$
Brand	Cognitive	f_{BC}	$\mathbf{X}_{BC} = (X_{BC1}, X_{BC2}, X_{BC3})$
	Emotional	f_{BE}	$\mathbf{X}_{BE} = (X_{BE1}, X_{BE2}, X_{BE3}, X_{BE4})$
	Behavioral	f_{BB}	$\mathbf{X}_{BB} = (X_{BB1}, X_{BB2}, X_{BB3}, X_{BB4}, X_{BB5})$
Sales assistant	Cognitive	f_{SC}	$\mathbf{X}_{SC} = (X_{SC1}, X_{SC2}, X_{SC3})$
	Emotional	f_{SE}	$\mathbf{X}_{SE} = (X_{SE1}, X_{SE2}, X_{SE3}, X_{SE4})$
	Behavioral	f_{SB}	$\mathbf{X}_{SB} = (X_{SB1}, X_{SB2}, X_{SB3}, X_{SB4}, X_{SB5})$

Let f_{FCE}, f_{BCE} and f_{SCE} denote the latent factors of focal objects of CEs: Fashion, Brand and Sales assistant, respectively. We describe the structural equation model:

$$\begin{cases} (f_{FC}, f_{FE}, f_{FB}) = \boldsymbol{\alpha}_F f_{FCE} + \mathbf{e}_F \\ \qquad = (\alpha_{FC}, \alpha_{FE}, \alpha_{FB}) f_{FCE} + (e_{FC}, e_{FE}, e_{FB}), \\ (f_{BC}, f_{BE}, f_{BB}) = \boldsymbol{\alpha}_B f_{BCE} + \mathbf{e}_B \\ \qquad = (\alpha_{BC}, \alpha_{BE}, \alpha_{BB}) f_{BCE} + (e_{BC}, e_{BE}, e_{BB}), \\ (f_{SC}, f_{SE}, f_{SB}) = \boldsymbol{\alpha}_S f_{FCE} + \mathbf{e}_S \\ \qquad = (\alpha_{SC}, \alpha_{SE}, \alpha_{SB}) f_{SCE} + (e_{SC}, e_{SE}, e_{SB}), \end{cases} \quad (1)$$

where $\boldsymbol{\alpha}_F$, $\boldsymbol{\alpha}_B$ and $\boldsymbol{\alpha}_S$ are vectors of directed path coefficients, and $\mathbf{e}_F$, $\mathbf{e}_B$ and $\mathbf{e}_S$ are vectors of errors associated with the latent factors. These vectors are computed from the model (1).

We give the measurement equation model:

$$
\begin{cases}
\mathbf{X}_{FC} = \boldsymbol{\lambda}_{FC} f_{FC} + \mathbf{e}_{FC} \\
\quad = (\lambda_{FC1}, \lambda_{FC2}, \lambda_{FC3}) f_{FC} + (e_{FC1}, e_{FC2}, e_{FC3}), \\
\mathbf{X}_{FE} = \boldsymbol{\lambda}_{FE} f_{FE} + \mathbf{e}_{FE} \\
\quad = (\lambda_{FE1}, \lambda_{FE2}, \lambda_{FE3}, \lambda_{FE4}) f_{FE} + (e_{FE1}, e_{FE2}, e_{FE3}, e_{FE4}), \\
\mathbf{X}_{FB} = \boldsymbol{\lambda}_{FB} f_{FB} + \mathbf{e}_{FB} \\
\quad = (\lambda_{FB1}, \lambda_{FB2}, \lambda_{FB3}, \lambda_{FB4}) f_{FB} + (e_{FB1}, e_{FB2}, e_{FB3}, e_{FB4}), \\
\mathbf{X}_{BC} = \boldsymbol{\lambda}_{BC} f_{BC} + \mathbf{e}_{BC} \\
\quad = (\lambda_{BC1}, \lambda_{BC2}, \lambda_{BC3}) f_{BC} + (e_{BC1}, e_{BC2}, e_{BC3}), \\
\mathbf{X}_{BE} = \boldsymbol{\lambda}_{BE} f_{BE} + \mathbf{e}_{BE} \\
\quad = (\lambda_{BE1}, \lambda_{BE2}, \lambda_{BE3}, \lambda_{BE4}) f_{BE} + (e_{BE1}, e_{BE2}, e_{BE3}, e_{BE4}), \\
\mathbf{X}_{BB} = \boldsymbol{\lambda}_{BB} f_{BB} + \mathbf{e}_{BB} \\
\quad = (\lambda_{BB1}, \lambda_{BB2}, \lambda_{BB3}, \lambda_{BB4}, \lambda_{BB5}) f_{BB} \\
\qquad + (e_{BB1}, e_{BB2}, e_{BB3}, e_{BB4}, e_{BB5}), \\
\mathbf{X}_{SC} = \boldsymbol{\lambda}_{SC} f_{SC} + \mathbf{e}_{SC} \\
\quad = (\lambda_{SC1}, \lambda_{SC2}, \lambda_{SC3}) f_{SC} + (e_{SC1}, e_{SC2}, e_{SC3}), \\
\mathbf{X}_{SE} = \boldsymbol{\lambda}_{SE} f_{SE} + \mathbf{e}_{SE} \\
\quad = (\lambda_{SE1}, \lambda_{SE2}, \lambda_{SE3}, \lambda_{SE4}) f_{SE} + (e_{SE1}, e_{SE2}, e_{SE3}, e_{SE4}), \\
\mathbf{X}_{SB} = \boldsymbol{\lambda}_{SB} f_{SB} + \mathbf{e}_{SB} \\
\quad = (\lambda_{SB1}, \lambda_{SB2}, \lambda_{SB3}, \lambda_{SB4}, \lambda_{SB5}) f_{SB} \\
\qquad + (e_{SB1}, e_{SB2}, e_{SB3}, e_{SB4}, e_{SB5}).
\end{cases}
\tag{2}
$$

As in factor analysis, $\boldsymbol{\lambda}$ represents a vector of factor loadings and is estimated in the measurement equation model (2). We also derive the estimates of the latent factors f_{Fk}, f_{Bk} and f_{Sk} $(k = C, E, A)$ in the model.

We specify second-order SEM as the structural equation model for $\{H1, H2\}$. Then, the model is described as follows:

$$
\begin{cases}
f_{BCE} = \beta_{FCE} f_{FCE} + e_{BCE}, \\
f_{SCE} = \beta_{BCE} f_{BCE} + e_{SCE},
\end{cases}
\tag{3}
$$

where β_{FCE} and β_{BCE} are directed path coefficients, and e_{BCE} and e_{SCE} are errors associated with the latent factors. These coefficients and errors are computed in the model (3).

Table 2 presents observed variables and latent factors related to the involvement of Fashion, Brand and Sales assistant. The observed variables for each involvement are associated with importance, excitement and attractiveness. We denote the variables as Y_{**I} for importance, Y_{**E} for excitement and Y_{**A} for attractiveness in each involvement.

We give the measurement equation model:

$$
\begin{cases}
\mathbf{Y}_{FI} = \boldsymbol{\lambda}_{FI} f_{FI} + \mathbf{e}_{FI} \\
\quad = (\lambda_{FII}, \lambda_{FIE}, \lambda_{FIA}) f_{FI} + (e_{FII}, e_{FIE}, e_{FIA}), \\
\mathbf{Y}_{BI} = \boldsymbol{\lambda}_{BI} f_{BI} + \mathbf{e}_{BI} \\
\quad = (\lambda_{BII}, \lambda_{BIE}, \lambda_{BIA}) f_{BI} + (e_{BII}, e_{BIE}, e_{BIA}), \\
\mathbf{Y}_{SI} = \boldsymbol{\lambda}_{SI} f_{SI} + \mathbf{e}_{SI} \\
\quad = (\lambda_{SII}, \lambda_{SIE}, \lambda_{SIA}) f_{BI} + (e_{SII}, e_{SIE}, e_{SIA}).
\end{cases}
\tag{4}
$$

Table 2. Observed variables and latent factors with involvement.

Object	Factor	Observed variables
Fashion	f_{FI}	$\mathbf{Y}_{FI} = (Y_{FII}, Y_{FIE}, Y_{FIA})$
Brand	f_{BI}	$\mathbf{Y}_{BI} = (Y_{BII}, Y_{BIE}, Y_{BIA})$
Sales assistant	f_{SI}	$\mathbf{Y}_{SI} = (Y_{SII}, Y_{SIE}, Y_{SIA})$

In the measurement equation model (4), we estimate the vectors of factor loadings $\boldsymbol{\lambda}_{FI}$, $\boldsymbol{\lambda}_{BI}$ and $\boldsymbol{\lambda}_{SI}$ and the latent factors f_{FI}, f_{BI} and f_{SI}. The structural equation model for $\{H3, H4\}$ is given by

$$\begin{cases} f_{BI} = \beta_{FI} f_{FI} + e_{BI}, \\ f_{SI} = \beta_{BI} f_{BI} + e_{SI}. \end{cases}$$

We describe the structural equation model investigating the effect of involvement on CE for $\{H1, H2, H5\}$:

$$\begin{cases} f_{FCE} = \gamma_{FFI} f_{FI} + \gamma_{FBI} f_{BI} + \gamma_{FSI} f_{SI} + e_{FCE}, \\ f_{BCE} = \gamma_{BFI} f_{FI} + \gamma_{BBI} f_{BI} + \gamma_{BSI} f_{SI} + \gamma_{FCE} f_{FCE} + e_{BCE}, \\ f_{SCE} = \gamma_{SFI} f_{FI} + \gamma_{SBI} f_{BI} + \gamma_{SSI} f_{SI} + \gamma_{BCE} f_{BCE} + e_{SCE}. \end{cases} \quad (5)$$

The path coefficients $\gamma_{FI} = (\gamma_{FFI}, \gamma_{BFI}, \gamma_{SFI})$, $\gamma_{BI} = (\gamma_{FBI}, \gamma_{BBI}, \gamma_{SBI})$ and $\gamma_{SI} = (\gamma_{FSI}, \gamma_{BSI}, \gamma_{SSI})$ represent the causal effects of the latent factors of involvement on the latent factors of CE and are related to $H5$. The coefficients γ_{FCE} and γ_{BCE} are directed paths associated with $\{H1, H2\}$. In the structural equation model (5), we compute these coefficients and errors e_{FCE}, e_{BCE} and e_{SCE}.

3.2 Structural Equation Modeling with Optimal Scaling

Likert scale data are not exactly quantitative data but ordinal qualitative data. In SEM, Likert scale data are treated as quantitative data and are assumed to be approximately normal distributed. When they do not resemble a normal distribution, applying SEM to the data may not be appropriate. Then, we employ quantification methods. Optimal scaling is a quantification technique and can nonlinearly transform such ordered qualitative data into quantitative data. Nonlinear principal component analysis (NPCA) of Young et al. [11] is PCA with the optimal scaling. Appendix A introduces NPCA and gives the alternative least squares (ALS) algorithm used in NPCA.

NPCA obtains optically scaled data and computes principal component scores of the data. The measurement equation model replaces factor analysis with NPCA and treats principal component scores as observed data. Therefore, we do not examine the relationship between latent factors and observed variables in factor analysis but instead construct composite variables of observed variables in NPCA. This approach is referred to as NPCA-SEM (Kuroda et al. [7]).

Let $\mathbf{x}$ denote the observed Likert scale data. NPCA obtains optimally scaled data $\mathbf{x}^*$ by quantifying $\mathbf{x}$ and computes a vector of principal component scores $\mathbf{z}$ and a component loading vector $\mathbf{a}$ on $r = 1$ component. The ALS algorithm finds the least squares estimates of $\mathbf{x}^*$, $\mathbf{z}$ and $\mathbf{a}$ by minimizing the loss function $\sigma(\mathbf{z}, \mathbf{a}, \mathbf{x}^*)$ defined by Equation (7). Then, the loss function for each object is given as follows:

– Fashion:

$$\sigma_F = \sigma(\mathbf{z}_{FC}, \mathbf{a}_{FC}, \mathbf{x}^*_{FC}) + \sigma(\mathbf{z}_{FE}, \mathbf{a}_{FE}, \mathbf{x}^*_{FE}) + \sigma(\mathbf{z}_{FB}, \mathbf{a}_{FB}, \mathbf{x}^*_{FB}).$$

– Brand:

$$\sigma_B = \sigma(\mathbf{z}_{BC}, \mathbf{a}_{BC}, \mathbf{x}^*_{BC}) + \sigma(\mathbf{z}_{BE}, \mathbf{a}_{BE}, \mathbf{x}^*_{BE}) + \sigma(\mathbf{z}_{BB}, \mathbf{a}_{BB}, \mathbf{x}^*_{BB}).$$

– Sales assistant:

$$\sigma_S = \sigma(\mathbf{z}_{SC}, \mathbf{a}_{SC}, \mathbf{x}^*_{SC}) + \sigma(\mathbf{z}_{SE}, \mathbf{a}_{SE}, \mathbf{x}^*_{SE}) + \sigma(\mathbf{z}_{SB}, \mathbf{a}_{SB}, \mathbf{x}^*_{SB}).$$

Let the composite variables of $(\mathbf{X}_{FC}, \mathbf{X}_{FE}, \mathbf{X}_{FB})$, $(\mathbf{X}_{BC}, \mathbf{X}_{BE}, \mathbf{X}_{BB})$ and $(\mathbf{X}_{SC}, \mathbf{X}_{SE}, \mathbf{X}_{SB})$ denote as $\mathbf{Z}_F = (Z_{FC}, Z_{FE}, Z_{FB})$, $\mathbf{Z}_B = (Z_{BC}, Z_{BE}, Z_{BB})$ and $\mathbf{Z}_S = (Z_{SC}, Z_{SE}, Z_{SB})$, respectively. Principal component scores are the values of the composite variables. Then, the measurement equation model (2) is replaced with the following one:

$$\begin{cases} \mathbf{Z}_F = \boldsymbol{\eta}_F f_{FCE} + \mathbf{e}_F = (\eta_{FC}, \eta_{FE}, \eta_{FB}) f_{FCE} + (e_{FC}, e_{FE}, e_{FB}), \\ \mathbf{Z}_B = \boldsymbol{\eta}_B f_{BCE} + \mathbf{e}_B = (\eta_{BC}, \eta_{BE}, \eta_{BB}) f_{BCE} + (e_{BC}, e_{BE}, e_{BB}), \\ \mathbf{Z}_S = \boldsymbol{\eta}_S f_{SCE} + \mathbf{e}_S = (\eta_{SC}, \eta_{SE}, \eta_{SB}) f_{SCE} + (e_{SC}, e_{SE}, e_{SB}). \end{cases}$$

Factor analysis computes the vectors of factor loadings $\boldsymbol{\eta}_F$, $\boldsymbol{\eta}_B$ and $\boldsymbol{\eta}_S$ for $\mathbf{Z}_F$, $\mathbf{Z}_B$ and $\mathbf{Z}_S$. Equation (3) is used as the structural equation model for $\{H1, H2\}$. We give the procedure of NPCA-SEM for each hypothesis.

NPCA-SEM for $\{H1, H2\}$ We show NPCA-SEM for $\{H1, H2\}$.

– **NPCA:** Compute matrices of principal component scores $\mathbf{z}_F = (\mathbf{z}_{FC}, \mathbf{z}_{FE}, \mathbf{z}_{FB})$, $\mathbf{z}_B = (\mathbf{z}_{BC}, \mathbf{z}_{BE}, \mathbf{z}_{BB})$ and $\mathbf{z}_S = (\mathbf{z}_{SC}, \mathbf{z}_{SE}, \mathbf{z}_{SB})$ using the ALS algorithm. Obtain $(\mathbf{z}_F, \mathbf{z}_B, \mathbf{z}_S)$ as observed data.
– **SEM:** Estimate $(f_{FCE}, f_{BCE}, f_{SCE})$ using $(\mathbf{z}_F, \mathbf{z}_B, \mathbf{z}_S)$ in the measurement equation model. Compute $(\beta_{FCE}, \beta_{BCE})$ in the structural equation model.

NPCA-SEM for $\{H3, H4\}$ Let $\mathbf{y}^*_{FI}$, $\mathbf{y}^*_{BI}$ and $\mathbf{y}^*_{SI}$ represent the optimally scaled data of the observed variables in Table 2. NPCA computes the vectors of principal component scores of $\mathbf{y}^*_{FI}$, $\mathbf{y}^*_{BI}$ and $\mathbf{y}^*_{SI}$. We denote these vectors as $\mathbf{w}_{FI}$, $\mathbf{w}_{BI}$ and $\mathbf{w}_{SI}$. NPCA-SEM for involvement is similar to that for CE and is given as follows:

- **NPCA:** Compute the vectors of principal component scores $\mathbf{w}_{FI}$, $\mathbf{w}_{BI}$ and $\mathbf{w}_{SI}$ using the ALS algorithm. Obtain $(\mathbf{w}_{FI}, \mathbf{w}_{BI}, \mathbf{w}_{SI})$ as observed data.
- **SEM:** Estimate (f_{FI}, f_{BI}, f_{SI}) using $(\mathbf{w}_{FI}, \mathbf{w}_{BI}, \mathbf{w}_{SI})$ in the measurement equation model. Compute $(\beta_{FI}, \beta_{BI}, \beta_{SI})$ in the structural equation model.

NPCA-SEM for $\{H1, H2, H5\}$ SEM describes the interplay between CEs and involvements. NPCA computes matrices and vectors of principal component scores of the optimally scaled data. SEM estimates latent factors in the measurement equation model and path coefficients among latent factors in the structural equation model. Then, NPCA-SEM is given as follows:

- **NPCA:** Compute $\mathbf{z}_F$, $\mathbf{z}_B$ and $\mathbf{z}_S$ for $\{H1, H2\}$, and $\mathbf{w}_{FI}$, $\mathbf{w}_{BI}$ and $\mathbf{w}_{SI}$ for $\{H3, H4\}$ using the ALS algorithm. Obtain $(\mathbf{z}_F, \mathbf{z}_B, \mathbf{z}_S)$ and $(\mathbf{w}_{FI}, \mathbf{w}_{BI}, \mathbf{w}_{SI})$ as observed data.
- **SEM:** Estimate $(f_{FCE}, f_{BCE}, f_{SCE})$ for $\{H1, H2\}$ using $(\mathbf{z}_F, \mathbf{z}_B, \mathbf{z}_S)$, and (f_{FI}, f_{BI}, f_{SI}) for $\{H3, H4\}$ using $(\mathbf{w}_{FI}, \mathbf{w}_{BI}, \mathbf{w}_{SI})$ in the measurement equation model. Compute $(\gamma_{FCE}, \gamma_{BCE}, \gamma_{FI}, \gamma_{BI}, \gamma_{SI})$ for $\{H1, H2, H5\}$ in the structural equation model.

4   Data Analysis and Results

We collected data related to CE and involvement in January 2018 through an online survey of members registered with an internet research company and enjoying fashion. Responses were obtained from 263 males and 234 females. Likert scales, as provided in Hollebeek et al. [4], were used to measure CE and involvement. Likert scales for all variables have five levels. We apply SEM and NPCA-SEM to the data. SEM is performed by the R package lavaan of Rosseel [10]. The R package homals of de Leeuw and Mair [2] computes principal component scores in NPCA.

We check the normality of the data using a skewness test. Table 3 shows the skewness of the data of involvement. The results indicate that none of the data are normally distributed. We obtained the same results for the data of CE. Therefore, the use of maximum likelihood estimation is not appropriate for the data. The robust maximum likelihood estimation method is applicable to second-order SEM, and the robust weighted least squares method is available for NPCA-SEM.

Table 3. Skewness of the data of involvement.

	Fashion			Brand			Sales assistant	
	skewness	p-value		skewness	p-value		skewness	p-value
Y_{FII}	1.200	0.000	Y_{BII}	0.961	0.000	Y_{SII}	0.445	0.000
Y_{FIE}	0.776	0.000	Y_{BIE}	0.736	0.000	Y_{SIE}	0.285	0.000
Y_{FIA}	1.178	0.000	Y_{BIA}	1.345	0.000	Y_{SIA}	0.678	0.000

Figure 4 shows the standardized parameter estimates of the structural equation model for $\{H1, H2, H5\}$ obtained from second-order SEM. The asterisk in the figure indicates a statistically significant difference at $p < 0.05$. Therefore, we can not find (i) the effect of involvement with Fashion on CE with Sales assistant, (ii) the effect of involvement with Brand on CE with Fashion, (iii) the effect of involvement with Sales assistant on CE with Fashion and (iv) the effect of involvement with Sales assistant on CE with Brand.

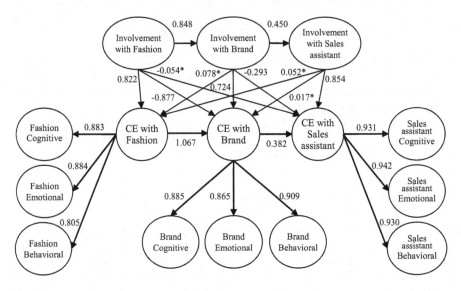

Fig. 4. The standardized parameter estimates of the structural equation model for $\{H1, H2, H5\}$ obtained from second-order SEM.

We apply NPCA-SEM to fit the conceptual model for $\{H1, H2, H5\}$. The optimal scaling in NPCA assigns numerical values to Likert scale levels. The values are called category quantification. Table 4 shows the category quantifications for the data of involvement $\mathbf{y}_{FI}$, $\mathbf{y}_{BI}$ and $\mathbf{y}_{SI}$. The five levels Likert scales are replaced with the corresponding category quantifications. For example, Levels 3 to 5 in $\mathbf{q}_{FII}$ are assigned the same category quantification value of 0.02. This means that the five level Likert scale data are replaced with three values data, such as -0.02, 0.01 and 0.02.

In NPCA-SEM, NPCA computes the principal component scores of the optimally scaled data of the category quantifications, and SEM estimates the latent factors and path coefficients using these scores as observed data. Note that NPCA-SEM does not need to estimate the parameters of the measurement equation model in second-order SEM, and thus, its number of parameters is much fewer than that of the SEM. Figure 5 represents the standardized parameter estimates of the structural equation model for $\{H1, H2, H5\}$ obtained from

Table 4. Category quantifications for $\mathbf{y}_{FI}$, $\mathbf{y}_{BI}$ and $\mathbf{y}_{SI}$.

Level	q_{FII}	q_{FIE}	q_{FIA}	q_{BII}	q_{BIE}	q_{BIA}	q_{SII}	q_{SIE}	q_{SIA}
1	−0.02	−0.02	−0.01	0.02	0.02	0.01	−0.01	−0.02	−0.01
2	0.01	0.00	0.02	−0.01	−0.00	−0.01	−0.01	−0.01	−0.01
3	0.02	0.02	0.03	−0.03	−0.02	−0.03	0.00	0.00	0.00
4	0.02	0.02	0.04	−0.03	−0.02	−0.03	0.01	0.00	0.01
5	0.02	0.04	0.04	−0.04	−0.04	−0.05	0.05	0.05	0.05

NPC-SEM. We can not identify the effects (i), (iii) and (iv) as shown in the second-order SEM.

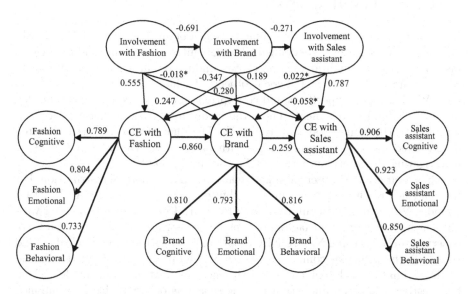

Fig. 5. The standardized parameter estimates of the structural equation model for $\{H1, H2, H5\}$ obtained from NPCA-SEM.

We measure the goodness of fit of the conceptual model to the data by using indexes SRMR, RMSEA, GFI and AGFI. Table 5 shows the index values of the conceptual models for $\{H1, H2\}$, $\{H3, H4\}$ and $\{H1, H2, H5\}$ obtained from second-order SEM and NPCA-SEM. We see that all index values of NPCA-SEM are better than those of second-order SEM. The results illustrate that the use of the principal component scores as observed data can improve the goodness of fit of the models to the data.

Table 5. Index values of goodness of fit of the conceptual models for $\{H1, H2\}$, $\{H3, H4\}$ and $\{H1, H2, H5\}$ obtained from second-order SEM and NPCA-SEM.

	Hypothesis	SRMR	RMSEA	GFI	AGFI
Second-order SEM	$\{H1, H2\}$	0.06	0.06	0.90	0.87
	$\{H3, H4\}$	0.05	0.11	0.92	0.86
	$\{H1, H2, H5\}$	0.06	0.06	0.86	0.84
NPCA-SEM	$\{H1, H2\}$	0.05	0.00	0.99	0.99
	$\{H3, H4\}$	0.02	0.00	1.00	1.00
	$\{H1, H2, H5\}$	0.04	0.00	0.99	0.99

5   Concluding Remarks

In this paper, we focused on researching the effect of involvement on CE in a fashion consumption context. We defined CE as Cognitive, Emotional and Behavioral investments. In the qualitative research, we conducted semi-structured interviews with consumers and extracted focal objects, Fashion, Brand and Sales assistant. We developed hypotheses and conceptual models concerning the interplay between CE and involvement. Then, the involvement was defined as the commitment to the same focal objects as CE. The quantitative research collected data related to CEs and involvements with Likert scale. We employed SEM for investigating the interplay between CEs and involvements.

SEM assumes that observed Likert scale data have a normal distribution. For the data not resembling a normal distribution, we proposed NPCA-SEM that includes NPCA in SEM computation. NPCA-SEM does not use observed variables as indicator of latent factors but instead constructs composite variables of observed variables using NPCA. NPCA optimally scales the Likert scale data and computes the principal component scores of the optimally scaled data instead of the estimation of latent factors in the measurement equation model. Then, SEM estimates the parameters using the scores as observed data. We applied second-order SEM and NPCA-SEM to analyze our research data. The results demonstrated that NPCA-SEM improves the goodness of fit of the conceptual model to the data.

Acknowledgments. This study was funded by JSPS KAKENHI Grant Number JP21K11800.

A   Nonlinear Principal Component Analysis

Let $\mathbf{x} = (\mathbf{x}_1, \mathbf{x}_2, \cdots \mathbf{x}_p)$ be an observed data matrix on n objects and p variables. We code $\mathbf{x}_j$ of the qualitative variable j with K_j categories by using an $n \times K_j$ indicator matrix

$$\mathbf{G}_j = (\mathbf{g}_{j1} \ \cdots \ \mathbf{g}_{jK_j}) = \begin{pmatrix} g_{j11} & \cdots & g_{j1K_j} \\ \vdots & \vdots & \vdots \\ g_{jn1} & \cdots & g_{jnK_j} \end{pmatrix},$$

where

$$g_{jik} = \begin{cases} 1 \text{ if object } i \text{ belongs to category } k, \\ 0 \text{ if object } i \text{ belongs to some other category } k'(\neq k). \end{cases}$$

We find $K_j \times 1$ category quantifications $\mathbf{q}_j$ under restrictions imposed by the measurement level of variable j and transform $\mathbf{x}_j$ into the optimally scaled vector $\mathbf{x}_j^* = \mathbf{G}_j\mathbf{q}_j$. We can use the monotone regression method of Kruskal [6] for quantifying ordinal scale data due to the monotonicity restriction.

We consider PCA of $\mathbf{x}$ of n objects by p quantitative variables. We approximate

$$\mathbf{x} \approx \mathbf{z}\mathbf{a}^\top,$$

where $\mathbf{z}$ is an $n \times r$ matrix of n component scores on r $(1 \leq r \leq p)$ components and $\mathbf{a}$ is a $p \times r$ matrix of p component loadings on r components. Then, the PCA is formulated in terms of the loss function

$$\sigma(\mathbf{z}, \mathbf{a}) = \text{tr}(\mathbf{x} - \mathbf{z}\mathbf{a}^\top)^\top(\mathbf{x} - \mathbf{z}\mathbf{a}^\top). \tag{6}$$

The problem is solved to minimize the loss function (6) over $\mathbf{z}$ and $\mathbf{a}$ by means of the singular value decomposition of $\mathbf{x}$ or the eigen-decomposition of $\mathbf{x}^\top\mathbf{x}$.

In the presence of qualitative variables, we require the quantification of qualitative data for obtaining $\mathbf{x}^*$. Then, the loss function (6) is replaced by

$$\sigma(\mathbf{z}, \mathbf{a}, \mathbf{x}^*) = \text{tr}(\mathbf{x}^* - \mathbf{z}\mathbf{a}^\top)^\top(\mathbf{x}^* - \mathbf{z}\mathbf{a}^\top) \tag{7}$$

and is minimized over $\mathbf{z}$, $\mathbf{a}$ and $\mathbf{x}^*$ under the restrictions

$$\mathbf{x}^{*\top}\mathbf{1}_n = \mathbf{0}_p \quad \text{and} \quad \text{diag}\left[\frac{\mathbf{x}^{*\top}\mathbf{x}^*}{n}\right] = \mathbf{I}_p, \tag{8}$$

where $\mathbf{1}_n$ and $\mathbf{0}_p$ are vectors of ones and zeros of length n and p, respectively, and $\mathbf{I}_p$ is the $p \times p$ identity matrix. Optimal scaling for $\mathbf{x}^*$ can be performed for each variable separately and independently, and therefore the loss function (7) can be also rewritten as

$$\sigma(\mathbf{z}, \mathbf{a}, \mathbf{x}^*) = \sum_{j=1}^{p}(\mathbf{x}_j^* - \mathbf{z}\mathbf{a}_j^\top)^\top(\mathbf{x}_j^* - \mathbf{z}\mathbf{a}_j^\top) = \sum_{j=1}^{p}\sigma_j(\mathbf{z}, \mathbf{a}_j, \mathbf{x}_j^*).$$

Thus, we can obtain the minimum of $\sigma(\mathbf{z}, \mathbf{a}, \mathbf{x}^*)$ by independently minimizing each $\sigma_j(\mathbf{z}, \mathbf{a}_j, \mathbf{x}_j^*)$ under measurement restrictions on variable j. When solving the minimization problem of the loss function (7), we cannot simultaneously find the closed-form solutions. The alternative least squares (ALS) algorithm is utilized to obtain the least squares estimates of the solutions. The general formulation of the ALS algorithm is shown in Appendix B.

The loss function (7) is minimized over $\mathbf{z}$, $\mathbf{a}$ and $\mathbf{x}^*$ under the restriction (8). Then, the ALS algorithm alternates between two estimation steps. The first step finds optimally scaled data $\mathbf{x}^*$, and the second computes $\mathbf{z}$ and $\mathbf{a}$ for ordinary PCA. The procedure of the ALS algorithm is as follows:

Step 1: Obtain $\mathbf{a}^{(t+1)}$ by solving the eigen-decomposition of $\mathbf{x}^{*(t)\top}\mathbf{x}^{*(t)}/n$ or the singular value decomposition of $\mathbf{x}^{*(t)}$. Compute $\mathbf{z}^{(t+1)} = \mathbf{x}^{*(t)}\mathbf{a}^{(t+1)}$. Update $\hat{\mathbf{x}}^{*(t+1)} = \mathbf{z}^{(t+1)}\mathbf{a}^{(t+1)\top}$.

Step 2: Find $\mathbf{x}^{*(t+1)}$ by separately estimating $\mathbf{x}_j^*$ for each variable j. Compute $\mathbf{q}_j^{(t+1)}$ by

$$\mathbf{q}_j^{(t+1)} = \left(\mathbf{G}_j^\top \mathbf{G}_j\right)^{-1} \mathbf{G}_j^\top \hat{\mathbf{x}}_j^{*(t+1)}.$$

Recompute $\mathbf{q}_j^{(t+1)}$ by using the monotone regression method. Obtain $\mathbf{x}^{*(t+1)} = \mathbf{G}\mathbf{q}_j^{(t+1)}$. Check the convergence by

$$\sigma^{(t)} - \sigma^{(t+1)} < \delta,$$

where $\sigma^{(t)} = \sigma(\mathbf{x}^{*(t)}, \mathbf{z}^{(t)}, \mathbf{a}^{(t)})$ and δ is the desired accuracy.

In the description of the ALS algorithm in Appendix B, it corresponds to $\boldsymbol{\theta} = \mathbf{x}^*$ and $\boldsymbol{\eta} = \{\mathbf{z}, \mathbf{a}\}$.

We can find the detail derivation of the ALS algorithm for NPCA in Kuroda et al. [7].

B   The ALS Algorithm

We show the general procedure of the ALS algorithm. Let $\boldsymbol{\theta}$ and $\boldsymbol{\eta}$ be the parameters of a loss function σ. The problem is to minimize $\sigma = \sigma(\boldsymbol{\theta}, \boldsymbol{\eta})$ over $\boldsymbol{\theta}$ and $\boldsymbol{\eta}$. Let $\boldsymbol{\theta}^{(t)}$ and $\boldsymbol{\eta}^{(t)}$ denote the t-th estimate of $\boldsymbol{\theta}$ and $\boldsymbol{\eta}$, respectively. The ALS algorithm iterates to find the least squares estimates of $\boldsymbol{\theta}$ and $\boldsymbol{\eta}$ by updating each parameter in turn, keeping the other fixed:

$$\boldsymbol{\eta}^{(t+1)} = \arg\min_{\boldsymbol{\eta}} \sigma(\boldsymbol{\theta}^{(t)}, \boldsymbol{\eta}),$$

$$\boldsymbol{\theta}^{(t+1)} = \arg\min_{\boldsymbol{\theta}} \sigma(\boldsymbol{\theta}, \boldsymbol{\eta}^{(t+1)}).$$

Then, the estimates $\boldsymbol{\theta}^{(t+1)}$ and $\boldsymbol{\eta}^{(t+1)}$ decrease the value of σ such that it satisfies

$$\sigma^{(t+1)} = \sigma(\boldsymbol{\theta}^{(t+1)}, \boldsymbol{\eta}^{(t+1)}) < \sigma(\boldsymbol{\theta}^{(t)}, \boldsymbol{\eta}^{(t)}) = \sigma^{(t)}.$$

The inequality implies monotonic convergence of the algorithm.

References

1. Chandler, J.D., Lusch, R.F.: Service systems: a broadened framework and research agenda on value propositions, engagement, and service experience. J. Serv. Res. **18**, 6–22 (2015)
2. de Leeuw, J., Mair, P.: Gifi methods for optimal scaling in R: the package homals. J. Stat. Softw. **31**, 1–20 (2009)
3. Heinonen, K.: Positive and negative valence influencing consumer engagement. J. Serv. Theory Pract. **28**, 147–169 (2018)
4. Hollebeek, L.D., Glynn, M., Brodie, R.J.: Consumer brand engagement in social media: conceptualization, scale development and validation. J. Interact. Mark. **28**, 149–165 (2014)
5. Jaakkola, E., Alexander, M.: The role of customer engagement behavior in value co-creation a service system perspective. J. Serv. Res. **17**, 247–261 (2014)
6. Kruskal, J.B.: Nonmetric multidimensional scaling: a numerical method. Psychometrika **29**, 115–129 (1964)
7. Kuroda, M., Mori, Y., Iizuka, M., Sakakihara, M.: Alternating least squares in nonlinear principal components. WIREs Comput. Stat. **5**, 456–464 (2013)
8. Kuroda, M., Oyabu, A., Takahashi, R.: Structural equation modeling for the interplay among consumer engagements with multiple engagement objects in consumer's Fashion. In: Mori, H., Asahi, Y. (eds.) Human Interface and the Management of Information. HCII 2023. LNCS, vol. 14016, 114-126. Springer, Cham (2023). https://doi.org/10.1007/978-3-031-35129-7_8
9. Naumann, K., Bowden, J., Gabbott, M.: Expanding customer engagement: the role of negative engagement, dual valences and contexts. Eur. J. Mark. **54**, 1469–1499 (2020)
10. Rosseel, Y.: lavaan: an R package for structural equation modeling. J. Stat. Softw. **48**, 1–36 (2012)
11. Young, F.W., Takane, Y., de Leeuw, J.: The principal components of mixed measurement level multivariate data: an alternating least squares method with optimal scaling features. Psychometrika **43**, 279–281 (1978)
12. Zaichkowsky, J.L.: Measuring the involvement construct. J. Consum. Res. **12**, 341–352 (1985)

A Qualitative Research Approach to Collect Insights of College Students Engaging in A University Social Responsibility Project with Augmented Reality

Pei Shan Lee[1] , Meng-Jung Liu[2] , Le-Yin Ma[2], and Chia Hui Pan[3]( )

[1] Kaohsiung Municipal Tsoying Senior High School, Kaohsiung, Taiwan
[2] Department of Special Education, National Kaohsiung Normal University, Kaohsiung, Taiwan
[3] Department of Educational Psychology and Counseling, National Taiwan Normal University, Taipei, Taiwan
pennypantw@gmail.com

Abstract. Universities play a pivotal role not just in producing educational content but also in imparting socially recognized values to students and facilitating the integration of student youth into society. Demonstrating social responsibility, universities effectively utilize public resources to enhance their efficiency, ensuring a harmonious blend of teaching and education. In essence, universities operate as open social institutions, serving as the focal point for social policy in the region where they are located. This research focused on the project of National Kaohsiung Normal University Social Responsibility (NKNUSR) which established a cross-field teacher community and recruited college students from different departments to jointly produce augmented reality (AR) videos and went to Mass Rapid Transit (MRT) stations to promote on caring for the disadvantaged. The goal of this project is to optimize the environment for diverse groups to safely take the MRT. The diverse groups include: the elderly, young children, people with disabilities, and victims of sexual harassments. Augmented reality videos were shot and promotional activities were conducted on four themes of the safety of the elderly, the behavior of people with disabilities that may cause misunderstandings, sexual harassment incidents, and young children who may need help. Students were recruited from the Department of Special Education and the Department of Visual Design of NKNU. Seven college participants were recruited in a snowballing manner, and interested students were interviewed and invited to participate in the training. The college students participated in 5 basic stages of this project: 1. Shooting videos 2. Producing AR videos 3. Curating exhibitions at MRT stations 4. Interacting with the public 4. Completing project results. The impact of NKNUSR on students was evident in two key areas: personal development and self-awareness, both closely linked to perceived changes in civic and social engagement. Students attributed significant importance to these projects as vital learning spaces for their personal growth. Notably, they enhanced skills related to tolerance, acceptance of diverse perspectives, and foster a collaborative profile. This development extended beyond the university setting, influencing various spheres of their lives.

H. Mori and Y. Asahi (Eds.): HCII 2024, LNCS 14690, pp. 224–237, 2024.
https://doi.org/10.1007/978-3-031-60114-9_16

Keywords: University social responsibility · Augmented reality · Mass Rapid Transit

1 Introduction

The 1998 UNESCO World Declaration on Higher Education for the 21st Century mandates every higher education institutions (HEIs) to recognize its challenges, considering present and future societal needs. Emphasizing the importance of higher education for each nation or region, the declaration calls for aligning efforts with human rights, democracy, tolerance, and mutual respect. It underscores that to attain a sustainable and green economy, along with economic and social development, endeavors should focus on creative activities, enhancing knowledge, understanding cultural heritage, and elevating living standards (Tryma & Chervona, 2022). On the other hand, social responsibility stands out as a paramount competence in contemporary professional landscape, highly coveted by employers when considering graduates from HEIs. This proficiency is intricately woven into the fabric of societal expectations. These individuals are envisioned to not only work with effectiveness but also uphold moral values, embody social activism and responsibility, possess a well-defined civic stance, champion a healthy lifestyle, and demonstrate a capacity for critical thinking.

Tomlinson (2012) clarified the importance of social responsibility as a basic condition for the reflective integration of learned knowledge during the training process. The centrality of social responsibility emerges as a pivotal factor, assuming a crucial role in not only molding our worldview but also exerting a profound influence on how we perceive the world. Beyond its immediate impact on external perspectives, social responsibility becomes a linchpin, facilitating a meticulous and accurate interpretation of one's own identity. This intrinsic connection between an individual's sense of responsibility and their self-perception underscores the nuanced interplay between personal values and societal engagement. Furthermore, the significance of social responsibility transcends its immediate implications, extending into the realm of education and knowledge acquisition. It stands as a fundamental condition that intricately weaves into the fabric of the reflective integration process during training. The assimilation of acquired knowledge gains a deeper dimension, intertwining with a sense of responsibility to the broader community and the world at large. In this way, social responsibility not only shapes personal perspectives but also serves as a guiding principle for the ethical and thoughtful application of knowledge, fostering a holistic and socially conscious approach to education.

Universities play a pivotal role not just in producing educational content but also in imparting socially recognized values to students and facilitating the integration of student youth into society. Demonstrating social responsibility, universities effectively utilize public resources to enhance their efficiency, ensuring a harmonious blend of teaching and education. Moreover, they actively engage students and educators in diverse social practices. By utilizing their resources, universities contribute to the development and consolidation of society, champion democratic reforms, and establish connections with individual citizens, authorities, businesses, various organizations, and institutions. In essence, universities operate as open social institutions, serving as the focal point for social policy in the region where they are located. Universities have begun to adopt the Corporate Social Responsibility (CSR) approach in such a way that this strategy has already permeated numerous universities' functions (Adomssent et al., 2007; Ferrer-Balas et al., 2008; Latif, 2018; Minguet et al., 2014).

This research focused on University Social Responsibility (USR). Presently, universities articulate their mission, vision, values, principles, and corporate culture to guar-´antee socially responsible practices (Jorge et al. 2012a, 2012b). Within this framework, students' ethical outlook is influenced by many internal and external factors (Leonard & Cronan, 2005), fostering not only their comprehensive personal development but also augmenting their contributions through purposeful actions (Vallaeys, 2007). Based on the above reasons, the project of National Kaohsiung Normal University Social Responsibility (NKNUSR) established a cross-field teacher community and recruited college students from different departments to jointly produce augmented reality (AR) videos and went to Mass Rapid Transit (MRT) stations to promote on caring for the disadvantaged. The goal of this project is to optimize the environment for diverse groups to safely take the MRT. The diverse groups include: the elderly, young children, people with disabilities, and victims of sexual harassments. AR videos were shot and promotional activities were conducted on four themes of the safety of the elderly, the behavior of people with disabilities that may cause misunderstandings, sexual harassment incidents, and young children who may need help. The present study's objectives included three aspects. First, the research included evaluating university students' participation in the USR activities. Second, an analysis was conducted of students' perceptions of the USR practices in their university. Last, the study examined the causal relationship between the USR and students' empathy. The study adopted a qualitative research design.

This paper is structured as followed. After the present introduction, a preliminary review is presented of the literature on CSR and USR. Then, we propose the relationship of empathy and the USR, after which the study's methodology is explained. The results are given next, followed by the conclusions of research.

2 Literature Review

2.1 SR, CSR, and USR

The notion of Social Responsibility (SR) presently holds a progressively significant role, positioning itself as an integral component within the ongoing global discourse concerning competitiveness and sustainability in the context of globalization (Vasilescu et al., 2010). Despite its burgeoning importance, managerial thought has thus far failed to furnish a distinct and unequivocal concept of SR. Berman (1990) points out the formidable challenge in attaining a comprehensive diagnosis of social responsibility, emphasizing the inherent difficulty arising from the disparity between the expectations of the local community from these companies and the preparedness of these companies to fulfill those expectations.

Berman presents a detailed diagram - specifically labeled as Fig. 1 - elucidating the intricate dimensions encompassed within the concept of "educating for social responsibility". The diagram not only outlines the theoretical framework but also provides practical insights into how to effectively educate the younger generation. This pedagogical approach aims at fostering the development of social consciousness and instilling a profound understanding of social and ecological interdependence. The ultimate goal is to mold these individuals into integral contributors to their society, ensuring that they become indispensable members. Within this educational paradigm, there is an imperative need to nurture foundational social skills and cultivate a participatory understanding. Additionally, it is crucial to create opportunities for these individuals to make meaningful social contributions. Moreover, the educational strategy encourages students to delve into real-world issues that resonate with their concerns, thereby prompting active exploration and engagement (Berman, 1990: 77).

Fig. 1. The development of social consciousness (Berman, 1990: 77)

The experts from Europe, Africa, North America, Latin America and Asia concluded that the social responsibility of specific universities should be fostered promoting the preparation of specific Social Responsibility programs at institutional level, including three main dimensions: social, economic and environment CSR practices of universities. Universities have increasingly initiated the adoption of the CSR approach, manifesting a trend where this strategic framework has already deeply permeated and influenced a multitude of functions within university' operational frameworks (Latif, 2018; Minguet et al., 2014). CSR, in its essence, encompasses a holistic and comprehensive approach encompassing business management, production processes, marketing endeavors, and fostering relationships with diverse third parties, including but not limited to workers, customers, suppliers, distributors, and regional communities (Lafuente et al., 2003). When scrutinized from this particular standpoint, a company attains the status of social responsibility not merely by meeting but surpassing the expectations of a diverse array of stakeholders who are intricately affected by its day-to-day operations (Frooman, 1999; Van Marrewijk, 2003).

USR signifies an expansion of the conventional mission of the university, with the purpose of addressing economic, social, and environmental challenges by actively engaging with the community and society at large (Ali et al., 2021). This overarching concept assumes a pivotal role in educational development, contributing to and enabling positive societal impacts. USR is, therefore, a concept that is being continuously developed, including moving social cohesion to the fore as a primary objective. These institutions' proposals revolve around four key parameters: instruction, research, social leadership, and commitment (Beltrán-Llevador et al., 2014). This situation translates into a significant opportunity for change in terms of universities' strategic orientation toward social responsibility values (Bok, 2009). Vallaeys et al. (2009) articulate USR as the multifaceted influence of institutions on their surroundings, spanning organizational, educational, cognitive, and social domains. Quezada (2012) additionally posits that USR encompasses the assimilation of diverse interest groups into university administrations. Further insights from researchers, namely Larrán-Jorge and Andrades-Peña (2015), underscore the necessity for USR policies to embrace stakeholder theory. This approach aims to harmonize the diverse interests and expectations of various groups, encompassing students, professors, researchers, administration and service personnel, as well as managers (Fig. 2).

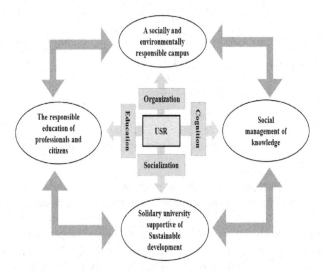

Fig. 2. Universities' Areas of Social Responsibility (Vallaeys, 2014: 95)

Vallaeys (2014) conducted a comprehensive examination of the impacts associated with universities, differentiating them into four distinct categories. The first category is organizational impacts, exerting influence on the university's environment and community, encompassing students, staff, and academics. The second category involves educational impacts, focusing on the crucial task of educating individuals while concurrently shaping their ethical perspectives and values. Moving on to the third category, cognitive impacts come into play, emphasizing the construction and dissemination of knowledge. This category solidifies the intricate relationship between the technological and social context of science and society. Lastly, the fourth category encompasses social impacts, highlighting the university's role in affecting society positively. This influence is achieved through fostering progress, building social capital, and preparing students for the challenges of the real world. Vallaeys' exploration of these four impactful dimensions serves as the foundation for delineating four key areas in the management of socially responsible universities.

2.2   Empathy, Transformative Learning Theory, and Community Engagement

Empathy is an important motivator of prosocial behavior (Batson et al., 1991; Feshbach, 1997) and a necessary condition for prosocial behavior (Sanders et al., 1978). The higher level of empathy, the better the interpersonal relationships (Coutinho et al., 2014). Davis (1980) believed that the multiple conceptualizations of cognitive and affective capacities of empathy are the basis of prosocial behavior, so he integrated the previous single cognitive or affective dimensions to construct empathy with a multi-dimensional structural model, which includes perspective taking, imagination, and imagination. Its connotations include perspective taking, fantasy, empathic concern, and personal distress. Empathy encompasses complex concepts of understanding, recognizing, and imagining, and is a position-shifting ability that can be divided into two levels: cognitive and emotional. On the cognitive side, empathy is the ability to understand what the other person is thinking as a result of an event, perspective taking, and imagination. Perceptual perspective taking is the ability to understand the person's internal experience, to put oneself in the other person's shoes, and to experience the other person's feelings as if they were one's own. Social perspective taking is the ability to recognize the thoughts, motives, or social behaviors and feelings of others. Imagination is the ability to project subjective states imaginatively onto characters in fictional situations, to imagine one's own feelings and behaviors as a result of various characters in books, movies, and novels, and to understand other people's situations or feelings.

On the emotional side, empathy is the ability to see the other person's expression or body language, etc., that is, the ability to understand the other person's current feelings and emotional state, to understand, predict and describe the other person's feelings and reactions, and to experience substitutive emotions, and "empathic care" and "personal distress" are the measurements of this ability. "Empathetic Care" is the tendency to show concern and sympathy for others' distress or misfortune from the perspective of others. The empathetic feelings that arise from the internal reaction of being motivated to relieve the suffering of others, which is directed by others. The empathic behavior of caring for others in response to experienced feelings. "Personal distress" refers to self-oriented negative emotions that are triggered by the negative emotional state of another person, in which one observes the emotions of another person's negative experience from one's own point of view, and the anxiety of the other person causes one to feel tense and anxious, making it difficult for one to calm down.

The process of community engagement, followed by reflection on personal experiences and a critical assessment of values and beliefs, aligns with Jack Mezirow's transformative learning theory. First proposed in 1978 and refined in the 1990s, Mezirow's theory serves as a foundational framework for understanding the outcomes observed in the current study. This theory consists of 10 phases of transformative development, wherein individuals integrate previous perspectives, beliefs, assumptions, and values, ultimately leading to the formation of new paradigms of thinking (Mezirow, 1978; Mezirow, 1991; Mezirow, 1995). Mezirow (1997) proposed that transformative learning is a process that triggers a change in the frame of reference, which is a meaning perspective, a hypothetical structure through which we make sense of experience, and which consists of habits of mind and their resulting perspectives. It is composed of habits of mind and the perspectives they lead to. Habits of mind are influenced by cultural, social, educational, economic, political, or psychological factors that shape our habits of thinking, feeling, and acting, and habits of mind are linked to particular perspectives, beliefs, value judgments, attitudes, and emotions that shape particular interpretations. In Furze and colleagues (2011) study, university students' reflections from community engagement experiences provided a greater understanding of how their perceptions about themselves and their professional role in society were transformed through experiential learning. Students demonstrated a more in-depth cognitive understanding of the role and responsibility of their future jobs in meeting a community need. They also found that the number of times they participate in the community affects self-insight and reflection.

In this study, participants were initially exposed to people who were at risk of experiencing distress on public transportation, who were suffering physically or emotionally, and many of the people who witnessed the scene may not have known how to react in the beginning. Our study participants noted that these diverse populations were exposed to danger while riding public transportation, which is supposed to be safe, and that each participant had family members or friends who were likely to be similarly situated. As a result, they were engaged in the process of identifying ways to help and were tasked with helping to conceptualize and advocate for ways to move from facing a dilemma to breaking through it.

3   Research Context and Methodology

3.1   Participants

This research was carried out in the context of the project of NKNUSR, composed of teams of teachers and students from multiple departments of National Kaohsiung Normal University (NKNU) in southern Taiwan. NKNUSR Involving students, teachers, researchers, and staff members as active agents in their universities, and professors from nearby Pingtung University and Shu-Te University of Science and Technology were invited to participate. This innovative project, based on experiential learning and student-centered learning, provided a unique opportunity to complement students' training by acquiring USR skills and other transversal and transferable competences. We aimed to develop a design to assist USR students in developing a community engagement project. This project consisted of five basic stages: 1. Shooting videos 2. Producing AR videos 3. Curating exhibitions at MRT stations 4. Interacting with the public 5. Completing project results.

Participants were recruited from the department of special education and the department of visual design of NKNU in the southern region of Taiwan. Seven college participants were recruited in a snowballing manner, and interested students were interviewed and invited to participate in the training. The rationale for the student training was a reference framework for USR (Bokhari, 2017) based on four benchmarks: 1. Research, teaching, support for learning, and public engagement; 2. Governance; 3. Environmental and societal sustainability and 4. Fair practices. The whole project involved two phases. In the first phase, all the student participants attended, in their host institution, intensive training based on the concepts of USR, auditing, research methods, and techniques. The curricula of this intensive training were conjointly developed by trainers from the three universities during training at the NKNU at the outset of the project. In the second phase, Students participated in groups, discussed the project activities, and conducted social participation work.

3.2 Interview

This study aimed to understand, more broadly, how students perceived the impact of participation in the NKNUSR, in general, in the development of their academic, civic, and professional lives. The project used individual interview discussions to address specifically the experience of students who participated in the NKNUSR audit exercises. Participants involved all the NKNUSR students who agreed, voluntarily, through written informed consent, to share their self-assessment reports (SAR) and to participate in individual interviews conducted immediately after the audits or after the completion of the assessment procedure. The majority of the participants were female (71.43%) and the medium age was 21.14 years (SD = 1.1 years); as seen on Table 1 participants' academic background was quite varied. The confidentiality of the participants has been guaranteed and the use of records and data was subject to standard data protection regulations of a local university Human Research Ethics Committee. All the interviews conducted were conducted by the first author and audio recorded, being subsequently transcribed verbatim and stored according to data protection procedures and with the support of MAXQDA software for data management and analysis.

Table 1. Participants' background

		Grade		Total
		sophomore	senior	
Gender	Male	-	2	2
	Female	1	4	5
Department	Special Education	1	4	5
	Visual Design	-	2	2
Total		1	6	7

3.3 Data Analysis

In coding and analyzing the data, we took a Descriptive-Interpretive Qualitative Approach (Elliott & Timulak 2005, 2021), which utilized features from both grounded theory

(Charmaz, 2014) and consensual qualitative research (Hill & Knox, 2021). This method was chosen to allow for a straightforward coding of the participants' responses, while also looking for convergence in perspectives on the themes and categories that were present in the data.

Coders. Three coders reviewed the recorded interviews and the transcripts, then line by line to identify paragraphs that were about the termination process. The text was then reviewed to identify open codes. These codes were brief descriptions that summarized the content as closely as possible to the informant's phrasing. Coders separately made an initial judgment of each paragraph and sentence, and when disagreements were present, consensus was reached through mutual discussion.

Axial Coding and Constant Comparative Analysis. In the cross-case analysis, codes that seemed closely related in meaning, theme, or content, were gathered into categories. The coders continuously discussed emerging categories and matched and checked code lists, striving for consensus in coding. During the process, each coder wrote memos describing the properties and scope of each category as well as the relations among categories.

Selective Coding. As the coding list developed, the coders discussed and examined theoretical memos integrating ideas about the comprehensive model structure. This made the coding more selective and guided by the categories. It also allowed core categories to emerge and meta-level essences to be captured, while still retaining a relationship to all other categories and integrating them into the conceptual model. The coders endeavored to refine the final set of categories by making them non-overlapping and distinguishing them from each other.

Credibility Checks and Triangulation. Although the coders performed their coding work separately, they discussed the coding architecture and precautions throughout the process. Randomly selected transcripts were checked for a consistency coefficient of coding categories greater than .80. This step of researcher triangulation aimed to increase the trustworthiness of the analyses and to check the conceptual model against the data (McLeod, 2013; Rennie, 2006). Category labeling and the conceptual model were also reviewed and revised by the three authors. To further enhance the validity of the study, the tentative model, descriptions of categories, and included quotations were sent to two other experienced researchers for external examination. They reported that the model and descriptions fit with their knowledge and experience.

4 Results

Empirical findings indicated that the NKNUSR project catalyzed "empowering students as critical agents of social responsibility" (Coelho et al., 2017, p. 1173). This implied that all students perceived engagement in the USR project as highly beneficial for their learning about social responsibility.

"The most important thing I learned in this project was part of civic responsibility because, in the past, I always thought that the people who needed help with public transportation were mainly the elderly, the weak, women, and children, but the

film of this project included the role of autistic people, so I realized that it is also very important to know how to help the disabled people in the right way!"(Male, Department of Special Education, Senior)

The students' feedback underscored the profound impact of USR participation on their perception of the university's vision. They exhibited a more positive sense of their role as students, driven by a heightened understanding of the university's initiatives, operations, and crucial societal role: "In this project, I gained knowledge in different fields, such as multimedia, photography, etc. I also had more opportunities to interact and learn with students from outside departments or people from different fields, and through the presentation of this project, so that the public can better understand people with disabilities or other ethnic groups. Notably, some students can bridge their academic knowledge with societal context, illustrating a strengthened connection between their college education and broader societal implications, and tend to think more positively about their role as students because they were more aware of university initiatives and how they operated.

"We may have had some understanding of disabilities when we were studying in the Department of Special Education. In the process of this project, we can be more truly aware of the challenges that people with disabilities face when integrating into society, and think about how to express themselves to others. People convey the correct way of coping with people with physical and mental disabilities." (Female, Department of Special Education, Senior)

Conversely, participants generally expressed that it was a pity that only two departments participated in the project. They expressed a desire for the university to expand access, enabling more students to engage in associated USR projects. This aspiration was rooted in the belief that broader participation would enhance students' comprehension of the intricate dynamics between the university and the community.

"If the school has other opportunities for cross-domain cooperation in the future, I think we can find professors from various fields to jointly execute the entire project at the beginning of the project, and students will also be able to learn more during the project."(Female, Department of Visual Design, Senior).

On the other hand, some participants were less aware of the clear connection between the USR and the university. In these cases, project involvement was seen as a valuable avenue for providing community services, refining teamwork skills, and gaining knowledge. This approach aimed to enhance participants' readiness for future professional endeavors.

"During the filming process, I saw people from different professional fields, each with different expertise, which made me realize that acting, filming or curating are not as simple as we imagined. We also asked professors or experts for their opinions during the process, hoping to make the results better." (Male, Department of Special Education, Senior)

Perceptions of students' roles were intricately tied to their views of the University's role and their experiences in the project of USR. Those who perceived the University as deeply connected to themselves and society tended to envision their role as more active, extending beyond academia into the community. For example, the curated content of this project included exploring the needs of diverse ethnic groups on the MRT. These were usually publicity matters, but because college students were personally involved, they have different meanings.

"There are many things happening in society that we cannot notice. Through this special topic, we not only let ourselves know about the occurrence of these issues, but also let more people understand these issues. Through the explanation of this topic, I understand the difficulties of people with hidden disabilities, and it allows me to understand and treat others with a normal heart." (Male, Department of Special Education, Senior)

In the past, some students viewed university as an insular institution and did not think that they could have a voice or influence, or even serve as a bridge between the university and the community. They might tend to request only the essentials and, even when recognizing issues, believe their opinions nonsense. For these students, they first engaged in SR projects. Despite meeting academic requirements, they transcended the role of "just a student". Actively participating in projects and training, they expressed opinions and took action on significant social issues.

"I am most impressed by a group of people who are passionate about this society and sincerely hope that through their efforts, more people can recognize the diversity of the ethnic groups, and that this society can be better and more tolerant of the diversity of the ethnic groups!" (Male, Department of Special Education, Senior)

In general, students emphasized the positive impacts of active civic participation on their growth, particularly in developing knowledge and awareness of social responsibility. This involvement also enhanced their ability to identify socially responsible companies and instilled a sense of obligation to make a positive difference. Those students who perceived their role with greater engagement were more likely to actively participate in the community and contributed to various social responsibility projects within their communities.

"For example, one student analyzed the USR process as if it were the epitome of a small theater group, in which everyone is an important screw, having to do clerical, administrative, and financial underwriting and other tedious administrative work, and having to have strong patience and stable emotions, in which abstract concepts and imaginations must be gradually materialized into feasible community outreach, and the results of the entire program are presented and promoted to the public."

The impact of NKNUSR on students was evident in two key areas: personal development and self-awareness, both closely linked to perceived changes in civic and social engagement. Students attributed significant importance to these projects as vital learning spaces for their personal growth. Notably, they enhanced skills related to tolerance, acceptance of diverse perspectives, and foster a collaborative profile. This development extended beyond the university setting, influencing various spheres of their lives.

5 Discussion

It is observed that a subset of students adopts a perspective characterized by an externalized focus, which is linked to teamwork or skill acquisition on social responsibility. This orientation prompts an inquiry into the nuanced dynamics that may or may not exist between collaborative endeavors or the cultivation of skills and with the broader societal construct. Implicit within this inquiry is a discerning exploration of the multifaceted interplay between acquired skills and the ethical dimensions of social responsibility.

Moreover, an integral facet of their perspective involves a contemplative evaluation of the appreciation accorded to these acquired skills and attendant concerns. Some students underscore the importance of acknowledging the potential impact of their acquired competencies on fostering a sense of social responsibility. This evaluative framework underscores a comprehensive understanding that transcends the insularity of skill acquisition, recognizing its intrinsic connection to broader sociotechnical considerations. In essence, the complex interrelationships between teamwork, skill learning, and the overarching ethos of social responsibility. This exploration serves to enrich our understanding of the multifaceted dimensions inherent in the USR process.

References

1. Adomssent, M., Godemann, J., Michelsen, G.: Transferability of approaches to sustainable development at universities as a challenge. Int. J. Sustain. High. Educ. **8**, 385–402 (2007). https://doi.org/10.1108/14676370710823564
2. Ali, M., Mustapha, I., Osman, S., Hassan, U.: University social responsibility: a review of conceptual evolution and its thematic analysis. J. Clean. Prod. **286**, 124931 (2021)
3. Batson, C.D., Batson, J.G., Slingsby, J.K., Harrell, K.L., Peekna, H.M., Todd, R.M.: Empathic joy and the empathy-altruism hypothesis. J. Pers. Soc. Psychol. **61**, 413–426 (1991). https://doi.org/10.1037/0022-3514.61.3.413
4. Beltrán-Llavador, J., Íñigo-Bajos, E., Mata-Segreda, A.: La responsabilidad social universitaria, el reto de su construcción permanente. Revista Iberoamericana de Educación Superior. **5**, 3–18 (2014)
5. Berman, S.: Educating for Social Responsibility. Educ. Leadersh. **48**, 75–80 (1990)
6. Bok, D.: Beyond the Ivory Tower: Social Responsibilities of the Modern University. Harvard University Press (2009)
7. Bokhari, A.A.: Universities' social responsibility (USR) and sustainable development: A conceptual framework. SSRG Int. J. Econ. Manage. Stud. (SSRG-IJEMS). (**4**)12, 8–16 (2017)
8. Charmaz, K.: Constructing Grounded Theory. Sage, Newcastle upon Tyne (2014)
9. Coelho, M., Rodrigues, F., Evans, P., Menezes, I., Martin, B.: Student auditing of university social responsibility-reform through reflective, experiential learning. In: Proceedings of the 3rd International Conference on Higher Education Advances, pp. 1165–1175. Editorial Universitat Politècnica de València (2017)

10. Coelho, M., Menezes, I.: University social responsibility, service learning, and students' personal, professional, and civic education. Front. Psychol. **12**, 617300 (2021). https://doi.org/10.3389/fpsyg.2021.617300

11. Coutinho, J.F., Silva, P.O., Decety, J.: Neurosciences, empathy, and healthy interpersonal relationships: recent findings and implications for counseling psychology. J. Couns. Psychol. **61**, 541–548 (2014). https://doi.org/10.1037/cou0000021

12. Elliott, R., Timulak, L.: Descriptive and interpretive approaches to qualitative research. In: Miles, J. Gilbert, P. (eds.), pp. 147–159. Oxford University Press (2005)

13. Elliott, R., Timulak, L.: Essentials of Descriptive-interpretive Qualitative Research: A Generic Approach. American Psychological Association, Washington (2021). https://doi.org/10.1037/0000224-000

14. Ferrer-Balas, D., et al.: An international comparative analysis of sustainability transformation across seven universities. Int. J. Sustain. High. Educ. **9**, 295–316 (2008). https://doi.org/10.1108/14676370810885907

15. Feshbach, N.D.: Empathy: The formative years-Implications for clinical practice. In: Bohart, A.C., Greenberg, L.S. (eds.), pp. 33–59. American Psychological Association (1997). https://doi.org/10.1037/10226-001

16. Frooman, J.: Stakeholder influence strategies. Acad. Manag. Rev. **24**, 191–205 (1999). https://doi.org/10.5465/amr.1999.1893928

17. Furze, J., Black, L., Peck, K., Jensen, G.M.: Student perceptions of a community engagement experience: exploration of reflections on social responsibility and professional formation. Physiother. Theory Pract. **27**, 411–421 (2011). https://doi.org/10.3109/09593985.2010.516479

18. Gallardo-Vázquez, D., Folgado-Fernández, J.A., Hipólito-Ojalvo, F., Valdez-Juárez, L.E.: Social responsibility attitudes and behaviors' influence on university students' satisfaction. Soc. Sci. **9**, 8 (2020). https://doi.org/10.3390/socsci9020008

19. Hill, C.E., Knox, S.: Essentials of Consensual Qualitative Research. American Psychological Association, Washington (2021). https://doi.org/10.1037/0000215-000

20. Jorge, M.L., Hernández, A.L., Calzado, Y.: Stakeholder expectations in Spanish public universities: an empirical study. Int. J. Humanit. Soc. Sci. **2**, 1–13 (2012)

21. Jorge, M.L., Hernández, A.L., Madueño, J.H., Peña, F.A.: Do Spanish public universities use corporate social responsibility as a strategic and differentiating factor? Int. J. Humanit. Soc. Sci. **2**, 29–44 (2012)

22. Lafuente, A., Edo, V.V., Pueyo, R., Llaría, J.: Responsabilidad social corporativa y políticas públicas. Documentos de trabajo (Laboratorio de alternativas) **3**, 1 (2003). https://dialnet.unirioja.es/servlet/articulo?codigo=8566237

23. Larrán-Jorge, M., Andrades-Peña, F.J.: Análise da responsabilidade social universitária desde diferentes enfoques teóricos. Revista Iberoamericana de Educación Superior **6**, 91–107 (2015)

24. Latif, K.F.: The development and validation of stakeholder-based scale for measuring university social responsibility (USR). Soc. Indic. Res. **140**, 511–547 (2018). https://doi.org/10.1007/s11205-017-1794-y

25. Leonard, L.N., Cronan, T.P.: Attitude toward ethical behavior in computer use: a shifting model. Ind. Manag. Data Syst. **105**, 1150–1171 (2005). https://doi.org/10.1108/02635570510633239

26. McLeod, J.: Qualitative Research: Methods and Contributions. In: Lambert, M.J. (eds.), pp. 49–84. Wiley (2013)

27. Mezirow, J.: Perspective transformation. Adult Educ. **28**, 100–110 (1978). https://doi.org/10.1177/074171367802800202

28. Mezirow, J.: Transformative Dimensions of Adult Learning. Jossey-Bass, San Francisco (1991)

29. Mezirow, J.: Transformative theory of adult learning. In: Welton, M.R. (eds.), pp. 39–70. State University of New York Press (1995)
30. Mezirow, J.: Transformative learning: theory to practice. New Dir. Adult Continuing Educ. **74**, 5–12 (1997)
31. Minguet, P.A., Piñero, A., Martínez-Agut, M.P.: La sostenibilidad en la formación universitaria: Desafíos y oportunidades. Educación XX1 **17**, 133–158 (2014). https://doi.org/10.5944/educxx1.17.1.10708
32. Nunez, I.: Aprendizaje-servicio y rendimiento académico del alumnado universitário. La evaluación de um programa (dissertation). Universidade Santiago de Compostela, Santiago de Compostela, Spain (2019)
33. Gaete Quezada, R.: Gobierno universitario pluralista. Una propuesta de análisis desde la teoría de los stakeholders. Int. J. Educ. Technol. High. Educ. **9**(2), 296–310 (2012). https://doi.org/10.7238/rusc.v9i2.1412
34. Rego, M.A.S., Losada, A.S., Moledo, M.D.M.L.: El aprendizaje-servicio en la educación superior: una vía de innovación y de compromiso social. Educacion y diversidad= Education and diversity: Revista inter-universitaria de investigación sobre discapacidad e interculturalidad. **10**, 17–24 (2016)
35. Rennie, D.L.: The grounded theory method: Application of a variant of its procedure of constant comparative analysis to psychotherapy research. In: Fischer, C.T. (eds.), pp. 59–78. Elsevier Academic Press (2006)
36. Ribeiro, R., Magalhães, A.M.: Política de responsabilidade social na universidade: conceitos e desafios. Educação, Sociedade & Culturas. **42**, 133–156 (2014). https://doi.org/10.34626/esc.vi42.285
37. Sánchez, A.V.: La innovación social en el ámbito universitario: una propuesta para su diagnóstico y desarrollo. RAES: Revista Argentina de Educación Superior **8**, 188–218 (2014)
38. Sanders, G.S., Baron, R.S., Moore, D.L.: Distraction and social comparison as mediators of social facilitation effects. J. Exp. Soc. Psychol. **14**, 291–303 (1978). https://doi.org/10.1016/0022-1031(78)90017-3
39. Tomlinson, M.: Graduate employability: a review of conceptual and empirical themes. High Educ. Pol. **25**, 407–431 (2012). https://doi.org/10.1057/hep.2011.26
40. Tryma, K., Chervona, L.: Social responsibility of university: the student aspect. Uluslararası Sosyal Bilimler ve Eğitim Dergisi. **4**, 641–656 (2022)
41. Vallaeys, F.: University social responsibility: a mature and responsible definition. High. Educ. World. **5**, 88–96 (2014)
42. Vallaeys, F., De la Cruz, C., Sasia, P.M.: Responsabilidad Social Universitaria: Manual de Primeros Pasos. Inter-American Development Bank (2009)
43. Van Marrewijk, M.: Concepts and definitions of CSR and corporate sustainability: between agency and communion. J. Bus. Ethics **44**, 95–105 (2003). https://doi.org/10.1023/A:102333 1212247
44. Vasilescu, R., Barna, C., Epure, M., Baicu, C.: Developing university social responsibility: a model for the challenges of the new civil society. Procedia Soc. Behav. Sci. **2**, 4177–4182 (2010). https://doi.org/10.1016/j.sbspro.2010.03.660

A Case Study on AI System Evaluation from Users' Viewpoints

Ryuichi Ogawa[1]([⊠]), Yoichi Sagawa[1], Shigeyoshi Shima[1,2], Toshihiko Takemura[1,3], and Shin-ichi Fukuzumi[4]

[1] Information-Technology Promotion Agency Japan, Tokyo 113-6591, Japan
r-ogawa@ipa.go.jp
[2] University of Nagasaki, Nagasaki 851-2195, Japan
[3] Josai University, Saitama 350-0295, Japan
[4] Riken AIP, Tokyo 103-0027, Japan

Abstract. This paper proposes a process of AI system evaluation from users' viewpoints, utilizing quality-in-use model adopted in ISO25029:2013. The proposed approach provides a method to map service requirement components of an AI service to quality-in-use components and sum up individual evaluation results to derive comprehensive results for three components, benefit, freedom from risk and adaptability. The authors applied the process to a use case of autonomous drone, which delivers luggage with autonomous control capability and have different stakeholder groups such as service provider, service user and residents of flight area. The case study showed that mapping of non-functional service requirement components (such as safety and other risk management) to quality-in-use components, and their comprehensive evaluation worked well, providing different evaluation results for each stakeholder. Also, it showed some refinement needed for the practical use of the process.

Keywords: AI System · Evaluation · Quality in Use · Requirement-quality Mapping

1 Introduction

1.1 Problem Definition

Building trustworthiness in AI has become a critical task of AI governance to provide safe, secure and beneficial AI systems/services. AI governance has been long discussed in terms of ethics and trust, and the term trustworthiness has been used to describe items that embody ethical and trust values such as fairness, accountability, sustainability, safety, and transparency.

Since the trustworthiness concept is highly broad, its evaluation and implementation are tough tasks for AI system/service providers. The evaluation is also critical and a tough task for AI users. In order to ease the load of evaluation/implementation, AI system management standards (such as ISO42001 et al.) have been including some of these items. Also, the items have been discussed as software engineering viewpoints, which resulted in the AI extension of software quality standard model (SQuaRE) [7]. However, these standards are described in general terms so that it is still difficult to practically evaluate and implement value items such as safety, security, privacy, sustainability, etc.

If we can rightly evaluate the value items, AI systems/services implementing the right value items will be seen as trustworthy and accepted by users and other stakeholders. However, our previous study shows it can become easily complicated. Through AI system/service supply chains, stakeholders such as AI vendor, AI service operator and AI user may require different level of quality in different value items. Since the current standards are written in general terms, they may not provide enough information on how to cope with this diversity.

1.2 Proposed Approach

The authors have been proposing and testing a new software quality standard model that includes acceptability item as one of three major quality characteristics, and we expect that it can better handle the trustworthiness value items as quality components [1, 2, 3]. One major advantage of the model is that it is designed to handle the diversity by developing individual quality models for different stakeholders in different circumstances. With this model we are attempting to design the process to specify trustworthiness-related quality components, including social acceptance. The process can be a useful tool to solve the complexity problem mentioned above.

In the paper we will attempt to define a process of specifying the quality components in a use case of autonomous drone. In the case autonomous drone is supposed to fly without a human operator, adjust their flying routes along with circumstance changes. In the severest case it will take an action such as emergency landing. Just like autonomous car-driving services, this service is required to have critical quality in safety, security and compliance to regulations, as well as its benefit. For this case, flying safety is a big issue and social acceptance for the safety rules, both technical and operational, is critical.

Assuming that the safety rules/regulations are accepted, we have to check if the autonomous drone has capabilities to fulfill the regulations/flight rules. However, such regulations are often described in abstract terms and there is difficulty in designing the evaluation, which requires specific quality parameters to measure and methods to determine the rule-conformance level of the measurements. Another issue is that such rules might not fully prepared in extreme cases, such as emergency landing. Still, the service provider needs to implement the safety capability and evaluate how safe it is or to what extent it is accepted by stakeholders.

In the following we tackle these problems. We specify evaluation attributes of the drone functions. The attributes and evaluation processes are specified according to the use case with a specified service type (delivery), specified stakeholders (service provider, delivery client, residents in the flying aera, etc.), environment (geographical and weather data, etc.), flight route (prohibited area, obstacles, etc.) and rules/ regulations. We then evaluate the parameters and sum up the result as a comprehensive value of the service from quality-in-use viewpoints: benefit, freedom from risk and acceptability.

We believe that this approach provides a process of trustworthiness-related quality evaluation design for specific AI service cases and fill the gap between abstract trustworthiness requirements and practical quality implementation.

2 Model Development Based on Quality-in-Use Components

2.1 Quality-in-Use Model

In our previous work [3], we developed a trust framework for AI system users to accept AI systems and use them by evaluating their quality-in-use attributes. For this purpose, we have employed a quality-in-use model proposed by Fukuzumi et al. [4, 5], comprising three components, Benefit, Freedom from risk and Acceptability with detailed attributes (e.g. Ease of use, Accessibility and Adaptability for Benefit component) as shown in Fig. 1. Here Acceptability represents the degree of favorable human response to an AI system when accepting and using it. This model is extensible to describe quality-in-use attributes for different category of users, such as an operator and an end user of the AI system.

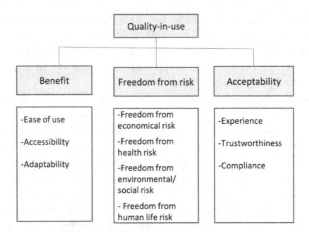

Fig. 1. Quality-in-Use Model

2.2 Trust Development to Accept an AI System

In the previous work we have assumed that users' intention to use an AI system is well explained by the quality-in-use attributes, and when the intention is enhanced by them so that the user accepts the system to use, we can say that the trust is built between the user and the system. We tested the effectiveness of the assumption by conducting a questionnaire asking answerers if they can accept a personal AI system making small mistakes. As shown in Fig. 2, we connected the system's judgment capability to 'freedom from economical risk' sub-component (since the mistake could bring additional cost) and designed a questionnaire. The result shows that if the questionnaire is well designed, its answers are valid to check the effectiveness of AI system's quality-in-use component attributes for the system acceptance.

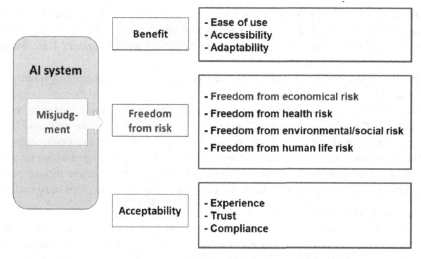

Fig. 2. AI system's misjudgment evaluated as freedom from risk component

2.3   Comprehensive Approach to Evaluate and Design Quality-in-Use Components of an AI System

The limitation of the above approach is the difficulties of questionnaire design, especially for complicated used cases in business and public/social application domain. For the evaluation of such cases, corresponding questionnaires might require answerers expert knowledge of related businesses, quality evaluation and related rules. Also, the connection between AI system capabilities and quality-in-use components could be complex and multiple. For example, the AI judgement precision capability can connect to benefit, freedom from risk and acceptability (e.g. misjudgment must not cause ethical problems) components at the same time. Moreover, such prioritization of the connectivity is dependent on for whom the quality-in-use components are designed and evaluated. For example, Privacy protection capability of AI drone which needs to visually recognize the point of landing is not a big issue for drone users but could be critical for residents on the flight route of the drone. Considering these, we need a comprehensive, systematic process to choose AI system's important service functions for each related stakeholder (system owner, operator, user, public/society, etc.), map the functions to quality-in-use components (and sub-components) based on stakeholder specific prioritization rules, and evaluate the level of fulfilment of each component (and subcomponent) in user-understandable manner (e.g. not requiring expert knowledge).

This is a tough task, since AI system application can be broad and so are stakeholder needs and backgrounds. As a starting step, we assume a case of AI drone that can autonomously fly, deliver a luggage and take emergency landing in adversarial conditions. The service includes stakeholders such as delivery service providers and service users. In this paper we attempt a thought experiment of the AI delivery drone flight to discuss how the above processes actually become possible. The procedure outline is summarized as follows:

1. Specify a service of an AI system whose service qualities need to be evaluated from user and social viewpoint. In this paper we adopt a luggage delivery service using a drone exclusively operated autonomously (without human operator). Here we say the service as 'AI drone delivery.'
2. Specify required levels of functions of the AI drone delivery that embody quality-in-use attributes of the service.
3. The function items are structured along with the service implementation viewpoint, but they do not necessarily correspond to quality-in-use components (sub-components) in simple, one-to-one manner. We need to develop a mapping diagram. The importance of function-quality connectivity can vary according to whom we want to design and evaluate the quality. For example, the quality for drone service owner and the quality for AI delivery users are different. Therefore, our steps must include:

   • Separate diagrams for each stakeholder.
   • Prioritize the connections of each diagram based on quality attributes differently prioritized by each stakeholder. For example, privacy protection capability can be highly valued by residents of expected flight area.

4. Evaluate levels of quality-in-use fulfillment for the abovementioned attributes in comprehensive manner, such as 5 grade evaluation from most to least. As for technology-oriented attributes (e.g. precision or error rate), they can be described in more detail, but we believe this evaluation should be done comprehensively so that the result can be summed up as a total value regardless of attribute details. Therefore, we adopt a level definition that is general, coarse-grained, and intuitively understandable for non-AI experts.

3 Use Case Analysis

3.1 Outline of Autonomous Drone Service

In this paper we assume a case that can achieved in the near future with AI assistance, so that the current drone technologies and regulations (e.g. rules described in [8]) are not necessarily applicable. For example current aviation rules for UA (unmanned aircraft) usually require human operators' control of drones. Here we that assume every operation actions are executed autonomously to avoid complexity of human-AI flight collaboration and to focus on the AI related quality-in-use components evaluation.

3.2 Service Requirement Details

First, we introduce a structured list of requirements to embody autonomous drone service quality. The requirements include both functional (such as weight/size of deliverable luggage, delivery speed and frequency, etc.) and non-functional (such as security and reliability of delivery flights based on flight plans, etc.). In general, scope of the requirements is broad, and the structured list could be large. Since functional requirement evaluation are rather understandable, we focus on the non-functional requirement evaluation, regarding the following points:

1. How well a delivery flight is prepared and planned. The evaluation includes the readiness of learning to perform autonomous control with required functional level (e.g. delivery cost/time) and safety level. Also, it includes the evaluation of individual flight plan to check its compliance, safety and privacy consideration as well as cost-efficient flight route selection.
2. How well the flight is operated as planned. The evaluation includes the easiness of flight control monitoring, appropriateness of consistency with the flight plan and, if any, appropriateness of emergency operation (e.g. landing due to weather change).

Service Requirement Structure.   Figure 3 shows a derived service requirement structure. It comprises three major blocks, Learning, Planning, Flight management.

Learning.   Learning subcomponent describes categories and depth of machine learning for drone's autonomous operations. In this case we define the following subcomponents.

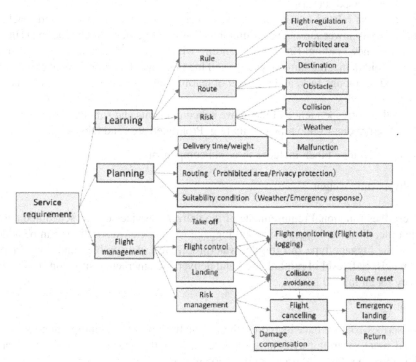

Fig. 3. Drone AI system's service requirement structure

– Rule

Fundamental knowledge of flight regulations and flight prohibited areas in the whole area of the service. Every drone needs to know the knowledge for safe and compliant flight. The regulation includes rules for safety, security, deliverable materials and their weights, privacy protection when using camera, etc.

– Route

For each delivery service learning the destination and geographical data of its route is required. The data must include machine (or camera) recognizable data of the destination, possible obstacles such as tall buildings, power lines, and machine recognizable data of prohibited areas.

– Risk

Learning risks include flight safety and the delivery material protection is required. In this case the learning is done by three cause factor, collision, weather change and mechanical (or software) trouble.

Collision avoidance learning includes obstacle (unknown object) detection via sensors (mostly camera), and collision avoidance action such as change directions or altitudes. The level of learning level can be variable based on the detection accuracy and available avoidance actions.

As for risks related to weather (such as local gust or thunderstorm) and machine trouble (such as power shortage or communication failure), the avoidance action is likely to be emergency landing. Emergency landing with safety and compliance restrictions (such as avoid damaging human, houses and luggage, avoid landing in residential area, etc.) would be a tough task, and the level of learning landing can be an issue of quality-in-use.

Note that correspondence of the above subcomponents and sub-subcomponents are not restricted to one-to-one relationship (e.g. Prohibited area and Obstacle).

Planning. Planning block includes three subcomponents.

– Delivery time/weight

Describes functional requirements of the delivery service such as scheduled deliverable time, distance, luggage size and luggage weight, etc. Restrictions can be added such as the luggage type (no fragile, waterproof, etc.), deliverable conditions (maximum windspeed, level of rainfall, etc.) and deliverable emergency situations (medicine delivery for an injured person, etc.).

– Routing

Describes routing data including the destination, proof of appropriateness of the selected route regarding avoiding prohibited area, tall obstacles and residential area where collision safety and privacy protection matter.

– Suitability conditions

Describes the degree of service coverage such as delivery frequency (available every hour, etc.), luggage type (no fragility, need waterproof, etc.), weather conditions (maximum windspeed, deliverable level of rainfall, etc.) and emergency situations (medicine delivery for an injured person, etc.). The bigger the coverage is, the better the service becomes from service users' viewpoint, but the preparation cost also becomes bigger.

Flight Management. Flight management block includes four subcomponents.

– Take off

Describes autonomous control of take-off operations, including check of drone settings/collision risks and communications with UA flight management system. All the operation data are recorded.

– Flight control

Describes autonomous control of a flight, where flight route and operations are checked if they are following its flight plan. If a new obstacle (for a temporal construction work, etc.) is detected and route correction is needed, additional operation is triggered. All the operation data are recorded.

– Landing

Describes autonomous control of landing operations, including risk detection of collision to human or things on the ground and, if necessary, triggering avoidance actions. All the operation data are recorded.

– Risk management

Describes safety/economical risk management of a flight. As for safety risk, it mostly describes collision detection/avoidance operations. As for economical risk, it describes compensation management for collision (or bad landing) incidents and accompanying human/material damages.

Note that two sub-subcomponents (Flight monitoring and Collision avoidance) are connected to three subcomponents (Take off, Flight control and Landing). Flight monitoring and collision avoidance are thought to be key safety elements of autonomous drone service.

3.3 Connecting Service Requirements to Quality-in-Use Components

Once we have a structured service requirements as shown in Fig. 3, we attempt to connect their subcomponents and sub-subcomponents to quality-in-use components in Fig. 2 to visualize to what extent the requirements can affect what quality-in-use components. The formalized connecting process is yet unknown, so we have attempted a trial-and-error style: draw arrow between them. The result is shown in Fig. 4. In the figure blue, orange and green arrows show connections related to learning, planning and flight management related, respectively.

Necessary Quality Evaluation Process. This connection relationship implies a simple way to evaluate quality-in-use subcomponents by summing up evaluation results of thus connected requirement subcomponents (and sub-subcomponents) or calculating an average value of the related evaluation results. In order to allow the summation and averaging, evaluation process of the requirement fulfillment needs to be common throughout the requirement components. One simple way is describing the degree of fulfillment for each required function (e.g. using 5 stage evaluation). Note that the degree of fulfillment could be expressed in meaningful manner. For example, the degree of learning can be presented by the coverage of learning (e.g. manageable legal issues

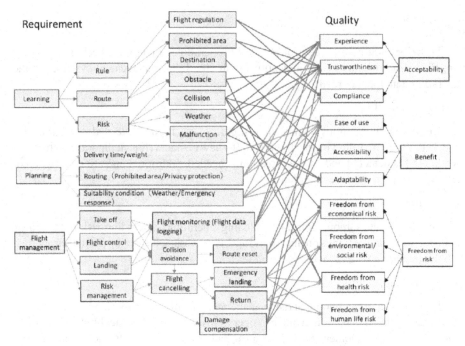

Fig. 4. Connecting drone service requirements and quality-in-use components

including privacy, obstacles, and risks etc.), so it would be useful to define fulfillment levels with thus specified learning areas.

On the other hand, this map is too simple for practical quality-in-use evaluation and analysis. For example, the current map is ignoring the prioritization of connections. The connection priority can vary along with at whom the quality-in-use evaluation is aimed. As we have seen, the importance of quality components for drone service provider, user and flight area residents would be different. While learning rules is as important as learning risks for service providers, learning risks might be more important for users and residents, since risk management failure can directly affect them rather than flight rule violation.

Another issue is that one requirement can have both positive and negative impact on quality-in-use component. For example, a risk-avoidance or safety requirement may negatively affect ease-of-use and accessibility subcomponent. Current map does not express this relationship.

For practical use, this connection map needs to be designed for each stakeholder group and only connections prioritized for the group should be used for the evaluation. Also, it should clarify negative/positive relationship.

Implications of the Requirement-Quality Map. Here we describe some implications of the requirement-quality map creation experience.

1. We have tested the case of mapping non-functional requirements and it turned out to be meaningful, since such requirements are hard to evaluate quantitatively. This

process provides a unified framework to evaluate them in numerically ordered form and is easier compared to preparing a sophisticated questionnaire.

2. In order to design levels of non-functional requirements, comparison of operation data with criteria would be useful. Logging and utilizing flight records as criteria are thought to be fundamental for evaluation process.

3. Also, the map implies that learning knowledge and flight logs are fundamental for adaptability quality. For delivery service stakeholders knowing the scope of learning and successful past flights can provide feel of experience and trustworthiness, etc.

4. On the other hand, effectiveness of mapping functional requirements is not clear. Although such requirements can be evaluated with more precise numeric data, we believe the proposed process provides comprehensive perspective for the functional requirements. How to harmonize evaluation levels between functional and non-functional requirements would be a future work.

5. The right side of Fig. 4 (quality) comprises terms taken from ISO25019:2023, so that the term 'trustworthiness' is used in that context. However, in AI community the word 'trustworthiness' is used in different way (such as in [8]). This type of mismatch can happen when we take service requirement terms in the left side where ISO25019 terminology (those given in [7, 8]) is not necessarily adopted. Terminology used for this connection map might need more work.

4 Conclusion

We have been working on the trust building method to accept and use an AI system that makes mistakes, so that user commitment to the quality-in-use evaluation is essential. Our previous approach focused on the evaluation of misjudgment of personal AI, using a questionnaire. It worked, but the questionnaire design was a tough task. In this paper we have attempted the evaluation of more complex use case, autonomous delivery drone, acceptance of many stakeholders and social rules/regulations are necessary. In order to focus on trustworthiness related quality evaluation, we adopted a mapping process of service requirements and quality-in-use components, so that we can comprehensively evaluate the quality in terms of benefit, freedom from risk and adaptability. A case study of autonomous drone showed that the process is useful for the evaluation of non-functional requirements and some necessary refinement.

For further investigation we are going back to survey work using questionnaire to refine the process, and develop a sound method of service requirement derivation and prioritization.

References

1. Shima, S., Ogawa, R., Sagawa, Y., Takemura, T.: Quantitative measurement of the decline in quality in use due to AI misjudgment (in Japanese). In: Proceedings of Computer Security Symposium 2022, pp. 759–766 (2022)
2. Shima. S., Ogawa, R., Sagawa, Y., Takemura, T.: Impact analysis of the influence of AI misjudgment risk on intention to use AI systems (in Japanese). In: Proceedings of 2023 Symposium on Cryptography and Security (SCIS2023), 4E-2 (2023)

3. Ogawa. R., Shima. S., Takemura. T., Fukuzumi. S.: A study on trust building in AI systems through user commitment. In: Human-Computer Interaction Design and User Experience (HCII2023), pp. 557–567. Springer (2023)
4. Fukuzumi, S., Hirasawa, N., Wada, N., Komiyama, T., Azuma, M.: Proposal of quality in use in software quality. In: Kurosu, M. (ed.) HCII 2020. LNCS, vol. 12181, pp. 431–438. Springer, Cham (2020). https://doi.org/10.1007/978-3-030-49059-1_31
5. ISO/IEC 25019:2023 Systems and software engineering - Systems and software Quality Requirements and Evaluation (SQuaRE) Quality-in-use model. https://www.iso.org/standard/78177.html.
6. ISO/IEC DIS 25059 Software engineering - Systems and software quality requirements and evaluation (SQuaRE) - quality model for AI systems. https://www.iso.org/standard/80655.html, (Accessed 5 Feb 2023)
7. Ministry of Land, Infrastructure, Transport and Tourism (MLIT), Flight Rules for Unmanned Aircraft (Drones and Model Aircraft, etc.). https://www.mlit.go.jp/en/koku/uas.html (Accessed 4 Mar 2024)
8. NIST, Artificial Intelligence and Risk Management Framework (AI RMF1.0), https://nvlpubs.nist.gov/nistpubs/ai/NIST.AI.100-1.pdf, (Accessed 4 Mar 2024)

Exploring Connections Between Eye Movements and the Big Five Personality Traits

Yuya Tahara[1], Issei Inaba[1], Yukio Saito[1], Toru Hitomi[2], Takuya Okada[2],
Yuka Honda[3], and Takusige Katura[1(✉)]

[1] Tokyo City University, Tamazutsumi, Setagaya-ku, Tokyo, Japan
tkatsura@tcu.ac.jp
[2] NeU Corp., Kanda 2-2, Chiyoda-ku, Tokyo, Japan
[3] Toppan Edge Inc., Higashi Shinbashi 1-7-3, Minato-ku, Tokyo, Japan

Abstract. This study investigates the connection between eye movements, as captured through eye-tracking technology, and personality traits, specifically focusing on the Big Five personality model (Openness, Conscientiousness, Extraversion, Agreeableness, Neuroticism). Utilizing a diverse set of images with clear meanings, such as pictures of animals and landscapes, the research explores how individual personality traits influence visual attention patterns. Participants rated images based on personal preferences while their eye movements were recorded, aiming to correlate these movements with their personality traits. The analysis revealed relationships between certain personality traits and specific aspects of eye movement, such as fixation duration and gaze patterns, suggesting that personality influences how individuals visually engage with content. This has implications for neuromarketing, educational content tailoring, and enhancing user engagement through personalized visual experiences.

Keywords: Eye movement · Personality trait · Neuromarketing

1 Background

1.1 The Role of Eye Tracking in Neuromarketing

Eye tracking technology has been widely used in neuromarketing research, taking advantage of the crucial role that eye movements play in shaping our thoughts and decisions. This method is based on the belief that by observing where and how long people focus on something, we can uncover their subconscious preferences and reactions. Such insights are extremely valuable for developing marketing strategies that connect at a subconscious level. For example, a significant study by Kaneko and colleagues made use of eye-tracking devices to watch how people selected products in a supermarket's fresh fish section [1]. This research brought to light the differences in engagement between students and housewives with the products, especially how the duration of their gaze impacted their purchasing choices. Additionally, eye tracking has been shown to be effective in understanding how consumers perceive the size and color of text in ads [2], further highlighting its potential to improve marketing efforts.

H. Mori and Y. Asahi (Eds.): HCII 2024, LNCS 14690, pp. 249–261, 2024.
https://doi.org/10.1007/978-3-031-60114-9_18

1.2 How Personality Influences Observation Behavior

Recent studies have shown that observational behaviors are strongly influenced by participants' personality traits. Xu et al. [3] conducted research where subjects were asked to view photographs of faces and rate their impressions of those faces. They then collected data on the subjects' personality traits (Big Five) and examined the relationship between the areas of the face the subjects focused on during observation and their personality traits. The results indicated that individuals with specific personality traits tend to focus on certain facial regions. For example, participants with high extraversion were more inclined to look at the eyes, while those with high neuroticism tended to focus on the nose. Participants with high openness did not show a tendency to look at the eyes, nose, or mouth.

This research concludes that while facial features play a crucial role in impression formation, the observer's personality traits also determine their observational behavior, which, through directed gaze, can affect impression inferences. This provides significant insights into how personality traits influence impression formation through observational behavior.

Personality traits not only influence how we perceive others but also how we engage with visual stimuli, including abstract moving images. Research by Rauthmann et al. [4] delved into this phenomenon through an experiment involving 242 participants (172 females and 70 males) aged between 18 and 46. These individuals were exposed to a unique visual task where they watched animations in red and blue for a minute, followed by a fixation symbol. The study aimed to understand how personality affects the way we observe and interact with these animations by measuring various aspects of eye movement, such as the time to first fixation, total number of fixations, average fixation time, and overall dwell time. Participants' personalities were assessed through questionnaires following the eye-tracking session, which used the pupil-centered corneal reflex method for accurate gaze data collection. The animations themselves were designed to be visually striking, utilizing contrasting colors and cellular automaton sequences to draw and hold attention. The findings indicated a clear link between personality traits and observation behavior. For instance, individuals with higher levels of emotional instability showed a tendency towards longer gazing and dwell times, suggesting a deeper engagement or processing of the visual content. In contrast, those with high extraversion showed less fixation and shorter dwell times, possibly indicating a quicker or less focused visual engagement. Interestingly, traits like cooperativeness and sincerity did not significantly alter observation patterns. This study not only highlights the intricate ways in which our personality can guide our visual attention but also suggests practical applications, such as tailoring marketing or educational content to better suit individual personality profiles. Moreover, it underscores the importance of further exploring the connections between our psychological traits and how we interact with the world visually, offering valuable insights for both business and psychological research.

2 Objective

This study aimed to explore how individuals' personality traits influence their eye movements when looking at different types of images with clear meanings, such as animal pictures and landscapes. The research builds on previous findings about how people observe abstract videos and static images of faces. It seeks to understand if and how personality affects our perception and processing of various still images.

3 Method

3.1 Experiment Procedure

In this study, participants were asked to rate a variety of still images based on their personal preferences using a simple three-point scale: 'like,' 'dislike,' or 'neutral.' Throughout the experiment, an eye-tracking device called Pupilyzer [5] was used to monitor and record their gaze behavior. The images shown to the participants covered a range of categories, including abstract icons, photographs of animals, landscapes, and people. Each image was displayed for six seconds, followed by a 20-s break before the next image appeared. In total, 70 different images were presented, and the order of these images was randomized for each participant to avoid any sequence bias.

After viewing all the images, participants completed a personality questionnaire based on the Big Five personality traits model. This questionnaire was designed to assess their personality characteristics in areas such as openness, conscientiousness, extraversion, agreeableness, and neuroticism. The group of participants consisted of 10 individuals, ranging in age from 20 to 40 years, with a majority being male. The goal of this method was to correlate the participants' eye movement patterns, such as where they looked, how long they focused on certain parts of the images, and their overall engagement with each image, with their personality traits as identified by the Big Five questionnaire. This approach aimed to provide insights into how personality influences visual preference and attention.

3.2 Information on Personality Traits (Big Five)

The Big Five personality model is a widely recognized framework that breaks down personality into five major domains: Extraversion, Neuroticism, Conscientiousness, Agreeableness, and Openness [6]. This model has been a cornerstone in psychological research and applications since its popularization in the 1990s, contributing to our understanding of human behavior and individual differences [7].

In Japan, the Big Five model has inspired several localized versions of the personality scale. Notably, Wada [6] introduced a Big Five scale in 1996, which was followed by the development of the FFPQ-50 by Fujishima [8] in 2005. Additionally, the Ten Item Personality Inventory (TIPI), created by Gosling et al. in 2003 [9], was adapted into Japanese as TIPI-J [10], further demonstrating the model's adaptability and relevance across cultures.

For this study, the Japanese translation of the IPIP-50 was utilized, a scale based on the work of Karen Holcombe Ehrhart et al. [11]. This translation was conducted in line with Hirabayashi's study [12] and comprises 50 items that participants rate on a 5-point scale. This choice reflects the study's commitment to employing a robust and culturally relevant measure of personality traits, ensuring that the insights derived from the analysis of gaze data and personality assessments are grounded in a well-established psychological framework. The application of the IPIP-50 in this context allows for a detailed exploration of how individual differences in personality may influence visual attention patterns, enriching our understanding of the intricate relationship between personality and perception.

3.3 Eye Tracking

The study incorporated the "Pupilyzer," an eye-tracking device that uses the pupil-centered corneal reflection (PCCR) method for measuring where people are looking. This method involves capturing the reflection of near-infrared light on the cornea and aligning it with the center of the pupil to accurately determine gaze direction. The device records this information at a frequency of 90 Hz. To ensure accuracy, participants were asked to look at nine specific points on a screen to calibrate the device before starting the experiment.

4   Analysis Methods

4.1   Data for Analysis

The analysis strategy for this study focuses on interpreting gaze data collected during a 6-s viewing period of each still image. This comprehensive data set is instrumental in understanding participants' visual attention and preferences towards the images, which are subjectively rated as "like," "dislike," or "neutral." Additionally, the analysis takes into account the response times to these images and participants' personality traits as determined by the Big Five Personality Inventory.

The gaze data consists of two-dimensional coordinates tracking where on the screen participants looked, as well as changes in pupil diameter, sampled at a rate of 60 Hz. This data provides a granular view of eye movement and attention focus over the 6-s exposure to each image. The primary dataset encompasses 700 sets of observations, derived from 10 participants viewing 70 images each. The eye movement data included a significant number of error points, leading to the exclusion of data files with a high error proportion to prevent outliers in model construction. Only files with an error rate below 20% were analyzed. Instances lacking an impression evaluation within the 6-s viewing window or those with insufficient eye movement data due to excessively short evaluation times were also omitted. Consequently, the dataset for model construction was narrowed down to 400 instances, accounting for 57.1% of the total data collected.

4.2 Eye Movement Features

In this research, specific features were derived from the raw eye gaze data to analyze participants' viewing patterns. Gaze features generally encompass the count of gazing instances and the average duration of each gaze. However, the precise definition of "gazing" varies among researchers, with each adopting criteria suited to their analytical needs. Following the guidelines set by Amano and Tomime [13], gazing is typically identified when the gaze remains steady at a single point for a duration ranging from 0.1 to 0.2 s. Previous studies have also suggested that for moving objects, such as when driving, a gaze shift slower than 11° per second qualifies as gazing, whereas a slower rate of 5° per second is used for stationary objects.

For the purposes of this study, gazing is specifically defined as a scenario where the gaze's angular velocity is 5° per second or less, and the gaze remains fixed for at least 0.15 s. This definition aims to quantitatively assess the manner in which participants view images, focusing more on the act of viewing itself rather than the specific points being viewed. The 70 images used in this study were not abstract but comprised a diverse set of images with specific meanings, leading to a focus on the universal parameter of 'how' the images were viewed.

Furthermore, to enhance the reliability of machine learning models used for regression and classification in this analysis, features were selected with an eye toward minimizing multicollinearity, as evidenced by the Variance Inflation Factor (VIF) values.

Number of Gazing Points

The concept of "gazing points" in this study refers to the distinct points that participants focus on during a specified 6-s observation period of each image. A critical aspect of this definition is the dynamic nature of gazing points: even if a participant's gaze remains on what appears to be the same point, any movement at a speed of 5° per second or faster qualifies the point as a new gazing point. Moreover, if a participant shifts their gaze away from a point and then returns to a spot near the initial point, this action is classified as two separate gazing points.

Average Gaze Time

Average gaze time is defined as the mean duration spent gazing at a single point.

Smooth Pursuit Duration

The duration of smooth pursuit eye movements, which occur when the eyes follow a moving object. The benchmark for these movements is set at a maximum speed of approximately 30° per second. In this study, the focus was on capturing the duration of eye movements that did not exceed this speed, over the course of a 6-s viewing period.

Gaze Movement Area

This metric calculates the area covered by eye movements within a 6-s interval using the concept of convex hull area. A convex hull refers to the smallest convex polygon that completely encloses a set of points, in this case, the points where the gaze has moved during the observation period. By measuring the area of the convex hull formed by these gaze points, the study quantifies the spatial extent of visual attention over the image, providing insight into how broadly or narrowly a participant explores the visual field.

Gaze Transition Entropy

Gaze Transition Entropy [14] is an analytical measure utilized in eye-tracking studies to measure the randomness and intricacy of how a gaze moves across different areas within an image. This method involves identifying specific Areas of Interest (AOIs) on the image and then calculating the entropy based on the likelihood of gaze transitions between these designated AOIs. Equation (1) presents the definition of Gaze Transition Entropy.

$$H_t = -\sum_{i \in S} p_{ii} \sum_{i \in S} p_{ij} \log_2 p_{ij} \tag{1}$$

Here, S represents the set of states, where i and j denote the indices of different Areas of Interest (AOIs). p_{ii} Indicates the stationary probability at state i, and p_{ij} represents the transition probability from state i to state j. This equation quantifies the randomness and complexity of gaze movements as entropy, with the results expressed in bits. A higher entropy value suggests that gaze transitions are more random and exploratory, indicating a complex pattern of visual attention. Conversely, a lower entropy value indicates a more deterministic and predictable sequence of gaze movements. The screen was divided into four AOIs of equal size by splitting it vertically and horizontally, ensuring that there are no unset or overlapping areas within the screen. This structured approach enables a precise analysis of how individuals' gaze patterns vary in terms of randomness and exploration, providing insights into their attentional and cognitive processing while viewing images.

4.3 Model Development

The Multiple Regression Model was developed using the scores of the Big Five personality traits as dependent variables and eye movement features as independent variables, aiming to analyze how participants' gaze behavior contributes to their impression evaluations. Concurrently, the Binary Classification Model was designed to categorize participants based on their personality trait scores as either "high" or "low" By calculating the average scores of the 10 participants for each trait and classifying scores above this average as "high" and below as "low," this model leverages eye movement features to explore their influence on personality traits. Employing a logistic regression model, this method simplifies the analysis of how independent variables affect personality traits, mirroring the multiple regression model's use of pre-impression evaluation data to ensure a focused investigation into the relationship between gaze behavior and personality assessment.

5   Results

5.1   Big Five Personality Traits

The personality traits analyzed from the Big Five for each participant are presented in Table 1. There was variability in each personality trait, with different participants showing the highest and lowest values for each trait. This variation indicates that there is a distinct individuality among participants.

Table 1. Big Five Personality Trait Scores Among Ten Participants

Subject	Extraversion	Neuroticism	Conscientiousness	Agreeableness	Openness
sub1	34	26	28	40	30
sub2	27	33	44	37	29
sub3	33	39	40	35	38
sub4	39	32	42	42	29
sub5	27	28	29	36	38
sub6	16	29	35	32	33
sub7	34	28	33	41	35
sub8	18	25	37	41	31
sub9	34	27	23	36	34
sub10	28	41	34	30	26
Average	29	30.8	34.5	37	32.3
SD	7	5.2	6.2	3.8	3.8

5.2 Impression Evaluation Data

Out of the 700 responses collected from the experiment, 279 (39.9%) were "like," 281 (40.1%) were "neutral," 94 (13.5%) were "dislike," and 46 (6.6%) had no response. The response times ranged from 0.3 s to 5.7 s, with an average of 2.2 s and a standard deviation of 1.2.

5.3 Multiple Regression Analysis

The coefficient of determination (R^2) for each model were as follows: Extraversion at 0.07, Neuroticism at 0.01, Conscientiousness at 0.22, Agreeableness at 0.33 (Fig. 1), and Openness at 0.16. While Agreeableness showed some explanatory potential, the overall explanatory power of the models was low, indicating a challenge in directly correlating eye movement features with specific personality traits.

5.4 Eye Movement Features Visualization

In Fig. 2, we present how different eye movement features are related, using colors to indicate levels of Agreeableness (blue for high Agreeableness, orange for low). We observe distinct patterns in variables such as gaze duration, the scope of gaze movement, the number of focus points, and the length of time tracking moving objects. These patterns suggest that eye movement behaviors may be associated with personality traits. When analyzing the charts that compare these features, we identify two main clusters. This indicates the potential for classifying individuals into groups based on their eye movement patterns, without implying causation or deeper psychological insights directly from the observed data.

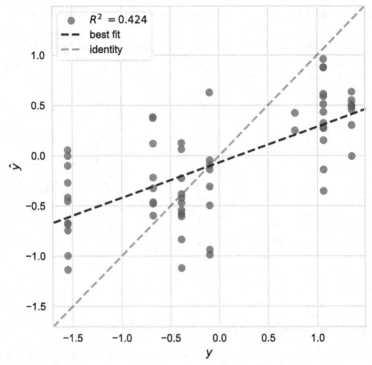

Fig. 1. Estimation Using the Agreeableness Personality Trait Model. This figure presents the analysis results of a multiple regression model used to estimate personality traits from eye movement features, focusing specifically on agreeableness, where the model fit was found to be the best. The x-axis displays the original agreeableness personality trait indicators from the data, while the y-axis shows the predicted values of each participant's agreeableness personality trait indicators, based on eye movement features as explanatory variables. Each image corresponds to one estimated data point.

5.5 Binary Classification Analysis

Extraversion. In the model that used Extraversion as the outcome variable, the results from the training data showed an accuracy of 0.61 and an AUC (Area Under the Curve) of 0.53. These results point to challenges in solely using eye movement data to explain Extraversion. This outcome is somewhat in contrast with the findings from research like that conducted by Rauthmann et al. [4], which proposed a link between Extraversion and eye movement patterns. However, such a connection wasn't clearly shown in our experiment.

Neuroticism. The model targeting Neuroticism resulted in an accuracy of 0.52 and an AUC of 0.48 with the training data, suggesting that classification based on the presented eye movement features is challenging. Similar to Extraversion, previous research by Rauthmann et al. [4] indicated a potential link between Neuroticism and eye movement data, which was not corroborated by the findings of this study.

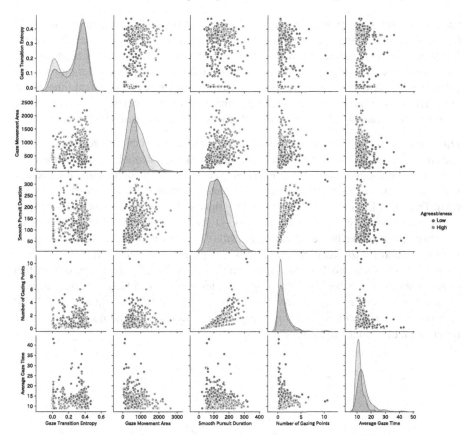

Fig. 2. This matrix illustrates the relationships among various eye movement metrics, with colors indicating levels of Agreeableness (blue for high, orange for low). Variations in gaze duration, movement patterns, and focal points hint at possible connections between eye movement behaviors and personality traits. The formation of two distinct clusters suggests the potential for categorizing individuals by their eye movement characteristics.

Conscientiousness. For the model with Conscientiousness as the dependent variable, the training data yielded an accuracy of 0.59 and an AUC of 0.43, suggesting difficulties in classification based on the eye movement features presented. A potential reason for the inability to classify effectively could be the imbalanced ratio of 'low' to 'high' in the training data. However, this finding is consistent with Rauthmann et al.'s [4] research, which also indicated no significant relationship between Conscientiousness and eye movement data.

Agreeableness

The model with Agreeableness as the dependent variable showed an accuracy of 0.75 and an AUC of 0.84 (Fig. 3), indicating the potential to explain Agreeableness through eye movement data. Examination of the partial regression coefficients reveals the following: the average gaze duration was −1.14 (p = 0.00), gaze movement area was 0.73 (p = 0.00),

Gaze Transition Entropy was −0.75 (p = 0.00), the number of gaze points was −2.18 (p = 0.00), and tracking eye movement time was 2.00 (p = 0.00). These results suggest that subjects with a high tendency towards Agreeableness have greater gaze movement areas and longer tracking eye movement times, but lower average gaze durations, Gaze Transition Entropy, and fewer gaze points. A longer tracking eye movement time, lower Gaze Transition Entropy, and fewer gaze points indicate a tendency to observe a wide area in a short amount of time, reflecting characteristics associated with Agreeableness.

Openness. In the model with Openness as the dependent variable, an accuracy of 0.71 and an AUC of 0.78 (Fig. 4) were achieved, suggesting the potential to explain Openness through eye movement data. Upon examining the regression coefficients, the average gaze duration was found to be 0.66 (p = 0.00), gaze movement area was −0.45 (p = 0.00), Gaze Transition Entropy was 0.52 (p = 0.00), the number of gaze points was 1.94 (p = 0.00), and tracking eye movement time was −1.06 (p = 0.00). These findings indicate that participants with a higher tendency towards Openness have higher Gaze Transition Entropy, average gaze duration, and number of gaze points, but shorter tracking eye movement times and smaller gaze movement areas, showing a trend opposite to that of Agreeableness. Furthermore, this suggests a tendency to carefully observe a limited range of points before quickly forming an impression. While Rauthmann et al.'s [4] research concurred with the finding of higher gaze durations, it did not align with the observation of shorter eye movement times.

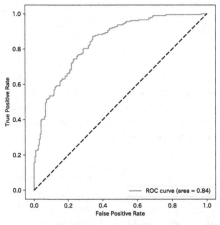

Fig. 3. Eye Movement Data Analysis on Agreeableness. This figure shows the model's performance in explaining Agreeableness through eye movement data, achieving accuracies of 0.78 (training) and 0.63 (validation) with an AUC of 0.82 for both. Regression analysis reveals that more agreeable individuals have larger gaze movements and longer tracking times, yet shorter gaze durations, lower Gaze Transition Entropy, and fewer gaze points, indicating a tendency for broader yet focused exploration characteristic of a cooperative nature.

Summary of Relationships with Personality Traits. The findings of this study, summarized in Table 7 alongside Rauthmann et al.'s [4] results, suggest that while there

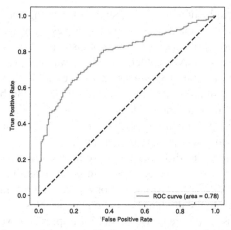

Fig. 4. Eye Movement Data on Openness. This figure shows a model's ability to use eye movement data to predict Openness, achieving 0.79 accuracy and 0.89 AUC in training, and 0.75 accuracy with 0.79 AUC in validation. It suggests eye movement can explain Openness, with individuals showing higher Openness having greater Gaze Transition Entropy and longer gaze times but shorter tracking times. This indicates a tendency for detailed observation of fewer points before quickly forming impressions, partly aligning with previous research on gaze duration, yet diverging in tracking times.

are some consistencies, differences in the interpretation and definition of eye movement metrics, such as dwell time and tracking eye movement time, indicate they share similar characteristics as total screen recognition time. These insights contribute to our understanding of how personality traits may influence visual attention and cognitive processing during observation tasks.

6 Discussion

The results of this experiment indicate the possibility of explaining certain personality traits measured by the Big Five using eye movement data. While it was not possible to directly model the scores of the Big Five traits, which range from 10 to 50 in this experiment, converting these scores into a binary format of "high" and "low" enabled some level of explanation. One reason the multiple regression models may have failed to explain the personality traits could be the lack of variation in the independent variables, as there were only eight unique values for the personality traits among the 340 data points used for training.

Among the constructed models, the one for Agreeableness showed the highest potential for accurate explanation. Regression coefficient analysis suggests that individuals with high Extraversion tend to carefully examine each point, those with high Openness quickly view many locations before making an impression evaluation, and those with high Agreeableness, similar to high Extraversion, tend to carefully examine each point. The models could not explain Neuroticism and Conscientiousness.

Comparing with Rauthmann et al.'s [4] study, the findings on Openness align, and the inability to explain Conscientiousness also matches. However, while Rauthmann et al. were able to predict Extraversion and Neuroticism, this experiment did not achieve the same results. Conversely, Agreeableness, which was not predicted in Rauthmann et al.'s study, was most accurately predicted here. The differing results, even for traits that matched, suggest different influencing factors, which could be due to the stimuli used. Rauthmann et al. used abstract videos from automata, while this study included various types of still images, including abstract and concrete stimuli, possibly leading to different observational behaviors among participants.

Another factor could be the different eye movement features used. Rauthmann et al. focused on gaze count, dwell time, and gaze time, whereas this study also included gaze movement area and Gaze Transition Entropy, potentially contributing to improved accuracy but also affecting the influence of the other variables.

The attempt to construct a predictive model for impression evaluations was unsuccessful, suggesting the inability to explain the mechanism where differences in observers' personality traits result in changes in observation behavior, thereby affecting impression ratings, as proposed by Xu et al. [3]. This study asked participants to rate images as "like," "dislike," or "neutral," differing from Xu et al.'s approach of rating impressions of individuals in images on five traits. This difference in evaluation method could have contributed to the differing results. Additionally, the mechanism suggested by Xu et al. might not apply in scenarios where impressions of images are rated simply as "like" or "dislike," as in this study.

This research indicates the possibility of inferring observers' personality traits through their observation behavior in situations requiring impression evaluations, which could have applications in marketing. By tracking consumers' gaze as they view product packaging or advertisements, it might be possible to infer their personality traits. This could enable personalized marketing strategies, such as product recommendations, by predicting consumer behavior. For instance, impatient individuals might prioritize information like price or functionality and make quick decisions, while more relaxed individuals may consider design or brand and make more careful choices.

Future studies should explore gaze measurement in actual buying scenarios, develop predictive models linking gaze behavior with personality traits, examine the impact of psychological and social states on gaze and decision-making, and expand participant diversity to validate findings. This research could improve marketing strategies by offering deeper insights into consumer behavior.

7 Summary

In this study, we examined the relationship between eye movement data and personality traits while observing static images. By generating eye movement features from the data, we demonstrated the potential for predicting whether certain personality traits—Extraversion, Agreeableness, and Openness—are higher or lower than average. Additionally, through verification with data from additional experiments, we confirmed that it is possible to apply the model to Agreeableness.

This research highlights the intricate link between how individuals visually engage with images and their underlying personality characteristics. The findings offer promising implications for fields such as marketing, where understanding consumer behavior and preferences is crucial. By leveraging eye tracking technology, it may be possible to infer personality traits from the way consumers view product packaging and advertisements, potentially guiding more personalized and effective marketing strategies.

Acknowledgments. A third level heading in 9-point font size at the end of the paper is used for general acknowledgments, for example: This study was funded by X (grant number Y).

Disclosure of Interests.   It is now necessary to declare any competing interests or to specifically state that the authors have no competing interests. Please place the statement with a third level heading in 9-point font size beneath the (optional) acknowledgments, for example: The authors have no competing interests to declare that are relevant to the content of this article. Or: Author A has received research grants from Company W. Author B has received a speaker honorarium from Company X and owns stock in Company Y. Author C is a member of committee Z.

References

1. Kondo, Y., Ishibashi, K., Yada, K.: Analysis of consumer in-store purchasing behavior using eye tracking data. J. Retail. **2**(5), 99–110 (2018)
2. Satomura, T.: Understanding consumer behavior through eye tracking. Oper. Res. **12** (2017)
3. Xu, K., Matsuka, T.: Effects of observers' characteristics on impression formation on face. In: Asia-Pacific Signal and Information Processing Association Annual Summit and Conference (APSIPA ASC), pp. 1293–1298 (2018)
4. Rauthmann, J.F., Seubert, C.T., Sachse, P., Furtner, M.R.: Eyes as windows to the soul: gazing behavior is related to personality. J. Res. Pers. **46**, 147–156 (2012)
5. NeU Co. Ltd. Homepage, Introduction of Pupilyzer. https://neu-brains.co.jp/information/press/2020/12/23/1779.html. Accessed 18 Dec 2023
6. Wada, S.: Development of Big Five scale using personality trait terms. Jpn. J. Psychol. **67**(1), 61–67 (1996)
7. Narikawa, T., Tani, I., Wakita, T., Kumagai, R., Nakane, A., Noguchi, Y.: Development and validation of a short version of the Big Five scale. Psychol. Res. **83**(2), 91–99 (2012)
8. Fujishima, Y., Yamada, N., Tsuji, H.: Construction of short form of five factor personality questionnaire. Jpn. J. Pers. **13**(2), 231–241 (2004)
9. Gosling, S.D., Rentfrow, P.J., Swann, W.B.: A very brief measure of the Big-Five personality domains. J. Res. Pers. **37**(6), 504–528 (2003)
10. Koshio, S., Abe, S.: Catroni: Attempt to create a Japanese version of the Ten-Item Personality Inventory (TIPI-J). J. Pers. Stud. **21**(1), 40–52 (2012)
11. Ehrhart, K.H., Roesch, S.C., Ehrhart, M.G., Kilian, B.: A test of the factor structure equivalence of the 50-item IPIP Five-factor model measure across gender and ethnic groups. J. Pers. Assess. **90**(5), 507–516 (2008)
12. Hirabayashi, N.: Designing a marketing framework to stimulate purchasing behavior of English learners using personality traits. Glob. Bus. J. **5**(2) (2019)
13. Amano, K., Toma, M.: Literary considerations on eye tracking with movement. Doshisha Nurs. **3**, 21–29 (2018)
14. Krejtz, K., et al.: Gaze transition entropy. ACM Trans. Appl. Percept. **13**(1), Article 4 (2015)

A Study of Factors Having Suicidal Thoughts in the Japanese

Kinoka Takashima[✉] and Yumi Asahi

Department of Management, Graduate School of Management, Tokyo University of Science, 1-11-2, Fujimi, Chiyoda-KuTokyo 102-0071, Japan
kinoka1122@outlook.jp, asahi@rs.tus.ac.jp

Abstract. Japan's suicide death rate is one of the highest in the world, especially among young people. According to a 2022 survey, about half of young people have had feelings of wanting to die in the past. In order to solve this problem, it is necessary to listen to the actual voices of those who have suicidal thoughts and understand their backgrounds and factors. The purpose of this study is to capture the events that contribute to Japanese people having suicidal thoughts from the actual text data submitted. In addition, by creating time-series data, we will visualize how the factors that cause people to have suicidal thoughts are changing. Using the data of questions posted on Yahoo! Chiebukuro, we extracted questions containing *"Shinitai"* (English: wanting to die) and conducted co-occurrence network analysis by nouns. From the co-occurrence network analysis, we were able to divide the nouns that frequently occur in the actual statements of people who have suicidal thoughts into six groups. Next, for each of the extracted nouns, we obtained the TF value (Term Frequency) over a period of time and observed its change over time in order to measure how much the word accounted for the sentences posted over a given period of time. There was a strong change in values from month to month, and no significant increase or decrease in the yearly transition was observed. Observations by time period showed that some words had higher TF values at certain times of the day.

Keywords: Q&A site · suicidal thoughts · text mining

1 Introduction

1.1 Social Issues Related to Suicide in Japan

One of the problems facing Japan is the high number of suicides. According to a 2022 study by the World Health Organization, Japan has the highest suicide death rate among the seven major industrialized countries (G7), with 15.7 suicides per 100,000 population [1]. A particularly serious problem is suicide by youth. While the overall number of suicides in Japan has declined from 1998–2011, when it had been consistently above 30,000, the number of suicides among elementary, middle, and high school students has been on the rise for many years [2]. In 2022, 514 elementary, junior high, and high school students died by suicide, the highest number since 1980, when statistics began to be compiled [2].

H. Mori and Y. Asahi (Eds.): HCII 2024, LNCS 14690, pp. 262–275, 2024.
https://doi.org/10.1007/978-3-031-60114-9_19

It is not only the high suicide mortality rate that is a problem. In recent years, the number of young people with suicidal thoughts has been increasing and has become a social problem in Japan. Suicidal thoughts are the will to commit suicide [3]. In 2022, the Nippon Foundation conducted a survey of 14,555 men and women between the ages of 18 and 29 on suicidal thoughts among young people [4]. The results showed that the percentage of those who have had suicidal thoughts was 44.8%, with the devastating result that about one out of every two young people has thought of "I want to die [4]."

The Japanese government enacted the Basic Act on Suicide Countermeasures in 2006, which was amended in 2016 to require prefectures and municipalities to have a suicide prevention plan [5]. In addition to this, in 2022, the Cabinet approved the Comprehensive Suicide Prevention Program Outline, which aims to further strengthen measures against youth suicide [5]. In this way, the government is continuing its efforts in suicide prevention, but in order to ensure that this serious social problem is addressed, it is essential to pay attention to the actual statements of people who have suicidal thoughts and to understand the factors behind them.

Suicide-related events can be divided into several stages, focusing on their different levels of risk [6]. In order of decreasing risk level, the following categories were identified: (1) self-injury (self-injurious behavior without intention of death), (2) suicidal thoughts (feelings of wanting to die without the intention of suicidal behavior), (3) suicidal thoughts (suicidal thoughts, including cases involving a concrete plan or intention to commit suicide), (4) suicide in progress (suicide attempts interrupted by others or oneself), (5) suicide attempt (survival after suicidal behavior), and (6) suicide attempt (death after suicidal behavior) [6]. Although it is difficult to determine the extent to which suicidal thoughts are psychologically defined, this study will focus on suicidal thoughts in (2) and (3), and in particular, those who said *"Shinitai"* (English: wanting to die) will be analyzed as having suicidal thoughts.

1.2 Q&A Site in Japan

The subject of the survey is the data of questions posted on Yahoo! Chiebukuro [7]. Yahoo! Chiebukuro is Japan's largest knowledge search service provided by Line Yahoo Corporation since April 2004 [8]. As of 2017, approximately 180 million questions and more than 440 million answers have been posted [9]. It is said that there are two types of people who post questions on Yahoo! Chiebukuro: those who seek clear answers and those who simply want to know other people's opinions without needing answers, with the latter being more common [9].

In addition to Yahoo! Chiebukuro, social media such as X (former service name: Twitter) are also used in Japan. However, Yahoo! Chiebukuro does not have a follow function like X (as of February 2024), which allows users to ask questions and seek advice without building a community like a friendship. Furthermore, the ability to keep one's identity private has the added benefit of allowing users to post posts related to mental health and illnesses without any personal information being disclosed at all [9].

Research on the relationship between anonymity and self-disclosure has found that self-anonymity tends to reduce anxiety, and that anonymity is more effective when participants have concerns or problems that they are unable to tell others about [10]. Another previous study has reported that in medical settings, patients are more likely to accurately communicate their own medical conditions when they are anonymous [11]. For these reasons, it is thought that the hurdle for posting serious questions, such as those involving suicidal thoughts. Will be much lower in Yahoo! Chiebukuro.

1.3 Previous Studies on Yahoo! Chiebukuro

There have been a great many studies using data from Yahoo! Chiebukuro. In a study on questions posted regarding the abuse of over-the-counter drugs, questions were extracted from the text data using the product names of over-the-counter drugs and the keywords "overdose" and "OD" to conduct a qualitative analysis [12]. In a study on marital conflict resolution strategies, questions were extracted using the keyword "marital conflict" to study the presence or absence of statements regarding the gender of the questioner and respondent, age at marriage, and number of children, as well as the severity of marital conflict [13]. In this study, the same method of extracting research subjects by keywords was applied as in these studies.

In a study that extracted trendy words from the Yahoo! Chiebukuro dataset, the frequency of occurrence of words over a certain period of time was examined from questions posted from 2004 to 2009, and how it changes over time was visualized [14]. In this study, we referred to this analysis method in the process of extracting the frequency of occurrence.

There is a study that analyzed the mental health and school refusal categories as a study of Japanese mental health issues using Yahoo! Chiebukuro [15]. However, no analysis has yet been conducted on questions that focus on those that directly manifesting suicidal thoughts.

1.4 Purpose

In this study, we will explore the factors that cause them to have feelings of suicidal thoughts by analyzing what kind of words are frequently written in the counseling content of people with suicidal thoughts posted on Q&A sites. In addition, by creating time-series data, we will visualize how the factors that cause people to have suicidal thoughts are changing (or not changing).

2 Target Data and Analysis Method

2.1 Target Data

The data used in this study is the Yahoo! Chiebukuro data (3rd edition) [7]. This data is provided by the National Institute of Informatics Research Data Repository from Line Yahoo Corporation, which distributes to us 10% of the questions and answers that have been resolved. The data collection period is approximately 6 years, from April 1, 2015 to March 31, 2021. The total number of questions is 4,865,520. Although this study does not deal with the answer data, the number of responses is also shown in Table 1. Yahoo! Chiebukuro data includes the question text, the category name that the questioner can select by himself or herself, and the date and time of the question submission, but does not include information such as the attributes of the submitter. Table 2 shows the contents of the data items provided.

Table 1. Number of questions and answers.

	Questions	Answers
FY 2015–2017	2,697,906	8,383,256
FY 2018–2020	2,167,614	5,591,283
Total	4,865,520	13,974,539

Table 2. Items included in the question data.

	Item name
1	Question ID
2	Category name
3	Category path
4	Title
5	Text
6	Date and time of post (yyyymmddhhmmss)
7	Date and time of solving (yyyymmddhhmmss)
8	Having or not having an image (1: Having, 0: Not having)
9	Type of device used for the post

2.2 Software

We used Sakura Editor (Nakatani) and Excel (Microsoft) for reading the data, KH Coder (Higuchi) and Python (Guido van Rossum) as text mining software for data analysis.

2.3 Analysis Method

The flow of the analysis method is as follows.

1. From a total of 4,865,520 questions, we extracted questions containing the keyword *"Shinitai."* This word means "I want to die" in English. A keyword search was conducted for both *kanji* and *hiragana* representations, resulting in the extraction of 7,406 questions. The categories to which these questions belong are illustrated in Table 3.
2. After conducting morphological analysis [16] of the text data with the KH coder, we created a co-occurrence network diagram with nouns. Our aim was to capture events impacting suicidal thoughts, and therefore, we focused exclusively on nouns.
3. We used Python to analyze how often the nouns displayed in the co-occurrence network diagram appeared and how they changed over time. The morphological analysis tool we used in KH Coder and Python was MeCab.

The above is the category structure defined in Yahoo! Chiebukuro, and each question belongs to a secondary or tertiary category.

Table 3. Categories of questions extracted (numbers in parentheses: n is the number of submissions, only those with $n \geq 10$ are shown)

Primary category	Secondary category	Tertiary category
>Lifestyle and love, relationships	Love advice, relationships(1495)	Family(1016)/School(509)/Friend(354)/Workplace(262)/Love advice(153)/Neighborhood relations(10)
	Way of life, life counseling(1067)	Dream(39)/Living alone, single life(23)/Senior life, silver life(15)
>Health, beauty and fashion	Mental health(242)	Depression(351)/Counseling, treatment(82)/Stress(58)/Developmental disorder(30)
	Health, sickness, hospital(69)	Sickness, symptoms(310)/Hospital, medical tests(27)/Menstruation(20)/Acne care(18)/Eye disease(16)/Dental care(10)/Skin disease, eczema(10)
	Diet, fitness	Diet(39)
	Sexual problems, advice(15)	
>Yahoo! JAPAN	Yahoo!Chiebukuro(149)	
>Child care and school	Examinations	University entrance exam(75)/High school entrance exam(25)
	Parenting, childbirth	Parenting(28)/Pregnancy, childbirth(17)
	School refusal(26)	
	Elementary and junior high school, high school	Highschool(17)/Junior high school(16)
	University, graduate school	University(14)
>News, politics, international affairs	Politics, social issues(40)	
	News, incidents	Incidents, accident(16)
>Other	Adult(36)	
	Gambling	Horse racing(14)
>Entertainment and hobbies	Prize contest, raffle(36)	
	Game	Amusement arcade(31)
	Fortune telling, the paranormal	The paranormal, occult(16)/Fortune telling(10)
>Occupations and careers	Employment, job change	Job hunting(33)
>Living and living guide	Legal, consumer issues	Legal problem(21)
	Welfare, nursing care(20)	
>Manners, ceremonial occasion	Religion(18)	
>Liberal arts and academics, science	Arts, literature, philosophy	Philosophy, ethics(16)
	Language	English(13)
>Internet, telecommunications	Communication services	Twitter(13)

3　Co-occurrence Network Analysis Using Text Mining Software

3.1　Morphological Analysis

Morphological analysis for Japanese is the process of taking a Japanese sentence as input and dividing it into morphemes defined as the direct product of notation and part-of-speech [16]. Since there is no explicit separation between words in Japanese, morphological analysis is a fundamental process in Japanese language processing that divides input sentences into words and adds parts of speech [16].

　　We conducted a morphological analysis of the sentences in the 7,406 target datasets, and the top 20 most frequently occurring nouns are shown in Fig. 1. Here, the extracted Japanese nouns were translated by English to mean as close as possible. Direct translation into English sometimes resulted in a meaning different from the original usage in the text data, and sometimes there were several candidates for English translation. Therefore, in some cases, two or more words were arranged by slashes to convey the meaning of a Japanese word from multiple angles. Since the number of occurrences was simply counted, a large number of nouns that are necessary to explain a situation, such as "I/Myself" and "Person," were represented. Next were "Parents," "School," "Friend," "Work/Job," and "Mother" also appeared frequently. It can be inferred that school, work, and family are often related to the concerns of those who have suicidal thoughts. Serious words such as "Suicide" were also relatively high on the list.

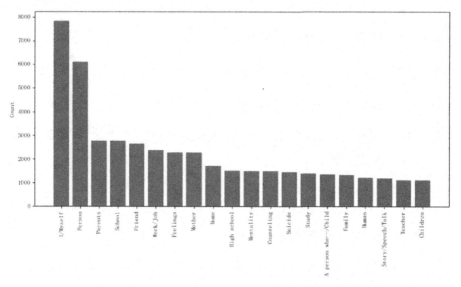

Fig. 1. Top 20 most frequently occurring nouns

3.2 Jaccard Coefficient

The Jaccard coefficient is a coefficient used to express the strength of the relationship between keywords [17]. When the sentence containing the word "a" is A and the sentence containing the word "b" is B, the Jaccard coefficient $J(A, B)$ can be expressed as in the following Eq. (1), and this is the Jaccard coefficient of "a" and "b."

$$J(A, B) = \frac{|A \cap B|}{|A \cup B|} = \frac{|A \cap B|}{|A| + |B| - |A \cap B|} \tag{1}$$

3.3 Results of Co-occurrence Network Analysis

Co-occurrence network analysis is a method to visually understand the relationship between words by calculating the Jaccard coefficients for morphologically analyzed text data and displaying the words and occurrence patterns with strong co-occurrence relationships as a diagram. The diagram drawn by co-occurrence network analysis is called a co-occurrence network diagram. Figure 2 shows a co-occurrence network diagram created using the KH coder. The size of the circles in the co-occurrence network diagram varies depending on the number of times a word occurs, and circles of the same color mean that the words belong to the same group, while white ones mean single words that do not form a group with other words [18]. It should also be noted that

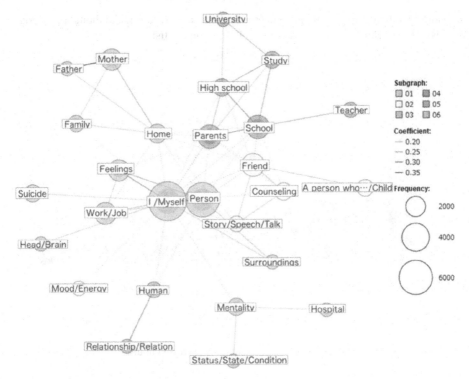

Fig. 2. Co-occurrence network diagram by nouns in the questions

the stronger the co-occurrence relationship, the denser the line of association, but the distance between the circles has no special meaning.

From the results seen in Fig. 2, we were able to divide the frequently occurring nouns into six groups. Subgraph01 consists of "I/Myself," "Person," "Feelings," "Work/Job," "Suicide," "Head/Brain," and "Surroundings." Subgraph01 is centered on "Person" and "I/Myself". Since "Work/Job" is included, it can be judged that this group is mainly for consultations by working people. Subgraph02 consists of "Friend," "Counseling," "Story/Speech/Talk," and "A person who.../Child." This is a group for consultation about friends. Subgraph03 consists of "Mentality," "Hospital," and "Status/State/Condition." Since Subgraph03 contains the word "Mentality," we can assume that it is a group for consultation on mental illness. Subgraph04 consists of "School," "Parents," "High school," "Teacher," "Study," and "University." It is immediately obvious that this is a group of student's school and study concerns. Subgraph05 consists of "Human" and "Relationship/Relation." This is a group consisting only of "Human" and "Relationship," but since the co-occurrence of the two is strong, we interpreted it as a "Human relationship" concern. Subgraph06 consists of "Mother," "Father," "Family," and "Home." This is a group of family problems.

4 Visualization of Term Frequency as Time Series Data

4.1 TF (Term Frequency)

The TF value is an index of the relative frequency of the word t in a sentence d, which allows us to determine how much a particular word occupies in the sentence. When $f_{t,d}$ is the number of times the word t appears in the sentence d, the TF value is generally defined as (2).

$$tf(t, d) = \frac{f_{t,d}}{\sum_{t' \in d} f_{t',d}} \tag{2}$$

In this study, we set the sentence d as period p and consider the index $tf(t, p)$, which represents the relative frequency of the word t in the period [14]. Therefore, we define it as (3).

$$tf(t, p) = \frac{f_{t,p}}{\sum_{t' \in p} f_{t',p}} \tag{3}$$

By changing p, it is possible to measure TF values within various time periods. In this study, three visualizations were conducted: visualization of 6-year changes in TF values by taking p every month, visualization of 1-year changes in TF values by taking p every month, and visualization of 1-day changes in TF values by taking p every hour.

4.2 Six-Year Changes in TF Values

First, we observed how the frequencies of nouns that frequently appear in the statements of people with suicidal thoughts changed (or did not change) over the six-year period.

Since the values of "I/Myself" and "Person" were significantly larger than those of the other words, and there was no clear change, we excluded them in favor of observing the change in the other words. The results are shown in Figs. 3, 4, 5, 6, 7 and 8 below.

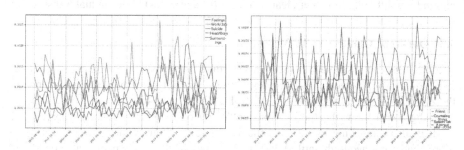

Fig. 3. Results of Subgraph01 analysis   **Fig. 4.** Results of Subgraph02 analysis

Subgraph 01 shows that "Work/Job" and "Feelings" have been slightly higher in TF values since May 2019 (Fig. 3). We judged that the number of respondents who have feelings of suicidal thoughts due to their job has slightly increased. In Subgraph02, we

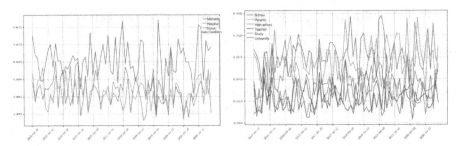

Fig. 5. Results of Subgraph03 analysis   **Fig. 6.** Results of Subgraph04 analysis

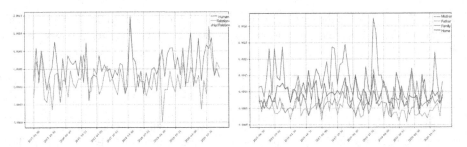

Fig. 7. Results of Subgraph05 analysis   **Fig. 8.** Results of Subgraph06 analysis

looked at changes in TF values for "Friend" and other factors and found that there was no significant increase or decrease in "Friend" over the six-year period, only a sharp change from month to month (Fig. 4). However, the TF value for "A person who…/Child" tended to be low for about two years after November 2018 (Fig. 4). "A person who…/Child" is a word that was mainly used to discuss relationship problems. "School" and "Parents" included in Subgraph04 have been taking relatively high TF values since around May 2018 (Fig. 6). "Mother" in Subgraph06 had the highest TF value in December 2018, but had lower values since April 2019 (Fig. 8). Overall, the TF values varied widely from month to month, with no other clear increases (or decreases) in the annual transition.

4.3 One-Year Changes in TF Values

After looking at the six-year changes in TF values, we considered the monthly changes to be too drastic, so we decided to look at the seasonality regarding the occurrence of these words. The results are in Figs. 9, 10, 11, 12, 13 and 14 below.

Subgraph01 shows that the TF value for "Work/Job" is sharply higher in May (Fig. 9).

It is also interesting to note that the TF value for "Surroundings" rose sharply in March and remained high until May (Fig. 9). It may be that many people are consulting with an awareness of their surroundings as they begin their new life. The "Head/Brain" is also changing in the same way as the "Surroundings (Fig. 9)." The word "Head/Brain" was used mainly to mean "not very smart". It is thought that many people are worried about how smart or dumb they are compared to their surroundings at this time of year, when new life begins. In Subgraph02, the monthly TF values for "Friend" and "A person

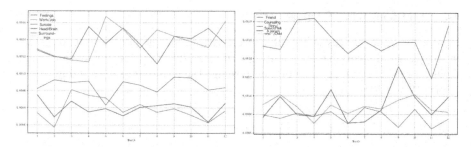

Fig. 9. Results of Subgraph01 analysis   **Fig. 10.** Results of Subgraph02 analysis

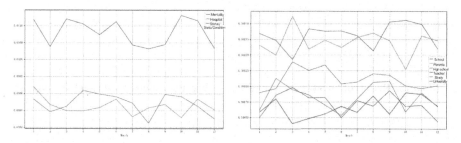

Fig. 11. Results of Subgraph03 analysis   **Fig. 12.** Results of Subgraph04 analysis

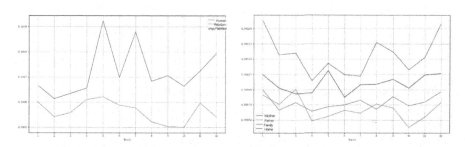

Fig. 13. Results of Subgraph05 analysis   **Fig. 14.** Results of Subgraph06 analysis

who…/Child" varied widely. The value for "Friend" was noticeably higher from March to April, while the value for "A person who…/Child" was higher in September (Fig. 10). In Subgraph04, "School" and "Parents" also showed a strong monthly change.

The TF value for "School" was higher in the fall, while that for "Parents" was higher in March (Fig. 12). It was also interesting to note the contrast in the way these two words changed (Fig. 12). The change in TF values for "Parents" is similar to that for "University," "Study," and "High school." From this result, it can be inferred that the examination worries of high school students, in which parents are likely to be involved, increase during the spring and summer vacation seasons. In Subgraph 06, there was a large monthly change in the TF value for "Mother." "Mother" showed a similar behavior to that of "Father," with higher TF values in December, January, and August (Fig. 14).

4.4   24-h Changes in TF Values

Finally, the 24-h changes in TF values were visualized. The purpose was to see how the frequency of nouns that commonly appear in the statements of people with suicidal thoughts changed with the time of their posting. The results are shown in Fig. 15, 16, 17, 18, 19 and 20 below.

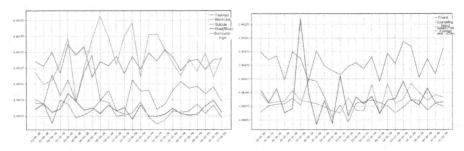

Fig. 15. Results of Subgraph01 analysis   **Fig. 16.** Results of Subgraph02 analysis

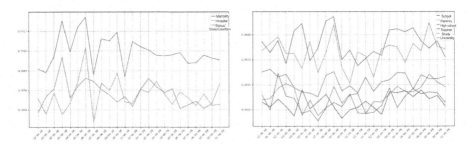

Fig. 17. Results of Subgraph03 analysis   **Fig. 18.** Results of Subgraph04 analysis

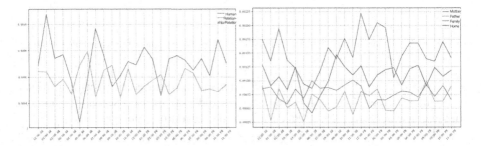

Fig. 19. Results of Subgraph05 analysis   **Fig. 20.** Results of Subgraph06 analysis

In Subgraph01, the TF value for "Work/Job" was high and concentrated at certain times of the day, such as 8:00 AM, 12:00 PM, and 2:00–3:00 PM (Fig. 15). The highest values were also recorded in the early morning hours at 4:00 AM (Fig. 15). The TF value for "Suicide" was highest in the early morning hours at 7:00 AM (Fig. 15). In Subgraph02, the TF value for "A person who.../Child" was found to be sharply higher at 5:00 AM (Fig. 16). All of the words in Subgraph03 had high TF values from midnight to morning (Fig. 17). These words often appear in questions from people with mental illness. It is likely that serious people who have trouble falling asleep, waking up early in the morning, or thinking during the night tend to seek help during the night and in the morning.

In Subgraph04, the TF value for "School" was higher in the early morning around 5 AM, around 9 AM when people commute to school, and from 4 PM to 7 PM when they go home (Fig. 18). "Study" showed higher values late at night and in the middle of the night (Fig. 18). In Subgraph 05, "Human" had high TF values at 1:00 AM and 7:00 AM (Fig. 19). "Mother" in Subgraph 06 were relatively divided into various time periods except from 3:00 to 7:00 AM (Fig. 20).

5 Conclusion

5.1 Consideration

In this study, we examined the nouns that frequently appear in the statements of people with suicidal thoughts by using the data of questions posted on Yahoo! Chiebukuro. Furthermore, by examining the occurrence of these nouns over a certain period of time, we examined the events that trigger people's suicidal thoughts. The topics of people with suicidal thoughts were divided into six major groups, and we suspected that the events that cause them to feel like they want to die could also be grouped into these six groups.

Observations throughout the six years revealed that the words "Work/Job" appeared more frequently after May 2019 and "School" and "Parents" appeared more frequently after May 2018 than before. Although it is difficult to say for sure, it can be assumed that suicidal thoughts have been increasing in recent years due to worries about work and school that involve parents. While there were other minor changes, there was no monotonous increase or decrease from year to year due to the strong seasonality.

Looking at the changes throughout the year, it is interesting to note that words such as "Surroundings" and "Head/Brain" appear more frequently from March to May. It can be inferred that before the start of a new environment, and for some time after the start of a new environment, Japanese people become hopeless to the point of suicidal thoughts when they compare their abilities with those of others. In addition, words such as "A person who.../Child" and "School" appear relatively frequently in the fall, indicating that Japanese students feel a desire to die in the fall, after summer vacation, due to school worries. Incidentally, September 1 is said to be the day when the largest number of Japanese students commit suicide [19]. Perhaps the resumption of school after the summer break has become an emotional burden for Japanese students, and in fact many Japanese with suicidal thoughts included the word "School" in their statements in September. Other results included more nouns related to examinations and studying in March, the exam season, and more nouns related to mothers and fathers during the winter and summer vacation seasons, when they are likely to spend more time at home, which is a natural result considering the events in Japan.

Observation throughout the 24-h period showed that certain words appeared more frequently at times that could be expected given people's lives: nouns related to work appeared more frequently during commuting and lunchtime, nouns related to school appeared more frequently during the commute to school and after going home, and nouns related to study appeared more frequently during the late evening. On the other hand, nouns related to suicide and mental illness tended to increase in concentration from midnight to morning, but the reason for this was not known.

Thus, the results suggest that observing changes in TF values can provide a variety of insights.

5.2 Future Tasks

The actual text data submitted by people with suicidal thoughts in this study provided a variety of insights into the nouns that are often expressed, but the study also found some inadequacies.

First, while these nouns are undoubtedly triggers for people to want to die, they are in fact intertwined with the person's potential personality and other problems they originally have, making the cause of their suicidal thoughts complex rather than simple. We felt keenly that this could not be solved by the text mining we conducted alone.

In addition, the analysis in this case was conducted by simply counting the frequency of occurrence of nouns, but there are some problems, such as overlooking words that have the same meaning but are called in completely different ways. In essence, words have many different ways of being called. Some words can be considered the same even if they have slightly different meanings. For example, "Test" and "Examination" should be considered the same word, but this time, they were recognized as different words. Therefore, in the future, in order to improve the accuracy of the analysis, we would like to analyze the frequency of words that are similar to the word in addition to the frequency of occurrence of the word.

We hope to continue our research and provide new knowledge that will lead to the prevention of the suicide problem among the Japanese.

Acknowledgments. In this paper, we used "Yahoo! Chiebukuro data (3rd edition)" provided by LY Corporation via IDR Dataset Service of National Institute of Informatics.

Disclosure of Interests. The authors have no relevant financial or non-financial interests to disclose.

References

1. LNCS Homepage. https://www.mhlw.go.jp/stf/seisakunitsuite/bunya/hukushi_kaigo/seikat suhogo/jisatsu/sesakugaiyou.html. Accessed 3 Feb 2024
2. LNCS Homepage. https://www.nippon.com/ja/japan-data/h01624/. Accessed 15 Feb 2024
3. Kamizawa, T., Nakata, R., et al.: Research on relation of self-harm and psychological distress of young people (2016)
4. LNCS Homepage. https://www.nippon-foundation.or.jp/who/news/pr/2023/20230406-87204.html. Accessed 2 Feb 2024
5. LNCS Homepage. https://www.mhlw.go.jp/content/000527996.pdf. Accessed 3 Feb 2024
6. Eto, N., Kawasaki, H.: Actual situation of adolescent suicide and consideration of suicide prevention for them. Kyushu Neuro-Psychiatry **63**(2), 75–82 (2017)

7. LNCS Homepage. https://chiebukuro.yahoo.co.jp/. Accessed 3 Feb 2024
8. LY Corporation (2020, 2023): Yahoo! Chiebukuro Data, 3rd edn. Informatics Research Data Repository, National Institute of Informatics. https://doi.org/10.32130/idr.1.3
9. LNCS Homepage. https://about.yahoo.co.jp/info/blog/20171129/chiebukuro.html. Accessed 2 Feb 2024
10. Sato, H., Yoshida, F.: Self-disclosure on the Internet: the effects of anonymity of the self and the other. Jpn. Psychol. Res. **78**(6), 559–566 (2008)
11. Ferriter, M.: Computer aided interviewing and the psychiatric social history. Soc. Work. Soc. Sci. Rev. **4**(3), 255–263 (1993)
12. Kariya, A., Okada, H., et al.: Internet-based inquiries from users with the intention to overdose with over-the-counter drugs: qualitative analysis of Yahoo! Chiebukuro. JMIR Form. Res. **7**(e45021), JMIR Publications Inc. (2023)
13. Kawashima, A.: Marital conflict resolutions expressed in "Yahoo! Answers." Bull. Faculty Educ. Chiba Univ. **61**, 185–191 (2013)
14. Sakai, Y., Ito, E.: Extracting buzzwords from the Yahoo! Chiebukuro dataset. In: 2019 Kyushu Section Joint Convention of Electrical and Information Related Societies (2019)
15. LNCS Homepage. https://www.nii.ac.jp/dsc/idr/userforum/poster/IDR-UF2022_P01.pdf. Accessed 1 Feb 2024
16. Mori, S., Nagao, M.: An improvement of a morphological analysis by a morpheme clustering. Nat. Lang. Process. **5**(2), 75–103 (1998)
17. Ida, A., Kitamura, Y., et al.: Discovered rule filtering method using MEDLINE information retrieval. Technical report, **102**(710), 5–10 (2003)
18. Higuchi, K.: A two-step approach to quantitative content analysis: KH coder tutorial using Anne of green gables (Part I). Ritsumeikan Soc. Sci. Rev. **52**(3), 77–91 (2016)
19. LNCS Homepage. https://www.mext.go.jp/content/20200824-mext_jidou01-000009294_011.pdf. Accessed 1 Feb 2024

Research on Situations in Which It is Difficult to Communicate What You Want to Say - Assertiveness from a Contextual Perspective

Nono Taniai[1]([✉]), Keiko Kasamatsu[1], and Takeo Ainoya[2]

[1] Tokyo Metropolitan University, Tokyo 191-0065, Japan
`taniai-nono@ed.tmu.ac.jp`
[2] Tokyo University of Technology, Tokyo 144-0051, Japan

Abstract. There are many situations in which it is difficult to communicate what you want to say. And it has been suggested that this is also related to depression. In this study, we focused on situations where it is hard to communicate to others who seems busy. The purpose is to clarify why it is difficult to communicate.

To achieve this, we conducted survey and interview research when communicating and being communicated. Subsequently, qualitative analyses were performed on behaviors, thoughts, and emotions.

As a result, participants who exhibited a tendency towards non-assertive behavior (not expressing their opinions) were suggested to self-impose limitations on their behaviors and to engage in self-blame in their thoughts and emotions. On the contrary, participants with lower scores did not show a tendency for their thoughts and emotions to turn negative.

Therefore, in situations where it is difficult to communicate, the relationship between behavior, thoughts, and emotions and assertion was recognized. It was found that assertion is related to differences in behavior, thoughts, and emotions.

Keywords: Communication · Qualitative analysis · Assertiveness · Emotion · Seems busy

1 Introduction

1.1 Research Background

There are many situations in which it is difficult to communicate what you want to say.

In previous studies, it was suggested that approximately 40% of nursing students in their 2nd to 4th years did not consult anyone about difficulties related to their relationships with instructors or mentors during their clinical practicum [1]. Furthermore, individuals with high levels of depression tend to anticipate negative outcomes regarding such help-seeking (which involve seeking help from others when dealing with problems they cannot solve alone [2]). It has been shown that depression directly inhibits the intention to seek assistance [3].

Therefore, there are situations where individuals are unable to communicate even when they are in distress, and this may be influenced by depression. Furthermore, from a communication perspective, we have focused on assertion (self-expression with self-respect and respect for others [4]). According to Hiraki (2021), assertion types can be classified into three categories: non-assertive (not expressing one's opinion or using ambiguous expressions), aggressive (asserting oneself while imposing one's opinion on others), and assertive (expressing oneself while respecting both oneself and others) [4].

Based on assertion types, we investigate individuals with different assertion types, focusing on those who find it difficult to express themselves and those who can express themselves. By focusing on the differences between these types, I consider it is necessary to focus on these differences to clarify why some people feel difficult to communicate.

1.2 Purpose of Research

The purpose of this research is to clarify why it is difficult to communicate.

To achieve this, in Survey 2.1, we collected episodes in which it is difficult to communicate and be communicated. In investigation 2.2, we focused on differences based on the recipient and assertion tendencies, conducting a survey using questionnaires. In investigation 3, we conducted semi-structured interviews to explore the behaviors, thoughts, and emotions experienced in situations where it is difficult to communicate and be communicated.

1.3 Previous Research

About Assertions. According to Hiraki (2021), assertion refers to "self-respecting self-expression" and can be categorized into non-assertive, aggressive, and assertive types [4]. The following describes the classification conducted by Hiraki (2021) for each of these types [4].

Non-assertive (NA) refers to feelings and attitudes where individuals suppress themselves and prioritize the other person's feelings or attitudes by not expressing their opinions, using ambiguous expressions, or adopting passive attitudes.

Aggressive (AG) behavior involves asserting oneself but doing so by imposing one's opinions onto others.

In assertive (AS) self-expression, individuals assert themselves by exercising their right to self-expression while simultaneously respecting the rights and freedoms of others to express themselves.

Research on scales to measure these assertion types has been conducted by Hamaguchi (1994) for children's versions [5] and by Tamase et al. (2001) for versions tailored to young adults [6], among others. In this study, which targeted students, the scale created by Kageyama (2009) specifically for students [7] was utilized. To investigate whether there are differences in behaviors, thoughts, and emotions when feeling difficult to communicate based on assertion tendencies, the scale was used to examine the assertion tendencies of the participants in the study.

Benefits and Costs of Help-Seeking. One of the behaviors associated with communication is Help-seeking behavior. According to Daibo et al. (1990), it is defined as "actions performed with the intention of providing benefits to others or other groups facing unsolvable or difficult problems for problem resolution" [2].

According to Nagai et al. (2018), it is suggested that when individuals anticipate benefits and costs, and the benefits of action outweigh the costs of action, or when the costs of avoidance exceed the benefits of avoidance, help-seeking is indicated [1].

In this study, we used the perceptions of benefits and costs when help-seeking to examine whether there is a relationship with feeling difficult to communicate.

Reasons Why People Feel Busy. According to a study by Yomura et al. (2013) on factors regulating the sense of busyness in industrial organizations, workload density is a direct cause. The more individuals perceive a sense of workload density, the more they feel unable and unsupported, leading to a greater sense of busyness [8]. In this study, we examined which factors individuals perceive more strongly when they feel that the other person seems busy or when they themselves feel busy. We also utilized this information to investigate how it relates to the feeling of being difficult to communicate.

2   Investigation of Situations that People Are Reluctant to Communicate

2.1   Survey on Situations Where You Can't Communicate Someone Because They Seem Busy

Purpose. We conducted a questionnaire survey regarding situations where individuals feel difficult to communicate because the other person seems busy. The purpose was to investigate the types of episodes that occur when considering the other person's situation. This situation was selected because it was observed frequently in the preliminary survey.

Method. Firstly, the author listed and classified the situations they had experienced so far. As a result, the author felt that the approach varied depending on the urgency level of the message to be communicated. Therefore, the author created a scale to assess the urgency level on a five-point rating scale (see Table 1). The questionnaire items were then used to conduct a survey via Google Forms (see Table 2). There were 6 participants, with an average age of 21.5 years old.

Result. Participants provided 23 episodes of their own experiences in communicating and 26 episodes of their experiences in being communicated. The responses from both the post-survey and the preliminary questionnaire were tagged using Notion (an application for note-taking) to categorize the reasons for feeling busy under the "1st tag" label (see Table 3).

Tags were also applied to the factors indicated in Yomura et al.'s (2013) study [8].

Based on the content participants wanted to communicate, along with the urgency level and tagging results, the content they wanted to communicate was classified into four categories: "Help-seeking," "Request," "Explanation of Situation," and "Other."

The situations that fit the definition of help-seeking behavior [2] were categorized as "Help-seeking."

Table 1. Crisis Level.

	Experience to communicate	Listening experience
Level 1	I have to tell you someday	I can listen to any content anytime
Level 2	It's okay if I don"t tell you today	I can respond to any content when it's convenient
Level 3	I have to tell you today	I can respond at anytime if there is a high degree of urgency
Level 4	Things I should tell you right away when it's convenient	I can only respond when it's convenient if there is a high degree of urgency
Level 5	What I need to tell you right now	I can't listening anything

Table 2. Question matters.

	Friend	seminars, club activities, circles	part-time job
Situation	Free description		
Relationship	Single selection : peer, senior, junior	Single selection : peer, senior, junior, teacher	Single selection : peer, senior, junior, master or president, full-time employee
Crisis level	Single selection : level 1 to 5		

Table 3. 1st code

1st code
When I / the other person is busy (job hunting, before exams, etc.)
I /the other person don't know what the other person/I am doing
When I / the other person is relaxed
frown at me
unwell
others

Instances where individuals had something they wanted to ask for or request were classified under "Request."

"Explanation of Situation" was used when individuals wanted to explain the situation because the other person didn't know what was going on.

Instances that did not fit into any of the three categories were classified under "Other."

The results were as follows: "Help-seeking" was classified as 6 instances in communicating experiences and 4 instances in being communicated experiences. "Request" was classified as 15 instances in communicating experiences and 4 instances in being communicated experiences. "Explanation of Situation" was classified as 2 instances in communicating experiences and 1 instance in being communicated experiences. "Other" was classified as 13 instances in communicating experiences and 18 instances in being communicated experiences.

Discussion. Among the situations categorized as "Help-seeking," 3 out of 4 instances communicated during part-time job were at crisis level 4, indicating a high level of urgency in the content. "Request" in communicating experiences included various situations such as part-time jobs, seminars, clubs, and circles, with diverse recipients including superiors, seniors, seminar members, parents, and shop attendants, among others, yielding a wide range of results. Additionally, there was a tendency to feel less urgency regarding crisis levels compared to "Help-seeking." "Explanation of Situation" varied in each instance, as did the recipients involved. Regarding the crisis level, the communicating experiences ranged from level 3 to 4, while the being communicated experiences were at level 5. Therefore, it is suggested that even when individuals feel the urgency to explain the situation, the recipients may be unable to respond to the situation, indicating a potential mismatch in urgency levels.

From the above, it was possible to analyze differences in "one's own state" and "aspects of the content" within the context of "relationship with the others."

On the other hand, regarding the "relationship with the other party," it is believed that making "one's own state" and "aspects of the content" similar in situations may clarify the differences based on the recipient, facilitating a clearer understanding.

2.2 Investigation of Different Thought Patterns and Assertion Tendencies Towards Different Individuals

Purpose. The objective is to focus on the "relationship with the other party" and the "Help-seeking" classified in investigation 2.1, aiming to verify whether responses vary depending on the recipient.

Method. The survey for "Help-seeking" situations was conducted, and responses were collected using Google Forms (see Table 4).

Furthermore, focusing on assertion [4], we conducted a simultaneous survey using the 15 questions investigating assertion tendencies created by Kageyama (2009) [7] for NA, AG, and AS (see Table 5). There were 5 participants, with an average age of 22.2 years old.

Table 4. Question matters.

	Seniors and full-time employees at part-time jobs	Group work (Manufacturing-related university classes)
Situation	· I don't know how to do it while working part-time and want to ask for advice. · There is an urgency · The person I want to ask seems busy.	· I am in charge of tasks that I have no experience with before · I am the only one in charge · I don't know how to do it. But the deadline is approaching · I would like to ask them, but they are also busy with other classes.
Behavior	Single selection : · ask immediately · ask when it's convenient · express what is bothering me · ask my peers because it's hard to ask theres (I don't know if my peers know how to do it) · deal with it my way · free description	Single selection : · ask immediately(using SNS) · ask directly the next time we meet · express what is bothering me the next time we meet · ask my friend who seems to be familiar with my task (not a group member) · Investigate and deal with it yourself · free description
Thoughts (Benefit and Cost)	Multiple selection : · If I ask now, it will be easier to ask the next time · It will be a burden and nuisance for them · learn how to do it · they will cooperate · Being told something unpleasant or being rejected · Later, I might be talked behind my back, "That person didn't even know this" · ask immediately (I feel stressed when I think about whether to ask) · By solving problems on my own, I can grow and develop the ability to think	Multiple selection : · If I ask now, I will be able to get along better with them · It will be a burden and nuisance for them · learn how to do it · they will cooperate · Being told something unpleasant or being rejected · Later, I might be talked behind my back, "That person didn't even know this" · ask immediately (I feel stressed when I think about whether to ask) · By solving problems on my own, I can grow and develop the ability to think

Table 5. 1st code.

AS	NA	AG
You can ask a friend for a favor or ask for advice	I can't refuse an unreasonable request from my senior	Other people's opinions and claims are secondary; only my own opinions are important
When you can't hear what the teacher is saying, ask him to speak again	Even if I am asked to do something that I don't think I can do, I have no choice but to accept it	When something happens that I can't do on my own, I force my friends to help me
I start talking to people I like	I can't refuse even if my friend's forces his own schedule upon me	When I ask a friend for a favor, I force myself to do it
When my friends are talking about something I don't know, I ask them to tell me	Even if I want to ask a friend something, it's hard to tell him	When I don't understand something, I complain that the other person's explanation is bad
If someone misunderstands you, talk to them to clear up the misunderstanding	If I get interrupted while I'm talking about something important, I will end up stammering	When I come across an opinion that contradicts what I think during a discussion, reject that opinion

Result. In part-time jobs, all responses resulted in situations where individuals observed the situation and waited for the right timing to listen. On the other hand, in group work situations, results showed a division between those who immediately consulted with others or consulted at the next meeting, and those who did not consult and instead researched on their own. Individually, individuals with a strong assertive (AS) tendency tended to choose "consulting immediately (including non-members)" as their preferred option.

Consistent with the results of previous studies, there were 2 responses where the benefits of action and the costs of avoidance outweighed, and 1 response where despite feeling the costs of action (apology), the benefits were perceived as greater.

On the contrary, individuals with low assertive (AS) tendencies tended to choose not to consult immediately. There was 1 response where the individual chose to resolve the issue without consulting due to the benefits of avoidance, and 1 response where the costs of action outweighed, making it impossible to consult immediately.

Discussion. From the results, among the 5 participants, only 1 person felt the costs of action during part-time jobs. Therefore, it is suggested that in high-crisis situations such as part-time jobs, few individuals feel the costs of action.

Furthermore, the number of individuals who chose "I think it would burden or inconvenience the staff (or members)" was 1 in part-time jobs and 3 in group work situations. Therefore, it is suggested that individuals are more likely to feel a sense of apology towards friends rather than towards supervisors.

2.3 Discussion on Hypotheses

The factors contributing to the difficulty in communicating, such as the relationship with the recipient and the context of communication, were found to be closely related. Particularly, there were numerous episodes concerning "considering the recipient's situation," suggesting its significance in communication challenges.

Furthermore, it was found that "Help-seeking" situations also had a high level of crisis in their content.

In communicating experiences categorized as "Request," various situations and recipients indicated a tendency to feel less urgency compared to "Help-seeking," suggesting a lower level of crisis.

"Explanation of Situation" situations indicated urgency where individuals felt the need to explain the situation; however, recipients were unable to respond, suggesting a mismatch in urgency levels.

Furthermore, in high-crisis situations such as part-time jobs, few individuals felt the costs of action, and it was suggested that individuals are more likely to feel a sense of apology towards friends rather than towards supervisors. From the above results, it is suggested that responses vary depending on the situation and the recipient, and there are differences in approaches based on assertion tendencies as well. It is necessary to investigate what thoughts and emotions arise and why individuals feel difficult to communicate.

3 Investigation on Factors Which Make People Feel Difficult to Communicate

3.1 Purpose

The objective is to elucidate why individuals feel unable to communicate. To achieve this, an analysis of behaviors, thoughts, and emotions in the three representative situations categorized as "Help-seeking," "Request," and "Explanation of Situation" based on the results of Investigation 2.2 was conducted.

3.2 Method

The three situations, "Help-seeking," "Request," and "Explanation of Situation," were investigated via Google Forms (see Table 6), and the responses were further explored through semi-structured interviews.

Table 6. 1st code.

Category	Situation	Experience	Detailed situation	Action
Request help-seeking	I want to ask a question during my part-time job, but everyone around me seems busy			
Be requested help-seeking	I'm asked a question by another employee during a busy part-time job			
Request	I want confirmation that the work is completed, but the other person seems to be concentrating on the work			
Be requested	I was asked to confirm something while I was concentrating on my work	Yes or No	Free description	Free description
Please explain the situation	I promised to play with a friend, but he didn't show up when the time came (He said he had plans before that)			
Asked to explain the situation	I have plans to play with a friend, but I think I'm going to be late because my previous appointment go over time			

The full set of 35 questions regarding assertion tendencies created by Kageyama (2009) was examined [7], and self-assessments were collected using a 5-point scale (5 indicating fully able to communicate, 1 indicating unable to communicate at all) via Google Forms (see Table 7).

Table 7. Question matters.

AS	NA	AG	Self-evaluation
You can ask a friend for a favor or ask for advice	When a store clerk enthusiastically recommends something, I end up buying it	Other people's opinions and claims are secondary; only my own opinions are important	I can communicate in situations that is difficult to communicate
When you can't hear what the teacher is saying, ask him to speak again	When I agree with a friend's opinion, it's hard to express my agreement	If I like the other person, I prioritize my own feelings over the other person's feelings	I can communicate in everyday life
I start talking to people I like	When the money I lent is not returned, it's hard to say what I want to get my money back.	When something happens that I can't do on my own, I force my friends to help me	
Honestly express your love for someone you like	I can't say "I can't do it" to your seniors even if you can't do it	Even if I see good things about my friends, I don't particularly evaluate them.	
When my friends are talking about something I don't know, I ask them to tell me	I can't refuse an unreasonable request from my senior	When my teacher says something that makes me angry, say firmly, "That's too loud!"	
When the teacher writes incorrectly on the blackboard, tell them about it	Even if I am asked to do something that I don't think I can do, I have no choice but to accept it	When I ask a friend for a favor, I force myself to do it	
If there is a defect in the product you purchased, please politely inform them of the defect and request a replacement	When someone invites me out to play and I can't go, I end up doing without being able to refuse	When I don't understand something, I complain that the other person's explanation is bad	
If someone misunderstands you, talk to them to clear up the misunderstanding	I can't refuse even if my friend's forces his own schedule upon me	If the product I bought is defective, I get angry and complain and ask for a replacement	
	Even if I want to ask a friend something, it's hard to tell him	Forcibly forcing my opinion through a small group discussion	
	When my parents oppose me, I don't say anything and just follow their opinion	When I come across an opinion that contradicts what I think during a discussion, reject that opinion	
	If I get interrupted while I'm talking about something important, I will end up stammering	If someone brazenly acts dishonestly, yell, "Stop it!"	
		When a friend doesn't return the money he lent, I strongly demands, "Give it back!"	
		If someone interrupts me while I'm talking about something important, I get angry and say, "Shut up!"	
		When someone misunderstands me, I curse and criticize them	
		If someone is making a noise next to me while I'm studying, I get angry and say, "It's noisy!"	
		When asked to do something that I don't think I can do, I get angry and say, "You should do it!	

3.3   Result and Analysis

"The behaviors," "thoughts," and "emotions" of the participants in each situation were coded using MAXQDA (a qualitative data analysis software) (see Table 8).

Table 8. 1st, 2nd and 3rd code.

1st code	2nd code	3rd code
Situation	I, you	c1risis level
Who	I, you, Disinterested person	relationship
Action	I, you, Disinterested person	ask, tell, suggest, make an appeal, self-solving, don't action
Thinking	I, you, Disinterested person	why I need to tell, why is it told, calm thinking, positive thinking, negative thinking, I want to do xxxx, I want you to do xxx, sympathize
Emotions	I, you, Disinterested person	positive emotions, negative emotions, emotionless

Based on these codes, UX maps were created for each episode. The phases included "Normally," "Before expressing," "From wanting to express," and "After expressing," with only the relevant parts described. A total of 46 UX maps were created. Among them, typical examples are as follows (see Fig. 1) (see Fig. 2) (see Fig. 3).

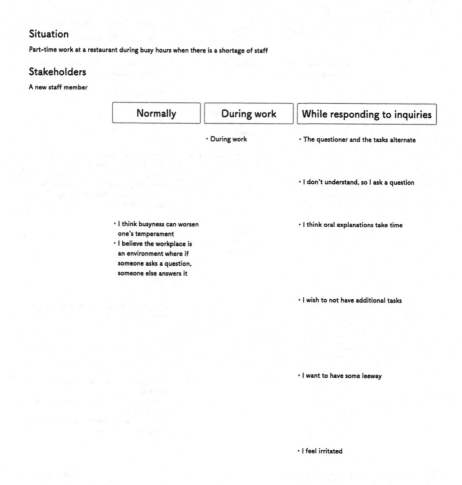

Situation

Part-time work at a restaurant during busy hours when there is a shortage of staff

Stakeholders

A new staff member

Normally	During work	While responding to inquiries
	· During work	· The questioner and the tasks alternate
		· I don't understand, so I ask a question
· I think busyness can worsen one's temperament · I believe the workplace is an environment where if someone asks a question, someone else answers it		· I think oral explanations take time
		· I wish to not have additional tasks
		· I want to have some leeway
		· I feel irritated

Fig. 1. Participant 01 (with average NA score) 's UX map (Be requested Help-seeking). It shows that they get irritated when asked questions.

The scores for the assertion types yielded the following results respectively (see Table 9).

The inclination degree of assertion types was measured based on the average and standard deviation calculated when creating the scale for the assertion questionnaire [7].

Situation

Online internship

Stakeholders

The supervisor

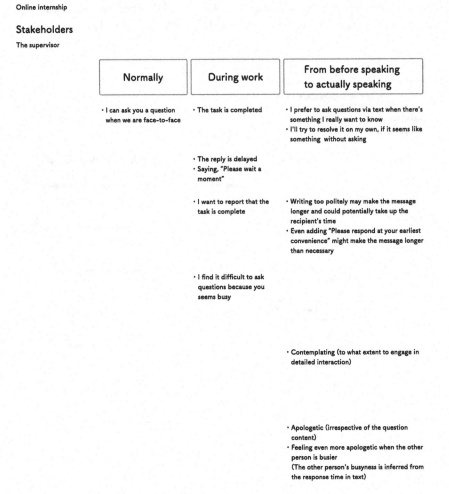

Fig. 2. Participant 07 (with high NA score) 's UX map (Request). It shows a strong sense of empathy and consideration towards others.

If nearly half of the data falls within (mean − standard deviation) to (mean + standard deviation), and most of the data falls within (mean − 2 * standard deviation) to (mean + 2 * standard deviation), the scores were classified as follows: (see Table 10).

Focusing on the NA scores, it was observed that participants 03 and 06 had low scores, participant 05 had slightly higher scores, while participants 07 and 08 had high scores.

Furthermore, the NA scores were compared with self-assessment scores. Participants 03 and 06 had low NA scores and high self-assessment scores. Participants 01, 02, and

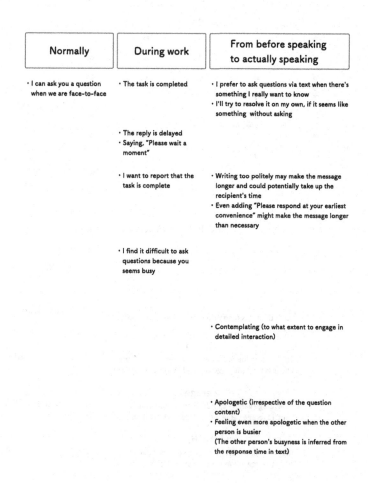

Fig. 3. Participant 03 (with slightly lower NA score) 's UX map (Be requested Help-seeking). It is indicated that there is no emotion towards others.

04 had average NA scores and did not feel difficult to communicate themselves based on their self-assessment.

Participant 08 had a high NA score and a low self-assessment. Participant 07 obtained a high NA score, indicating difficulty in communicating themselves, yet their self-assessment is low in normal circumstances.

On the other hand, Participant 05 has a slightly high NA score but does not have a low self-assessment, feeling capable of communicating themselves under normal circumstances.

Table 9. Score.

Participant number	AG score	NA score	AS score	Assertion score	Self-evaluation 1	Self-evaluation 2
01	36	21	25	-32	4	4
02	35	25	19	-41	3	4
03	24	16	35	-5	4	5
04	36	20	26	-30	4	3
05	30	30	32	-28	3	5
06	32	14	36	-10	4	4
07	21	37	28	-30	2	3
08	35	42	20	-57	1	2
09	23	22	28	-17	2	4
10	44	22	25	-41	2	3

Table 10. NA score evaluation.

	NA
Low Less than (average value - standard deviation*2)	score <12.6
a little Low (Average value - Standard deviation *2) or more and less than (Average value - Standard deviation)	12.6≦ score <18.3
Average Average value - standard deviation) or more and (average value + standard deviation) or less	18.3≦ score ≦29.7
a little High Greater than (average value + standard deviation) and (average value + standard deviation*2) or less	29.7< score ≦35.4
High Greater than (mean value + standard deviation *2)	score <35.4

Additionally, Participants 09 and 10 have average NA scores, but their self-assessment in difficult communication situations is low.

From the above, Participants 01, 02, 03, 04, 06, 07, and 08 generally showed a correlational relationship between their NA scores and self-assessment. However, Participants 05, 09, and 10 exhibited an inverse relationship.

3.4 Discussion

Participants with average NA scores tend to communicate themselves without much hesitation, as they perceive both the benefits and costs of execution when asking questions, such as "Because it is what the other person is instructing," indicating a balanced approach between the benefits of action and the avoidance of costs [3]. Moreover, when asked questions, many respondents expressed negative emotions towards the others, such as "Feeling irritated when given additional work," suggesting a prevalent tendency to harbor negative sentiments towards the others (see Fig. 1). Participants 08 and 10 responded with "The other person gets irritated when I ask questions," with participant 08 feeling unable to express themselves as a result. Therefore, it is speculated that feeling difficult to communicate might stem from experiences where negative emotions were elicited from the other person upon asking questions.

Participant 07, who scored high on the NA scale, expressed sentiments such as "feeling sorry for customers attended by other staff" and "worrying about taking up the other person's time unnecessarily during message exchanges" (see Fig. 2). From these, it can be inferred that Participant 07 exhibits a strong sense of empathy and consideration towards others. Similarly, Participant 08, with high scores, displays passive behavior such as "not expressing the desire to end the conversation" and "not contacting even when no communication is received." Participant 05, with slightly higher scores, tends to internalize situations such as "regretting not confirming beforehand" and "tightening up to prevent mistakes from snowballing."

Therefore, participants with higher NA scores tend to exhibit a tendency to restrict their own behaviors and to blame themselves in their thoughts and emotions compared to average participants. It is speculated that this tendency might be a contributing factor to feeling difficult to communicate.

Furthermore, the notion that the individuals 08 and 10 expressed, about "the recipient getting irritated when questioned," could also be considered a factor contributing to the feeling of being difficult to communicate.

The participants with average NA scores also responded with negative emotions when questioned. On the other hand, Participant 03, who had slightly lower NA scores, responded with statements like "I don't think anything about the other person" (see Fig. 3) and "It's okay not to know," suggesting a more neutral or accepting attitude towards the situation. Therefore, it can be inferred that Participant 03 does not dwell on thoughts or concerns about either the other person or themselves. Similarly, Participant 06, whose scores are slightly lower, expressed feelings such as "feeling happy" and "being pleased to have some waiting time." So, it is considered that Participant 06 perceives the situation positively. Therefore, participants who tend to have low NA scores are suggested to have a tendency where their thoughts and emotions do not tend towards negativity compared to average or high-scoring participants.

Consequently, it is considered that incorporating these thoughts and emotions can help individuals communicate without feeling overly pressured. Furthermore, it is speculated that even when be communicated by others, they can engage in communication without feeling difficult to communicate.

Based on the results, Participant 09, although having an average NA score, exhibits passive behavior due to feelings of fear, as indicated by responses such as "think it's faster to ask, but I'm afraid so I research it myself." One contributing factor is that the Assertion Scale [7] is not specifically tailored to address difficult communication situations. Participant 09 also self-assesses as someone who can communicate in everyday life, which correlates with the results of the Assertion Scale [7].

There were episodes of experiences where help-seeking was initiated, but episodes where help was offered were not obtained. Therefore, it was not possible to compare experiences of help-seeking with experiences of offering help. This aspect warrants further consideration.

4 Conclusion

The purpose of this study was to identify the reasons behind the difficulty in communication. The study focused on situations where communication could not be achieved due to the perceived busyness of others. Surveys and interviews were conducted, followed by qualitative analysis of the data.

At the outset, episodes where communication was hindered due to the perceived busyness of the recipient were collected. Based on the results, the desire to communicate the situation was classified into four categories: "Help-seeking," "Request," "Explanation of Situation," and "Other."

Next, we conducted a survey to investigate whether behavior changes depending on others. The results indicated that "Help-seeking" situations exhibited high levels of urgency in the content. On the other hand, in "Request" situations, various circumstances and different others led to a tendency not to perceive the urgency as much as in "Help-seeking" scenarios. Additionally, "Explanation of Situation" suggested that despite feeling the urgency to explain the situation, others might not be able to respond. Furthermore, it was suggested that in high-crisis situations like part-time work, individuals felt fewer costs associated with behaviors, and they were more likely to feel a sense of guilt towards friends rather than towards supervisors. Therefore, it was suggested that responses vary depending on the situation and the individual involved, and that there are differences in response strategies based on assertion tendencies.

Furthermore, semi-structured interview surveys were conducted to explore behaviors, thoughts, and emotions in three typical situations: "Help-seeking," "Request," and "Explaining Situations." The results suggested that feeling difficult to communicate may stem from experiences where negative emotions were elicited by the recipient upon questioning.

Additionally, participants with higher NA scores tended to restrict their own behaviors and blame themselves more in their thoughts and emotions compared to average participants. This suggests that they feel difficult to communication. Furthermore, participants with lower NA scores tend not to lean towards negative thoughts and emotions compared to average or higher-scoring participants. This suggests that they may feel more capable of communicating.

Therefore, incorporating the thoughts and emotions of participants with lower NA scores may facilitate easier communication without feeling overly pressured when communicating. Additionally, it may contribute to smoother communication where the recipient does not feel difficult to be communicated.

5 Future Work

The clear identification of differences in behavior, thoughts, and emotions in this study suggests that computer-based systems could be utilized to create environments that are easier to communicate in.

As an example, consider the case where one struggles with determining the appropriate amount of text. Computers can organize the key points to communicate. Furthermore, developing a service that generates messages communicating apologies and gratitude. This is expected to enable individuals to communicate what they want to communicate others without hesitation. The outlook involves utilizing computers to provide support for tailored communication methods according to individual needs.

References

1. Kondo, F., et al.: Study on the help-seeking behaviors of nursing students during clinical practicum. Northern Kanto Med. Soc. **73**(1), 61–68 (2023)
2. Daibo, F., Ando, S., Ikeda, T.: Social Psychology Perspective 1 - From the Individual to Others. Seishin Shobo, Tokyo (1990)
3. Nagai, F., Suzuki, S.: Effects of anticipated costs and benefits on help-seeking intentions: university students. Educ. Psychol. Res. **66**, 150–161 (2018)
4. Hiraki, F.: Third Edition Assertion Training-For Refreshing <Self-Expression>-. Japan Mental Technology Research Institute, Tokyo (2021)
5. Hamaguchi, F.: Construction of assertiveness scale for children. Educ. Psychol. Res. **42**(4), 463–470 (1994)
6. Tamase, F., et al.: Development of an Assertion Scale for Adolescents and its reliability and validity. Nara Univ. Educ. Bull. **50**(1), 221–231 (2001)
7. Kageyama, F.: A study of constructing a scale of assertion behavior for a university student -validation research by PF-study. Bull. Graduate School, Soka Univ. **31**, 185–214 (2009)
8. Yomura, F., et al.: A study of the influential factors on the sense of busyness in the industrial organization: towards the construction of a cognitive structure model of busyness. Labor Sci. **89**(5), 166–173 (2013)

Co-creation for Space Development: Case Studies of Student and Staff Collaborations in University Administration Space Proposals

Sakie Tasaki[1], Toshihide Kuzuhara[1], Takashi Funayama[1], Misaki Uchida[1], and Takeo Ainoya[2(✉)]

[1] Tokyo University of Technology, 5-23 Nishikamata, Ota, Tokyo, Japan
[2] Tokyo University of Technology the Graduate School of Design, Ota, Tokyo, Japan
ainoyatk@stf.teu.ac.jp

Abstract. In response to the dynamic landscape of higher education, accelerated by the COVID-19 pandemic, this study investigates the transformative potential of co-creation in reimagining university administrative spaces. By integrating modern technologies such as Computer-Aided Design (CAD) and CG (Computer Graphics), the research aims to foster collaborative partnerships between students, staff, and designers. Through iterative design processes and immersive virtual reality experiences facilitated by HMDs, stakeholders engage in refining and evaluating multiple administrative space proposals. Key findings highlight the significance of visibility, accessibility, and multifunctionality in design, favoring proposals that embrace these principles. Co-created designs featuring modular layouts and prioritizing well-being and collaboration resonate strongly with stakeholders. This groundbreaking approach emphasizes co-creation as a driving force behind user-centric spatial solutions. As future prospects emerge, the study's insights hold promise for revolutionizing educational space design and advancing the integration of VR technology in architectural practice.

Keywords: Co-creation · Collaborative Design Processes · User-Centric Design · Participatory Design Methods · Virtual Reality in Architecture

1 Research Background

In the evolving landscape of higher education, the COVID-19 pandemic has served as a catalyst for significant changes in university administration and space utilization. This period has witnessed a radical transformation in students' lives and learning environments, with a rapid shift towards online platforms and digital interactions. The distinction between physical and virtual spaces has become increasingly blurred, prompting a reevaluation of the role and design of university administrative spaces.

Historically, these spaces have been designed with traditional face-to-face interactions in mind. However, the pandemic's onset has underscored the need for flexible, adaptive, and multifunctional spaces that can cater to a diverse range of activities, from administrative tasks to student support and engagement. This shift is not merely about physical space rearrangement but involves rethinking the very essence of how university spaces are perceived and utilized by students, faculty, and staff.

Furthermore, the pandemic has highlighted the importance of creating environments that are not only functional but also conducive to well-being and collaboration. This has led to an increasing interest in exploring innovative ways to design spaces that are responsive to the changing needs of the university community.

Additionally, there's a growing recognition of the necessity to move beyond traditional administrative approaches where universities take the lead, towards a more collaborative process involving faculty members serving as designers and students engaged in design education. This co-creative design process ensures that the perspectives and insights of end-users are integrated from the outset, promoting a sense of ownership and relevance among stakeholders. By incorporating the voices and experiences of those who will ultimately utilize the spaces, the design process becomes more inclusive and aligned with the diverse needs of the university community.

2 Purpose of the Research

2.1 Research Objective

The primary objective of this study is to reimagine and optimize the design of university administrative spaces by integrating modern technologies, specifically CAD (Computer-Aided Design) and CG (Computer Graphics). The ambition is to transcend traditional architectural practices by employing virtual reality (VR) technology, enabling a more dynamic and interactive design process.

This study aims to create administrative spaces that are not only efficient and practical but also adaptable to the evolving needs of students and staff. By harnessing the power of CAD and VR, the project seeks to develop detailed and innovative design proposals. These proposals will be evaluated in a virtual environment, allowing stakeholders to experience and interact with the designs in a way that traditional blueprints and models cannot provide.

Furthermore, the study aims to facilitate mutual understanding through technology, embedding this aspect within the development process itself. By showcasing case studies where technology facilitates collaborative design processes and fosters mutual understanding among stakeholders, the research highlights the potential of integrating technology not only to enhance spatial design but also to promote a deeper level of engagement and cooperation among all involved parties. The ultimate goal is to foster an environment that enhances productivity, fosters collaboration, and supports the diverse needs of the university community while promoting mutual understanding and inclusivity throughout the design process.

2.2 Objective Summary

The study aims to articulate and verify spatial design requirements from a student perspective in reception areas, in collaboration with university administration, to propose high-quality spatial designs. This involves deeply understanding the actual usage of spaces by conducting interviews and onsite observations to form a grounded requirement definition.

2.3 Methodology Summary

Three student groups (A, B, C) received specific needs from the university administration and conducted interviews and observations with staff and students to deeply understand the administrative usage and inform their design requirements.

Based on these requirements, students developed spatial designs. University administration provided feedback on these proposals, which were then used to evaluate and refine the accuracy and appropriateness of the requirements.

The process of analyzing the issues identified by each group and their improvement strategies clarified the understanding of spatial problems, moving from tacit knowledge to explicit knowledge. This was achieved by comparing the requirements identified by each group with those recognized by the administration.

The collaborative design and co-creation process were facilitated by using CAD-generated CG as a communication tool, which proved to be an excellent example of fostering mutual understanding through technology.

The process allowed for a clear design that met user requirements, with digital simulations aiding in advancing mutual understanding throughout the development.

Process Summary:

1. University administration compiled space-related requirements.
2. Students proposed designs based on these requirements.
3. University administration provided feedback on these design proposals.
4. Students redesigned based on this feedback.
5. Students created multiple design proposals, which were then voted on by the administration to determine the chosen design.

3 Research Method

3.1 Requests from the University Office

The requests from the university office were communicated to the student groups. This was used as a reference in the initial stage of each group's design activities.

Proposal of a method (panel, sign, etc.) to guide students from the entrance of the office to each department (Business Division, Academic Affairs Division, Career Support Center) Proposal of how to use the space used by students, furniture and arrangement (Fig. 1).

3.2 Requirements from the University Administration

- Functionality

- Ensure easily identifiable pathways for each department.
- Maintain an orderly environment.
- Consolidate carts.

- Comfort

- Create a bright atmosphere that is welcoming and easy for students to use.

Fig. 1. Before the renovation of the university administration office, where students analyzed the actual usage of the space through observations of users and the responses of university administration staff.

3.3 Survey of Each Group Each Student Group Conducted Interviews with the Administrative Office

Each student group interviewed the secretariat. This enabled us to gain a deeper understanding of the actual conditions of use, requests and issues of the secretariat.

The student groups were asked to exchange opinions with the staff in charge of the secretariat, and to make proposals based on the students' viewpoints and opinions.

The dark atmosphere, the cluttered situation, and the difficulty for students to understand the proposal were considered as problems (Fig. 2).

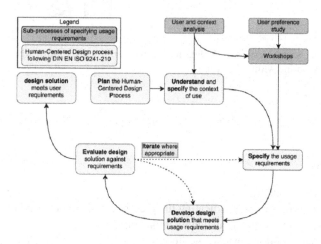

Fig. 2. Diagram of ISO 9241-210 referenced after a thorough understanding of the actual usage of the space obtained through interviews and on-site observations.

3.4 Examination of Design Requirements for Student Groups

Each group examined their specific design requirements based on the results of the survey, using online services such as miro (Fig. 3). Here, each group's interpretation and ideas were reflected, and initial design concepts were formed. Group A focused on visibility and functionality, Group B on flow lines and friendliness, and Group C on information communication and a relaxed atmosphere (Fig. 4).

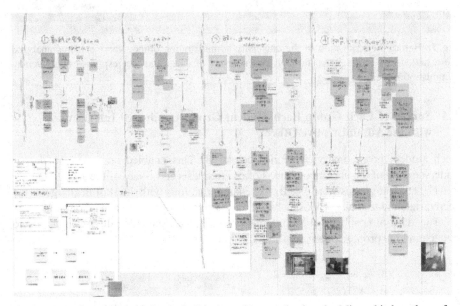

Fig. 3. Analyzing survey results, including interviews, and using the Miro whiteboard app for compilation and sharing within the group.

Group A.

• Functionality

- Identify departments by color.
- Place a map at the entrance indicating the presence of three departments.
- Install eye-catching signs immediately upon entry.
- Apply signage on pillars, walls, and floors.
- Provide chairs for writing and waiting.

• Comfort

- Use natural and bright colors or materials.
- The concept emphasized ease of department identification and a natural ambiance.

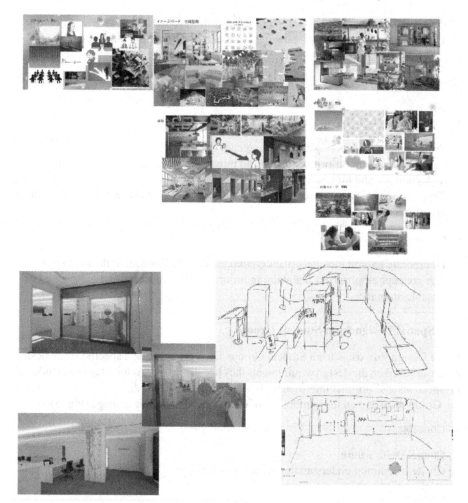

Fig. 4. Forming initial design concepts reflecting each group's interpretation and ideas, creating mood boards to share and decide on design aesthetics. Phase of concretizing ideas through sketches and CG.

Group B.

- Functionality
- Apply signage that is visible from outside the entrance (with clear identification for Operations, Academic Affairs, CSC).
- Include a directory (signage) on the pillars.

- Comfort
- Create an enjoyable atmosphere by decorating the walls with illustrations.

- Place potted plants and use wood grain furniture.
- The concept focused on eye-catching signs and creating a fun atmosphere.

Group C.

- Functionality

- Provide clear guidance using digital signage.
- Create spaces for non-primary users and those who just need to fill out forms (install high counters and high stools).
- Keep storage below eye level so that only those who need it can access it, maintaining orderliness.

- Comfort

- Incorporate natural elements (background music and plants) into the atmosphere.
- The concept emphasized maintaining an orderly environment and creating a comfortable ambiance.

3.5 Spatial Design from Student Groups

Space Design Proposals from Student Groups Each group made a specific space design proposal based on the design requirements they had discussed. At this stage, the students' perspectives and original interpretations were strongly reflected.

Group A discussed the symbolism of each section and floor signage (Fig. 5).

- Concept

- Connect with nature
- Create a common understanding through symbols

- Features

- Symbols for each department with flower motifs, mindful of the language of flowers.
- Signs on floors and pillars that follow the traffic flow, expressed with plant patterns.
- A symbolic circular bench designed for writing and waiting.

Group B made effective use of the walls (Fig. 6).

- Concept

- Eliminating boundaries and expanding circles

- Design

- The administration office as a place of connection Simple × Pop

- Features

- Graphics covering the entire wall.

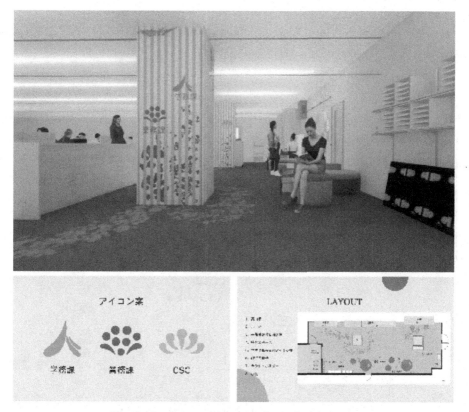

Fig. 5. Space proposal panel suggested by Group A

- Protruding signs from pillars to highlight traffic flow.
- Listing related items for each department on pillars.
- Use of colorful hues to create a bright atmosphere.

   Group C used wood as a base while incorporating signage and music (Fig. 7).

- Concept

- A space where students "feel and move"
- Natural Modern
- Transforming into a peaceful and user-friendly space for students
- Signage design as a guide for students

- Features

- A tranquil space with a wood-based theme.
- Use of signage for information dissemination to keep the space uncluttered.
- A soft atmosphere created with plants and background music.
- Symbols based on the initials and related elements of each department.

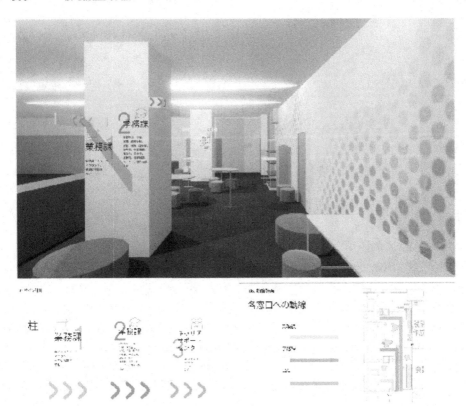

Fig. 6. Space proposal panel suggested by Group B

3.6 Feedback from the Secretariat on the Space Design Proposals from the Student Groups

The secretariat provided detailed feedback on the proposed designs. The feedback clarified the degree to which the students' proposals matched the actual needs and constraints in the field, and what improvements could be made. Based on the feedback from the secretariat, Group A identified areas that need to be reconsidered, such as the lack of entry tables, the feasibility of floor signage, and the need to improve the design of the building.

Group B had concrete measures for flow lines, and Group C had effective use of walls and pillars.

Feedback for Group A

- Positives

- The overall image, concept, and the creation of symbols are good. They can significantly change the current impression.
- Drawing guiding images on pillars and floors is a good idea.

Fig. 7. Space proposal panel suggested by Group C

– The guidance sign placed at the entrance is good.

• Areas for Improvement

– The louvers on pillars may make the guidance difficult to see.
– There is insufficient space for filling out documents.
– There is no perceived need to read flyers etc., via QR codes. Prefer to implement in a way that is closer to traditional methods.
– The waiting area needs tables for face-to-face interactions.

High praise for the symbols and signage for guidance, but there are challenges on the functional side.

Feedback for Group B

• Positives

– The bright and pop imagery is good.
– The idea of utilizing pillars for traffic flow planning is good.

– The selection of furniture that makes desks accessible and document shelves low and easy to see and reach is good.

● Areas for Improvement

– While detailed simulations of traffic flow are done, specific strategies to ensure movement as expected are weak.
– There is no place to put belongings when writing at high tables.
– Rethinking is needed for the placement of shelves and where materials are kept.
– High praise for creating a bright atmosphere, with challenges identified in traffic flow management.

Feedback for Group C

● Positives

– The use of earth tones in the imagery is good.
– The clean and uncluttered image is appealing.
– The color-coded signage is easy to understand.
– The idea of incorporating potted plants is good.

● Areas for Improvement

– The impression that the design is led too much by the image itself.
– Walls and pillars could be utilized more effectively.
– The use of signage and potted plants could pose challenges in terms of operation and maintenance.
– High praise for the overall image, with challenges noted in operational aspects.

4   Research Results

Through the student design proposal process, a requirements definition based on design thinking was confirmed to be very effective. The process showed how the Secretariat's requirements and validity considerations could be facilitated.

The student's proposal demonstrated the potential to bring new perspectives and solutions, as well as to verify the degree of conformity with the daily operation and actual requirements of the office.

Unlike the usual furniture selection process by office equipment manufacturers, the students were able to make pure space design proposals based on their observations and interviews.

The students' activities had an educational effect and enabled proposals based on the principles of human-centered design in accordance with ISO 9241-210.

The CG created using CAD facilitated collaborative design and co-creation and served as an important communication tool in promoting mutual understanding.

The design process was better adapted to user requirements and mutual understanding was facilitated through digital simulation.

The combined application of CAD and CG has proven to be a groundbreaking approach in the realm of spatial design for university administrative offices. This methodology has shown that it's possible to achieve a delicate balance between innovative design and practical functionality. It allows for a participatory design process, where feedback from actual users plays a central role in shaping the final outcome.

This approach also highlights the benefits of using VR technology in architectural design, particularly in terms of cost efficiency and flexibility. It opens up new possibilities for designing spaces that are more aligned with the actual needs and experiences of users.

5 Future Challenges and Prospects

Looking ahead, the study's findings offer exciting prospects for applying these insights to real-world construction projects. There is potential for extending this methodology to other universities and institutions, potentially revolutionizing how educational spaces are designed. Additionally, as technology continues to advance, the increasing integration of VR in space planning and design is anticipated.

References

1. Sakai, T., Ainoya, T.: Practice report on HyFlex exercise classes in industrial design education. In: Proceedings of the 7th ADADA Japan National Conference. [in Japanese]
2. Liedtka, J.: Why Design Thinking Works. Harvard Business Review (2018). [Translated to Japanese as "Design Thinking de Souzoutekikai wo Michibiku Houhou" in DAIAMOND Harvard Business Review, June 2019]

Model for Subjective Evaluation of Video Quality Considering User Perception of 5G Technology

Kenta Tsukatsune[✉]

Okayama University of Science, 1-1 Ridai-cho, Kita-ku, Okayama-shi, Okayama, Japan
k-tsukatsune@ous.ac.jp

Abstract. In this study, we conducted a subjective evaluation experiment on video quality. We assumed a situation where 5G technology is deployed in video distribution services, and analyzed the factors that influence the evaluation. A group of 24 videos was generated using an orthogonal array, with conditions such as resolution, waiting time, presence of a logo "5G" (implying that 5G technology is used in the video), and content (a train or lecture). We obtained 240 sets of evaluation data from our experiments. The results of our analysis verify the effect of the 5G logo in significantly reducing the overall satisfaction in a model where the relationship between satisfaction levels is considered with multilevel structural equation modeling (ML-SEM). Independent of the process of evaluating image quality and waiting tolerance, the overall satisfaction of users is lower when the 5G logo is mentioned explicitly. Presenting the name of an advanced technology for quality assurance purposes may occasionally not have the effect intended by the designers. It may rather result in a more severe evaluation by users.

Keywords: quality of experience (QoE) · video quality · 5G · brand · ML-SEM

1 Introduction

In the research on communication quality, the quality of service (QoS) and quality of experience (QoE) perceived by users have been considered. QoE research has also demonstrated that a user's attributes and past experiences, as well as the environment surrounding both technology and user, influence the quality evaluation [1–4].

Currently, fifth generation (5G) technology has passed the trial phase and is advancing into the practical phase. With reference to the observations on QoE, a similar approach focusing on the user side of acceptance would be required for 5G technology [5]. For example, it is necessary to consider the physical performance improvements in video and online gaming (low latency, high capacity, and multiple connections) and factors such as the user's daily frequency of contact with communication technologies and the amount of relevant knowledge. However, the impacts of users' individual characteristics on 5G QoE are occasionally unpredictable. It is likely that the more knowledgeable a user is regarding a technology, the more exhaustively he/she would perceive the advantages of

© The Author(s), under exclusive license to Springer Nature Switzerland AG 2024
H. Mori and Y. Asahi (Eds.): HCII 2024, LNCS 14690, pp. 304–319, 2024.
https://doi.org/10.1007/978-3-031-60114-9_22

5G, and the higher would be his/her evaluation of its quality. However, there is also a reverse possibility: his/her assessment of the technology would be more detailed and the rating more severe.

In addition, technology is not accessible to the average user. It is provided by specific operators (e.g., companies, government departments, and universities). Given that many of these are paid services, users also have a position as customers or contractors. Therefore, a business perspective is also required in the verification of QoE mechanisms [1]. Certain users may have a preconceived notion of the term "5G" as being superior without awareness of the details. They may consider it as a brand that ensures high quality, similar to well-known corporate brands.

This study presents a model of the evaluation process by analyzing data from video evaluation experiments and a questionnaire survey. It assumes a situation where 5G technology has been introduced to video services. We measure users' evaluation of the video quality and examine the influence of video conditions (such as the resolution, waiting time, and presence of stimuli related to 5G technology) on the evaluation results. In addition, we apply a statistical method to appropriately separate the value of the quality rating from the part that varies depending on the video characteristics and the part caused by the users. Tsukatsune [6] used data common to this study and the linear mixed model (LMM) in which the explanatory variables directly explain the values of individual evaluation items. Meanwhile, this study applies the multilevel structural equation modelling (ML-SEM) used in Tsukatsune and Niida [7]. It adopts a model that more appropriately follows the process of user cognition, thereby reflecting the ordinal relationship between the evaluation items.

2 Related Works

Various elements necessary to understand QoE have been discussed. These include methods of reliable measurement and analysis, explanatory variables that affect it, and its relationship with QoS [1–4]. In the research on QoE involving video evaluation experiments, comprehensive analyses have also been conducted considering individuality on the user side [3, 7–11]. As specific examples of factors, the influence of the evaluator's level of interest in the content [8, 9], viewing environment such as with whom and where the content is watched [3, 10], and influence of personality characteristics known as Big5 [3, 11] have been examined. The analysis by Tsukatsune and Niida [7] revealed that the users' preference regarding whether to prioritize high image quality or short waiting time also influenced their evaluation of the actual waiting time. Other demographic attributes such as age and gender can also be taken into account [1–3]. Furthermore, it is considered that business-related dimensions of QoE should also be identified. Models have been proposed that include the impact of advertisement, pricing, etc. [1].

The research to measure the user QoE of services using 5G technology is proceeding in various domains and is being developed at a large scale and automated. For example, Nightingale et al. [12] proposed a framework for predicting user QoE for ultra-high-definition (UHD) video application. They presented results that can be predicted with good accuracy. Meanwhile, the literature [5] discusses various factors and measurement methods to be considered as challenges for 5G research. In the literature, the need to focus on the user-side factors has been indicated. In this study, among the various feasible 5G research approaches, we focus on the approach that evaluates factors such as user's experience and psychological states, which remain largely unexplored.

In recent years, certain questionnaire studies have been conducted to investigate users' attitudes and opinions regarding 5G technology, including their backgrounds. For example, the studies [13, 14] addressed the approval of 5G technology by Indonesian users; Suryanegara [13] asked survey respondents regarding their experiences of satisfaction or dissatisfaction with existing 2–4G technology and their expectations regarding 5G, in the form of a questionnaire. The combination of these answers was used to categorize the users (respondents) into six clusters. Each cluster predicted a different likelihood of acceptance of 5G in the future. Given this observation, the introduction of 5G is unlikely to improve the QoE for all users. Moreover, the QoE would differ depending on a user's background. The questionnaire by Mardian et al. [14] also addressed 10 factors on attractiveness, perspicuity, etc., for each of experiences with existing 4G technologies and expectations regarding future 5G technologies. The relationships between the factor groups were then analyzed using structural equation modelling (SEM). It revealed significant correlations between the 4G experience and 5G expectations.

As a case from a different country, Ejdys and Soler [15] conducted a questionnaire survey of Poles from the perspective of the social theory of science and technology and analyzed factors that define their attitudes toward 5G technology. The results illustrate that a high internet usage frequency, young age, higher education, and alcohol consumption frequency resulted in positive attitudes regarding 5G technology.

Finally, we evaluate studies that may be of interest when considering the cognitive and psychological effects of the term "5G". To the author's knowledge, research has not been conducted on the term 5G. However, research examining the influence of the brand's name, logo, keywords, etc., on the evaluation of the quality of a particular product or service has been conducted extensively, particularly in the fields of psychology and marketing. For example, Klink [16] performed an experimental questionnaire survey to examine the relationship between the linguistic features of a brand's name and its logo, and the impact of their combination on evaluations of the product. Suzuki and Yamamoto [17] and Yamashita et al. [18] also conducted experiments in which participants were instructed to subjectively evaluate logos of highly popular companies and brands. They observed that the evaluations varied depending on various conditions such as the shape of the logo and the symbols that were combined.

3 Experiment and Survey

3.1 Overview of Experiment and Survey

In this study, an experiment and a survey were conducted with undergraduate and postgraduate students at Tokyo Metropolitan University (TMU). A situation was assumed where students use local 5G facilities installed in the school building to watch video content, e.g., online lectures. TMU is planning to introduce local 5G and considering its future use in education. In conjunction with the equipment preparation, the effectiveness of 5G technology as a user experience needs to be verified. This study is part of that effort. However, at the time this research started (November 2021), local 5G had not begun operation within the university. Therefore, anticipating the future environment, this study generated an experimental video assuming that 5G technology is in use and instructed participants to evaluate its quality. Although the 5G networks operated by major telecommunications operators and local 5G differ, these are not directly related to the main purpose of this study. Therefore, all these would henceforth be referred to as "5G".

The period of our experiment and survey was initially set as February 21–March 16, 2022. Participants who appeared on any day during the period were recruited within the university. The first and last actual participants came on February 22 and March 10, respectively. The location of the event was a small seminar room on the TMU campus. A tranquil environment was maintained there.

The number of participants was 10 (7 males and 3 females). In ML-SEM, LMM, and other methods to effectively handle individual differences between respondents, a minimum of 20 participants (total number of responses obtained = 100) is considered preferable. However, the number of participants in this experiment was low owing to an overlap between the implementation period and university holidays. Although sufficient data were obtained (sum of the final number of responses obtained = 240 sets), we executed our further procedures considering that this would pose limitations in detecting individual differences between users.

The participants' ages ranged from 21 to 25 years. This study envisaged undergraduate and postgraduate students as users of 5G in educational settings. Therefore, younger individuals were recruited. In addition, each participant had a major in information science, information technology, or mechanical engineering. They were more familiar with communications technology than the average student. However, the data obtained from them is considered sufficient to understand the overall evaluation trends and the aspects of individual differences between participants within the same major.

3.2 Experimental Contents and Survey Items

The process of data acquisition in this study consisted of two main parts: an experiment on video evaluation and a subsequent questionnaire survey. The first half of the experiment measured participants' evaluations of the videos presented. The questionnaire survey in the second half had questions on aspects such as experience and knowledge of ICT use. Of the experimental and survey tasks, the processing of the videos corresponding to the experimental conditions, design of web pages for responding to the video evaluation items, and automatic recording of the answers were outsourced to an internet research company. The other tasks were conducted manually by the author. The following section describes in detail the experiment/survey and the hypotheses underlying the experimental conditions set.

Video Evaluation Experiments. The experiment involved one participant at a time. The author prepared 24 videos for the conditions and played these on a laptop (viewing laptop) placed in front of each participant. After each completed viewing of a video, the participant completed a rating on a web page displayed on a second laptop (response laptop) adjacent to him/her.

The evaluation was based on three items for each video, "image quality", "waiting tolerance", and "overall satisfaction", on a five-point scale (5: very satisfied; 4: satisfied; 3: neither satisfied nor dissatisfied; 2: dissatisfied; 1: very dissatisfied). The format for item names and option words is identical to that in Niida et al. [20] and Tsukatsune and Niida [7] (as an exception, we use "image quality" instead of "picture quality"). These items follow the absolute category rating (ACR) method in ITU-T [19] for measuring the mean opinion score (MOS). The results of responses using discrete rating words were used as is. After all the ratings for a video were completed and the participant was prepared to watch, the next video was played.

The following four factors were adopted as the experimental conditions. These are likely to be highly relevant for both video services and 5G technology: (1) resolution (three levels): high/middle/low; (2) waiting time (latency) (four levels): 0 s/2 s/4 s/6 s; (3) 5G presentation conditions (two levels): "5G" logo is/is not displayed on the screen; and (4) video content (two levels): video of an online lecture/video of a transportation medium (a train). However, if researchers attempt to prepare videos by the book corresponding to the experimental conditions, a larger number of these would be required. For example, a simple calculation would reveal that if there are four experimental conditions with three levels, 81 videos are required to correspond to all the combinations. Therefore, in this study, an orthogonal array of experimental design was used to reduce the number of videos. Based on Table 1, 24 patterns of videos were prepared (identical to Table 1 in Tsukatsune [6]). Examples of the videos used (nos. 8 and 15 in Table 1) are shown in Fig. 1.

The conditions of resolution and waiting time have been demonstrated to have a strong influence on video-quality assessment [7, 20]. Therefore, the experimental conditions of Niida et al. [20] and Tsukatsune and Niida [7] were also used as a reference in this study. In the resolution condition, the quality was expressed in three levels (resolution, compressed, and processed) and then, played back in the full-screen display mode of an equivalent 14-inch laptop to reproduce the image's denseness/roughness. However, for participants familiar with video services in the 2020s, when dramatic improvements in image quality are being made, the presentation of significantly low quality images in the context of cutting-edge technology may generate a perception of it being unrealistic. Therefore, three levels of resolution were set while maintaining a level of high quality. The high, medium, and low quality of uncompressed videos was at 1920×1080 pixels, 1680×944 pixels, and 1440×810 pixels, respectively.

The waiting time conditions were also reconsidered similarly as for resolution. Four levels were determined. The waiting time in the experimental data of Tsukatsune and Niida [7] was 5/10/15/20 s. However, these values are excessively long for a video that assumes 5G, which advocates low latency. Therefore, we adopted a shorter waiting time. Based on recommendations of experts in network technology and user interfaces both inside and outside the university, we finally adopted 0/2/4/6 s. The length of the video is 10 s. A waiting time was added to it. In the videos with waiting time, the screen stops 2 s

Table 1. The orthogonal array used.

Video no.	Resolution	Waiting time	5G logo	Contents
1	Middle	6 s	Yes	Lecture
2	Low	2 s	Yes	Train
3	Low	0 s	Yes	Lecture
4	High	4 s	Yes	Lecture
5	High	4 s	Yes	Train
6	High	0 s	No	Lecture
7	Low	6 s	No	Lecture
8	High	6 s	No	Train
9	Middle	4 s	Yes	Lecture
10	Low	2 s	No	Lecture
11	Middle	2 s	Yes	Train
12	Low	0 s	Yes	Lecture
13	Low	4 s	No	Train
14	High	0 s	No	Train
15	Low	6 s	Yes	Train
16	Middle	6 s	No	Lecture
17	Middle	0 s	Yes	Train
18	High	2 s	No	Lecture
19	Middle	0 s	No	Train
20	High	6 s	Yes	Train
21	Middle	4 s	No	Lecture
22	Middle	2 s	No	Train
23	High	2 s	Yes	Lecture
24	Low	4 s	No	Train

after the start, and a circular loading animation is displayed in the middle of the screen for each second. After this, it moves again.

For the condition wherein the use of 5G technology is implied in the video, two levels were adopted: displaying/not displaying a logo with the letters "5G" in white block letters on a black rectangle at the top-left corner of the screen. This was adopted to examine the likelihood that an indication of 5G would influence the subjective quality evaluation. For example, participants who perceived the term 5G as a brand that assures high quality may rate the logo particularly highly when it is included in the video under high quality and low latency conditions. Meanwhile, it was assumed that when the logo 5G is included in a video under low quality and high latency conditions, the rating may be rather low owing to the discrepancy between the brand and actual quality. Participants

Fig. 1. Example of videos used (above: no. 8 with loading animation; below: no. 15).

were not provided prior explanation regarding the logo. At the end of the entire process including the questionnaire, it was clarified to them that the main purpose of the 5G logo was for experimentation and that 5G technology was not applied in the video used in this study. Unlike previous studies on logos and brands [16–18], it was infeasible to examine the characteristics of the logo in detail in this study. However, as a first step, we verified whether its presence was related to the QoE or not.

For the video content conditions, two levels (online lecture video and transportation video) were adopted. The experiments by Yamamoto and Yamazaki [21] demonstrated that even when the physical conditions are identical, the subjective quality of the video varies significantly depending on its genre. Differences such as the speed of object movement and presence/absence of textual information are considered to be related to video evaluation. Therefore, in this study as well, in addition to videos of online lecture scenes, videos of rapidly moving objects were prepared for comparison. Such an object was selected for filming because it is more convenient to detect disturbances in such a video than in one displaying a speaking human. For the lecture videos, scenes of an individual (lecturer) explaining an academic concept using a whiteboard were filmed. For the comparison and verification, videos of a transportation medium were used. These are common scenes in everyday life. Moreover, the difference between moving and stationary objects is apparent in these. Among several candidates, a video of a train entering a station was selected. The recording function of a mirrorless digital camera (Canon EOS M3) was used for these videos.

The 24 videos filmed and processed according to the above conditions were played back in a different, randomly assigned order for each participant. In addition, these were played back on mute. Notwithstanding the fact that the scenes are from an online lecture, the images without sound appear marginally unnatural. Nonetheless, an evaluation that includes sound would require the consideration of the conditions related to acoustics and the complex composite conditions of image and sound. Therefore, the present experiment focused only on simple visuals.

Questionnaire Survey. After the experiment, a questionnaire survey was conducted. It contained questions regarding knowledge of the characteristics of 5G technology and its use, frequency of use of ICTs such as internet services, and experience of attending online lectures. The influence of the users' experiences and habits on their attitudes and expectations regarding 5G technology has been demonstrated in previous studies [13–15] using questionnaires with explicit question items. In this study, the questionnaire survey was delayed given the need to ensure a more unconscious psychological state during the quality evaluation experiment.

4 Analysis

4.1 Basic Analysis

First, we identified the general evaluation trends of the 10 participants. The intra-individual averages for the ratings of image quality, waiting tolerance, and overall satisfaction for the 24 videos are shown in Fig. 2 (identical to Fig. 1 in Tsukatsune [6]). The numbers on the horizontal axis identify the participants. The figure reveals that in general, the overall satisfaction tends to be lower than the individual quality ratings (image quality and waiting tolerance) for the same respondent. However, individual differences such as high and low values can also be observed.

Figure 3 displays the average value of the corresponding video (e.g., eight videos with "High" image quality) for each experimental condition and its level, obtained from the 10 participants (identical to Fig. 2 in Tsukatsune [6]). Here, a clear trend is observed wherein the better the physical resolution and waiting time conditions, the higher is the evaluation of image quality and waiting tolerance. Meanwhile, a significant uncertainty exists regarding the other experimental conditions and overall quality trends.

4.2 ML-SEM

Analytical Methods. Having identified trends in the basic results, we performed a more advanced analysis. As stated at the beginning of this study, we used ML-SEM. SEM has also been used in studies explaining the QoE of video viewers [8]. It is a method that enables analysis that considers complex pre- and post-relationships between variables. In addition, because the results of multiple responses by the same respondent are data with a hierarchical structure, it is also necessary to consider means of appropriately separating the total variance of the rating values into the variance between raters and that between rating objects. LMM is a part of the generalized linear mixed model (GLMM) framework applied in recent related research [3, 11]. Tsukatsune [6] used it to measure variations attributable to individual differences (participants) and experimental conditions (videos). However, the analysis was limited to examinations of relatively simple

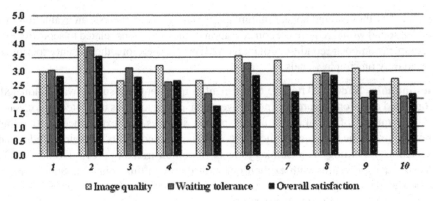

Fig. 2. Averages of each participant.

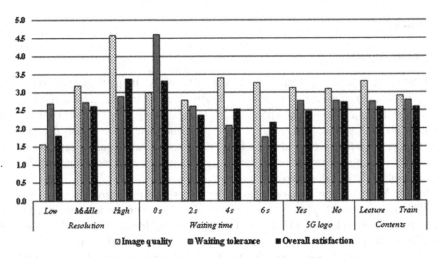

Fig. 3. Averages of each experimental condition.

influence relationships for only the observed variables. In this study, rather than LMM, we adopted the ML-SEM used in Tsukatsune and Niida [7] and considered the influence relationships between the objective variables. ML-SEM is a method that has elements of SEM. However, it also allows for an appropriate processing of hierarchical data, similar to LMM. The software Mplus ver. 7 is used. Maximum likelihood with robust standard errors (MLR) is used for estimation.

Models and Variables. Tsukatsune [6] analyzed a model in which explanatory variables directly influence the image quality, waiting tolerance, and overall satisfaction. However, in this study, in line with Tsukatsune and Niida [7], we examined a model in which overall satisfaction is the final objective variable. In this model, each explanatory variable influences the image quality and waiting tolerance. Ultimately, these two influence the overall satisfaction. In addition, ML-SEM divides the variance of the objective variable into two levels: one for the response unit and the other for the individual. The effects of the explanatory variables corresponding to each level can be verified[1]. This study also expressed and analyzed the relationship between variables in the two levels as a model[2].

The explanatory variables for the response units of evaluation (Level 1, within level) were those corresponding to each experimental condition. The impact was not necessarily monotonically increasing/decreasing. Therefore, all the conditions, in conjunction with the resolution and waiting time conditions, were used as dummy variables separated by levels, rather than continuous variables. Low quality (1440 × 810p), 0 s, "no logo", and "lecture" were used as the reference categories for the resolution condition, waiting time condition, 5G logo condition, and content condition, respectively. In Tsukatsune and Niida [7], the paths to image quality and waiting tolerance were subtracted from the resolution and waiting time. Therefore, a similar process was conducted in our model. The 5G logo and content were also conducted in a similar manner. To control for the influence of the order of presentation of each video (which differs for each participant), it was also put into Level 1 as a continuous variable.

The explanatory variables for participant units (Level 2, between levels) were not entered in the present analysis. The first reason for this was that it was difficult to effectively verify the effects of the Level 2 explanatory variables because data from a small number of participants (10) were used. Moreover, there was concern that this difficulty would be higher in ML-SEM, where the number of paths is large. In addition, although the age, gender, and eyesight variables and the "knowledge regarding 5G" (the number of features and use-cases of 5G technology that participants could remember, as revealed by their responses to the free-answer questions; maximum value $= 7$, minimum value $= 2$) was incorporated into the analytical model in the LMM of Tsukatsune [6], a negligible effect was observed. Therefore, although it was disadvantageous that the user background could not be verified as in previous studies [13–15], we prioritized the analysis stability. In Level 2, we analyzed only the relationship between the variables image quality, waiting tolerance, and overall satisfaction[3]. However, the main purpose of these processes was also to obtain more robust Level 1 analysis results by controlling for individual differences, rather than to reveal individual differences between participants and gain new insights.

Note that again, the small number of participants hindered the application of complex models that assume variance between individuals in this case. Therefore, models including random slopes and cross-level interactions such as Tsukatsune and Niida [7] were not implemented. Rather, only random intercept models were tested. The descriptive statistics of the variables used are presented in Table 2.

Model Improvement and Selection. Before conducting the main analysis, the intra-class correlation (ICC1) was calculated with participants as group variables by a model with no explanatory variable. The ICC1 for image quality, waiting tolerance, and overall

---

[1] The term "level" here does not indicate the level of condition or height of value of response results. It rather indicates each stratum of the nested data.

[2] In the analysis of LMM in Tsukatsune [6], a level of video units (independent of response units) was also set up. However, the order of videos was randomized, and the level did not have a significant influence. Therefore, this level is not reflected in our ML-SEM.

[3] It should be mentioned in advance that there was no significant effect when the variable "knowledge regarding 5G" was incorporated into the analytical model on a trial basis.

Table 2. Descriptive statistics.

Level	Variable	Mean	S.D.	Min	Max
Lv.1/Lv.2	Image quality	3.108	1.454	1.000	5.000
	Waiting tolerance	2.767	1.346	1.000	5.000
	Overall satisfaction	2.596	1.060	1.000	5.000
Lv.1 (Response)	High (1920 × 1080)	.333	.471	.000	1.000
	Middle (1680 × 944)	.333	.471	.000	1.000
	2 s	.250	.434	.000	1.000
	4 s	.250	.434	.000	1.000
	6 s	.250	.434	.000	1.000
	5G logo	.500	.500	.000	1.000
	Train	.500	.500	.000	1.000
	Presentation order	12.500	6.922	1.000	24.000

satisfaction was .047, .141, and .165, respectively[4]. For image quality, the ICC1 was small, and the response trends were consistent across participants. Meanwhile, in the last two items, an inter-participant variance was observed that could be considered significant for applying ML-SEM. For example, 16.5% of the total variance in the value of overall satisfaction was the difference in evaluation between participants. Based on the above, we applied ML-SEM while also considering the variance in image quality.

A relatively simple model based on Tsukatsune and Niida [7] was then applied. This model is denoted Model 1 (M1). As mentioned earlier, in this model, all the Level 1 explanatory variables are affected by the image quality and waiting tolerance, and the experimental conditions and presentation order do not directly affect the overall satisfaction. As a result, robust effects of the resolution and waiting time conditions were detected[5]. A content influence (a train video has lower image quality than a lecture video) was also detected. However, the 5G logo was not significant.

Meanwhile, the goodness-of-fit of M1 remained low. Therefore, considering that the direct effect of the 5G logo on the overall satisfaction was detected in Tsukatsue [6], we aimed to improve and test a model in which the paths for 5G logo, video content, and presentation order (these do not have directly corresponding evaluation items) were drawn to overall satisfaction. It is denoted as Model 2 (M2). Furthermore, as a comparison, another model was analyzed in which the paths for the explanatory variables of resolution and waiting time conditions were also directly drawn to overall satisfaction. This is denoted as Model 3 (M3). However, in the case of M3, although image quality

---

[4] After adding the explanatory variables, the ICC1 for each evaluation item was .069, .167, and .187 for image quality, waiting tolerance, and overall satisfaction, respectively.

[5] In each of the subsequent models, a non-linear effect of the waiting time on the image quality (a significant positive effect at 4 s) was identified. This is difficult to interpret. However, a mechanism by which a moderate waiting time impresses an improvement in image quality is likely to exist (such as a subjective perception of cost-effectiveness).

Table 3. Results for each model.

	AIC	BIC	aBIC	RMSEA	CFI	TLI	SRMR Lv.1	SRMR Lv.2
M1	1264.371	1372.271	1274.009	.174	.936	.759	.027	.002
M2	1223.994	1342.336	1234.564	.100	.987	.920	.010	.000
M3	1222.482	1358.227	1234.606	.000	1.000	1.000	.000	.000

and waiting tolerance were affected appropriately by the resolution and waiting time, those experimental conditions also directly affected the overall satisfaction. This model represents a path structure that is mechanically analyzable but logically impractical.

The values of the above M1–M3 information criteria and various absolute goodness-of-fit indices are shown in Table 3. From the information criteria (AIC, BIC, and adjusted BIC (aBIC)), M2 or M3 have high validity. The values of the goodness-of-fit indices are low for M1, good for M2 (but its RMSEA low), and highest for M3. Meanwhile, it is difficult to use M3 as a model of realistic user perceptions because as mentioned above, the model reflects unnatural assumptions. Hence, M2 would be adopted from an overall perspective and subject to interpretation (the results of M3 are also mentioned where necessary). The results for M2 are shown in Fig. 4. The path coefficients in the figure are for all the variables standardized simultaneously.

In M2, the resolution and waiting time conditions via image quality and waiting tolerance eventually result in overall satisfaction. The model also demonstrated that the appearance of the 5G logo does not influence the evaluation of individual technical qualities such as image quality. Rather, it results in a more severe overall evaluation[6]. Although the direct effect of the 5G logo was also verified by Tsukatsune [6], the relationship between the 5G logo and overall satisfaction became more evident when the model was re-examined based on the model of Tsukatsune and Niida [7]. Their model also incorporated the pre- and post-relationships between the quality evaluation items.

With regard to the impact of the video content, it was observed that the image quality decreased while the overall satisfaction increased, in the case of videos of moving trains. It is convenient to interpret that the reduced visibility of rapidly moving objects compared with humans moving slowly and speaking in class results in more severe evaluations. However, the effect on the overall satisfaction is difficult to interpret. This is likely to be owing to unaccounted-for technical factors such as the color and contrast of the video as a landscape image.

The presentation order variable also illustrated that the later that a video is displayed, the lower is the level of satisfaction. This indicates that participants provide more severe evaluations as they become more familiar with the experimental environment. This is not a result of QoE. It is rather a reaffirmation of the factors that should be controlled while conducting an experiment.

---

[6] Note that the results of M3, where all the explanatory variables directly affected the overall satisfaction, were approximately similar to those of M2, with the direct effect of waiting time lowering the overall satisfaction but weakening the effect of waiting tolerance (no direct effect of resolution).

Level 1 (Response)

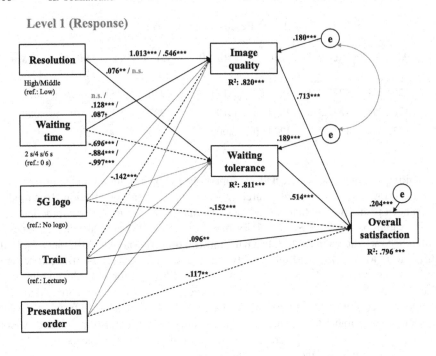

Level 2 (Participant)

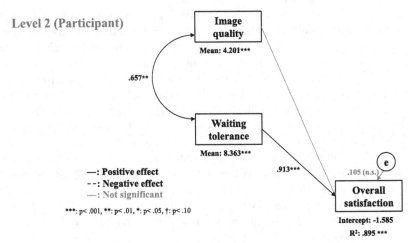

Fig. 4. Result of ML-SEM (Model 2).

Finally, a strong effect of the waiting tolerance on the overall satisfaction was detected at Level 2. Meanwhile, the effect of the image quality was not significant. Although the coefficient of Level 2, which describes differences between users, cannot be interpreted positively at this time, this result may have been influenced by the fact that the values of image quality were close for the participants in the first place.

5 Conclusion and Future Work

5.1 Conclusion

In this study, a subjective evaluation experiment using video and survey was conducted to examine the factors influencing the evaluation. It assumed the introduction of 5G into the university educational environment. This time, a model was analyzed by ML-SEM, which also considered the pre- and post-relationships between quality evaluations. The results revealed inter-variable relationships (such as a lower evaluation of overall satisfaction when the 5G logo was presented in the video) independent of the individual image quality and waiting time evaluation structures. This result implies that presenting the name of an advanced technology for quality assurance does not necessarily have a positive effect as intended. Rather, it may result in higher challenges in evaluation by users.

The fact that the 5G logo did not affect the evaluation of image quality and latency indicates that the difference between the specific reputation of 5G (such as the low latency) and the service at hand was not calculated. Rather, it is related to the overall impression and expectation/dissatisfaction with the service, similarly as with brand logos[7]. However, the above is a tentative conclusion based only on the explanatory variables or main effects examined in this study.

5.2 Future Work

Many tasks remain for this study. Issues related to the need for new experiments and surveys should be described and addressed. The first of these is the issue of the number and diversity of respondents/participants. The number of participants in our experiments was significantly small, and their age (in the 20 s) and field of study (information science, information technology, or mechanical engineering) were exceptionally limited. To construct a more universal model for the quality assessment of 5G environments, it is necessary to secure many participants and seek the participation of individuals with a wide range of attributes. The analysis in this study had significant limitations including the inability to test the impact of explanatory variables derived from participants (Level 2). Ejdys and Soler [15] analyzed over 1000 responses. They observed significant effects of the indicators such as education, age, and frequency of internet use. These should be considered as factors that may influence the variance between individuals in future QoE models. In addition, the evaluation of random slopes and interaction effects between 5G presentation conditions and resolution, waiting time, etc., also need to be studied.

Next is the issue of the 5G presentation condition. In this study, only the presence or absence of a simple logo was used as the experimental condition. However, experiments should also be conducted under different external conditions such as the color, shape,

---

[7] Other practical aspects of university education were also indicated by the results of this study regarding the content: the image quality of the lecture video was rated higher than that of the train video. This may imply that users may be relatively more tolerant of image disturbances when the video is provided online (however, the relative tolerance, and the accurate conveyance of the lesson content would be a prerequisite).

and size of the logo [17, 18], or under conditions where the brand or name of the operator is presented [16].

Acknowledgments. This study was supported by the Tokyo Metropolitan University (TMU) local 5G research support. I also wish to thank Dr. Sumaru Niida (KDDI Research, Inc.), Prof. Masaki Aida (Tokyo Metropolitan University), and Dr. Naoki Hirakura (Toyama Prefectural University) for their recommendations for this study.

Disclosure of Interests. The author has no competing interests to declare that are relevant to the content of this article.

References

1. Laghari, K.U.R., Connelly, K.: Toward total quality of experience: a QoE model in a communication ecosystem. IEEE Commun. Mag. **50**(4), 58–65 (2012)
2. Streijl, R.C., Winkler, S., Hands, D.S.: Mean opinion score (MOS) revisited: methods and applications, limitations and alternatives. Multim. Syst. **22**(2), 213–227 (2016)
3. Zhu, Y., Guntuku, S.C., Lin, W., Ghinea, G., Redi, J.A.: Measuring individual video QoE: a survey, and proposal for future directions using social media. ACM Trans. Multim. Comput. Commun. Appl. **14**(2s), 30, 1–24 (2018)
4. Yamazaki, T.: Quality of experience (QoE) studies: present state and future prospect. IEICE Trans. Commun. **E104-B**(7), 716–724 (2021)
5. Wang, Y., et al.: A data-driven architecture for personalized QoE management in 5G wireless networks. IEEE Wirel. Commun. **24**(1), 102–110 (2016)
6. Tsukatsune, K.: An experiment on subjective evaluation of video quality assuming a 5G environment and verification of effects of personal characteristics and a presentation condition. IEICE Tech. Rep. **122**(275), CQ2022-49, 13–18 (2022) (in Japanese)
7. Tsukatsune, K., Niida, S.: Model for subjective evaluation of video quality considering individual differences and interfactorial relationships. J. IEICE **J106-B**(7), 424–437 (2023) (in Japanese)
8. Eguchi, M., Miyoshi, T., Yamori, K., Yamazaki, T.: Practical QoE model considering delay condition and content preference. J. IEICE **J92-B**(12), 1810–1822 (2009) (in Japanese)
9. Kortum, P., Sullivan, M.: The effect of content desirability on subjective video quality ratings. Hum. Factors **52**(1), 105–118 (2010)
10. Zhu, Y., Heynderickx, I., Redi, J.A.: Understanding the role of social context and user factors in video quality of experience. Comput. Hum. Behav. **49**, 412–426 (2015)
11. Scott, M.J., Guntuku, S.C., Lin, W., Ghinea, G.: Do personality and culture influence perceived video quality and enjoyment? IEEE Trans. Multim. **18**(9), 1796–1807 (2016)
12. Nightingale, J., Salva-Garcia, P., Calero, J.M.A., Wang, Q.: 5G-QoE: QoE modelling for ultra-HD video streaming in 5G networks. IEEE Trans. Broadcast. **64**(2), 621–634 (2018)
13. Suryanegara, M.: Managing 5G technology: using quality of experience (QoE) to identify the innovation enhancement pattern according to the Indonesian market. IEEE Access **8**, 165593–165611 (2020)
14. Mardian, R.D., Suryanegara, M., Ramli, K.: User experience of 5G video services in Indonesia: predictions based on a structural equation model. Information **13**(3), 155 (2022)
15. Ejdys, J., Soler, U.: The society's attitude toward 5G technologies–a case study of Poland. Technol. Econ. Dev. Econ. **29**(5), 1539–1558 (2023)

16. Klink, R.R.: Creating meaningful brands: the relationship between brand name and brand mark. Mark. Lett. **14**(3), 143–157 (2003)
17. Suzuki, Y., Yamamoto, H.: A study of trade marks, symbols and logotypes of Japanese corporations: by means of perspective on visual evolution. Trans. Jpn. Soc. Kansei Eng. **12**(1), 109–113 (2013)
18. Yamashita, T., Eibo, A., Kasamatsu, K.: Psychological effects of English and Arabic in global corporate logos. Trans. Jpn. Soc. Kansei Eng. **21**(2), 175–179 (2022) (in Japanese)
19. ITU. ITU-T Recommendation P.910 Subjective Video Quality Assessment Methods for Multimedia Applications (1996)
20. Niida, S., Ano, S., Uemura, S.: User study of the subjective quality of mobile streaming service. In: Proceedings of the 14th international Conference on Human-Computer Interaction with Mobile Devices and Services Companion (Mobile HCI 2012), pp. 83–88 (2012)
21. Yamamoto, R., Yamazaki, T.: Analysis of quality of experience in consideration of the color information in the video streaming. J. Inst. Image Inf. Televis. Eng. **71**(7), J199–J206 (2017) (in Japanese)

Research on Factors Influencing Self-medication from UX Perspective

Sirui Zhang[1(✉)], Keiko Kasamatsu[1], and Takeo Ainoya[2]

[1] Tokyo Metropolitan University, 6-6 Asahigaoka, Hino, Tokyo, Japan
zhangsiruidesign@yeah.net
[2] Tokyo University of Technology, 5-23-22 Nishikamata, Ota City, Tokyo, Japan

Abstract. Self-medication is highly prevalent across various countries worldwide. According to the World Health Organization (WHO), one-third of patients globally die due to improper self-medication practices, and one-seventh of patients are hospitalized as a result. This study primarily focused on China and Japan, utilizing User Experience (UX) analysis methodology, and conducted face-to-face interviews with 17 participants from nine countries regarding their experiences with self-medication in their respective nations. The investigation analyzed the reasons behind self-medication practices among patients in different countries and identified commonalities, summarizing them into a five-stage behavioral process. Self-medication behaviors are significantly associated with the laws, healthcare policies, and cultural customs of each country. To ensure safe self-medication practices, this study emphasizes the indispensability of health literacy for both patients and pharmacists.

Keywords: Self-Medication · User experience · Health literacy

1 The Definition and Current Status of Self-medication

According to the definition provided by the World Health Organization (WHO), self-medication refers to the individual's choice and use of drugs (including herbs and traditional products) to treat self-perceived diseases or symptoms.

Self-medication is a component of self-care, as defined by the World Health Organization (1998) [1]. In Japan, the Ministry of Health, Labour, and Welfare defines self-medication as concern for one's own health and self-treatment of minor physical discomfort [2]. The China Association of Enterprises with Foreign Investment in the Medical and Healthcare Industry mentions that self-medication involves individuals using over-the-counter drugs, health supplements, home medical devices, medicinal diets, etc., for self-treatment, prevention, and healthcare. While definitions may vary among countries, the concept of self-medication has broadened in many nations to include not only the relief of mild symptoms but also the self-management of common diseases that individuals can determine themselves, as well as addressing various issues related to daily healthcare [3].

© The Author(s), under exclusive license to Springer Nature Switzerland AG 2024
H. Mori and Y. Asahi (Eds.): HCII 2024, LNCS 14690, pp. 320–333, 2024.
https://doi.org/10.1007/978-3-031-60114-9_23

The "self-medication behavior" defined in this study encompasses the elements of "mild symptoms," "over-the-counter drugs," and "patient's autonomous decision-making."

With the advancement of healthcare standards and the increasing awareness of health among the global population, self-medication has become a prevalent approach to health management worldwide. Relevant studies indicate that self-medication with both over-the-counter and prescription drugs is common in 21 developing countries [1]. The escalating aging population and the consequent rise in complications from chronic diseases are placing substantial pressure on families and societies. There is a growing societal focus on controlling healthcare costs [4]. In pursuit of the strategic goal of achieving an "extended healthy life expectancy for the nation," Japan, for example, implemented a "self-medication tax system" in January 2017. This initiative aims to encourage the use of over-the-counter drugs as alternatives to prescription medications under appropriate health management [2].

In China, the production of over-the-counter drugs has seen rapid development, with diverse distribution channels for over-the-counter products, including online, telephone, and mail-order options. This has led to the establishment of an open and competitive over-the-counter market [3]. The successful advancement of self-medication relies on both the enhancement of public awareness regarding self-health management and the support provided by national policies in the health industry. Self-medication demonstrates high cost-effectiveness.

Temin's study [6] reveals the impact of transitioning many cough and cold medications from prescription to over-the-counter status in the United States from 1976 to 1989, based on analysis using IMS Health data. The research indicates a yearly reduction of approximately 110,000 doctor visits related to common cold during these 14 years. In the final year, there was a decrease of 1.65 million visits, translating to an estimated savings of $70 million in consultation fees alone (with an estimated cost of $42 per visit in 1989, comprising a $30 fee, $2 for public transportation, and $10 for the patient's time). Implementing self-medication not only increases patients' access to treatment but also significantly enhances patients' autonomy in managing their symptoms and health [7].

For society, promoting self-medication sensibly can alleviate the burden on the national healthcare service system, directing limited health resources more towards the treatment of severe illnesses, reducing pressure on the healthcare system, cutting waiting times, and improving medical efficiency [8]. This, in turn, lowers time and economic costs for both patients and healthcare providers.

Despite the social and economic benefits of self-medication, there are potential risks due to insufficient public awareness of its hazards [9]. For example, the widespread belief in the minimal side effects of herbal medicine has led many residents in China to choose herbal remedies independently, contributing to a gradual increase in patients experiencing acute renal failure and nephritis [10]. In the usage of over-the-counter medications without professional guidance, cases of adverse effects from inappropriate drug combinations have been widely reported [11].

Community pharmacy practitioners, as easily accessible professionals providing health consultation services, play a crucial role in meeting the public's needs for safe and rational medication [7]. However, challenges such as limited time for physicians to provide detailed medication information to patients, a shortage of pharmacy personnel, and a lack of individuals to explain medication usage can lead to instances of patients engaging in inappropriate self-medication [12]. Therefore, ensuring the safety of self-medication requires not only societal policy support and increased user awareness but also the active involvement of pharmacists.

2   Comparison of the Medical Systems Background Between China and Japan

2.1   The Medical System in China

China's healthcare system operates on a prepayment system, primarily composed of community pharmacies and hospitals with pharmacies that can dispense prescription medications. Community pharmacies include chain pharmacies, standalone pharmacies, and online pharmacies, all of which sell over-the-counter medications and can dispense certain prescription medications online [2]. Physical chain and standalone pharmacies require the legal entity or person in charge to be a licensed practicing pharmacist, and the quality management personnel at the stores should also be pharmacists [14]. A practicing pharmacist is a pharmacy technician who has undergone national vocational qualification recognition and is registered to practice. Practicing pharmacists undertake professional technical tasks such as drug management, prescription review and dispensing, and providing guidance on rational medication use.

In China, there are issues with the varying quality of education for practicing pharmacists, with training organizations and examinations often being seen as formalities, making it difficult for practicing pharmacists to genuinely improve their professional skills [15]. According to research by Wang Shuling, the number of practicing pharmacists in China has been increasing each year, but their distribution is uneven, with significant differences between urban and rural areas [16]. In more than 80% of provinces (autonomous regions, direct-controlled municipalities), rural retail pharmacies have a scarcity of registered practicing pharmacists compared to urban areas.

As of 2022, China's total healthcare expenditure as a percentage of GDP is approximately 7.0% (up from 6.70% in the previous year) [17]. However, China's current healthcare system faces challenges related to a situation known as "medicine supporting medicine," where the high added value of drugs is achieved through the labor of doctors, driving the economic benefits of hospitals through the high profits of pharmaceuticals, sustaining the normal operation of hospitals [18]. While Chinese laws and regulations touch on social pharmacies, practicing pharmacists, and pharmaceutical services, these provisions are scattered across different documents. There is no comprehensive and authoritative pharmacist law, and the service standards for social pharmacies are not clearly defined. The imperfection of laws and regulations adds to the difficulty of enhancing public awareness and implementing safe pharmaceutical services in society [19].

2.2 The Medical System in Japan

Japan's healthcare system operates under a division of medical functions and is primarily composed of community pharmacies and hospital institutions. Community pharmacies consist mainly of dispensing pharmacies, drugstores, drugstores, and online pharmacies. Among them, dispensing pharmacies sell both prescription and over-the-counter medications, and the staff must be licensed pharmacists.

The staff in drugstores, drugstores, and online pharmacies are categorized as registered sellers, pharmacists, and staff [20]. Pharmacists, as pharmaceutical experts, are responsible for dispensing medications based on doctor prescriptions and explaining the correct usage and precautions to patients. Registered sellers emerged due to a shortage of pharmacists and are responsible for assisting in the sale of general pharmaceuticals (OTC drugs) and providing medical advice to patients [21]. Japan enacted the Pharmacist Law in 1925 (Taisho 14), and relevant laws have since matured and become relatively comprehensive [22].

As of 2022, the total national medical expenditure in Japan accounts for approximately 7.99% of the GDP (up from 7.97% in the previous year) [23]. Although it is anticipated that there may be an oversupply of pharmacists in the future, there are still challenges such as imbalances in the regional distribution of pharmacists and a lack of communication skills among pharmacists [2].

3 The Current Situation of Self-medication in China and Japan

3.1 The Phenomenon of Self-medication Is Widespread in China, But It Lacks Policy Support

Self-medication is a widespread phenomenon in China, but it comes with numerous safety issues. For instance, a study conducted by Hu Yinhuan et al. [24] employed a stratified random sampling method to conduct household interviews and questionnaire surveys on 2,160 community residents in six cities in eastern, central, and western China. The findings revealed that Chinese residents often engage in self-medication with issues such as arbitrary use of antibiotics, an inability to accurately assess the severity of their condition, and arbitrary adjustments to the medication regimen. The proportion of the general population reading drug instructions is relatively low. Research by Feng Xuemei and others on self-medication behavior among rural women in the Baoding region of China showed that only 19.1% of individuals could comprehensively read drug instructions [25].

In August 2018, the National Health Commission of China issued a notice on "Carrying out 'Internet + Medical Health' Convenience and Benefit Activities" to facilitate residents' drug purchases. The initiative encourages medical institutions to promote the construction of smart pharmacies [26]. Against the backdrop of rapid developments in mobile internet technology, the widespread use of smartphones is driving changes in consumer habits, leading to higher expectations for drug purchasing services. China's drug purchasing services are moving towards more intelligent, scientific, and systematic development [27].

While self-medication holds a significant position in China's healthcare system, due to insufficient dissemination of relevant educational knowledge and the lack of targeted measures, inadequate supervision of self-medication among special population groups, and the absence of pharmacist-related training, residents still lack offline guidance suitable for the general public. As a result, self-medication behaviors carry a higher risk factor [28].

3.2   Self-medication in Japan Is Supported by Relevant Policies

In an effort to control the rise in medical expenses and alleviate the pressure on the healthcare insurance system, the Japanese government introduced the Self-Medication Tax System in 2017. This system encourages individuals to engage in self-medication by deducting specified drug prices [2]. With the promotion and widespread adoption of the self-medication tax system, the awareness of self-medication among the Japanese population has been increasing annually, and there is a growing trend in the purchase of over-the-counter (OTC) drugs [2]. It is evident that the combination of relevant tax reduction policies to promote self-medication has had a significant impact on public knowledge dissemination and encouragement of self-medication behaviors.

However, there are also various challenges in the actual implementation of self-medication in Japan. Surveys indicate that the rate of general practitioners in Japanese households is relatively low, lacking health prevention education compared to Europe and the United States. The primary healthcare system in Japan is incomplete, leading to a lower level of health literacy among the population [29]. Research by Takabayashi Fumiyoshi [30] on first-year female students at a junior college in Japan revealed that while most respondents believed they were generally healthy, there was often a lack of awareness and effort to actively maintain good health. According to the survey results from the Ministry of Health, Labour and Welfare, when purchasing medication at pharmacies, only 14% of people reported receiving explanations from pharmacists, and 36% claimed to have rarely or never received such explanations. There is also a lack of a culture in Japan where consumers interact and communicate with healthcare experts while purchasing products [2].

4   Worldwide Research on the Current Situation of Self-medication

In the United States, the United Kingdom, and Australia, during the sale of over-the-counter (OTC) medications, there is frequent face-to-face consultation between pharmacists and patients [2]. In the UK, online consultations for non-prescription drug advice are uncommon, and patients typically visit pharmacies to consult with pharmacists and simultaneously purchase OTC non-prescription drugs. UK pharmacists not only provide medication consultations but also offer services such as responding to symptoms and assessing the condition. For instance, if certain symptoms are attributed to a lack of sleep or nutrition, pharmacists may suggest lifestyle changes, like increased water intake and sufficient sleep, to alleviate the patient's symptoms [2].

Sweden follows a similar approach. The types of OTC medications available for self-medication are limited in Sweden. Even if individuals decide to seek medical attention, obtain a referral letter, and schedule treatment at a comprehensive hospital, appointments are often delayed due to time constraints, with specialized doctor appointments requiring advanced scheduling for several months. Consequently, many citizens in Sweden resort to taking sick leave and consuming beverages like tea to recover from common ailments such as colds and headaches [31].

Nordic countries like Denmark and Finland focus extensively on the education of pharmacists' professional knowledge and customer consultation in self-medication. These countries have widely adopted electronic prescriptions, and the extensive use of IT technology and robotic dispensing has significantly improved communication service efficiency between pharmacists and patients [32].

On the other hand, South Korea, also part of the pharmaceutical division system like Japan, provides many opportunities for pharmacists in drugstores to interact with consumers regarding OTC drug sales. However, staff members are often passive in selling non-prescription drugs, with their attention primarily focused on dispensing prescription medications (for which pharmacists receive a small commission) [33]. This situation leads to a scenario where the general public in South Korea may be able to assess their own health conditions, but there is a higher risk of misuse and abuse due to the need for individuals to make their own judgments about the specific usage and dosage of medications [34].

In Western countries, including Europe and the United States, there is a greater emphasis on communication between pharmacists and patients in the context of self-medication. This goes beyond satisfying patients' immediate medication needs and takes into consideration recommendations for their future health development to ensure the safety of current self-medication practices and the healthiness of their future bodies. Nordic countries, similar to East Asia, are facing challenges of an aging population and labor shortages.

However, by effectively utilizing IT technology to reduce manual costs, they have successfully maintained the quality of interaction between pharmacists and patients. Analyzing the current status and approaches to self-medication in various countries worldwide provides valuable insights for the future promotion of self-medication in China, Japan, and other East Asian nations.

5   Unexplored Areas in Past Research and the Significance of the Current Study

Many studies have also analyzed factors influencing self-medication, finding a positive correlation between health literacy and the safety of self-medication. For example, differences in cultural levels have a significant impact on safe medication behaviors. The health risk level of residents engaging in self-medication is influenced by factors such as health conditions, geographical location, and attitudes toward self-medication. Residents with lower levels of education tend to have higher health risk levels [29]. Researchers have also studied self-medication from the perspective of patients, identifying tendencies when patients engage in self-medication. For instance, individuals confident in their health may be careless in self-care and self-medication, while anxious individuals may be more cautious [30].

Existing preliminary studies have relatively fewer analyses that compare the self-medication status and similarities and differences across different countries. Studies analyzing the self-medication process from the patient's perspective using user experience (UX) methods are scarce. Therefore, this study aims to compare the medical backgrounds and self-medication situations in China and Japan. Using interview methods and employing UX analysis, the study seeks to analyze the reasons for patients in China and Japan choosing self-medication and the interaction patterns between patients and pharmacists. The goal is to identify the similarities and differences in self-medication behaviors between China and Japan and propose a self-medication support method that is applicable to China, user-friendly, and facilitates user understanding.

At the current stage, this research not only focuses on China and Japan but also includes interviews with people from other countries. The objective is to derive insights into the experiences of people in various countries when engaging in self-medication, providing valuable reference points.

6   Experimental Method

6.1   Procedure

This study conducted a qualitative research approach through user interviews, utilizing both face-to-face interviews and video calls. Through these interviews, information was gathered regarding users' motivations for choosing self-medication, specific behaviors related to self-medication, and interactions with pharmacists while in their respective home countries. The interview content mainly covered whether users practiced self-medication, the motivations behind their self-medication behaviors, the process of purchasing medications, interactions with pharmacists, and expectations for future guidance on self-medication. The study was conducted with the consent of randomly selected individuals from various nationalities. Participants were approached on the streets, introduced through friend connections, and ultimately selected for the study. The interviewees represented diverse regions, including East Asia (China, Taiwan, Japan, South Korea), North America (Utah, Iowa, Canada), Southeast Asia (Thailand, Indonesia, Malaysia), the Middle East (Iran), and Europe (Germany). In total, there were 17 participants, comprising 9 males and 8 females.

6.2 Analysis of the Reasons for Self-medication

The responses of the 17 participants in this study were analyzed to understand the reasons influencing their choice of self-medication over seeking prescription medication from medical institutions. These reasons were ranked in order of importance as indicated by the interviewees and are presented in Table 1.

Table 1. The reasons for choosing self-medication.

Reason	Count and Nationalities
Mild symptoms, trust in body's self-healing, no need for strong medication	9 (China 3, Japan 3, Canada 1, USA 1, South Korea 1)
Long waiting times at hospitals	6 (China 1, Japan 1, Canada 1, Thailand 1, Indonesia 1, Malaysia 1)
Previous hospital visit, aware of corresponding methods	5 (China 2, Canada 1, Indonesia 1, Germany 1)
Family member or self has medical background	4 (China 1, Iran 1, USA 1, Thailand 1)
Complicated procedures before diagnosis	3 (Taiwan China 1, Germany 1, USA 1)
Traveling abroad, unfamiliar with local hospitals	2 (Germany 1, Japan 1)
Too unwell to leave the house	2 (USA 1, Japan 1)
Previous hospital visit but found it unhelpful	1 (USA 1)
OTC medication cheaper than prescription drugs	1 (Thailand 1)
Disease-related shame	1 (Iran 1)

Among the responses from the 17 interviewees, all mentioned that they would not choose to visit a hospital or clinic that can prescribe medications when their symptoms are mild. The study found that among the interviewed individuals who chose self-medication, the reason "mild symptoms, belief in the body's self-healing ability, and no need for strong medications" was repeatedly mentioned regardless of nationality. Additionally, six individuals mentioned that "hospital visits are too cumbersome and time-consuming," which is another reason for choosing self-medication. Furthermore, a participant from Iran mentioned, "In Iran, some illnesses make women feel ashamed, making it difficult to accurately communicate and describe their condition to a pharmacist." The psychological factor of "disease-related shame," which was rarely mentioned in past literature on self-medication, was highlighted.

Through the interview responses from people in different countries, the study discovered that the reasons for engaging in self-medication are highly correlated with individuals' health literacy and the healthcare system, medical-related laws, educational culture, and ideologies of their respective countries. Analyzing the reasons for individuals autonomously choosing self-medication, regardless of nationality or gender, people tend to exhibit varying degrees of "trust in the body's immune ability" during the initial stages of choosing self-medication. In terms of health self-efficacy, the belief in one's ability to resist temptation and adopt a healthy lifestyle plays a crucial role [37]. Hu Yinhuan's [38]research indicates that residents' self-efficacy in medication is a primary influencing factor on residents' attitudes toward self-medication, with residents in better health having the strongest intention for self-medication.

Regardless of country and cultural background, strengthening education and enhancing self-efficacy can better encourage the public to spontaneously and correctly adopt self-medication practices.

6.3   Interaction Analysis with Pharmacists

Community pharmacy pharmacists are the most accessible professionals for the public, providing health consultation services and directly meeting the public's needs for safe and rational medication [39]. Therefore, pharmacists play an indispensable guiding role in self-medication. In this study, when asking about the interaction between users and pharmacists, the responses were analyzed. Following the user experience (UX) user mapping method, the process of users purchasing over-the-counter (OTC) prescription drugs was roughly divided into five stages: "feeling unwell," "going to the pharmacy," "selecting medications," "counter checkout," and "taking medications." As shown in Fig. 1.   In these five stages, the author chose "pharmacist" as a touchpoint and, through analysis, concluded that the interaction between pharmacists and users is most intense

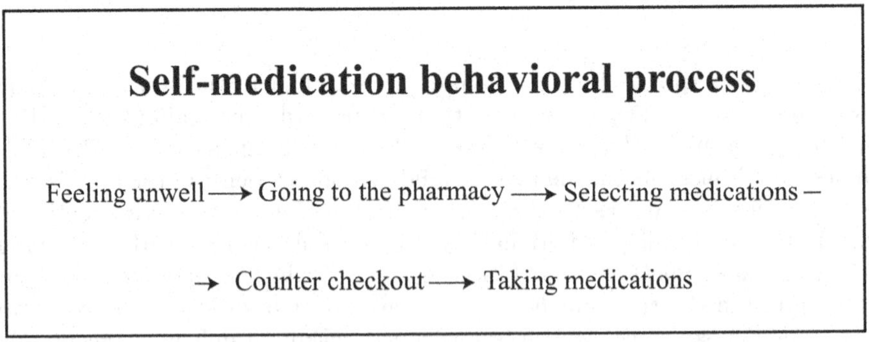

Self-medication behavioral process

Feeling unwell ⟶ Going to the pharmacy ⟶ Selecting medications –

⟶ Counter checkout ⟶ Taking medications

Fig. 1. Five stages of Self-medication behavior

during the "selecting medications" and "counter checkout" stages. During these two stages, based on the responses of the interviewees, the interaction types between pharmacists and users were categorized into "user-initiated inquiries" and "pharmacist-initiated inquiries."

Table 2. The interaction Between Users and Pharmacists

Situation	User Initiates Inquiry	Pharmacist Initiates Inquiry
When Selecting Medicines	4	4
At Checkout	0	1

The specific interaction scenes and the number of mentions are shown in the Table 2. In the interaction with pharmacists, four individuals mentioned that they "hope to receive concise and effective medication guidance and recommendations, and do not want pharmacists to provide lengthy and complicated explanations." One interviewee, in particular, stated, "If the pharmacist tells me information and precautions about the medication that I already know, I would feel very annoyed, and it seriously wastes my time." Additionally, three individuals expressed the desire for pharmacists to "tell them something they don't know, such as methods outside of medications that can alleviate and prevent diseases." It can be observed that users attempting self-medication have both the need for practical and useful advice from pharmacists and the desire for concise recommendations.

It is noteworthy that there are differences in the trust level towards pharmacists when asked about trust. Two interviewees from China expressed a certain degree of distrust in pharmacists, citing reasons such as "pharmacists receiving kickbacks" and "feeling that pharmacists are not professional enough." This is largely attributed to the inadequate reward system that reflects the value of practicing pharmacists in China. Pharmacists are unable to provide more effective assistance to the public, leading to a perception of pharmacists as mere dispensers without the necessary respect and trust [40].

In contrast, Japanese interviewees tended to show more trust in pharmacist recommendations, with one participant stating, "I would be happy to listen if the pharmacist recommends medication."

The safety of self-medication and the patient's experience with self-medication are highly correlated with the individual health literacy of both pharmacists and patients. Countries should improve relevant laws regarding self-medication while promoting the importance of the role of practicing pharmacists and emphasizing pharmacist education. Continuous enhancement of their professional competence can elevate societal recognition of the pharmacist industry in our country. Pharmacists also need to enhance their information gathering skills by inquiring about patients' lifestyles, psychological aspects, and social backgrounds to better understand patients. This enables them to provide more secure self-medication options [35]. Moreover, the safe promotion of self-medication in China requires pharmacists to proactively inquire about patients' thoughts, establish a communication system and environment conducive to both parties, and provide practical and effective assistance, thereby increasing patient trust and enthusiasm for self-medication.

7   Discussion

Currently, countries worldwide are actively promoting self-medication. Although the definitions of self-medication may vary slightly among different national institutions, the overall concept is similar.

Through an extensive literature review, three predominant factors influencing the decision to engage in self-medication were identified. These factors include residents' health conditions, geographical location, and attitudes toward self-medication. Consequently, the reasons people choose self-medication behaviors are highly complex. In addition to considering improvements in relevant medical policies and promoting public knowledge about diseases and drug principles, it is crucial to provide education on individuals' understanding of their own health conditions and guide them correctly on a psychological level.

Additionally, this study has organized and collected other responses from users, as shown in Table 3 and 4.

Table 3. Survey Results: Gender, Nationality

Category	Subcategory	Number of People
Gender	Male	9
	Female	8
Nationality	Mainland China	4
	Taiwan	1
	Japan	3
	USA (Canada)	1
	USA (Iowa)	1
	USA (Utah)	1
	Indonesia	1
	Iran	1
	Malaysia	1
	Thailand	1
	Germany	1
	South Korea	1

Table 4. Survey Results: Health Status and Other Categories

Category	Subcategory	Number of People
Health Status	Very Healthy	8
	Average	5
	Not Very Healthy	4
Concern About Health	Very Concerned	8
	Occasionally Concerned	6
	Not Very Concerned	3
Medicine at Home	Yes	15
	No	2
Medical Education Background	Yes	4
	No	13
Read Medicine Instructions	Yes	3
	No	14
Reason for Choosing This Medicine	Price	3
	Brand/Advertising	4
	Pharmacist Recommendation	2
	Random Choice	8
Concern About Side Effects	Concerned	3
	Not Concerned	14
Guidance from Pharmacist	Yes	8
	No	2
	Depends	7
Effectiveness of OTC Drugs	Yes	13
	No	3
	Unsure	1

8   Conclusion and Future Work

This study employed user interviews to explore the behaviors and thoughts of 17 individuals from various countries around the world, excluding China and Japan, regarding self-medication. It revealed that self-medication is highly prevalent globally and is influenced to some extent by factors such as national healthcare systems and laws. However, beyond national factors, it is also closely associated with the health literacy of social groups and relevant healthcare professionals. In the future, promoting communication between doctors and patients could be considered to effectively enhance patients' enthusiasm and satisfaction with self-medication.

Currently, the study is constrained by a small sample size and a bias towards younger interviewees. In the future, it will focus on conducting in-depth interviews with social groups and professionals in relevant industries in China and

Japan, with a particular emphasis on exploring the similarities and differences in self-medication behaviors between the two countries.

Through a comparison between China and Japan and based on the existing medical systems and backgrounds in China, a platform facilitating communication between doctors and patients will be developed. This platform will not only provide recommendations for over-the-counter (OTC) medications but also offer knowledge about diseases and related medications, as well as other health advice, thereby improving the health literacy and quality of life (QOL) of the general public.

References

1. Al-Worafi, Y.: Drug Safety in Developing Countries, pp. vii–xiv. Academic Press (2020). https://doi.org/10.1016/B978-0-12-819837-7.00046-7. ISBN 9780128198377
2. Ministry of Health, Labour and Welfare (Japan). https://www.mhlw.go.jp/
3. China Pharmaceutical Enterprise Management Association. (n.d.). http://m.cpema.org/
4. Zhaohui, L.I.: Discussion on the role of licensed pharmacists in self-medication. Chin. J. Med. Guide **23**(7), 542–545 (2021)
5. China Pharmaceutical Equipment Management Association. (n.d.). http://m.cpema.org/
6. Noone, J., Blanchette, C.M.: The value of self-medication: summary of existing evidence. J. Med. Econ. **21**(2), 201–211 (2018). https://doi.org/10.1080/13696998.2017.1390473
7. Li, C.: Exploration of the role of licensed pharmacists in public self-medication. Chin. Med. Guide **23**(07), 542–545 (2021)
8. Hu, Y., Zhang, L.: Exploring intervention strategies for health risk behaviors in self-medication among Chinese residents. Chin. Pharm. **18**, 1437–1439 (2005)
9. World Health Organization (WHO). (n.d.). http://apps.who.int/medicinedocs/
10. China Pharmaceutical Network. http://m.cnpharm.com/
11. Kimura, M., et al.: Insufficiency of OTC drug information; a pilot study with pharmacists, regulatory science of medical products **6**(3), 307–318 (2016)
12. Rongmei Health. (2022). http://www.rmzxb.com.cn/
13. China Business Industry Research Institute (2018). http://pdf.dfcfw.com/
14. National Medical Products Administration (NMPA), China. https://www.nmpa.gov.cn/
15. Ministry of Human Resources and Social Security, China. (2024). http://www.mohrss.gov.cn/
16. Shuling, W., Li, L., Zhaohui, L., et al.: Current distribution of registered pharmacists in urban and rural retail pharmacies in 14 provinces (autonomous regions, municipalities). Medical Tribune **39**(07), 1021–1025 (2020)
17. The State Council of China. https://www.gov.cn/
18. Wang, X., Yan, L., Bi, J.: Breaking through the drug-oriented medical system mechanism by streamlining medical service prices [News]. Econ. Ref. News 005 (2022). https://doi.org/10.28419/n.cnki.njjck.2022.005733.
19. Liu, R., Cao, Y., Chu, A., et al.: Current situation of community pharmacy services and the integration of pharmacists into family doctor team in Shanghai. Chin. Gen. Pract. **26**(31), 3922 (2023)

20. Yasuda, Y.: Study on distribution of non-prescription drugs. J. Human. Soc. Sci. Soc. Sci. Edn. **8**, 105–114 (2002)
21. Kazuo Toriizuka, F.: Registered seller system and responsibilities of pharmacists (topic). **45**(4), 348–352 (2009). Released on J-STAGE 26 August 2018, Online ISSN 2189-7026, Print ISSN 0014-8601
22. Oita City Phrmaceutical, Pharmacist History. http://www.oitasiyaku.net/
23. Ministry of Health, Labour and Welfare (Japan). https://www.mhlw.go.jp/toukei/saikin/
24. Hu, Y., Fang, P., Tao, H., et al.: Assessment of health risk levels in self-medication behavior among urban residents in China. Chin. J. Public Health **25**(11), 1328–1330 (2009)
25. Feng, X., Lu, F., Yang, Z., et al.: Analysis of the current situation of self-medication behavior among rural women in baoding area. Med. Res. Educ. **29**(05), 28–32 (2012)
26. Notice on the In-Depth Implementation of "Internet + Medical and Health" Convenience and Benefit Activities. Bulletin of the National Health Commission of the People's Republic of China 7 April 2007
27. Du, M., Zhang, L.: Research on the design of a smart pharmacy drug purchase service system. Design **36**(10), 28–32 (2023). https://doi.org/10.20055/j.cnki.1003-0069.000678
28. Ren, J., Kan, H., Duan, G.: Current situation, existing problems, and countermeasures and suggestions of self-medication. Chin. Pharm. **27**(34), 4888–4890 (2016)
29. Japan OTC Medicines Association. https://www.jsmi.jp/info/data/
30. Takabayashi, F.: Relationship between health status and the image of drug and self-medication of female students of junior college. J. Jpn. Soc. Nurs. Res. 12(1), 1_63–1_73 (1989)
31. Ministry of Health, Labour and Welfare (Japan). https://mhlw-grants.niph.go.jp
32. Daiko, T.: Overseas Pharmacy Training in Sweden and Denmark. http://id.nii.ac.jp/
33. Prospects for Reform in the South Korean Pharmaceutical Retail Industry. Chin. Pharm. 46–47 (2006)
34. Ministry of Health, Labour and Welfare (Japan). https://mhlw-grants.niph.go.jp
35. Hanya, M., et al.: Applying the roter method of interaction process analysis system to patient-pharmacist communications in triaging OTC drugs. Iryo Yakugaku (Jpn. J. Pharmaceut. Health Care Sci.) **34**(11), 1059–1067 (2008)
36. Hu, Y., Fang, P., Tao, H., et al.: Assessment of health risk levels in self-medication behavior among urban residents in China. Chin. J. Public Health **25**(11), 1328–1330 (2009)
37. Bandura, A.: Self-efficacy. The Exercise of Control, pp. 123–126. Freeman, New York (1997)
38. Hu, Y.-H., Chen, H.: Investigation on attitude towards self-medication in Chinese urban residents. Chin. J. Publ. Health **24**(12), 1503–1505 (2008)
39. Li, C.: Discussion on the role of practicing pharmacists in self-medication among the public. Chin. J. Med. Guide **23**(07), 542–545 (2021)
40. Wang, L., Liang, N.: Introduction to the social trust and income situation of pharmacists in the United States and Canada and their implications for the development of pharmacy in China. Chin. Pharm. **29**(23), 3174–3178 (2018)

Author Index

Printed in the United States
by Baker & Taylor Publisher Services